The Double Eagle Guide to

1,000 GREAT!
WESTERN
RECREATION
DESTINATIONS

VOLUME 1
WEST COAST

WASHINGTON
OREGON
CALIFORNIA

A DOUBLE EAGLE GUIDE™

DISCOVERY PUBLISHING BILLINGS, MONTANA USA

The Double Eagle Guide to
1,000 Great! Western Recreation Destinations
Volume 1 West Coast

Published by:

Discovery Publishing
Post Office Box 50545
Billings, Montana 59105 USA

Discovery Publishing is an independent, private enterprise. The information contained
herein should not be construed as reflecting the publisher's approval of the policies
or practices of the public agencies listed.

Information in this book is subject to change without notice.

Frontispiece: Yaquina Bay State Park, Oregon

10 9 8 7 6 5 4 3 2 1

May 12, 1998   4:37 PM Mountain Time

Produced, printed, and bound in the United States of America.

ISBN 0-929760-58-1

820305

▤ TABLE OF CONTENTS

(Continued...)

Table of Contents (continued)

Double Eagle™ *Guides*

❦ INTRODUCTION TO THE *Double Eagle*™ SERIES ❦

Whether you're a veteran of many Western trips or are planning your first visit, this series is for you.

In the four volumes of *The Double Eagle Guide to 1,000 Great! Western Recreation Destinations* we've described what we have determined to be outstanding recreation areas along or conveniently near the highways and byways of the 17 contiguous Western United States. Our goal is to provide you with accurate, detailed, and yet concise, *first-hand* information about the recreation areas you're most likely to want to know about. Places worth going out of your way to visit.

The volumes which comprise the *Double Eagle*™ series constitute a significant departure from the sketchy, plain vanilla approach to recreation information provided by so many other guidebooks. Here, for the first time, is the most *useful* information about the West's most *useable* public recreation areas. We've included a broad assortment of recreation sites from which you can choose: From simple, free parks with terrific scenery, to areas with complete facilities in deluxe, landscaped surroundings.

The name for this critically acclaimed series was suggested by the celebrated United States twenty-dollar gold piece—most often called the *"Double Eagle"*—the largest and finest denomination of coinage ever issued by the U.S. Mint. The *Double Eagle* has long been associated with the history of the West, as a symbol of traditional Western excellence.

So, too, the *Double Eagle*™ series seeks to provide you with information about what are perhaps the finest of all the West's treasures—its public recreational lands.

We hope you'll enjoy reading these pages, and come to use the information in the volumes to enhance your own appreciation for the outstanding outdoor recreation opportunities available in the West.

Enjoy your adventure!

Tom and *Liz Preston*
Publishers

🏕 CONVENTIONS USED IN THIS SERIES Δ

The following conventions or standards are used throughout the *Double Eagle*™ series as a means of providing a sense of continuity between one destination and the next.

Whenever possible, the destinations within each state have been arranged in what we have determined to be a reasonable progression, and based on *typical travel patterns* within a region. Generally speaking, a north to south, west to east pattern has been followed. In certain cases, particularly those involving one-way-in, same-way-out roads, we have arranged them in the order in which they would be encountered on the way into the area, so the standard plan occasionally may be reversed.

State Identifier: The state name and number combination in the upper left corner of each destination's description provides an easy means of cross-referencing the written information to the numbered locations on the maps in the Appendix.

Recreation Area Name: The officially designated name for the recreation area is listed in boldface, followed by the specific category in which it is classified by its state. ("National Park", "National Forest", "Corps of Engineers Park", "State Historic Park", "County Park", and so forth.) In most instances, the name was transcribed directly from the signpost planted at the recreation area entrance; it may (and often does), vary slightly from the name as it appears in other printed sources, (especially in 'official' literature). One example: Throughout the West, it's quite common to find places with a 'possessive' noun in their names to be spelled without the possessive apostrophe ("Clarks Camp" vs "Clark's Camp"). We have retained that convention whenever we determined it to be historically appropriate. Evidently, the apostrophe was considered a grammatical frill by many of our forebears.

Larger recreation areas with distinctively different major units may be divided into two or more separate descriptions. For example, if "Big River Regional Park" consists of two large areas, the "Mountain Valley" unit and the "Great Plains" unit, each with different access, facilities, and natural features, the two sections might be titled:

<table>
<tr><td align="center">**MOUNTAIN VALLEY**
BIG RIVER REGIONAL PARK</td><td align="center">**GREAT PLAINS**
BIG RIVER REGIONAL PARK</td></tr>
</table>

Location: This section allows you to obtain a quick approximation of a place's location in relation to nearby key communities, as depicted on the maps in the appendix.

Access: Our *Accurate Access* system makes extensive use of highway mileposts in order to pinpoint the location of access roads, intersections, and other major terminal points. (Mileposts are about 98 percent reliable—but occasionally they are mowed by a snowplow or an errant motorist, and may be missing; or, worse yet, the mileposts were replaced in the wrong spot!) In some instances, locations are noted primarily utilizing mileages between two or more nearby locations—usually communities, but occasionally key junctions or prominent landmarks.

Since everyone won't be approaching a destination from the same direction, we've provided access information from two, sometimes three, points. In all cases, we've chosen the access points for their likelihood of use. Distances from communities are listed from the approximate **midtown** point (very often the city hall, couthouse, or post office), unless otherwise specified. Mileages from Interstate highways and other freeway exits are usually given from the approximate center of the interchange. Mileages from access points usually have been rounded to the nearest mile, unless the exact mileage is critical. All instructions are given using the *current official highway map* available free from each state.

Directions are given using a combination of compass and hand headings, i.e., "turn north (left)" or "swing west (right)". This isn't a bonehead navigation system, by any means. When the sun is shining or you're in a region where moss grows on tree trunks, it's easy enough to figure out which way is north. But anyone can become temporarily disoriented on an overcast day or a moonless night while looking for an inconspicuous park turnoff, or while being buzzed by heavy traffic at a key intersection, so we built this redundancy into the system.

Day Use Facilities: Picnic area sizes and number of tables are categorized as: (1) small—up to a dozen; (2) medium—up to 50; (3) large—more than 50. The capacities of parking areas are similarly described. (These are *very* approximate figures because we weren't about to try to *count* all the picnic tables and parking spaces!)

Toilet facilities have been listed thusly: (1) Restrooms—'modern', i.e., flush toilets and usually a wash basin; (2) Vault facilities—'simple', i.e., outhouses, pit toilets, call them what you like. (A rose by any other name.....).

Camping Facilities: Campgrounds are by far the most common type of overnight facilities offered in public recreation areas. The items in this section have been listed in the approximate order in which a visitor might observe them during a typical swing through a campground. Following the total number of individual camp units, items pertinent to the campsites themselves are listed, then information related to 'community' facilities. It has been assumed that each campsite has a picnic table.

Site types: (1) Standard—no hookup; (2) Partial hookup—water, electricity; (3) Full hookup—water, electricity, sewer.

We have extensively employed the use of *general* and *relative* terms in describing the size, separation, and levelness of the campsites ("medium to large", "fairly well separated", "basically level", etc.). Please note that "separation" is a measure of relative privacy and is a composite of both natural visual 'screens' and spacing between campsites. The information is presented as an *estimate* by highly experienced observers. Please allow for variations in perception between yourself and the reporters.

Parking Pads: (1) Straight-ins, (sometimes called "back-ins" or "spurs")—the most common type, are just that—straight strips angled off the driveway; (2) Pull-throughs—usually the most convenient type for large rv's, they provide an in-one-end-and-out-the-other parking space; pull-throughs may be either arc-shaped and separated from the main driveway by some sort of barrier or 'island' (usually vegetation), or arranged in parallel rows; (3) Pull-offs—essentially just wide spots adjacent to the driveway. Pad lengths have been categorized as: (1) Short—a single, large vehicle up to about the size of a standard pickup truck; (2) Medium—a single vehicle or combination up to the length of a pickup towing a single-axle trailer; (3) Long—a single vehicle or combo as long as a crew cab pickup towing a double-axle trailer. Normally, any overhang out the back of the pad has been ignored in the estimate, so it might be possible to slip a crew cab pickup hauling a fifth-wheel trailer in tandem with a ski boat into some pads, but we'll leave that to your discretion.

Fire appliances have been categorized in three basic forms: (1) Fireplaces—angular, steel or concrete, ground-level; (2) Fire rings—circular, steel or concrete, ground-level or below ground-level; (3) Barbecue grills—angular steel box, supported by a steel post about 36 inches high. (The trend is toward installing steel fire rings, since they're durable, relatively inexpensive—60 to 80 dollars apiece—and easy to install and maintain. Barbecue grills are often used in areas where ground fires are a problem, as when charcoal-only fires are permitted.)

Certain recreation areas also offer other types of overnight facilties, such as a park-operated lodge, cabins, or group buildings.

Travelers' supply points have been described at five levels: (1) Camper Supplies—buns, beans and beverages; (2) Gas and Groceries—a 'convenience' stop; (3) Limited—at least one store which approximates a small supermarket, more than one fuel station, a general merchandise store, hardware store, and other basic services; (4) Adequate—more than one supermarket, (including something that resembles an IGA or a Safeway), a choice of fuel brands, and several general and specialty stores and services; (5) Complete—they have a major discount store.

   ♿ Recreation areas reported by public agencies to have facilities for physically challenged persons that conform to the requirements of the Americans with Disabilities Act of 1990 (ADA) have been highlighted with this familiar symbol. In most parks, a minimum you can expect is equal access to restrooms. In many places, special handicapped-access picnic or camp sites, fishing piers and other recreational facilities are also provided, especially in larger parks. Some places which are not listed as having handicapped access may indeed have some facilities that offer it on a limited basis, usually at restrooms, but they may not technically conform to the rigid standards of the ADA. If you rely on these facilities, it might be a good idea to double check for their existence and condition prior to visiting the park, using the ☎ information.

Recreation area managers, attendants and camp hosts can be expected to be on-site or readily available during the regular season in more than 75 percent of the listed areas.

Activities & Attractions: As is mentioned a number of times throughout this series, the local scenery may be the principal attraction of the recreation area (and, indeed, may be the *only* one you'll need). Other nearby attractions/activities have been listed if they are low-cost or free, and are available to the general public. An important item: *Swimming and boating areas very often do not have lifeguards.*

Natural Features: Here we've drawn a word picture of the natural environment in and around each area. Please remember that seasonal, even daily, conditions will affect the appearance of the locale. A normally "sparkling stream" can be a muddy torrent for a couple of weeks in late spring; a "deep blue lake" might be a nearly empty hole in a drought year; "lush vegetation" may have lost all its greenery by the time you arrive in late October. In the interest of simplicity and easy readability, we list broadleaf trees (i.e., "deciduous" trees, such as cottonwood, maple, oak) as "hardwoods"; cone-bearing needle trees (pines, Western cedar, spruce, etc.) as "conifers". We typically call the relatively small Eastern redcedar and Western junipers "evergreens". This information might be especially helpful to you in determining the amount of shade you can expect to find to help cool you in midsummer. Elevations above 500´ are rounded to the nearest 100´; lower elevations are rounded to the nearest 50´. (Some elevations are estimated, but no one should develop a nosebleed or a headache because of a 100´ difference in altitude.)

Season, Fees & Phone: Seasons listed are approximate, since weather conditions, particularly in mountainous or hilly regions, may require adjustments in opening/closing dates. Day use areas are generally available sunrise to sunset; historic sites are typically open during standard business hours; campground entrance gates are usually unlocked from 6:00 a.m. to 10:00 p.m. Fee information listed here and in the Appendix was obtained directly from the responsible agencies a few hours before press time. Fees should be considered *minimum* fees since they are always *subject to adjustment* by agencies or legislatures. Discounts and special passes are usually available for seniors and disabled persons. A local telephone number is listed which can be called in order to obtain information about current conditions in that recreation area. We've accented the phone number with a ☎ symbol for quick reference. It could be very helpful while you're in a highwayside phone booth fumbling for a quarter or your 'calling card', poking the buttons on the touch-tone pad, and simultaneously trying to hold the handset up to your ear as you're calling a park for reservations, current weather info, or whatever.

Trip Log: Consider this section to be somewhat more subjective in nature than the others. In order to provide our readers with a well-rounded report, we have listed personal comments related to our field observations. (Our enthusiasm for the West is, at times, unabashedly proclaimed. So if the text sometimes reads a bit like a tourist promotion booklet, please bear with us—there's a lot to be enthusiastic about!)

Throughout the series, certain small, undeveloped 'satellite' areas are given abbreviated 'thumbnail' descriptions in the *Trip Log* section of a principal recreation area. Since these spots often are little-used outback areas, it might pay to check them out if you're in the neighborhood and looking for a simple, tranquil place to sit for a while.

Editorial remarks (Ed.) occasionally have been included.

A Word About Style...

Throughout the *Double Eagle*™ series, we've utilized a free-form writing style. Complete sentences, phrases, and single words have been incorporated into the park descriptions as appropriate under the circumstances. We've adopted this style in order to provide our readers with detailed information about each item, while maintaining conciseness, clarity, and conversationality.

A Word About Print...

Another departure from the norm is our use of print sizes which are 20 percent larger (or more) than ordinary guidebooks. We also use more efficient page layouts for less paper waste. It's one thing to read a guidebook in the convenience and comfort of your well-lit living room. It's another matter to peruse the pages while you're bounding and bouncing along in your car or camper as the sun is setting; or by a flickering flashlight inside a breeze-buffeted dome tent. We hope this works for you, too.

A Word About Maps...

After extensive tests of the state maps by seasoned travelers, both at home and in the field, we decided to localize all of the maps in one place in the book. Travelers felt that, since pages must be flipped regardless of where the maps are located, it would be more desirable to have them all in one place. We're confident that you'll also find this to be a convenient feature. Likewise, we determined that states should be shown in their entirety, rather than fragmented into regions. Although this makes for 'cramped quarters' in a few high-density recreation areas, map readers preferred the overall 'big picture' approach. Cities shown on the maps are keyed to the cities listed in the *Location* and *Access* sections of the text.

Furthermore, details on the maps have been limited not only for clarity, but to discourage blatant photocopying and distribution of access information. You or your library paid someone's hard-earned greenbacks for this information. You'll probably not want to compete with hordes of 'second-hand' users for what you hope is a tranquil outdoor recreation experience.

A Word About 'Regs'...

Although this series is about public recreatiom areas, you'll find comparatively few mentions of rules, regulations, policies, statutes, decrees or dictates. Our editorial policy is simply this: (1) It's the duty of a citizen or a visitor to know his legal responsibilities (and, of course, his corresponding *rights*); (2) Virtually every recreation area has the appropriate regulations publicly posted for all to study; and (3) If you're reading this *Double Eagle*™ Guide, chances are you're in the upper ten percent of the conscientious citizens of the United States or some other civilized country and you probably don't need to be constantly reminded of these matters.

And a Final Word...

We've tried very, very hard to provide you with accurate information about the West's great recreation opportunities. But occasionally, all is not as it's supposed to be.....

If a place's access, facilities or fees have been recently changed, please let us know. We'll try to pass along the news to other travelers.

If the persons in the next picnic or camp site flip a frisbee that periodically plops into your potato salad, or keep their generator poppety-popping past midnight so they can cook a turkey in the microwave, blame the bozos, not the book.

If the beasties are a bit bothersome in that beautiful spot down by the bog, note the day's delights and not the difficulties.

Thank you for reading—and using—our book. We hope you'll have many terrific trips!

Washington Destinations

If it Rains, We Go Anyway

Washington is a fine state.

It can be argued, quite successfully, we believe, that few, if any, other states can top Washington in the area of scenic variety. From the rain forests of the Olympic Peninsula, to the emerald isles of Puget Sound, to the misty Cascades, to the arid Columbia Basin, to the golden Palouse Hills—Washington packs a lot more into a lot less territory than other western states. (You could spend a month, a year, or more just getting to know the Sound alone.)

And in spite of all the stories told of the state's incessant rain (many of which, we suspect, are fabricated by Southern Californians), it doesn't rain *all* the time, *all* over Washington. (Ask any tenured Washingtonian what he does when he plans a a trail hike, a picnic or a camping trip, and it *does* rain, he'll reply, "We go anyway".)

Even with a population density that's greater than average for the Western states, Washington has a surprisingly large number of excellent outdoor recreation areas.

And while many cite Oregon as being the western leader in state park development, Washington certainly doesn't take second place to its sister to the south in that area. It *may* be our misconception, but Washington's state parks, unlike those of some other states, don't have an overused look; somehow, most of the parks maintain a fresh appearance.

A lot of the credit for the excellent recreational environment in Washington has to go to the untold number of outdoor-oriented individuals who have made a concerted, and effective, effort to maintain Washington's highly desirable natural environment.

Washington *is* a fine place.

 Washington Ⓧ
Olympic National Park

Olympic National Park has a multi-faceted personality. Although most often thought of as a rugged alpine wilderness park, its thousands of acres encompass vast, lowland rain forest and scenic seashores as well. The following major park areas are all accessible by vehicles.

⚐ Washington 1 ♿

KALALOCH
Olympic National Park

Location: Western Washington on the west coast of the Olympic Peninsula south of Forks.

Access: From U.S. Highway 101 at milepost 157 +.7 in the small settlement of Kalaloch (34 miles south of Forks, 70 miles north of Hoquiam), turn west into the recreation area.

Day Use Facilities: Medium-sized picnic area; shelters; drinking water; restrooms; several small parking areas.

Camping Facilities: 179 campsites in 6 loops; (a group camp is also available, by reservation only); majority of the sites are small+ and fairly well separated; parking pads are paved, short to short+, reasonably level straight-ins, a few are pull-offs; most sites have medium to large, level tent spaces; fireplaces; b-y-o firewood; water at faucets in each loop; restrooms; paved driveways; ranger station nearby; camper supplies at a nearby resort; adequate supplies and services are available in Forks.

Activities & Attractions: Beachcombing; amphitheater for scheduled ranger-naturalist programs during the summer.

Natural Features: Located on a windswept bluff above the ocean beach; campground vegetation consists of short to medium height trees and leafy bushes which provide a fairly good windbreak; several inviting beaches are accessible from here; elevation 50´.

Season, Fees & Phone: Open all year; $10.00; 14 day limit; Olympic National Park Headquarters, Port Angeles, ☎(360) 452-4501.

Trip Log: Most of the sites are well-sheltered from oceanside weather; those that aren't have the advantage of good ocean views. The beaches in the Kalaloch (*Klay´-lock*) area are varied in their nomenclature and points of interest. Some have proper nouns for names, like Ruby Beach; most are merely numbered: Beach 2, Beach 3, Beach 6, and so on. Each beach has its own special appeal: Ruby beach is adorned with spires of stone called "seastacks"; steep, colorful cliffs rise above Beach 6; the shoreline north of Beach 4 is noted for its tidepools.

♣ **Washington 2** ♿

HOH
Olympic National Park

Location: Western Washington on the west side of the Olympic Peninsula east/southeast of Forks.

Access: From U.S. Highway 101 at milepost 178 +.5 (13 miles south of Forks, 21 miles north of Kalaloch), turn east onto Hoh Valley Road (paved, winding); travel easterly for 19 miles to the recreation area; (allow a minimum of 45 minutes for the trip).

Day Use Facilities: Medium-sized picnic area; shelters; drinking water; restrooms; several small to medium-sized parking areas.

Camping Facilities: 95 campsites in 3 loops; most sites are generously sized, level, and well spaced; parking pads are paved, short to medium-length straight-ins, plus some medium to long pull-throughs; most units offer good tent-pitching opportunities; fireplaces; b-y-o firewood from outside the park; water at central faucets; restrooms; holding tank disposal station; paved driveways; ranger station; nearest supplies (very limited) at a small store, 12 miles west on Hoh Valley Road; adequate supplies and services are available in Forks.

Activities & Attractions: Visitor center; 2 self-guided nature trails; paved mini-trail; hiking trail along the river; amphitheater for evening campfire programs during the summer.

Natural Features: Located on a moderately forested flat on the Hoh River deep in the Olympic Mountains; a number of campsites are along the edge of the riverbank; the Hoh Rain Forest, with its incomparable variety of flora and fauna, encircles the campground; elevation 600´.

Season, Fees & Phone: Open all year, with limited services in winter; $10.00; 14 day limit; Hoh Ranger Station & Visitor Center ☎(360) 374-6925.

Trip Log: Hoh is so truly unique that it's worth just about any amount of time and effort you need to get here. Spend a day or two listening to the river and silently walking the rain forest trails, and you'll remember the experience for a lifetime.

♣ **Washington 3** ♿

MORA
Olympic National Park

Location: Western Washington on the west side of the Olympic Peninsula west of Forks.

Access: From U.S. Highway 101 at milepost 193 +.2 (2 miles north of Forks, 9 miles south of Sappho), turn west-southwest onto LaPush Road and drive 8.4 miles to the Quilliute Prairie Fire Department building; turn west (right) onto Mora Road, and continue for 3.3 miles to the recreation area.

Day Use Facilities: Small picnic area; shelters; drinking water; restrooms; several small parking areas.

Camping Facilities: 90 campsites in 5 loops; sites are medium-sized, level, with fair separation; parking pads are paved, of assorted lengths and types; adequate space for medium to large tents in most sites; fireplaces; b-y-o firewood; water at central faucets; restrooms; holding tank disposal station; paved driveways; groceries, gas, laundromat and showers at the intersection of LaPush & Mora Roads, 3.3 miles east; adequate supplies and services are available in Forks.

Activities & Attractions: Ocean beaches 1.5 miles west, with trails that lead north and south along the coast; riverside campfire circle for evening nature programs; fishing.

Natural Features: Located on the north bank of the swift, deep Quilliute River; very dense rain forest with lots of ferns and twiggy hardwoods; cloudy/rainy throughout the year, but somewhat less in summer than during other seasons; elevation 100´.

Season, Fees & Phone: Open all year; $10.00; 14 day limit; Olympic National Park Headquarters, Port Angeles, ☎(360) 452-4501.

Trip Log: Mora is located in the narrow coastal section of Olympic National Park. There is a very quiet, (some might say somber) atmosphere associated with this area. Several of the most scenic beaches in the park are near here. There are some particularly nice campsites on the bank of the Quilliute River.

♠ Washington 4 &

FAIRHOLM
Olympic National Park

Location: Western Washington on the north side of the Olympic Peninsula west of Port Angeles.

Access: From U.S. Highway 101 at milepost 220 +.9 at Fairholm (26 miles west of Port Angeles, 33 miles east of Forks), turn north onto the paved campground access road and proceed 0.3 mile to the recreation area.

Day Use Facilities: Small picnic area; drinking water; restrooms; medium-sized parking area.

Camping Facilities: 87 campsites in three loops, including 16 walk-in sites just above the lake shore; most sites are small+, quite sloped, with nominal to fair separation; parking pads are gravel, mostly short to medium-length straight-ins; small to medium-sized tent areas; fireplaces; b-y-o firewood; water at central faucets; restrooms; holding tank disposal station; paved driveways; small store and gas station on the highway near the campground turnoff; adequate supplies in Forks, complete supplies and services are available in Port Angeles.

Activities & Attractions: Self-guiding 0.75 mile nature trail; other trails lead through the campground loops and down to the lake; designated swimming area; boat launch and docks; fishing.

Natural Features: Located on a moderately steep hillside at the west end of Crescent Lake; dense conifer and hardwood forest, plus enough low-level brush in the campground for some campsite separation; the entire area is surrounded by densely forested mountains; elevation 600´.

Season, Fees & Phone: Open all year; $10.00; 14 day limit; Olympic National Park Headquarters, Port Angeles, ☎(360) 452-4501.

Trip Log: Crescent Lake is perhaps the most picturesque of the easily accessible lakes on the Peninsula. There are some truly spectacular mountain vistas in this area. Many campers consider the walk-ins to be the best campsites.

♠ Washington 5 &

ELWHA
Olympic National Park

Location: Western Washington on the north side of the Olympic Peninsula west of Port Angeles.

Access: From U.S. Highway 101 at milepost 239 +.5 (at the east end of the Elwha River bridge, 9 miles west of Port Angeles), turn south onto Elwha Valley Road (paved); proceed 3.1 miles to the campground entrance on the east (left) side of the road; or continue for another 0.2 mile to the day use area.

Day Use Facilities: Small picnic area; drinking water; restrooms; small parking area.

Camping Facilities: 41 campsites, including 7 walk-ins; most sites are very level and of average size for a park service campground, with minimal separation; parking pads are paved, mostly short to medium straight-ins, plus a few pull-throughs; excellent tent-pitching opportunities for small to medium sized tents; fireplaces; b-y-o firewood; water at several faucets; central restrooms; shelter with a large stone fireplace; paved driveways; ranger station 1 mile south; limited supplies (and showers) at a resort on the main highway; complete supplies and services are available in Port Angeles.

Activities & Attractions: Elwha Campground Trail, a 0.7 mile loop; nearby amphitheater for scheduled ranger-naturalist programs in the summer; fishing.

Natural Features: Located on a wooded flat in the Elwha River Valley; Elwha River is 200 yards west of the campground; moderately dense conifer and hardwood forest (in slightly more open forest than many other campgrounds in the Olympics); elevation 400´.

Season, Fees & Phone: Open all year; $10.00; 14 day limit; Olympic National Park Headquarters, Port Angeles, ☎(360) 452-4501.

Trip Log: Although this place is very popular in the summer, it's nearly deserted in winter. That's unfortunate, since this valley can be enjoyed year 'round. Bring your rain gear.

♣ Washington 6 ♿

ALTAIRE
Olympic National Park

Location: Western Washington on the north side of the Olympic Peninsula west of Port Angeles.

Access: From U.S. Highway 101 at milepost 239 +.5 (at the east end of the Elwha River bridge, 9 miles west of Port Angeles), turn south onto the Elwha Valley Road (paved); travel south for 4.5 miles (0.5 mile past the Elwha Ranger Station) to the campground access road; turn west (right), go down a steep paved road 0.1 mile to the campground.

Day Use Facilities: None.

Camping Facilities: 32 campsites; sites are small+ to medium-sized, level, with nominal separation; parking pads are paved, most units have straight-ins, some have pull-throughs; good tent-pitching possibilities; fireplaces; b-y-o firewood; water at several faucets; restrooms; spacious shelter with a large stone fireplace; paved driveways; nearest supplies (and showers) at a resort on the main highway; complete supplies and services are available in Port Angeles.

Activities & Attractions: Whiskey Bend Trail leads off from the ranger station; scenic drive to the south on the Elwha Valley Road; fishing.

Natural Features: Located on a small flat on the bank of the swiftly flowing Elwha River; fairly dense conifer and hardwood forest, but little ground-level vegetation; high, heavily timbered hills on either side of the river; typically quite damp/wet; elevation 400´.

Season, Fees & Phone: May to October; $10.00; 14 day limit; Olympic National Park Headquarters, Port Angeles, ☎(360) 452-4501.

Trip Log: This is really a pretty nice little campground: very level, somewhat off the beaten path, with the sound of the rushing river for background music.

♣ Washington 7 ♿

HURRICANE RIDGE
Olympic National Park

Location: Western Washington on the north side of the Olympic Peninsula south of Port Angeles.

Access: From U.S. Highway 101 in midtown Port Angeles, turn south onto South Race Street (street signs will indicate that this is the way to Hurricane Ridge); travel south for 6.3 miles to the park entrance station, and Heart O' the Hills Campground just beyond; continue past the campground turnoff for another 13 miles to the Hurricane Ridge Visitor Center; (the last 16 miles of the park road are steep and winding.)

Day Use Facilities: Small picnic area, drinking water, restrooms, large parking area at the visitor center.

Camping Facilities: *Heart O' the Hills Campground*: 105 campsites in 5 loops; overall, the camp units are small+ to medium-sized, with nominal to fair separation; parking pads are paved, short to medium-length straight-ins or pull-offs, which will probably require additional leveling; adequate space for medium-sized tents; fireplaces; b-y-o firewood; water at central faucets; restrooms; paved driveways; complete supplies and services are available in Port Angeles.

Activities & Attractions: Visitor centers at park headquarters in Port Angeles and at Hurricane Ridge; several trailheads nearby; amphitheater for scheduled ranger-naturalist programs.

Natural Features: Located atop windswept Hurricane Ridge in the Olympic Mountains (visitor center), or in dense conifer forest on the north slope of the Olympics (campground); wide, deep valleys and sharply defined mountains are in the vicinity; elevation 1800´.

Season, Fees & Phone: Open all year; $10.00; 14 day limit; Olympic National Park Headquarters, Port Angeles, ☎(360) 452-4501.

Trip Log: Perhaps the park's most notable vistas are viewed from atop Hurricane Ridge. If you manage to get here during clear weather, you won't soon forget the astounding panoramas which can be enjoyed from here. If the weather turns a bit foul, the visitor center's huge windows will allow you to watch passing squalls in comfort

♣ Washington 8 ♿

STAIRCASE
Olympic National Park

Location: Western Washington on the east side of the Olympic Peninsula west of Hoodsport.

Access: From U.S. Highway 101 at milepost 331 +.7 (on the north edge of the community of Hoodsport, 15 miles north of Shelton), turn west onto Lake Cushman Road (paved) and travel northwest then north for 9.3 miles to a 'T' intersection; turn west (left) onto Forest Road 24 and drive another 7 miles (mainly gravel) to the park entrance station; continue for another 0.2 mile to the recreation sites.

Day Use Facilities: Small picnic area; drinking water; restrooms; medium-sized parking area.

Camping Facilities: 59 campsites; sites are small to small+, with nominal to fair separation; parking pads are gravel, short to short+ straight-ins; most pads will require additional leveling; small to medium-sized tent spots; fireplaces; limited firewood is available for gathering in the area; water at central faucets; restrooms; paved driveways; ranger station; gas and groceries+ are available in Hoodsport.

Activities & Attractions: Several hiking trails, some of which go deep into the heart of the Olympic Mountains; day use area.

Natural Features: Located on hilly terrain along the North Fork of the Skokomish River on the east slope of the Olympic Mountains; sites are well sheltered by tall conifers and hardwoods; elevation 800´.

Season, Fees & Phone: Open all year; $10.00; 14-day limit; Olympic National Park Headquarters, Port Angeles, ☎(360) 452-4501.

Trip Log: "Staircase" is an intriguing name for a recreation site and it evokes images of man-made or natural features. According to historical reports, the first trail along the North Fork was blazed by U.S. Army soldiers in 1889. The steep, densely forested terrain presented a multitude of trail-building barriers, including a rocky bluff along the riverbank at the site of the present-day campground. The troops fabricated a precarious wooden stairway of cedar logs to cross a steep gap near the top of the bluff. Miners, loggers, settlers, and others soon dubbed it "Devil's Staircase". A new trail eventually bypassed the old wooden contraption. "Staircase" remains as a link with the Peninsula's past.

⚘ Washington 9 ♿

SEQUIM BAY
Sequim Bay State Park

Location: Olympic Peninsula east of Port Angeles.

Access: From U.S. Highway 101 at milepost 269 +.1 (5 miles southeast of Sequim, 13 miles northwest of Discovery Bay), turn north into the park.

Day Use Facilities: Large picnic area; small and large shelters; (large shelter is reservable by groups); drinking water; restrooms; large parking area.

Camping Facilities: *Campground*: 86 campsites, including 26 with full hookups, in 2 loops; (3 hiker-biker/primitive sites are also available); sites in the upper loop are primarily for large vehicles—paved, level, pull-through parking pads; lower loop has smaller sites with better separation—parking pads are short straight-ins which may need additional leveling; small, but nice, tent spots in the lower loop; fireplaces; b-y-o firewood; water at several faucets; restrooms with showers; paved driveways; adequate supplies and services are available in Sequim. *Environmental Learning Center*: 8 Adirondak shelters can sleep up to 75 campers; lodge has indoor sleeping for 15, kitchen, eating and meeting areas; central restrooms; athletic field; picnic area; campfire circle; (ELC is available only to organized groups and only by reservation).

Activities & Attractions: Boating; boat launch, moorage buoys and floats; fishing; swimming beach; scuba diving; nature trails; playground; large, open, grass recreation areas; Ramblewood Environmental Learning Center can accommodate up 100 for day use (open to organized groups, only by reservation).

Natural Features: Located on the forested shore of Sequim Bay in the 'rain shadow' of the Olympic Mountains; picnic and camp sites receive medium to moderately dense shade/shelter from tall conifers; nearby, Dungeness Spit, a 7-mile long natural sand jetty, juts out from the Peninsula into the Strait of Juan de Fuca; sea level.

Season, Fees & Phone: Open all year; please see Appendix for ELC reservation information and campground fees; ☎(360) 683-4235.

Trip Log: Because of the 'rain shadow' effect of the Olympic Mountains, considerably less rain falls here than in the rest of the Olympic Peninsula—only 10-15 inches of annual precipitation, versus rain measured with a log-scaling pole elsewhere. Because of its mild, dry climate, the Sequim Bay area is occasionally termed the 'Banana Belt of the Pacific Northwest'. Lest you get your hopes too high, however, we should point out that the area does get a good share of cloudy, cool weather. This isn't Palm Springs. (Incidentally, drop the 'e' when you pronounce the name: "squim".)

⚜ Washington 10 ♿

SEAL ROCK
Olympic National Forest

Location: Western Washington on the east side of the Olympic Peninsula north of Shelton.

Access: From U.S. Highway 101 at milepost 305 +.4 (10 miles south of Quilcene, 2 miles north of Brinnon), turn east then immediately north and follow the paved access road for 0.2 mile to the recreation area.

Day Use Facilities: Small picnic area; drinking water; restrooms; small parking area.

Camping Facilities: 41 campsites in 3 tiers; sites are small to medium-sized, with nominal to fairly good separation; parking pads are hardened gravel, mostly short to medium-length straight-ins or pull-offs; additional leveling may be necessary; tent spots are fairly clear of underbrush and adequate for medium-sized tents; some sites have framed-and-graveled tent pads; fireplaces; some firewood is available for gathering on nearby forest lands (none in the campground area), so b-y-o is recommended; water at several faucets; restrooms; paved driveways are narrow, with limited space for large vehicles to maneuver; gas and groceries+ in Quilcene; nearest sources of adequate supplies and services are Sequim and Shelton.

Activities & Attractions: Self-guided nature trail; steep trails to the beach; designated swimming area; beachcombing, clamming and crabbing; boating; boat launch; fishing.

Natural Features: Located on a forested hillside overlooking Dabob Bay and Hood Canal on Puget Sound; vegetation in the campground consists of fairly dense, tall conifers, hardwoods, bushes and ferns; rocky beach; the Olympic Mountains rise to the west; elev. 50´.

Season, Fees & Phone: April to October; $7.00 to $8.00-$12.00; 14 day limit; Quilcene Ranger District ☎ (360) 765-3368.

Trip Log: Indians lived at Seal Rock as long as 700 years ago, and the short interpretive trail explains how they used local resources. The campground is on a sheltered bay with good to great views through the trees from virtually all sites. The drive along U.S. 101 in this region is superscenic—between the bay to the east and the Olympics to the west.

(Note: Although this state park and the forest camp described in the foregoing two sections are not within the national park, they offer excellent, saltwater alternatives to the park's inland recreation areas.)

 Washington ⛺
Southwest Corner

⚜ Washington 11 ♿

OCEAN CITY
Ocean City State Park

Location: Olympic Peninsula west of Aberdeen-Hoquiam.

Access: From the junction of Washington State Highways 109 & 115 (16 miles west of Hoquiam), travel south on Highway 115 for 1 mile; turn west into the park.

Day Use Facilities: Medium-sized picnic area; shelter; drinking water; restrooms; medium-sized parking lot.

Camping Facilities: 178 campsites, including 29 with full hookups, in 3 loops: (3 hiker-biker/primitive sites and a small group camp are also available); 130 standard sites (located in 2 loops which flank the entrance station) are small to medium-sized, level, with minimal to nominal separation; most parking pads are short to medium-length straight-ins; large, grassy areas ideal for tent-pitching; 48 hookup units (in a third loop west of the entrance station) are small to small+, level, with nominal to fair separation; parking pads are paved, medium to long, straight-ins or pull-throughs; fireplaces; b-y-o firewood; water at faucets; restrooms with showers; holding tank disposal station; paved driveways; limited supplies are available in Ocean City, 2 miles north, or Ocean Shores, 2 miles south.

Activities & Attractions: Beachcombing; fishing (boat or surf fishing on the ocean, freshwater fishing southeast of the park on Duck Lake); clamming and crabbing; short hiking trails; Ocean Shores Environmental Interpretive Center, near the south end of Ocean Shores, has exhibits and programs which focus on the history, wildlife and land use of Point Brown.

Natural Features: Located on a fairly level stretch of Pacific Ocean coastline on Point Brown; standard camp loops have large conifers which provide light to medium shelter/shade; hookup loop is a little more open, with a beach view from some sites; expansive ocean beach; typically breezy; sea level.

Season, Fees & Phone: Open all year; please see Appendix for campground fees; ☎(360) 289-3553.

Trip Log: There are a couple of other state parks on this stretch of the coast. Griffiths-Priday State Park is located at the mouth of the Copalis River near the hamlet of Copalis Beach. It has a day use area with a medium-sized shelter which is reservable by groups. (Call the Ocean City park office for reservations.) The other park is Pacific Beach State Park, in the burg of Pacific Beach. The park is operated by a concessionaire and it has nearly 140 unsheltered campsites (a few with hookups) packed together along the edge of an open beach.

♣ **Washington 12** ♿

FORT CANBY
Fort Canby State Park

Location: Southwest Washington west of Illwaco.

Access: From U.S. Highway 101 in midtown Illwaco at the corner of First Street and Spruce Street, head west on Spruce Street (Fort Canby Road) and out of town on a winding, hilly road for 3.4 miles to the park

Day Use Facilities: Several small picnic areas: at the beach, near the end of the jetty, at the interpretive center, and in the north end of the park near the North Head Lighthouse; drinking water; restrooms; small to medium-sized parking lots at the beach, at the boat launch, at the end of the jetty and at the interpretive center.

Camping Facilities: 250 campsites, including 60 with full hookups; sites are small to small+ in size, essentially level, with fair to very good separation; parking pads are paved, short to medium-length, mostly straight-ins; adequate space for medium to large tents; b-y-o firewood is recommended; water at several faucets; restrooms with showers; holding tank disposal station; paved driveways; camper supplies at the park concession; limited+ to adequate supplies and services are available in Illwaco.

Activities & Attractions: Lewis and Clark Interpretive Center; swimming/wading in a small cove on Waikiki Beach (really); Cape Disappointment Lighthouse, constructed in the 1850's, is the oldest West Coast lighthouse still in operation; four hiking trails; good beachcombing, particularly in winter; boat launch; fishing.

Natural Features: Located on more than 1700 acres along the Pacific Ocean at the mouth of the Columbia River; picnic sites vary from unsheltered to moderately sheltered; campsites receive light to moderately dense shade/shelter by medium-high shrubbery and bushy pines, and some large hardwoods; sea level to 100´.

Season, Fees & Phone: Open all year; interpretive center open daily during the summer, and weekends by appointment during the winter; campsite reservations accepted, recommended for anytime during the summer; please see Appendix for reservation information and campground fees; ☎(360) 642-3078 or ☎(360) 642-3029.

Trip Log: Fort Canby was operated as a Columbia River defense post from the 1870's to the end of World War II. The interpretive center features exhibits about frontier foods, early medicine, trade goods, biographical information about Lewis and Clark and other principal members of the Corps of Discovery, and info about the expedition. Lewis and Clark spent most of their time on the Coast at their winter home at Fort Clatsop in Oregon. Fort Canby is large enough, though, and has enough items of interest, that you'll probably spend more time than Meriwether & William did on this side of the Columbia.

♣ **Washington 13** ♿

MILLERSYLVANIA
Millersylvania State Park

Location: Western Washington south of Olympia.

Access: From Interstate 5 exit 95 for Maytown/Little Rock (12 miles south of Olympia, 11 miles north of Centralia), drive east on Maytown Road SW for 2.5 miles; at a 'T' intersection, turn north (left) onto Tilley Road and proceed 0.7 mile; turn west (left) into the park.

Day Use Facilities: Several medium to large picnic areas; several large shelters; drinking water; restrooms/bathhouses; large parking lots.

Camping Facilities: *Campground*: 187 campsites, including 52 with partial hookups; sites are small to medium-sized, essentially level, with minimal to fairly good separation; parking pads are gravel, mostly short to medium-length straight-ins; ample space for a large tent in most sites; fire rings; firewood is usually for sale, or b-y-o; water at several faucets; restrooms with showers; kitchen shelter; holding tank disposal station; paved driveways; camper supplies at a small local store; complete supplies and services are available in the Tumwater-Olympia area. *Environmental Learning Center*: 16 cabins (8 each for boys and girls), plus 3 staff cabins can accommodate 158 persons; restrooms with showers; dining hall with kitchen; parking lot; (ELC is available only to organized groups, only by reservation).

Activities & Attractions: Swimming beaches with swim platforms; playgrounds; several hiking trails, including Timber Island Ecology Trail; jogging and fitness trails; athletic field; limited boating (5 mph); boat launch; fishing; Environmental Learning Center has a sheltered outdoor classroom and an athletic field (available only to groups, only by reservation).

Natural Features: Located on a forested flat; park vegetation consists of very tall conifers which provide moderate to dense shelter/shade for picnic and camp sites, plus sections of mown grass, and some hardwoods, bushes and ferns; Deep Lake and Spruce Creek are the park's water features; elevation 100´.

Season, Fees & Phone: Open all year; please see Appendix for ELC reservation information and campground fees; ☎ (360) 753-1519.

Trip Log: Millersylvania's name was coined from the three members of the *Miller* family who donated this *sylvan* (forested) location for the park. The CCC lent a hand in constructing some of the facilities in the 1930's and 1940's.

♠ Washington 14 ♿

BATTLE GROUND LAKE
Battle Ground Lake State Park

Location: Southwest Washington north of Vancouver.

Access: From the junction of Washington State Highways 502 and 503 (west of the city of Battle Ground), drive east on Highway 502 (Main Street) for 0.8 mile to midtown Battle Ground; turn north onto 142nd (Grace Street); drive 0.6 mile north and turn east (right) onto 229th (Heissen Road); drive east, then north, then west on Heissen Road for 2.3 miles to 249th; at the intersection just after the railroad tracks, jog a few yards south (left) then west (right) into the park.

Day Use Facilities: Medium-sized picnic area; large shelter (reservable by groups); drinking water; restrooms/bathhouse; 2 medium-sized parking lots; concession stand.

Camping Facilities: 50 campsites, including 15 walk-in tent sites; (a horse camp and a group camp with 4 shelters is also available, by reservation); sites are small+ to medium-sized, with fair to fairly good separation; parking pads are paved, reasonably level, medium-length straight-ins or medium+ pull-throughs; fireplaces; b-y-o firewood; water at several faucets; restrooms with showers; disposal station; paved driveways; adequate supplies and services are available in Battle Ground.

Activities & Attractions: Fishing for stocked trout; limited boating; small boat launch; sandy swimming beach; nature trail; 5 miles of hiking trails; 5 miles of hiking/equestrian trails.

Natural Features: Located around the shore of 28-acre, spring-fed Battle Ground Lake in the western foothills of the Cascade Range; the lake's waters have collected in the caldera (basin) of an extinct volcano; (chunks of lava—called 'lava bombs'—have been found in the park where they landed after the volcano erupted); park vegetation consists of tall conifers, hardwoods, ferns and shrubs, with some mown lawns in the day use area; bordered by densely forested hills; elevation 100´.

Season, Fees & Phone: Open all year; please see Appendix for campground fees; ☎ (360) 687-4621.

Trip Log: The name for the park, the lake and the nearby town is actually a tongue-in-cheek term which resulted from a battle that never happened. Back in 1855 an Army captain named Strong was sent from Fort Vancouver to capture a band of Klickitat Indians who had escaped from the fort. When he caught up with the escapees, the Indians talked the captain into letting them go long enough to bury their chief, who had met with a fatal accident. The Klickitats said that they would turn themselves in after the funeral. Soft-hearted Captain Strong said OK to this plan, and returned to the fort empty-handed. For his "bravery and courage" he was awarded a petticoat, and the area became known as "Strong's Battle Ground".

 Washington
Puget Sound

♠ Washington 15 ♿

DECEPTION PASS
Deception Pass State Park

Location: Northwest Washington north of Oak Harbor.

Access: From Washington State Highway 20 at milepost 41 +.3 (0.5 mile south of the Deception Pass Bridge, 6.5 miles south of the junction of Highway 20 and the Highway 20 north spur to Anacortes, 9 miles north of Oak Harbor), turn west into the main park unit.

Day Use Facilities: Large picnic area, 2 small shelters and 1 large shelter, drinking water, restrooms and large parking area along the east shore of Cranberry Lake; restrooms/bathhouse and large parking lots at West Beach (parking at West Beach is for both the Cranberry Lake swimming beach and also for the saltwater beach); medium-sized picnic area, small shelter, drinking water, restrooms and large parking lot at North Beach.

Camping Facilities: 230 campsites; (5 hiker-biker sites and a reservable group camp are also available); sites are small to medium-sized, with nominal to good separation; parking pads are gravel, short to medium-length straight-ins or medium to long pull-throughs; most pads will require additional leveling; (the steepest pads are paved—probably so they won't be washed-away in a heavy rain); small to medium-sized tent spots; fireplaces; b-y-o firewood is recommended; water at several faucets; restrooms with showers; holding tank disposal station; paved driveways; adequate+ supplies and services are available in Oak Harbor. *Environmental Learning Center*: 16 sleeping cabins with a total capacity of 156 persons; restrooms; dining hall/kitchen; recreation hall; heated swimming pool; campfire circle; athletic fields; (ELC is available to groups, by reservation only).

(Camping and picnicking are also available in the park's Bowman Bay area, 1 mile north.)

Activities & Attractions: Swimming beach on Cranberry Lake; beachcombing; several miles of hiking trails; Deception Pass Nature Trail (guide pamphlet available); boating (electric or people-propelled on the lakes); boat launch; playground; fishing pier on Cranberry Lake; Cornet Bay Environmental Learning Center (available to organized groups, by reservation only; 250 persons can be accommodated for day use activities).

Natural Features: Located on forested, generally hilly terrain on the northwest corner of Whidbey Island; picnic sites at Cranberry Lake and North Beach are shaded by tall conifers; campsites are moderately shaded by tall conifers and well-sheltered by dense shrubbery; tall conifers tower over lush ferns and underbrush throughout much of the park;

the park encompasses a total of about 2500 acres; sea level.

Season, Fees & Phone: Open all year; please see Appendix for campground fees; ☎(360) 675-2417.

Trip Log: Your choice: freshwater or saltwater beaches within a few yards of each other, separated only by a low dune. The Cranberry Lake picnic area is quite nice. The huge campground is *very* much in demand during the summer. If you're a camper, it might take you a while to pick your way through what might seem to be a maze of driveways.

⚐ Washington 16 ⚐

FORT CASEY
Fort Casey State Park

Location: Northwest Washington south of Oak Harbor.

Access: From Washington State Highway 20 at the Keystone ferry terminal (3.4 miles west of the junction of State Highways 20 & 525 south of Coupeville), proceed northwest on Fort Casey Road for 0.45 mile; turn southwest (left) into the park.

(Special Note: if you're southbound to the park from Oak Harbor and Coupeville, you can save time, miles and fuel by taking a paved secondary road from Coupeville; from Highway 20 at milepost 21 +.9 in Coupeville, turn south onto South Main Street and proceed 0.3 mile through a small business district, then pick up Engle Road and continue traveling south for another 2.8 miles until you merge with Fort Casey Road; continue south on Fort Casey Road for a final 0.5 mile to the park entrance.

Day Use Facilities: Large picnic area; drinking water; restrooms; several medium to large parking lots.

Camping Facilities: 35 campsites; most sites are small, level, with very minimal to fair separation; parking pads are gravel, medium-length straight-ins or medium+ pull-throughs; small tent spaces on a grassy surface; fireplaces; b-y-o firewood; water at faucets; restrooms with showers; paved driveway; adequate supplies and services are available in Coupeville.

Activities & Attractions: Well-preserved coast artillery installation; interpretive- center features displays related to the history of the fort; self-guided walking tour (guide booklet available); hiking trails; access to 2 miles of beach; fishing; boat launch and scuba diving area nearby.

Natural Features: Located on and below a bluff/hill on the middle-west coast of Whidbey Island on Admiralty Inlet; picnic sites are on top of the hill and are lightly to moderately shaded/sheltered by hardwoods and conifers and bordered by dense forest; campground is at the base of the hill along an open shoreline on small Admiralty Bay, with vegetation that consists primarily of sparse grass, bushes and a few small conifers; a rocky beach skirts the shoreside campsites; sea level to 100´.

Season, Fees & Phone: Open all year; please see Appendix for campground fees; ☎(360) 678-4519.

Trip Log: The park's visitor center is located in the very nicely preserved Admiralty Head Lighthouse—a really neat idea. (The little, red-roofed, white-walled lighthouse could almost be called 'cute'.) The picnic sites are pleasant but don't offer a distant view; many of the campsites have reasonably good saltwater views; but the viewpoints from the shore batteries and from the lighthouse along the edge of the bluff are excellent. The campground is only a few yards across the bay from the ferry terminal. If you're a camper and like to take an afternoon snooze, plan your nap around the ferry schedule—the arrival and departure 'toots' from the boat's whistle could provide you with a startling awakening.

♣ **Washington 17** ♿

FORT WORDEN
Fort Worden State Park

Location: Olympic Peninsula north of Port Townsend.

Access: From Washington State Highway 20 (Sims Way) at the west edge of the downtown area in Port Townsend (0.5 mile west of the ferry terminal) turn north onto Kearney Street and continue for 0.4 mile to a 'T' intersection; turn east (right) onto Blaine Street for 0.15 mile; turn north onto Cherry Street and follow Cherry Street for 1.2 miles to another 'T'; jog east (right) onto W Street for 0.05 mile, then north (left) into the park.

Day Use Facilities: Small and medium-sized picnic areas; shelter; drinking water; restrooms; several small and large parking lots.

Camping Facilities: 50 campsites with full hookups; sites are small to medium-sized, level, with minimal separation; parking pads are paved, medium to long straight-ins or pull-throughs; large, grassy tent spots; fireplaces; b-y-o firewood; water at sites; restrooms with showers; paved driveways; adequate supplies and services are available in Port Townsend.

Additional Overnight Facilities: *Vacation Housing*: 23 houses, 'refurbished' or 'unrefurbished'; most units are furnished with Victorian-style 'repros' and are carpeted; units have 2 to 6 bedrooms, with queen-size or twin beds; bathrooms; good-sized, fully equipped kitchens; parlors with fireplaces in most units; (b-y-o TV if you don't want to miss your soaps and sports); limited telephone service; linen and towels are provided; rollaways are available; (no pets). *Dormitories*: Available for groups; accommodations include private rooms, 2 & 4-person rooms, or open bays with 21 bunks each; restrooms; optional linen service; dorms are available only with a meal plan; (a youth hostel is also in the park).

Activities & Attractions: National Historic Landmark District with renovated 1900 military buildings; meeting rooms with capacities of a few persons to hundreds of persons are available for rental and include seminar and conference rooms, a chapel, a theater, auditoriums, a gymnasium and a 15-room schoolhouse; recently renovated pavilion in the former balloon hanger; cafeteria; interpretive center in the Commanding Officers House; Coast Artillery Museum; boating; boat launch, dock and moorage buoys; beach access; 6 miles of hiking trails; playground; tennis courts; underwater park (no spear fishing).

Natural Features: Located on 340 acres on a hill and on the beach at Point Wilson; vacation housing is located on tree-lined streets; campground is on an open, grassy flat between and a forested hillside to the west and a beach on Admiralty Inlet; sweeping view across Admiralty Inlet toward Whidbey Island from the day use and camp areas, as well as just about anywhere else along the east edge of the park; sea level to 100´.

Season, Fees & Phone: Open all year; reservations accepted for conferences and vacation housing; please contact the park directly for current rate schedules and to make reservations; (expect to pay in excess of $100.00 per night for a typical refurbished house, or roughly 25 percent less for an unrefurbished unit); please see Appendix for campground fees; ☎(360) 385-4730.

Trip Log: Fort Worden is one of the West's most unusual state parks. Although there are other parks in the West with vacation and conference housing (Oklahoma's state resorts, for instance), none offer quite the breadth and depth of Fort Worden's. Essential info about the park's 'get-away' and conference lodging has been listed in the sections above, but for details you should call and request the applicable park brochures and rate cards. If you and your old Army buddies want to get together and swap war stories in a nostalgic setting, reserve one of the dorms—the remodeled barracks will provide an authentic atmosphere for your gathering.

⚑ Washington 18 ♿

FORT FLAGLER
Fort Flagler State Park

Location: Olympic Peninsula south of Port Townsend.

Access: From Washington State Highway 20 south of Port Townsend or Washington State Highway 104 northwest of the Hood Canal Bridge, follow the signs on local roads to the community of Port Hadlock (also called just 'Hadlock'); from midtown Port Hadlock at the corner of Irondale Road and Oak Bay Road, proceed easterly on Oak Bay Road for 0.9 mile; turn northeasterly (left) onto Flagler Road (watch for signs to Marrowstone Island and Fort Flagler), and travel on this winding road northeast, then southeast, then northerly (through the hamlet of Nordland) for a total of 8 miles to the park.

Day Use Facilities: Medium-sized picnic area; small shelter; drinking water; restrooms; large parking area.

Camping Facilities: 116 campsites in 3 loops; (hiker-biker sites, a group camp, and a youth hostel are also available); sites are small to medium-sized, with minimal to fair separation in the lower loops, and fair to fairly good separation in the upper loop; parking pads are gravel, short to medium-length straight-ins or medium to long pull-throughs; some pads will require a little additional leveling, especially in the upper loop; many good to excellent tent spots in the lower loops; fireplaces; b-y-o firewood is suggested; water at several faucets; restrooms with showers; holding tank disposal station; paved driveways; camper supplies at the park concession; adequate supplies and services are available in Port Hadlock.

Activities & Attractions: Self-guided tours of Fort Flagler; Roots of a Forest Interpretive Trail; hiking trails; beach access; boating; boat launches; dock and moorage buoys; fishing; clamming; playground; Environmental Learning Center (available to groups as large as 270 persons, by reservation).

Natural Features: Located at the northern tip of Marrowstone Island in Puget Sound; picnic sites are on an open, grassy beach area dotted with a few evergreens; campsites 1-47 are on a forested hillside with some scenic views through the trees; sites 48-96 are along the treeline near the beach; sites 97-116 are on an open, grass flat along the beach; historic area is on a huge, open, grassy flat and slope; great views of Admiralty Inlet and Whidbey Island from the park; sea level to 100´.

Season, Fees & Phone: Open all year; campsite reservations accepted, recommended for anytime during the summer, well in advance for weekends; please see Appendix for reservation information and campground fees; ☎ (360) 385-1259.

Trip Log: Of the triad of defense posts set up in the 1890's to guard the entrance to Puget Sound (also see Fort Worden and Fort Casey), Fort Flagler has, subjectively, the best picnicking and camping opportunities, and, overall, might also be the most attractive park as well. Although the east side of the Puget Sound region gets a lot of precipitation, Fort Flagler is in the 'rain shadow' of the Olympic Mountains and consequently the rainfall here is measured not in feet but in inches—an average of only 17 inches a year.

⚑ Washington 19 ♿

SCENIC BEACH
Scenic Beach State Park

Location: Western Washington northwest of Bremerton.

Access: From Washington State Highway 3 at milepost 43 +.5 (the Newberry Hill Exit, 8 miles north of Bremerton), travel west on Newberry Hill Road for 3 miles to a 'T' intersection; turn north (right) and follow the road 5 miles in a long sweeping 180 degree curve to Seabeck (you'll now be headed south); at a point 0.1 mile south of the Seabeck elementary school, turn west onto Scenic Beach Road and proceed 1.5 miles to the park.

Day Use Facilities: Large picnic area; large shelter (reservable by groups); drinking water; restrooms; 2 large parking lots.

Camping Facilities: 52 campsites in two loops; (2 hiker-biker/primitive sites are also available); most sites are medium to large, with fair to excellent separation; parking pads are medium+ to very long, packed/oiled gravel, pull-throughs or straight-ins; a little additional leveling may be required in some sites; adequate level space for large tents in most sites; fireplaces; b-y-o firewood; water at faucets every few sites; restrooms with showers in each loop; holding tank disposal station; paved driveways; gas and groceries in Seabeck; fairly complete supplies and services are available in Bremerton.

Activities & Attractions: Trails through the forest and down to the beach; beachcombing; swimming area; fishing; boating; public boat launch at Misery Point, 1 mile north; playgrounds in the day use area and campground.

Natural Features: Located on the Kitsap Peninsula along and above the east shore of Hood Canal, a major arm of Puget Sound; day use area is in a moderately forested section near the shore, campground is on a densely forested hillside; sea level to 150´.

Season, Fees & Phone: Open all year, but limited to weekends and holidays October to April; please see Appendix for campground fees; ☎ (360) 831-5079.

Trip Log: Scenic Beach is an extraordinarily well designed park. The environment here is superb. Many tables in the campground are installed on the hillside above the parking spots, with steps for easy accessibility, so campers in those sites get a slightly elevated view of the richly forested surroundings. It gets a little busy on summer weekends, so you may enjoy it more in spring or fall. (To be honest about it, the park can be pretty nice in winter too.) Fabulous views of the Olympic Mountains!

♣ Washington 20 ♿

BELFAIR
Belfair State Park

Location: Western Washington southwest of Bremerton.

Access: From the junction of Washington State Highways 3 and 300 in Belfair (10 miles southwest of Bremerton), drive southwest on Highway 300 for 3.1 miles; turn south (left) into the park.

Day Use Facilities: Large picnic area; drinking water; restrooms/bathhouse; large parking lot.

Camping Facilities: 184 campsites, including 47 with full hookups, in 3 loops; sites are very small to medium-sized, essentially level, with minimal to fairly good separation; parking pads are gravel, short to medium+ straight-ins or pull-throughs; tent areas vary from small to large; fireplaces; b-y-o firewood is recommended; water at several faucets; restrooms with showers; holding tank disposal station; paved driveways; adequate supplies and services are available in Belfair.

Activities & Attractions: Swimming lagoon; athletic field; volleyball court; beachcombing; crabbing, clamming, oystering; fishing; playground.

Natural Features: Located along the shore of Hood Canal, a major arm/inlet of Puget Sound; picnic sites and one camp loop are on a large, semi-open, grassy, soundside flat; most campsites are in a dense forest of very tall conifers, ferns and a considerable amount of underbrush; the loop closest to Hood Canal is more open and includes some lawn areas; Big Mission Creek flows past the day use area, Little Mission Creek drifts past the camp loops; over 2000 feet of Hood Canal shoreline are within the park; sea level.

Season, Fees & Phone: Open all year; campsite reservations accepted, suggested for anytime during summer; please see Appendix for reservation information and campground fees; ☎ (360) 478-4625

Trip Log: The park has a distinctive dual personality. The day use area and the camp loop along the shore, with their sections of mown grass dotted with hardwoods and evergreens, bear little resemblance to the two large camp loops back in the tall timber. The park is noted for its tideflats and the shellfishing and bird viewing activities they provide.

♣ Washington 21 ♿

PENROSE POINT
Penrose Point State Park

Location: Western Washington west of Tacoma.

Access: From Washington State Highway 302 at milepost 11 +.3 in Key Center (9 miles southwest of the Purdy/Shelton Exit on State Highway 16, 11 miles southeast of the junction of State Highways 302 and 3 south of Belfair), travel southerly on Key Peninsula Highway for 6.2 miles (through Lakebay); turn easterly (left) onto Delano Road and proceed 1.2 miles, then turn north (left) onto 158th Avenue for a final 0.3 mile to the park.

Day Use Facilities: Large picnic area; drinking water; restrooms; 2 large parking lots.

Camping Facilities: 83 campsites; (2 hiker-biker/primitive sites and a group camp are also available); sites are small, with fair to good separation; parking pads are gravel or paved, mostly short to short+ straight-ins, plus a few medium-length pull-throughs; many pads will require a little additional leveling; adequate space for medium to large tents in most sites; kitchen shelters; fireplaces; b-y-o firewood; water at several faucets; restrooms with showers; holding tank disposal station; paved driveways; gas and groceries in Lakebay.

Activities & Attractions: Beachcombing; clamming; swimming beach; 2.5 miles of hiking trails; A Touch of Nature Interpretive Trail (guide pamphlet available); boating; boat launch, 120´ dock, moorage buoys; fishing.

Natural Features: Located on Key Peninsula along Carr Inlet near the south end of Puget Sound; park vegetation consists of dense stands of tall conifers, hardwoods, ferns, and other dense ground cover, plus some large, open grassy areas; day use area is along the cove, campground is back in the forest, within a few minutes' walk of the shore; sea level.

Season, Fees & Phone: Open all year; please see Appendix for campground fees; ☎(360) 884-2514.

Trip Log: The park is named for Dr. Stephen Penrose, a prominent educational and church leader and long-time president of respected Whitman College in Walla Walla. Penrose and his family spent their summers vacationing on what is now park land. Penrose Point has one of the nicest day use areas on Puget Sound.

⚐ Washington 22 ⚐

KOPACHUCK
Kopachuck State Park

Location: Western Washington west of Tacoma.

Access: From Washington State Highway 16 (a 4-lane divided highway) at the Gig Harbor

City Center Exit near milepost 12 (4 miles northwest of the Tacoma Narrows bridge), turn southwest onto Wollochet Drive NW for 0.4 mile, then west (right) on Hunt Street NW for 0.2 mile, then north (right again) on 45th Avenue NW (Skansie Street) for 1 mile; turn west (left) onto Rosedale Street NW and travel 2.4 miles; turn southwest (left) onto Ray Nash Drive NW for 0.7 mile, then pick up Kopachuck Drive and continue southwest for 1.7 miles to the end of Kopachuck Drive; angle south (an easy left) onto Artondale Drive for 0.1 mile, then turn west (right) into the park.

Day Use Facilities: Medium-sized picnic area; shelters; drinking water; restrooms; large parking lot.

Camping Facilities: 41 campsites; (a group camp is also available); sites are small+ to medium-sized, reasonably level, with good to excellent separation; parking pads are gravel/paved, short to medium-length straight-ins; some pads will require a little additional leveling; adequate space for medium to large tents; fireplaces; b-y-o firewood; water at several faucets; restrooms with showers; holding tank disposal station; paved driveways; adequate supplies and services are available in Gig Harbor.

Activities & Attractions: Beachcombing; underwater scuba park; boating; moorage buoys; (nearest public boat launch is near the community of Arletta, 3 miles by land, 4 if by sea around Green Point.)

Natural Features: Located along, and on a slope above, the west shore of Henderson Bay, a major arm of Puget Sound, at the head of Carr Inlet, a small, secondary bay; park vegetation consists of light to medium-dense, towering conifers, plus hardwoods, dense bushes and ferns; sea level to 100´.

Season, Fees & Phone: Open all year; please see Appendix for campground fees; ☎(360) 265-3606.

Trip Log: Even if there were no picnic area or campground, a trip to the park could be justified on the basis of your being able to enjoy a walk among the giants in this fern-carpeted forest by the bay. *Kopachuck* is from an Indian phrase *kopa-chuk* which simply means "at the water".

♠ Washington 23

CAMANO ISLAND
Camano Island State Park

Location: Western Washington northwest of Everett.

Access: From Interstate 5 Exit 212 for Stanwood/Camano Island (17 miles north of Everett, 15 miles south of Mount Vernon), head west on Washington State Highway 532 for 9.5 miles to a fork; take the south (left) fork, continuing on Highway 532, which then becomes East Camano Drive and follow this road for 5.7 miles to another fork; continue southwesterly (i.e., straight ahead, on the right fork) onto Elger Bay Road for 1.9 miles; turn west (right) onto West Camano Drive and proceed 1.7 miles, then turn southerly (left) onto Park Drive for 0.9 mile into the park.

Day Use Facilities: Small and medium-sized picnic areas; shelter; drinking water; restrooms/bathhouse; large parking lots.

Camping Facilities: 87 campsites; (a large group camp is also available); sites are small or large, with fair to very good separation; parking pads are gravel, short straight-ins or medium to long pull-throughs; additional leveling will be required in some sites; medium to large, acceptably level tent areas; fireplaces; firewood is usually for sale, or b-y-o; water at central faucets; restrooms with showers; holding tank disposal station; paved driveways; gas and groceries at a local store; adequate supplies and services are available in Stanwood, 14 miles northeast.

Activities & Attractions: Hiking trails; Al Emerson Nature Trail (a guide pamphlet is available); boating; boat launch; swimming beach; amphitheater.

Natural Features: Located on hilly terrain along and above the middle-west shore of Camano Island; the west side of the island is situated on Saratoga Passage, north of Puget Sound; park vegetation consists of a dense blanket of ferns and bushes topped by tall conifers; (some of the Doug firs here are more than 600 years old); main day use area is along the beach on the southwest corner of the park; campground is on a short hill/bluff; the Olympic Mountains are in view to the southwest; sea level to 50´.

Season, Fees & Phone: Open all year; please see Appendix for campground fees; ☎(360) 387-3031 or ☎(360) 387-2575.

Trip Log: Back in 1949, after this land was first set aside to be developed as a park, 900 volunteers roughed-out the new park's facilities in one day. Nowadays, nearly that many visitors could come to camp, picnic or boat here on a single busy summer Saturday or Sunday. The island was named for a relatively obscure Spanish explorer, Jacinto Camano.

 Washington
North Western

♠ Washington 24 ♿

BIRCH BAY
Birch Bay State Park

Location: Northwest Washington northwest of Bellingham.

Access: From Interstate 5 Exit 266 for Custer/Grandview Road (3 miles north of Ferndale, 11 miles south of Blaine), travel west on Grandview Road for 7 miles (to the first side road past the refinery); turn north (right) onto Jackson Road; proceed 0.8 mile; turn west (left) onto Helwig Road and go 0.6 mile to the park.

Day Use Facilities: Picnic area; 3 shelters; drinking water; restrooms; large parking area; concession stand.

Camping Facilities: 167 campsites, including 20 with partial hookups; sites are small to small+, level, with nil to fair separation; parking pads are gravel, short to medium-length straight-ins, plus a few long pull-throughs; adequate space for a medium to large tent in most sites; fireplaces; b-y-o firewood; water at several faucets; restrooms with showers; holding tank disposal station; paved driveways; limited+ supplies and services are available in the city of Birch Bay, 5 miles north.

Activities & Attractions: Beachcombing; clamming and crabbing; swimming; Terrell Marsh Nature Trail, a half-mile loop which winds through a 40-acre freshwater marsh; (a guide pamphlet for the marsh trail is available , as well as a "Pictorial Guide to Marine Organisms at Birch Bay State Park" pamphlet).

Natural Features: Located at the south end of Birch Bay, east of the Strait of Georgia; park vegetation consists of tall conifers, hardwoods and a moderate amount of underbrush, which provide light to moderately dense shade/shelter; sea level.

Season, Fees & Phone: Open all year; (patrolled day and night); campsite reservations accepted; please see Appendix for reservation information and campground fees; ☎(360) 371-2800.

Trip Log: The entire park is at or just above high tide level, so it's an easy walk from anywhere in the place through the treeline and across the creek to the beach. You can catch glimpses of the shore from some campsites as well. Reportedly, about a million people a year visit the park. Birch Bay's clientele seems to be typically made up of approximately equal quantities of Yanks and Canucks, so if you want to become pals with someone from another country, this is the place to do it.

♣ **Washington 25**

LARRABEE
Larrabee State Park

Location: Northwest Washington south of Bellingham.

Access: From Interstate 5 (northbound), Exit 231 in Burlington, travel northwest on Washington State Highway 11 for 14 miles; turn west (left) into the park. **Alternate Access:** From Interstate 5 (southbound), Exit 250 (4 miles south of Bellingham), turn west onto Highway 11 and proceed west then south for 7 miles to the park entrance.

Day Use Facilities: Large picnic area; medium and large shelters (reservable by groups); drinking water; restrooms; large parking lot.

Camping Facilities: 87 campsites, including 26 with full hookups; (3 hiker-biker/primitive sites and a group camp are also available); sites are small to medium-sized, with nominal separation; parking pads are paved or gravel, mostly short to medium+ straight-ins; (longer pads are designated for trailers); many pads may require additional leveling; fireplaces; b-y-o firewood is recommended; water at several faucets; restrooms with showers; holding tank disposal station; paved driveway; complete supplies and services are available in Bellingham.

Activities & Attractions: 8 miles of hiking trails; (a shoreline guide pamphlet is available); swimming area; playground; fishing; boating; boat launch.

Natural Features: Located on a forested, hilly terrain along and above the shore of Samish Bay; there is a view of Puget Sound from some campsites; the camping area has a mown lawn with huge trees, ferns and shrubbery; sea level to 100´.

Season, Fees & Phone: Open all year; please see Appendix for campground fees; ☎(360) 676-2093.

Trip Log: If you enjoy hiking or just poking around on the beach, Larrabee offers a good choice of walks. Some trails lead to the shore where marine life can be observed in tidal pools; other trails lead to two mountain lakes. The scenic drive along Highway 11 (the highway is locally called Chuckanut Drive) is quite fascinating. It follows the shore and at times passes through a tunnel of lush, green vegetation. There are some excellent views of the San Juan Islands from the park. And if you're lucky enough to hit this place on a clear day, you'll be able to glimpse Mount Rainier waaaaaay off in the distant south.

♣ **Washington 26** ♿

MORAN
Moran State Park

Location: Northwest Washington southwest of Bellingham.

Access: From the Washington State ferry terminal at Anacortes, take the ferry to Orcas Island; from the Orcas ferry terminal, turn west (*left*) for 0.1 mile, then head northerly on Horseshoe Highway for 8 miles to and through the small community of Eastsound; continue southeasterly on Horseshoe Highway for another 3.5 miles to the park.

Day Use Facilities: Medium-sized picnic area; 5 shelters; drinking water; restrooms; medium-sized parking area.

Camping Facilities: 136 campsites in four areas—North End, Midway (Cascade Lake), South End (Cascade Lake), and Mountain Lake; (a dozen hiker-biker/primitive sites are also available in a fifth area along the road between the two lakes); sites are small to medium-sized, with nominal for fairly good separation; parking pads are mostly short to medium-length straight-ins, plus a few medium+ pull-throughs; tent space varies from small to large; fireplaces; b-y-o firewood; water at several faucets; restrooms with showers; holding tank disposal station; groceries in Eastsound and near the ferry landing; adequate+ supplies and services are available in Anacortes.

Activities & Attractions: 30 miles of hiking opportunities on more than a dozen trails (a guide pamphlet is available); swimming, sandy beach, limited lake boating (no gas motors), boat launch, windsurfing and fishing on Cascade

Lake; stone tower at the summit of Mount Constitution built in 1936 by the CCC, said to be designed to resemble the watch towers of the Caucasus Mountains in southeast Europe.

Natural Features: Located on and around Mount Constitution, at 2409´ the highest point in the San Juan Islands, and smaller Mount Picket; park vegetation consists of a conifer forest with dense undercover, plus some open grassy fields; 5 lakes, including sizable Cascade Lake and Mountain Lake, plus much smaller Summit Lake and Twin Lakes, are within the park; (road access to the first three lakes, trail access to Twin Lakes); a small section on the northeast corner of the park lies along the Strait of Georgia (very limited boat access only); sea level to 2409´.

Season, Fees & Phone: Open all year; campsite reservations accepted, recommended for weekends and holidays; please see Appendix for reservation information and campground fees; ☎(360) 376-2326.

Trip Log: This park's remoteness, it's abundance of fine scenery, it's varied activities—and, if nothing else, the ferry schedule—will frustrate your attempts to just pack it all in on a quick day-trip from the mainland. (Under the right set of circumstances that *can* be done during the summer; so can a one-day round trip from Seattle to Paris—but what's the point?) If you're not a camper, a call to the San Juan C of C in Friday Harbor, ☎(360) 378-5240, will get you the lowdown on conventional lodging and bed & breakfast houses on the island, but make your plans *well* in advance.

 # *Washington* ⛺

Mount Rainier National Park

⛺ **Washington 27**

SUNSHINE POINT
Mount Rainier National Park

Location: Southwest Washington in the southwest quadrant of Mount Rainier National Park.

Access: From Paradise Road at a point 0.2 mile east of the Nisqually Entrance Station and 6 miles west of Longmire, turn south into the campground. (Note: Paradise Road-Stevens Canyon Road is the main east-west route through the southern section of the national park; it links Washington State Highway 706 at the southwest corner of the park with State Highway 123 at the southeast corner of the park.)

Day Use Facilities: None.

Camping Facilities: 18 campsites; sites are small to medium-sized, level, with minimal to nominal separation; parking pads are gravel, mostly short to medium-length straight-ins; medium to large areas for tents; fireplaces; b-y-o firewood; water at faucets; vault facilities; paved driveways; minimal supplies in Longmire, limited supplies and services are available in Ashford, 7 miles west.

Activities & Attractions: Very large visitor center at Paradise; museum in Longmire; fishing and hiking.

Natural Features: Located on a large flat along the Nisqually River; campsites are either in the open right along the riverbank, or just at the forest's edge; vegetation consists primarily of some tall grass and medium-dense, tall conifers; Mount Rainier, visible to the north, is a glacier-clad 14,000´ dormant volcano surrounded by lush rain forests and alpine meadows; the Nisqually River, parented by the glaciers of Rainier, flows west past Sunshine Point on its way to Puget Sound; elevation 2000´.

Season, Fees & Phone: Open all year with limited services in winter; $8.00; 14 day limit; park headquarters ☎(360) 569-2211.

Trip Log: Sunshine Point is distinctively different from the other campgrounds in Mount Rainier National Park. Its climatic conditions allow for year-round camping, whereas most other camping areas are snowed-in for much of the year.

⛺ **Washington 28** ♿

COUGAR ROCK
Mount Rainier National Park

Location: Southwest Washington in the southwest quadrant of Mount Rainier National Park.

Access: From Paradise Road at a point 2.3 miles northeast of Longmire and 26 miles west of the junction of Paradise Road & State Highway 123 northeast of Packwood), turn north-west into the campground.

Day Use Facilities: Small picnic area, drinking water, restrooms, medium-sized parking area at Longmire.

Camping Facilities: 200 campsites in 6 loops; sites are generally small to small+, with nominal to fair separation; parking pads are gravel, mostly short to medium-length straight-ins, although about one-fourth are longer pull-throughs; some pads may require additional leveling; excellent tent-pitching opportunities; fireplaces; b-y-o firewood; water at faucets; restrooms; holding tank disposal station; paved driveways; camper supplies in Longmire.

Activities & Attractions: Wonderland Hiking Trail; Carter Falls; amphitheater for campfire programs; ranger-directed naturalist programs for children on summer weekends; Paradise Visitor Center and Viewpoint located a few miles east; Longmire also has a visitor center and museum.

Natural Features: Located in the Cascade Range on the south slope of Mount Rainier; the Paradise River flows into the Nisqually River at Cougar Rock; vegetation in the campground is predominantly tall conifers covered with hanging moss, plus a considerable quantity of ferns and underbrush; elevation 3200´.

Season, Fees & Phone: June to October; $10.00; 14 day limit; park headquarters ☎(360) 569-2211.

Trip Log: This campground is located in a rain forest-like atmosphere created by the moist maritime air flowing upward across the west slopes of Mount Rainier. If you're westbound on this route from Highway 123 to Cougar Rock and the other camp in the park's southwest quadrant, Sunshine Point, allow *at least* a couple of hours for the winding, hilly trip.

♠ **Washington 29** ♿

PARADISE
Mount Rainier National Park

Location: Southwest Washington in the south-central Mount Rainier National Park.

Access: From Paradise Road at a point 7 miles northeast of Longmire and 21 miles west of the junction of Paradise Road & State Highway 123 northeast of Packwood), turn north-west into visitor center parking lot. (Note: Paradise Road-Stevens Canyon Road is the main east-west route through the southern section of the national park; it links Washington State Highway 706 at the southwest corner of the park with State Highway 123 at the southeast corner of the park.)

Day Use Facilities: Medium-sized picnic area; drinking water; restrooms; large parking lot.

Camping Facilities: Nearest public campground is Cougar Rock (described above).

Activities & Attractions: Paradise Visitor Center and Viewpoint.

Natural Features: Located in the Cascade Range on the south slope of Mount Rainier; local vegetation consists primarily of tall conifers elevation 5200´.

Season, Fees & Phone: June to October; park headquarters ☎(360) 569-2211.

Trip Log: The drive along Paradise Road offers some truly *great* scenic views. Yet they pale in comparison to the awesome panoramas here at Paradise. If you want to see the sight of your life (it indeed may lengthen your years), do whatever it takes to spend time at the Paradise Visitor Center on a clear day. The captivating view of *The Mountain* through the visitor center's walls of glass and from the exterior observation decks is nothing short of absolutely astounding. Period.

♠ **Washington 30** ♿

OHANAPECOSH
Mount Rainier National Park

Location: Southwest Washington in the southeast corner of Mount Rainier National Park.

Access: From Washington State Highway 123 at milepost 3 +.7 (1.5 miles south of the junction of Highway 123 & Stevens Canyon Road, 2 miles north of the national park-national forest boundary, 3.7 miles north of the junction of Highway 123 & U.S. Highway 12 northeast of Packwood), turn west onto a paved access road; go a few yards to a fork, then bear right and proceed 0.3 mile to the recreation area.

Day Use Facilities: Small picnic area; drinking water; restrooms; small and medium-sized parking areas.

Camping Facilities: 220 campsites, including some walk-in sites, in several loops; campsites are generally small to small+, and closely spaced; parking pads are packed gravel, short to scant medium-length straight-ins; many pads may require additional leveling; a few sites will accommodate medium-sized rv's; many excellent tent spots; fireplaces; b-y-o firewood; restrooms; water at several faucets; holding tank disposal station; paved driveways; limited supplies and services are available in Packwood.

Activities & Attractions: Ohanapecosh Visitor Center offers historical information, plus exhibits about local animal life and vegetation; amphitheater for scheduled campfire programs in summer; self-guided and naturalist-guided walks to Silver Falls, Hot Springs, Laughing Water and Grove of the Patriarchs.

Natural Features: Located on hilly terrain in a densely forested valley along the glacier-fed Ohanapecosh River; Ohanapecosh Hot Springs is accessible by foot trail 0.1 mile east; campsite settings vary considerably: some sites are moderately forested, others have a few tall trees and no underbrush; some sites are situated on small knolls while others are on a creek's edge; elevation 1900´.

Season, Fees & Phone: May to October; $10.00; 14 day limit; park headquarters ☎(360) 569-2211.

Trip Log: Superscenic hikes, bikes and drives are important features of this park. Mount Rainier, at 14,410 feet, towers over the rest of the park and solicits spectacular views from numerous hiking trails and roadside pullouts.

 Washington 31 &

WHITE RIVER
Mount Rainier National Park

Location: Southwest Washington in northeast Mount Rainier National Park.

Access: From Washington State Highway 410 (Mather Memorial Parkway) at milepost 62 +.2 (4.5 miles north of Cayuse Pass summit, 39 miles southeast of Enumclaw), turn west onto a paved park road toward the national park's White River Entrance and Sunrise Point; travel 5.2 miles to a fork in the road; take the left fork and continue for another 2.5 miles to the campground.

Day Use Facilities: None.

Camping Facilities: 115 campsites in 4 loops; most sites are average in size and fairly well separated; parking pads are gravel, medium-length straight-ins or pull-offs; some pads will require additional leveling; some excellent tent-pitching opportunities; fireplaces; b-y-o firewood; water at several faucets; restrooms; paved driveways; camper supplies are available at Sunrise Point.

Activities & Attractions: Amphitheater for ranger-naturalist campfire programs on summer weekends; trailhead for Glacier Basin located at the west end of the campground; Sunrise Point Visitor Center located several miles north.

Natural Features: Located on a forested slope along the White River, which flows down from the heights of Mount Rainier; moderately dense vegetation consists of conifers, bushes and ferns over a somewhat rocky forest floor; nearby Sunrise Point offers a magnificent view of Mount Rainier; elevation 4400´.

Season, Fees & Phone: July to September; $10.00; 14 day limit; park headquarters ☎(360) 569-2211.

Trip Log: Mount Rainier National Park offers visitors a chance to commune with nature at its best. Subalpine meadows bloom with a myriad of flowers near the edge of acres of tenacious glaciers. White River Campground is at one of the closest drive-in points to the great dormant volcano which the Indians called *Tahoma*, simply "The Mountain".

Washington ▲
South Western

 Washington 32 &

LA WIS WIS
Gifford Pinchot National Forest

Location: Southwest Washington near the southeast corner of Mount Rainier National Park.

Access: From U.S. Highway 12 at milepost 138 (7 miles northeast of Packwood, 1 mile southwest of the junction of U.S. 12 and Washington State Highway 123), turn north (i.e., left if approaching from Packwood) onto a paved, but steep and twisty, access road; continue for 0.6 mile to the recreation area.

Day Use Facilities: Small picnic area; shelter; drinking water; restrooms; small parking area.

Camping Facilities: 101 campsites in 5 main loops plus 23 more in a "Hatchery" rv loop and a few walk-in tent sites; sites are average or better in size, mostly level, and fairly well separated; parking pads are paved, primarily very short to medium-length straight-ins; A Loop has longer pads; Hatchery Loop has paved, pull-off parking; fairly level, small to large tent spots; fireplaces or fire rings; some firewood is usually available for gathering in the area; water at several faucets; centrally located restrooms, plus auxiliary vault facilities; paved driveways; limited+ supplies and services are available in Packwood.

Activities & Attractions: Fishing; Blue Hole Trail; the surrounding forested region has many trails—including one for exploring an old growth forest; Ohanapecosh Visitor Center is nearby in Mount Rainier National Park.

Natural Features: Located in the Cascade Range in the narrow Ohanapecosh River Valley near the confluence of the Ohanapecosh and Cowlitz Rivers; rain forest-like vegetation predominates in this area; Mount Rainier National Park is 4 miles north; elevation 1400´.

Season, Fees & Phone: May to September; $8.00 for a standard site, $9.00 for a "premium" site (along the riverbank), $10.00 for a multiple site; 14 day limit; Packwood Ranger District ☎(360) 494-5515.

Trip Log: La Wis Wis is located in a lush forest of fir, hemlock and cedar, above a soft carpet of ferns and moss. The narrow valley between the Ohanapecosh and Cowlitz Rivers is a really lovely setting for a mountain retreat.

♣ **Washington 33**

IRON CREEK
Gifford Pinchot National Forest

Location: Southwest Washington northeast of Mount St. Helens National Volcanic Monument.

Access: From U.S. Highway 12 at milepost 115 in Randle (16 miles west of Packwood, 17 miles east of Morton), head south on Cispus Road/Forest Road 23 (paved) for 1 mile to a fork; take the right fork onto Forest Road 25 (paved) and continue southerly for another 8.6 miles; turn northeast (left) onto a paved access road into the recreation area.

Day Use Facilities: Small picnic area; drinking water; vault facilities; ; small parking area.

Camping Facilities: 98 campsites, including some double-occupancy units, in 4 loops; sites are small+ to medium-sized, with fairly good to excellent separation; parking pads are paved, short+ to long straight-ins; a touch of additional leveling may be needed in some sites; ample room for tents in most sites; fire rings; firewood is available for gathering; water at central faucets; vault facilities; paved driveways; limited+ supplies and services are available in Randle.

Activities & Attractions: Fishing; short trails lead down to the river; Big Trees Nature Trail; small amphitheater for campfire interpretive programs on summer weekends; scores of hiking trails and forest roads in the area, including Forest Road 99 to the Spirit Lake area just below Mount St. Helens; small visitor

information center, 4 miles north on Forest Road 25 at mile 4 +.7 (open during midsummer).

Natural Features: Located on gently rolling, sloping terrain above the confluence of the Cispus River and Iron Creek in the foothills of the west slope of the Cascade Range; sites receive medium to moderately dense shade/shelter from lofty conifers and abundant undercover; the active volcano, Mount St. Helens, rises to a foreshortened 8400´, 18 miles southwest; campground elevation 1100´.

Season, Fees & Phone: May to November; $8.00 for a single site, $10.00 for a double unit; 14 day limit; Randle Ranger District ☎(360) 497-7565.

Trip Log: Standing in the middle of an Iron Creek picnic or camp site and gazing skyward through the forest is like having a view from the lower deck of a 200-foot silo of light, air and space. Each site, in a nice-sized clearing encircled by towering trees, has its own natural cathedral ceiling, so to speak. A small visitor could stand under a giant fern and stay dry in a downpour in this forest. Whoever picked the location and designed the recreation area knew what they were doing.

♣ **Washington 34**

PLEASANT VALLEY
Snoqualmie/Wenatchee National Forests

Location: West-central Washington northwest of Yakima.

Access: From Washington State Highway 410 at milepost 80 +.3 (11 miles east of Chinook Pass, 15 miles east of the junction of State Highways 410 & 123, 40 miles northwest of Naches), turn south onto an oiled gravel access road; proceed 0.1 mile to the recreation area.

Day Use Facilities: Small picnic area; shelter; drinking water; vault facilities; small parking area.

Camping Facilities: 17 campsites in 2 loops; sites are medium+ to very large, with fair to very good separation; parking pads are gravel/dirt, mostly medium to very long straight-ins; a few pads may require additional leveling; large, mostly level areas for tents; fire rings or fireplaces; firewood is available for gathering; firewood is available for gathering; water at a hand pump; vault facilities; gravel/dirt driveways; gas and camper supplies in Cliffdell, near milepost 96; limited+ supplies and services are available in Naches.

Activities & Attractions: Kettle Creek Trail; footbridge across the stream; trout fishing.

Natural Features: Located on a slightly rolling flat along the bank of the American River in Pleasant Valley in the Cascade Range; campground vegetation consists of dense, very tall conifers and dense undergrowth, adjacent to a meadow; Norse Peak Wilderness lies to the north, William O. Douglas Wilderness (named for the late conservationist and U.S. Supreme Court Justice) lies to the south; elevation 3300´.

Season, Fees & Phone: May to October; $7.00; 14 day limit; Naches Ranger District ☎(509) 653-2205.

Trip Log: The large shelter could definitely come in handy on the not-infrequent rainy days around here. It comes complete with a good-sized, chimneyed barbecue grill—just the appliance you might need to help conquer rainy day appetites. Pleasant Valley is representative of the several riverside forest camp and picnic grounds along or near scenic Highway 410. Several nice 'grounds are also located along Bumping Road, east of here. The turnoff onto that road is near mile 88 +.5.

♣ Washington 35

INDIAN CREEK
Snoqualmie/Wenatchee National Forests

Location: South-central Washington between Mount Rainier National Park and Yakima.

Access: From U.S. Highway 12 at milepost 159 +.4 (9 miles east of White Pass, 26 miles west of the junction of U.S. 12 & Washington State Highway 410 near Naches), turn south into the campground.

Day Use Facilities: None.

Camping Facilities: 43 campsites; sites are medium to large, level, with fair to very good separation; parking pads are gravel, medium to long straight-ins; some large, level tent spots; fireplaces or fire rings; firewood is available for gathering in the area; water at faucets throughout; vault facilities; camper supplies at a small store on the north shore of Rimrock Lake; limited+ supplies and services are available in Naches.

Activities & Attractions: Boating; fishing; public boat launch located at the east end of Rimrock Lake; White Pass Recreation Area is 8 miles west; Mount Rainier National Park is 30 miles west.

Natural Features: Located on a large, timbered flat in the Cascade Range at the west end of Rimrock Lake, a beautiful mountain lake formed by a dam across the Tieton River about 5 miles east; high timbered ridges encircle the lake; some sites offer views of the lake through the trees; sites are separated by lofty conifers and a little underbrush; elevation 2900´.

Season, Fees & Phone: End of May to mid-September; $9.00; 14 day limit; Naches Ranger District ☎(509) 653-2205.

Trip Log: All the sites in this campground are level and nicely sheltered. The lake is accessible from the campground area, but lake views are limited because of the vegetation. The level of the lake varies considerably from one season to another. Indian Creek was selected to 'represent' the half dozen public campgrounds along and near this highway. The drive along Highway 12 through here and up over White Pass offers some of the best scenery in this part of the state.

♣ Washington 36 ♿

MARYHILL
Maryhill State Park

Location: South-central Washington along the Columbia River south of Goldendale.

Access: From U.S. Highway 97 at the north end of the Columbia River bridge (1.2 miles north of Interstate 84 Exit 104 in Oregon, 0.5 mile south of the junction of U.S. 97 and Washington State Highway 14 south of Goldendale), turn east into the park.

Day Use Facilities: Large picnic area; large shelters; drinking water; restrooms/bathhouse; 2 large parking lots.

Camping Facilities: 50 campsites with full hookups; (3 hiker-biker/primitive sites are also available); sites are medium-sized, level, with minimal separation; parking pads are packed gravel, medium to long straight-ins or pull-throughs; ample space for large tents; windbreaks for many sites; fireplaces; b-y-o firewood; water at sites and at several faucets; restrooms with showers; holding tank disposal station; paved driveways; nearest supplies (gas, groceries, cafes) are on the Oregon side of the river; adequate supplies and services are available in Goldendale.

Activities & Attractions: Swimming beach; boating; windsurfing; boat launch, docks and moorage buoys; old railroad locomotive and coal tender on display in the park; Maryhill

Museum of Fine Arts, 3 miles west; Stonehenge replica, 2 miles east, is visible from the park.

Natural Features: Located on a large flat on the north bank of the Columbia River; picnic and camp sites are lightly shaded by large hardwoods on mown and watered lawns; range grass and sage surround the park; high, fluted rock bluffs rise directly north of the park; typically windy; elevation 150´.

Season, Fees & Phone: Open all year; please see Appendix for campground fees; ☎(509) 773-5007 or ☎(509) 773-4957.

Trip Log: Maryhill State Park takes its name from the nearby community of Maryhill, which in turn had been named after the local estate-turned-museum called Maryhill. In the early 1900's Samuel Hill, son-in-law of the Great Northern Railroad magnate, J. J. Hill, built a palatial house high above the Columbia. The building, which is said to have been designed to resemble a French *chateau*, was turned into a museum to house Hill's art collection, and is now open to the public. Another of Hill's local projects was the full-scale Stonehenge replica perched on the bluff northeast of the park. Hill had the mysterious design of the original archaeological phenomenon in England replicated here as a World War I memorial.

 Washington ▲

North Cascades

▲ **Washington 37**

GOODELL CREEK
Ross Lake National Recreation Area

Location: Northwest Washington east of Mount Vernon.

Access: From Washington State Highway 20 at milepost 119 +.4 (0.5 mile west of Newhalem, 13 miles east of Marblemount), turn south, then immediately east (left) onto a paved campground access road, proceed 0.2 mile, then swing right, into the campground.

Day Use Facilities: Small parking area.

Camping Facilities: 22 campsites; (group camps are also available, in separate areas nearby); sites are small to small+, level, with fair to good separation; parking pads are gravel, short to short+ straight-ins; medium-sized tent areas; fireplaces; firewood is available for gathering in the vicinity; water at central faucets; vault facilities; paved driveway;

groceries in Newhalem, gas and groceries+ in Marblemount.

Activities & Attractions: Raft launch; fishing.

Natural Features: Located on a streamside flat at the confluence of the Skagit River and Goodell Creek in a valley in the western foothills of the Cascade Range; campground vegetation consists of dense hardwoods, scattered tall conifers and dense bushery; bordered by densely forested hills and mountains; North Cascades National Park lies north and south of here; elevation 600´.

Season, Fees & Phone: Available all year, subject to weather conditions, with limited services October to May; $7.00; 14 day limit; Ross Lake NRA Headquarters, Sedro Wolley, ☎(360) 856-5700.

Trip Log: One of the Pacific Northwest's principal streams, the Skagit River, is wide and fairly deep, and was navigable in the old days. Goodell Creek Campground is used as a launch point for rafters in modern times. Prepare for rain.

▲ **Washington 38** &

NEWHALEM CREEK
Ross Lake National Recreation Area

Location: Northwest Washington east of Mount Vernon.

Access: From Washington State Highway 20 at milepost 119 +.9 on the west edge of the hamlet of Newhalem (13 miles east of Marblemount, 38 miles west of Rainy Pass), turn south onto a paved access road, cross the narrow river bridge, and proceed 0.1 mile to the ranger/check-in station; just beyond the station, turn right or left to the camp loops.

Day Use Facilities: Large picnic area, drinking water, restrooms and large parking lot in Newhalem, 0.2 mile east.

Camping Facilities: 116 campsites in 4 loops, plus 13 walk-in sites; sites are small to medium-sized, level, with fairly good to very good separation; parking pads are paved, mostly medium-length straight-ins, plus some long pull-throughs; enough space for small to medium-sized tents in most sites; fireplaces; firewood is available for gathering in the vicinity, (b-y-o dry kindling); water at central faucets; restrooms; disposal station; paved driveways; groceries in Newhalem, gas and groceries+ in Marblemount.

Activities & Attractions: Nature trail; hiking trails; amphitheater for scheduled nature talks and children's programs; large playground at the day use area in Newhalem; visitor center and museum at the local hydroelectric plant.

Natural Features: Located on flats near the confluence of the Skagit River and Newhalem Creek on the west slope of the Cascade Range; campground vegetation consists of very dense, tall conifers and low shrubbery; bordered by forested hills and mountains; elevation 600´.

Season, Fees & Phone: May to October; $9.00; 14 day limit; Ross Lake NRA Headquarters, Sedro Wolley, ☎(360) 856-5700.

Trip Log: Like its much smaller sister camp, Goodell Creek, Newhalem Creek has a subdued, streamside environment, rather than a busy lakeside location, as you might expect in a national recreation area named for a major lake. Good views in most directions from in and around camp. Newhalem itself is a Seattle City Light 'company town' with a highwayside park that's quite a showplace, particularly for a small, remote location like this one. Midtown is just a couple-tenths of a mile from the campground.

♣ Washington 39 ♿

COLONIAL CREEK
Ross Lake National Recreation Area

Location: North-central Washington between Winthrop and Newhalem.

Access: From Washington State Highway 20 at milepost 130 +.2 (0.2 mile west of the Colonial Creek bridge and 0.2 mile east of the Diablo Lake crossing, 20 miles east of Newhalem, 63 miles west of Winthrop), turn south or north into the 2 respective sections of the recreation area.

Day Use Facilities: Small picnic area; drinking water; restrooms; medium-sized parking area.

Camping Facilities: 164 campsites in 2 sections; most sites are small+ to medium-sized, with fair to fairly good separation; parking pads are gravel, short to medium-length straight-ins or pull-throughs; some sites may require additional leveling; many small, private tent spots; a few walk-in tent sites; fireplaces; b-y-o firewood is recommended; water at several faucets; restrooms; holding tank disposal station; paved driveways; nearest reliable sources of supplies and services are Newhalem,

and Marblemount, 20 and 40 miles west, respectively.

Activities & Attractions: Boating and related water sports on Diablo Lake and Thunder Creek; self-guided nature trail; Thunder Creek Hiking Trail; evening interpretive programs in summer; Diablo Lake is at the southern tip of expansive Ross Lake National Recreation Area.

Natural Features: Located on a forested hillside near the south end of Diablo Lake; very tall conifers, hardwoods, and varying amounts of underbrush provide good separation; tall peaks of the Cascades tower over the lake and the campground; elevation 1200´.

Season, Fees & Phone: May to November; $9.00; 14 day limit; Ross Lake NRA Headquarters, Sedro Wolley, ☎(360) 856-5700.

Trip Log: This campground tends to fill early due to its location right beside the lake and on the highway. A few lakefront sites provide for tentside mooring of boats. Some sites may be a bit close to the highway or to a neighboring camper, but the dense vegetation helps to subdue extraneous noise. Of the trio of Ross Lake NRA campgrounds along Highway 20 (also see Newhalem Creek and Goodell Creek) only Colonial Creek is on a lake, and it's not actually on Ross Lake. The North Cascades Highway—Highway 20—passes through a corridor earmarked for easy public recreational access and very limited commercial development. The highway, which bisects North Cascades National Park, remained unpaved over Rainy Pass until the latter part of the Twentieth Century. The parklands have been set aside as a wilderness area.

♣ Washington 40

LONE FIR
Okanogan National Forest

Location: North-central Washington between Winthrop and Newhalem.

Access: From Washington State Highway 20 at milepost 168 +.4 (24 miles west of Winthrop, 49 miles east of Newhalem), turn southeast into the campground.

Day Use Facilities: None.

Camping Facilities: 27 campsites; sites are a bit small but quite well separated; parking pads are gravel, short to medium-length straight-ins or pull-throughs; many pads may require additional leveling; some secluded tent spots have been carved out of the dense vegetation; fireplaces; firewood is available for gathering in the vicinity; water at several faucets; vault facilities; gravel driveway; adequate supplies and services are available in Winthrop.

Activities & Attractions: A principal activity is hiking in the Cascades: Cutthroat Lake Trailhead is 1 mile west and the Pacific Crest Trail is accessible from near milepost 157 +.7 on Highway 20; stream fishing; the superscenic North Cascades Highway continues west from here over 5483´ Washington Pass.

Natural Features: Located on the east slopes of the North Cascades; tiny Pine Creek joins Early Winters Creek at this point; sites are surrounded by dense forest with tall conifers and considerable underbrush; elevation 5000´.

Season, Fees & Phone: June to September; $7.00; 14 day limit; Winthrop Ranger District ☎(509) 996-2266.

Trip Log: This is a high-altitude campground with a relatively short season. Near here are great views of several landmarks, including those with inspiring names like The Needles to the north, Silver Star Mountain to the east, and Liberty Bell Mountain to the west.

♣ Washington 41 &

KLIPCHUCK
Okanogan National Forest

Location: North-central Washington between Winthrop and Newhalem.

Access: From Washington State Highway 20 at milepost 175 +.1 (18 miles west of Winthrop, 55 miles east of Newhalem), turn northwest onto a paved access road; continue for 1.3 miles to the campground.

Day Use Facilities: None.

Camping Facilities: 46 campsites; sites are average-sized, with excellent separation; parking pads are gravel, short to medium-length straight-ins; some additional leveling will probably be required; small to medium-sized tents can be tucked into small nooks among the trees; stairs lead from parking pads to some table and tent areas; fireplaces; some firewood is available for gathering in the vicinity; water at several faucets; restrooms; paved driveway; adequate supplies and services are available in Winthrop.

Activities & Attractions: Stream fishing; hiking on several mountain trails, including those to Cedar Falls and Rattlesnake Creek,

which ultimately join the Pacific Crest Trail; the drive across the North Cascades Highway from here toward Newhalem offers magnificent mountain scenery.

Natural Features: Located on a forested hillside in a narrow valley along Early Winters Creek; vegetation consists of dense stands of conifers and hardwoods, with considerable grass and underbrush; high, timbered ridges flank the valley; peaks of the North Cascades rise just to the west; elevation 4300´.

Season, Fees & Phone: May to September; $7.00; 14 day limit; Winthrop Ranger District ☎(509) 996-2266.

Trip Log: A conscientious attempt was made in this campground to provide the most level sites possible, considering the steep terrain. The dense vegetation provides excellent privacy and a peaceful environment.

♣ Washington 42

EARLY WINTERS
Okanogan National Forest

Location: North-central Washington between Winthrop and Newhalem.

Access: From Washington State Highway 20 at milepost 177 +.7 (16 miles west of Winthrop, 58 miles east of Newhalem), turn left or right at the east end of the Early Winters Creek Bridge; (campsites are located on both sides of the highway.)

Day Use Facilities: None.

Camping Facilities: 7 campsites on the north and 7 sites on the south side of the highway; sites are small to average in size, with fair separation; parking pads are gravel, short to medium-length straight-ins; additional leveling may be necessary in some sites; medium-sized tent areas; fireplaces; firewood is available for gathering in the vicinity; water at several faucets; vault facilities; gravel driveways; adequate supplies and services are available in Winthrop, 16 miles east.

Activities & Attractions: Stream fishing; Cedar Creek Trailhead is 3 miles west; superscenic drive along the North Cascades Highway, over Washington Pass, past North Cascades National Park.

Natural Features: Located in a valley bordered by high rocky ridges on the east slope of the Cascade Range; Early Winters Creek joins the waters of the Methow River a few yards to the east; terrain along the river is level but a bit rocky; medium-sized conifers and moderate underbrush provide some shelter and separation for the campsites, many of which are creekside; elevation 4200´.

Season, Fees & Phone: May to September; $7.00; 14 day limit; Winthrop Ranger District ☎(509) 996-2266.

Trip Log: This is a good base-of-operations camp for exploration of the inviting mountain areas to the west. Many sites are so close to the creek that most highway noise would be moderated by the sound of the rushing water. Early Winters Creek is one of the main tributaries of the Methow River, and the highway hugs the swift creek from the summit of Washington Pass to the Methow-Early Winters confluence near here.

♣ Washington 43 ♿

PEARRYGIN LAKE
Pearrygin Lake State Park

Location: North-central Washington north of Winthrop.

Access: From Washington State Highway 20 (Riverside Avenue) at milepost 192 +.9 in midtown Winthrop, turn north onto Bluff Street and proceed 1.5 miles; turn east (right) onto the state park access road and continue for 1.7 miles, then turn southwest (right) into the park.

Day Use Facilities: Large picnic area; drinking water; restrooms/bathhouse; 2 medium-sized parking lots.

Camping Facilities: 83 campsites, including 27 with water hookups and 30 with full hookups; (3 hiker-biker/primitive sites are also available); sites are small to medium-sized, with minimal to nominal separation, (some lakeside sites are well separated); most parking pads are gravel, medium to long straight-ins or pull-throughs; large, fairly level, grassy tent spots; fireplaces; b-y-o firewood; water at several faucets; restrooms with showers; holding tank disposal station; paved driveways; adequate supplies and services are available in Winthrop.

Activities & Attractions: Boating; windsurfing; boat launch and docks; swimming area; fishing; cross-country skiing and snowmobiling.

Natural Features: Located on the north shore of Pearrygin Lake in the Methow Valley in the eastern foothills of the Cascade Range; the park has large sections of watered and mown lawns dotted with hardwoods which provide very light to light-medium shade for picnic and camp sites; sandy swimming beach; sage-and-grass covered, partially wooded hills surround the lake; lake area is 212 acres; elevation 1900´.

Season, Fees & Phone: General season April to November (available for winter day activities during the remainder of the year); campsite reservations accepted, especially recommended for weekends; please see Appendix for reservation information and campground fees; ☎(509) 996-2370.

Trip Log: At Pearrygin Lake, some lucky lakeside campers can tie up their boats within a few feet of their tents. There's an outstanding view up the valley toward the rugged peaks of the Cascade Mountains. The park is near the eastern terminus of the superscenic North Cascades Highway.

♣ Washington 44

LOUP LOUP
Okanogan National Forest

Location: North-central Washington between Twisp and Okanogan.

Access: From Washington State Highway 20 at milepost 214 +.7 (12 miles east of Twisp, 18 miles west of Okanogan), turn north onto Forest Road 42 (paved); proceed 0.5 mile north and west; turn north (right, still on Road 42) and continue for another 0.6 mile, then turn west (left) into the campground.

Day Use Facilities: None.

Camping Facilities: 27 campsites in 2 tiered loops; sites are generally quite large, level, with good separation; parking pads are gravel straight-ins or pull-throughs, some spacious enough for large rv's; most tent areas are large and level; fireplaces; ample firewood is available for gathering; water at several faucets; vault facilities; gravel driveways; limited supplies and services are available in Twisp.

Activities & Attractions: Nearby opportunities for backcountry exploration; Road 42 leads north to Conconully State Park and Reservoir; Loup Loup Winter Sports Area is close by.

Natural Features: Located in the foothills of the Cascades, between steep, forested slopes east and west; moderately dense vegetation in the campground's main loop consists of tall conifers with hanging moss; the lower 5 units, along the creek, have tall grass and typical creekside brush; elevation 4000´.

Season, Fees & Phone: May to September; $6.00; 14 day limit; Twisp Ranger District ☎(509) 997-2131.

Trip Log: This is a super stop, near a main highway, for a traveler seeking forest tranquillity; a secluded camp with lots of elbow room. The larger loop is close to the road, but the lower, smaller loop is further away, down along a creek. Which would you choose? If you're westbound on the North Cascades Highway, consider getting a few extra gallons of fuel and rounding-out your larder in one of the 'river' cities (Brewster, Chelan, Okanogan, Omak, Wenatchee) or at the very latest, Winthrop. It's slim pickin's' along the 130-some miles between Winthrop and Sedro Woolley at the other end.

♣ **Washington 45** ♿

LAKE WENATCHEE
Lake Wenatchee State Park

Location: West-central Washington northwest of Wenatchee.

Access: From the junction of U.S. Highway 2 and Washington State Highway 207 (at U.S. 2 milepost 84 +.7, 15 miles north of Leavenworth, 20 miles east of Stevens Pass), drive north on Highway 207 for 3.5 miles; turn west (left) and proceed 0.8 mile to the south unit; or continue north/northwest on Highway 207 for an additional mile, then turn south (left) into the north unit.

Alternate Access: From U.S. 2 at the east edge of Leavenworth, head north on Washington State Highway 209 for 19 miles to its junction with Highway 207; turn south (left) for 0.2 mile to the south unit, or turn north (right) and proceed 0.8 mile to the north unit. (The primary access is best if you're eastbound on U.S. 2; the alternate access could be used if you're westbound out of Wenatchee and would like a backroad approach with about the same mileage as the U.S. 2/Highway 207 route.)

Day Use Facilities: Large picnic area in the south unit; shelters; drinking water; restrooms; large parking lot; park concession stand.

Camping Facilities: *South unit*: 100 campsites; (a reservable group camp is also available); sites are generally small, sloped, with minimal to fair separation; parking pads are gravel, most are short to medium-length straight-ins; medium to large tent areas. *North unit*: 97 campsites; sites are small+ to medium-sized, most are marginally level, with nominal to fairly good separation; parking pads are gravel, medium-length straight-ins or long pull-throughs; large tent areas. *Both units*: fireplaces; some firewood is available for gathering on nearby national forest land, b-y-o to be sure; water at several faucets; restrooms with showers; holding tank disposal station; paved driveways; gas and camper supplies at a nearby store; adequate supplies and services are available in Leavenworth.

Activities & Attractions: Boating; boat launch; fishing; sandy swimming beach; several short hiking trails in the park, plus miles of national forest trails in the area; several miles of groomed x-c ski trails are in the vicinity; snowmobiling; playgrounds; amphitheater; boat and horse rentals from the park concession.

Natural Features: Located on the north and south shores of glacier-fed Lake Wenatchee; picnic sites receive medium shade from tall conifers; campground vegetation consists of medium-dense, tall conifers and moderate underbrush; the Wenatchee River flows out of the lake through the middle of the park; bordered by the heavily-timbered mountains of the Cascade Range; elevation 1800´.

Season, Fees & Phone: Open all year, with limited services October to April; please see Appendix for campground fees; ☎(509) 763-3101.

Trip Log: Because of its scenic superiority, Lake Wenatchee has always been a favorite spot for summer visits, but it is becoming one of the more popular winter parks in the state as well. Average annual snowfall is 145 inches, with a continuous snow cover of 3-4 feet. Since the park is right off a state highway, and only a few miles from a major trans-state route, it is usually readily accessible in winter.

♣ **Washington 46** ♿

WENATCHEE RIVER
Chelan County Park

Location: West Central Washington northwest of Wenatchee.

Access: From U.S. Highways 2/97 at milepost 115 +.2 at the intersection of U.S. 2/97 & Main Street in the hamlet of Monitor (7 miles northwest of Wenatchee, 3 miles southeast of Cashmere), turn south onto Main Street, then immediately east onto a paved park access road; proceed 0.2 mile to the park.

Day Use Facilities: Medium-sized picnic area; drinking water; restrooms; medium-sized parking lot.

Camping Facilities: 97 campsites, including 40 with full hookups, 40 with partial or electrical-only hookups, and 17 tent sites, in 6 areas; sites are small, level, with nominal separation; parking pads are paved, mainly medium-length straight-ins; adequate space for tents; fire rings; b-y-o firewood; water at faucets throughout; restrooms with showers; holding tank disposal station; paved driveways; limited supplies and services in Cashmere; complete supplies and services are available in Wenatchee.

Activities & Attractions: Fishing; sports field; playground; cycle path.

Natural Features: Located on a large flat along the north bank of the Wenatchee River; the park is very well landscaped with hardwood-dotted lawns and rows of hardwoods; most sites are nicely shaded; bordered by rocky, nearly treeless, semi-arid hills; elevation 900´.

Season, Fees & Phone: Open all year; $16.00 for a full hookup site, $14.50 for a partial hookup site, $12.50 for a tent site; 14 day limit; park office ☎(509) 662-2525.

Trip Log: If you prefer to enjoy an outing dressed in a threadbare plaid shirt and faded jeans, sitting by a fire of dried buffalo chips, eating beans from a soot-blackened can, 14 miles from the nearest blacktop, then this deluxe park probably isn't the spot for you. This local park is as magnificent as they come. A top-notch, competitively priced alternative to the region's well-appointed state parks.

⚐ **Washington 47** ♿

LINCOLN ROCK
Lincoln Rock State Park

Location: Central Washington north of Wenatchee.

Access: From U.S. Highway 2/ Washington State Highway 151 at U.S. 2 milepost 132 +.5 (on the east bank of the Columbia River, 9 miles north of East Wenatchee, 7 miles south of the Orondo junction) turn west onto the access road, then angle northwest and proceed 0.3 mile to the park.

Day Use Facilities: Large picnic area with shelters; 2 reservable group areas with shelters; drinking water; restrooms; medium-sized and very large parking lots.

Camping Facilities: 94 campsites, including 35 with partial hookups and 32 with full hookups, in 3 loops; most sites are small+ to medium-sized, tolerably level, with minimal to nominal separation; parking pads are paved, medium to medium+ straight-ins or long pull-throughs; adequate space for large tents; fireplaces; b-y-o firewood; water at hookup sites and at several additional faucets; restrooms with showers; holding tank disposal station; paved driveways; gas and groceries along the highway; complete supplies and services are available in Wenatchee, 10 miles south.

Activities & Attractions: Swimming beach; sports fields; tennis courts; volleyball courts; basketball courts; walk-bike trails throughout; boating; boat launch and docks; fishing; amphitheater for interpretive programs; playground; cross-country skiing.

Natural Features: Located on a large flat along the east bank of the Columbia River (Lake Entiat) just north of Rocky Reach Dam; park vegetation consists of watered and mown lawns dotted by small to medium-sized hardwoods and some pines, plus rows of tall poplars; picnic and camp sites are unshaded to lightly shaded and sheltered; the river is flanked by barren hills and bluffs; forested peaks are visible beyond the bluffs to the west; open and breezy; Lincoln Rock is in view across the river; elevation 700´.

Season, Fees & Phone: Open all year; campsite reservations accepted, suggested for anytime during the summer, recommended well in advance for weekends; please see Appendix for campground fees; ☎(509) 884-8702.

Trip Log: Lincoln Rock reportedly was named in 1889 when a crewman on a sternwheeler photographed the rocky outcropping and entered the picture in a photo contest conducted by the *Ladies Home Journal*. The *Journal* awarded first prize to the photo and published the resemblance of the presidential profile, captioned as "A Likeness of the Great Emancipator" or "Lincoln's Rock". Because of the *Journal's* widespread circulation, the name stuck. The park could be described as having a "country club" environment, with its manicured landscaping, tennis courts, soccer field—'the whole nine yards'—minus 18 holes.

⚐ **Washington 48** ♿

DENNY CREEK
Mt. Baker-Snoqualmie National Forest

Location: Western Washington east/southeast of Seattle.

Access: From Interstate 90 Exit 47 for Denny Creek Road and Tinkham Road (17 miles east of North Bend, 45 miles east of Seattle, 5 miles west of Snoqualmie Pass summit), go to the north/west side of the freeway to a 'T', then turn easterly onto Denny Creek Road/Forest Road 58 (paved) for 0.3 mile; turn northerly (left) continuing on Denny Creek Road (narrow, paved) for 2.1 miles, then turn left into the campground.

Day Use Facilities: Small picnic area, drinking water, vault facilities, small parking area in Asahel Curtis Recreation Area, 2 miles southwest, just off the highway.

Camping Facilities: 33 campsites, including several double units, in a complex loop; (a group site is also available, by reservation); sites are medium to large, reasonably level, with fair to good separation; parking pads are paved, medium-length straight-ins or medium+ pull-throughs; medium to large tent spots, including many large, framed-and-graveled tent pads; fireplaces; firewood is available for gathering (may be wet); water at a hand pump; vault facilities; paved driveways; pack-it-in/pack-it-out trash system; gas and snacks at Snoqualmie Pass; adequate supplies and services are available in North Bend.

Activities & Attractions: Footbridge across a side stream; trail to Franklin Falls and Asahel Curtis Recreation Area, 2 miles southwest.

Natural Features: Located on forested, terraced terrain high on the west slope of the Cascade Range along Denny Creek; local vegetation consists of very dense, very tall conifers over a thick undercover of bushes and ferns; several streamside sites; elevation 2700´.

Season, Fees & Phone: May to October; $9.00 for a single site, $14.00 for a double site; 14 day limit; North Bend Ranger District ☎ (206) 888-1421.

Trip Log: Even when the sun is high on a cloudless day (rare), you might be tempted to turn your headlights on as you approach the campground through the super dense tunnel of vegetation that engulfs the access road. Interesting touches of landscaping are evident throughout the campground. Even old, decaying, moss-shrouded logs add natural interest and beauty to this place. Considering the high elevation and very high winter precipitation levels, the campground isn't in a 'rain forest' as much as it is in a 'snow forest' environment. There's still a generous quantity of liquid precip here during the camping season, though. If you left your raingear at home, you could use one of the incredibly huge leaves of certain local plants for a bumbershoot.

⋀ Washington 49 ♿

WISH-POOSH
Wenatchee National Forest

Location: West-central Washington west of Ellensburg.

Access: From Interstate 90 Exit 80 for Roslyn/Salmon La Sac (28 miles west of Ellensburg, 9 miles east of Easton), travel north on a local paved connecting road for 2.9 miles to Roslyn; turn northwest (left) onto Washington State Highway 903 and proceed 7.7 miles; turn southwest (left) onto the paved recreation area access road for a few yards, then swing left into the recreation area (Note: Highway 903 officially ends after you've traveled 6 miles, but just continue beyond that point on the paved road for the remaining 1.7 miles of the total 7.7 miles to the recreation area.)

Day Use Facilities: Small picnic area; drinking water; small parking area.

Camping Facilities: 39 campsites, including several 2-family units; sites are small to medium-sized, with good to excellent separation; parking pads are gravel, short to medium-length straight-ins; a little additional leveling will be needed in some sites; small to large tent areas; fire rings or barbecue grills; firewood is available for gathering in the area; water at several faucets; restrooms; waste water receptacles; paved driveways; gas and groceries+ are available in Roslyn; limited+ supplies and services are available in Cle Elum.

Activities & Attractions: Boating; boat launch nearby; fishing.

Natural Features: Located on a slightly sloping, forested flat several hundred yards from the north-east shore of Cle Elum Lake, a reservoir on the Cle Elum River; sites are well-shaded/sheltered by tall conifers, ferns and a considerable amount of brush; the lake is bordered by high, forested mountains; elevation 2200´.

Season, Fees & Phone: May to October; $10.00 for a standard site; $18.00 for a 2-family unit; 14 day limit; Cle Elum Ranger District ☎ (509) 674-4411.

Trip Log: Lots of privacy, 'modern' facilities, a big lake, and 15 minutes from the Interstate. Need more be said?

🏠 *Washington* ⛺

Coulee Dam National Recreation Area

The vast majority of visitors to Coulee Dam National Recreation Area come from within 200 miles of here—from Washington and British Columbia. The tremendous variety of scenery and recreation opportunities are thus nearly untapped by travelers from other parts of the Continent.

🔺 Washington 50 ♿

EVANS
Coulee Dam National Recreation Area

Location: Northeast Washington north of Kettle Falls.

Access: From Washington State Highway 25 at a point 10.2 miles north of Kettle Falls and 30 miles south of the U.S.-Canada border, turn west onto a paved access road and proceed 0.1 mile to the recreation area.

Day Use Facilities: Medium-sized picnic area; drinking water; restrooms; large parking lot.

Camping Facilities: 56 campsites; sites are small+, level, with nominal separation; parking pads are paved, mostly short straight-ins, plus some pull-throughs; many good tent spots; fireplaces; b-y-o firewood; water at faucets throughout; restrooms; freshwater-rinse showers; holding tank disposal station; paved driveways; gas and groceries nearby on Highway 25; adequate supplies and services are available in Kettle Falls.

Activities & Attractions: Boating; boat launch; fishing for a wide variety of freshwater species (trolling is reportedly the most productive method); designated swimming area with swim platform; nice sandy beach; children's play area; amphitheater for scheduled ranger-naturalist programs.

Natural Features: Located on an open grassy/sandy flat on the east shore of Franklin D. Roosevelt Lake, a major impoundment on the Columbia River; sites are very lightly to lightly shaded by tall conifers; bordered by a small meadow; grass and evergreen-covered hills and high ridges border the lake; typically quite windy; elevation 1300´.

Season, Fees & Phone: Open all year, with limited services, October to May; $9.00; (no fee in winter); 14 day limit; Coulee Dam NRA Headquarters, Grand Coulee, ☎(509) 633-9441.

Trip Log: This very attractive, albeit well-used, recreation area affords tremendous views of the countryside. Definitely recommended, especially for weekday visits.

🔺 Washington 51

MARCUS ISLAND
Coulee Dam National Recreation Area

Location: Northeast Washington north of Kettle Falls.

Access: From Washington State Highway 25 at a point 5.6 miles north of Kettle Falls and 35 miles south of the U.S.-Canada border, turn west onto a paved road which leads 0.5 mile to the river level, doubles back around to the east for 0.5 mile, then crosses a short causeway northward into the recreation area.

Day Use Facilities: Small parking area.

Camping Facilities: 20 campsites; sites are small to medium in size, level, with minimal to fairly good separation; parking pads are paved, mostly short straight-ins, plus a few pull-throughs; most sites have adequate space for tents; fireplaces; b-y-o firewood is recommended; water at a hand pump; vault facilities; paved driveways; adequate supplies and services are available in Kettle Falls.

Activities & Attractions: Fishing for a variety of fresh water species including walleye, trout, salmon and sturgeon; trolling is probably the most effective means of taking fish; good boat launch and dock.

Natural Features: Located on a small island along the east shore of 150-mile-long Franklin D. Roosevelt Lake (part of the Columbia River system); campground vegetation consists of medium-dense moderately tall pine, plus tall grass; high grass and timber-covered mountains parallel the river; moderately dry climate; elevation 1300´.

Season, Fees & Phone: Open all year, subject to weather conditions, with limited services October to May; $9.00; (no fee in winter); 14 day limit; Coulee Dam NRA Headquarters, Grand Coulee, ☎(509) 633-9441.

Trip Log: All campsites are near the water's edge. A few sites at the tip of the point offer sweeping views of the local landscape. Skinny-dipping Canucks seem to favor the placid waters of the adjoining cove for refreshing midnight plunges.

⚑ Washington 52 ♿

KETTLE FALLS
Coulee Dam National Recreation Area

Location: Northeast Washington just west of Kettle Falls.

Access: From Washington State Highway 20 at the east end of the Columbia River bridge 3 miles west of Kettle Falls, turn south onto a paved two-lane road which parallels the river; follow this road for 1.8 miles to the ranger station and the campground. **Alternate Access:** From Washington State Highway 25 at a point 0.5 mile south of the junction of Highways 20 and 25, turn west at a sign indicating "Recreation Area 3 Miles"; follow this paved road for the specified distance to the recreation area.

Day Use Facilities: Large picnic area; drinking water; restrooms; large parking lot.

Camping Facilities: 76 campsites in 3 loops; most sites are of average size, level, with nominal to fair separation; parking pads are mostly short straight-ins, some are medium-length pull-throughs; excellent tent-pitching opportunities; fireplaces; firewood is a bit scarce in the immediate vicinity, so b-y-o is recommended; water at faucets throughout; restrooms with camper service sinks; holding tank disposal station near the ranger station; paved driveways; adequate supplies and services are available in Kettle Falls, 5 miles northeast.

Activities & Attractions: Playground and swimming beach in the day use area (0.2 mile south of the campground); fishing; marina nearby.

Natural Features: Located on a gently rolling flat along the east shore of Franklin D. Roosevelt Lake (actually the impounded Columbia River); area vegetation consists of moderately dense timber with little ground-level vegetation except tall grass; the lake is flanked by forested hills; elevation 1300´.

Season, Fees & Phone: Open all year, with limited services October to May; $9.00; (no fee in winter); 14 day limit; Coulee Dam NRA Headquarters, Grand Coulee, ☎(509) 633-9441.

Trip Log: Super-nice picnic spot here. The campground is in an agreeably pleasant, sheltered area. It's usually quite busy on midsummer weekends, but definitely worth considering due to its good facilities and proximity to the community of Kettle Falls. Of course, on major holiday weekends, all recreation sites along the lake play to a standing-room-only crowd.

⚑ Washington 53 ♿

GIFFORD
Coulee Dam National Recreation Area

Location: Northeast Washington south of Kettle Falls.

Access: From Washington State Highway 25 at milepost 56 +.4 (1.5 miles south of the hamlet of Gifford, 14 miles north of the community of Hunters), turn west onto a paved access road which leads 0.1 mile down to the campground.

Day Use Facilities: Small parking area.

Camping Facilities: 42 campsites; sites are medium-sized, with nominal separation; parking pads are gravel straight-ins or pull-throughs which may require a little additional leveling; a few walk-in sites are in a little cove at the south end of the grounds; fireplaces; very little firewood is available for gathering, so b-y-o is recommended; water at faucets; restrooms; holding tank disposal station; paved driveways; gas and groceries in Gifford.

Activities & Attractions: Boating; boat launch and docks; rock jetty; fishing for more than 30 species, including walleye (the number one game fish in the lake), rainbow trout, perch and kokanee.

Natural Features: Located on the east shore of Franklin D. Roosevelt Lake; most camp spots are right on the edge of the lake and/or have a lake view; campground vegetation consists of medium height pines and tall grass with a thick carpet of pine needles; usually quite windy; sites are fairly well sheltered, except for those closest to the lake shore; elevation 1300´.

Season, Fees & Phone: Open all year, with limited services October to May; $9.00; (no fee in winter); 14 day limit; Coulee Dam NRA Headquarters, Grand Coulee, ☎(509) 633-9441.

Trip Log: Camping in this very 'open' atmosphere provides you with excellent views north and south along the lake. The walk-in sites are a couple of the nicest you'll find in this part of the state. If you're a boater, there are lots of little coves and sandy beaches nearby for you to explore.

♣ Washington 54 ♿

HUNTERS
Coulee Dam National Recreation Area

Location: Northeast Washington south of Kettle Falls.

Access: From Washington State Highway 25 at milepost 42 +.3 in the small community of Hunters (37 miles south of Kettle Falls, 42 miles north of Davenport), turn west at the "Hunters Campground" sign onto a paved access road and proceed 0.8 mile to the recreation area.

Day Use Facilities: Small picnic area; drinking water; restrooms; medium-sized parking area.

Camping Facilities: 52 campsites, including some double-occupancy units; sites are medium to large, well leveled, with minimal separation; parking pads are gravel, mostly medium or medium+ pull-throughs; adequate space for large tents; several walk-in sites on the beach; fireplaces; very little firewood is available for gathering, so b-y-o is recommended; water at central faucets; restrooms with naturally cool and refreshing showers; holding tank disposal station; paved driveways; limited supplies and services are available in Hunters.

Activities & Attractions: Boating; boat launch and docks; rock jetty; fishing; designated swimming area; playground; Hunters community fair held annually in late August.

Natural Features: Located on the east shore of Franklin D. Roosevelt Lake on the Columbia River; vegetation consists of medium-dense conifers and a little undergrowth; sandy beach; interesting, heavily eroded bluffs are opposite the recreation area on the west shore of the lake; this spot is better-protected from the elements than other recreation areas near here; elevation 1300´.

Season, Fees & Phone: Open all year, with limited services October to May; $9.00; (no fee in winter); 14 day limit; Coulee Dam NRA Headquarters, Grand Coulee, ☎(509) 633-9441.

Trip Log: This is terrific country around here! In summer, its colors are rich green and gold and blue and brown. All picnic and camp sites have some sort of a lake view, and many are on or near the lake shore. The walk-in campsites, in particular, have a super view.

♣ Washington 55 ♿

FORT SPOKANE
Coulee Dam National Recreation Area

Location: Northeast Washington north of Davenport.

Access: From Washington State Highway 25 at milepost 23 +.1 (23 miles north of Davenport, 19 miles south of Hunters), turn east into the recreation area.

Day Use Facilities: Medium-sized picnic area; drinking water; restrooms; medium-sized parking area.

Camping Facilities: 62 campsites, including quite a few double-occupancy units, in several large loops; virtually all sites are quite spacious, level, with nominal separation; parking pads are paved pull-throughs; plenty of space for tents; fireplaces; b-y-o firewood; water at faucets throughout; restrooms; holding tank disposal station; paved driveways; limited supplies in Hunters; adequate supplies and services are available in Davenport.

Activities & Attractions: Visitor center and ranger station 0.2 mile south of the campground; self guiding tours around the well-maintained remnants of Fort Spokane; amphitheater on the bank of the Spokane River for planned ranger-naturalist programs; fishing; boat launch.

Natural Features: Located at the confluence of the Columbia and Spokane Rivers; light to medium-dense very tall pines shelter the campsites; ground cover consists of some shrubbery, but mostly pine needles and grass; the Spokane River is within easy walking distance of all campsites; elevation 1300´.

Season, Fees & Phone: Open all year, with limited services October to May; $9.00; (no fee in winter); 14 day limit; Coulee Dam NRA Headquarters, Grand Coulee, ☎(509) 633-9441.

Trip Log: Fort Spokane is a very popular place, but is it *nice*! There's a pleasant open-air feeling here. They really did a good job on this park. The drive down Highway 25 from the north passes through some of the most impressive scenery in this sparsely settled region.

♠ Washington 56 ♿

SPRING CANYON
Coulee Dam National Recreation Area

Location: North-central Washington southeast of Grand Coulee.

Access: From Washington State Highway 174 at milepost 24 +.2 (3 miles east of Grand Coulee, 20 miles west of Wilbur), turn north onto a paved access road; continue for 1.2 miles to the recreation area.

Day Use Facilities: Small picnic area; drinking water; restrooms; small parking area.

Camping Facilities: 78 campsites, including 66 for rv's; rv sites are very small, with short+ straight-ins in a reasonably level, paved parking lot arrangement; ramadas (sunshades) with 10´ of clearance for about 2-dozen rv sites; tent sites have short to medium-length gravel parking pads and large, mostly sloped, tent spaces; (using the somewhat leveled parking pad for a free-standing tent may be advisable); additional, paved parking for tenters; fireplaces; b-y-o firewood; water at central faucets; restrooms; holding tank disposal station; paved driveways; adequate supplies are available in Grand Coulee.

Activities & Attractions: Bunchgrass Prairie Nature Trail; interpretive programs scheduled during the summer; playground; swimming beach, boat launch and dock nearby; fishing; within view of Grand Coulee Dam; visitor center at the dam has auto tour information.

Natural Features: Located on a sage-and-grass slope overlooking Franklin D. Roosevelt Lake, created on the Columbia River by Grand Coulee Dam; campsites receive very light to light shade from large hardwoods on areas of watered-and-mown grass; typically breezy; bordered by dry hills and bluffs; elevation 1500´.

Season, Fees & Phone: Memorial Day to Labor Day; $9.00; 14 day limit; Coulee Dam NRA Headquarters, Grand Coulee, ☎(509) 633-9441.

Trip Log: Rv'ers have one of the most unusual setups to be found in a public campground, anywhere. The sunshades are in rows that resemble carports in an econo condo complex. Unconventional, but cheap and reasonably effective. Anything that sheds the blazing summer sun is welcome. The campground is within view of the massive hydroelectric powerhouse at 'Grand Cooler', but there's no juice here to run an rv's a/c. (Not even from a current bush.) Also very welcome is the big swimming beach with its nicely landscaped grounds. The recreation area provides a great view of the lake and the surrounding countryside. All things considered, Spring Canyon is one of the nicer recreation sites in semi-arid Central Washington.

♠ Washington 57 ♿

STEAMBOAT ROCK
Steamboat Rock State Park

Location: Central Washington southeast of Coulee Dam.

Access: From Washington State Highway 155 at milepost 15 +.6 (10 miles southwest of the city of Grand Coulee, 18 miles northeast of Coulee City), turn west onto a paved park access road; travel west then north for 2 miles to the park.

Day Use Facilities: Large picnic area; drinking water; restrooms/bathhouse; large parking lot; concession stand.

Camping Facilities: 105 campsites, including 100 with full hookups, in 2 clusters; sites are small, level, with minimal separation; parking pads are paved, medium-length straight-ins; adequate space for a large tent, only on the tent pad in each site; fireplaces; b-y-o firewood; restrooms with showers; paved driveways; gas and groceries in Electric City, adequate supplies and services are available in Grand Coulee.

Activities & Attractions: Swimming area; boating; boat launch and dock in the main park, and also at a park rest area just off Highway 155 at milepost 19; fishing; nature trail; hiking trail to the top of the Rock; playground; cross-country skiing and other winter sports.

Natural Features: Located along the west shore of Banks Lake in the great, canyon-like Grand Coulee; day use area has mown lawns well-shaded and sheltered by large hardwoods and rows of tall poplars; camp areas are similarly landscaped, with campsite shade which varies from minimal to moderate; high, rocky, sheer-walled bluffs flank the lake east and west; Steamboat Rock, a colossal, 700-foot high, treeless butte rises just west of the park; elevation 1500´.

Season, Fees & Phone: Main park open April to November, plus minimal day use and boat launch availability in winter; campsite reservations accepted, recommended for anytime in summer; please see Appendix for campground fees; ☎(509) 633-1304.

Trip Log: One of the neat things about the day use area is that it's virtually on an island. (A short, narrow isthmus connects the parking lot to the almost-isle.) The place is so nicely landscaped that it looks a lot like one of those lush and plush Sunbelt or South Coast resorts—big trees, acres of lawns, etc. The campground landscaping is also of good quality. For completely different surroundings, take the foot trail to the top of Steamboat Rock. There are striking views of Grand Coulee (the geological feature, that is, not the dam or the town of the same name). You can also wander around the top of the Rock's square mile of area. The country around Grand Coulee is unlike any other region in the Northwest—or anywhere else, when you come right down to it.

♣ Washington 58 &

SUN LAKES
Sun Lakes State Park

Location: Central Washington southwest of Coulee City.

Access: From Washington State Highway 17 at a point 17 miles north of Soap Lake and 4 miles south of the junction of Highway 17 & U.S. Highway 2, turn east and follow a winding, paved access road for 1 mile to the park.

Day Use Facilities: Medium and large picnic areas; large shelter (reservable by groups); drinking water; restrooms; 3 medium to large parking lots.

Camping Facilities: 190 campsites, including 18 with full hookups; (a reservable group camp is also available); sites are small, level, with minimal separation; most parking areas are short to medium-length pull-offs; large tent spaces; fireplaces; b-y-o firewood; water at several faucets; restrooms with showers; holding tank disposal station; paved driveways; camper supplies at a small store nearby; adequate supplies and services are available in Coulee City, 6 miles north.

Activities & Attractions: Boating; boat launch; trout fishing; swimming on a well-protected cove; playground; nature trail.

Natural Features: Located on a grassy flat at the base of steep, rocky walls deep in Grand Coulee; large hardwoods provide light to medium shade for picnic and camp sites; some sections are watered and mown; Mirror Lake, Park Lake, Dry Falls Lake, Deep Lake and other small lakes collectively are called Sun Lakes; elevation 1200´.

Season, Fees & Phone: Open all year; please see Appendix for campground fees; ☎ (509) 632-5583.

Trip Log: Another state park unit in the vicinity merits your consideration for a visit. Dry Falls Interpretive Center is located off the east side of Highway 17 just north of the Sun Lakes access road. It has exhibits describing the formation of an ancient waterfall, which, if active today, would make Niagara look like an overflowing rain gutter. A large picture window overlooks the 400-foot high, three-and-a-half mile wide precipice over which billions of gallons of water per minute plunged.

Washington ▲
Northeast Mountains

♣ Washington 59

OSOYOOS LAKE
Osoyoos State Park

Location: North-central Washington near the U.S.-Canadian border.

Access: From U.S. Highway 97 at milepost 332 +.7 (0.7 mile north of Oroville, 4 miles south of the international border), turn east into the park.

Day Use Facilities: Large picnic area; shelter; drinking water; restrooms; large parking lot; concession stand.

Camping Facilities: 80 campsites; (6 hike-bike/primitive sites are also available); sites are small to medium-sized, level, with minimal separation; parking pads are gravel, mostly medium-length straight-ins; excellent tent-pitching possibilities; fireplaces; b-y-o firewood; water at several faucets; restrooms with showers; holding tank disposal station; paved driveways; adequate supplies and services are available in Oroville.

Activities & Attractions: Boating; boat launch and dock; sandy swimming beach.

Natural Features: Located on a large, grassy flat along the south shore of Osoyoos Lake in the Okanogan Valley; picnic and camp sites receive minimal to light shade from large hardwoods on a grassy surface; adjacent marsh area is home for a variety of wildlife; dry hills and high mountains flank this very fertile valley; lake area is 5700 acres, about half of it in Canada; elevation 900´.

Season, Fees & Phone: Open all year; please see Appendix for campground fees; ☎(509) 476-3321.

Trip Log: The Okanogan Valley is renowned for its mild climate, long growing season, and delicious fruits and vegetables (grown and sold at roadside stands on both sides of the border). Boating campers may be pleased to know that, at a few lakeside campsites, their vessel can be moored right at their site. Since the north end of the lake is in Canada, many boaters take the opportunity to motor or sail across the border.

⚕ Washington 60 ♿

BONAPARTE LAKE
Okanogan National Forest

Location: Northeast Washington west of Republic.

Access: From Washington State Highway 20 at milepost 282 +.2 (20 miles east of Tonasket, 20 miles west of Republic), turn north onto Forest Road 396 (paved); travel northerly for 5.9 miles, then turn west (left) into the recreation area.

Day Use Facilities: Small picnic area; drinking water; restrooms; medium-sized parking area.

Camping Facilities: 24 campsites in 2 loops; sites are medium-sized, with fair separation; level parking pads are gravel, short to medium-length, straight-ins or pull-throughs; good tent spots; fireplaces; some firewood is available for gathering in the vicinity; water at central faucets; restrooms, plus auxiliary vaults; waste water receptacles for gray water; hard-surfaced driveways; limited supplies are available in Republic and Tonasket.

Activities & Attractions: Boating; boat launch; fishing; foot trail from the west end of the campground.

Natural Features: Located on the forested south shore of Bonaparte Lake; day use area is along the shore; many campsites have lake views through the trees; tall conifers tower over the campsites, with only a little underbrush and second growth to separate the sites; the lake is bordered by steep-sided, rocky, timbered mountains that rise to 7200´; elevation 4000´.

Season, Fees & Phone: May to October; $8.00 for a single unit, $10.00-$15.00 for a multiple unit; 14 day limit; Tonasket Ranger District ☎(509) 486-2186.

Trip Log: This is a really nice recreation area for any part of the country, but here in mostly dry eastern Washington, it's a very pleasant surprise! And this picturesque, tree-ringed lake is just a half dozen miles from the main highway, to boot.

⚕ Washington 61

SULLIVAN LAKE
Colville National Forest

Location: Northeast corner of Washington east of Metaline Falls.

Access: From Washington State Highway 31 at milepost 16 +.4 (1.5 miles north of Metaline Falls, 11 miles south of the Canadian border) turn east onto Sullivan Lake Road (Forest Road 9345); travel east, then south for 4.7 miles; turn east (left) onto Forest Road 22 and proceed 0.4 mile, then turn south (right) onto a gravel access road for a final 0.3 mile to the recreation area.
Alternate Access: From Washington State Highway 31 at milepost 3 +.1 (at the south edge of the town of Ione) turn east onto Elizabeth Street, which becomes Sullivan Lake Road and Forest Road 9345 (paved); travel east and north for 12.5 miles to Forest Road 22 and continue as above. (Note: The first Access is the shortest and most direct route from the main highway, and the preferred route for southbound travelers on Washington 31; the Alternate Access is a 'backdoor' approach and works very well for northbound travelers, and it is especially scenic.)

Day Use Facilities: Small picnic area; drinking water; vault facilities; medium-sized parking area.

Camping Facilities: 34 campsites in 2 sections (locally termed West and East); sites are fairly good-sized, level, with fair separation; parking pads are gravel, medium to long straight-ins; many large, level spots for tents; fireplaces; firewood is available for gathering in the area; water at several faucets; vault facilities; disposal station; gravel driveways; limited supplies and services are available in Metaline Falls.

Activities & Attractions: Boating; boat launch; fishing; designated swimming area; a foot trail leads south along the east shore of the lake for 4.1 miles to Noisy Creek Campground; benches along the shore line and a Sullivan Lake Viewpoint provide lake-watching opportunities; a grass airstrip makes fly-in camping possible.

Natural Features: Located near the north shore of glacially formed Sullivan Lake; tall conifers are the predominant vegetation, and the campsites are fairly well-cleared of underbrush; the lake is 3.5 miles long and up to 275´ deep;

encircled by forested hills and mountains; elevation 2600´.

Season, Fees & Phone: May to October; $8.00; 14 day limit; Sullivan Lake Ranger District ☎(509) 446-7500.

Trip Log: The relaxed atmosphere of this spot is due in part to its distance from population concentrations. The sight of this alluring mountain lake surrounded by pristine forested hills is, in itself, worth the trip.

⚜ Washington 62

NOISY CREEK
Colville National Forest

Location: Northeast corner of Washington northeast of Ione.

Access: From Washington State Highway 31 at milepost 3 +.1 (at the south edge of the town of Ione) turn east onto Elizabeth Street, which becomes Sullivan Lake Road and Forest Road 9345 (paved); travel east and north for 8.2 miles; turn east (right) and continue for 0.1 mile on gravel to a fork in the road; take the left fork for a final 0.3 mile to the campground.

Day Use Facilities: Small parking area.

Camping Facilities: 19 campsites in 2 tiered loops; (an adjacent overflow camp area is also available); sites are small to medium-sized, with fair to good separation; parking pads are gravel and may require additional leveling; some sites are designated for tents or small vehicles; tent spots are mostly small and sloped; fireplaces; firewood is available for gathering; water at several faucets; vault facilities; narrow, one-way, gravel driveway; limited supplies and services are available in Ione.

Activities & Attractions: Fishing; designated swimming beach; boating; boat launch; a foot trail leads north along the lake shore for 4.1 miles to Sullivan Lake Campground.

Natural Features: Located on the south shore of glacially formed Sullivan Lake; Noisy Creek tumbles past many of the sites on its way to the lake; moderately dense, tall conifers, hardwoods, and very little underbrush provide shade/shelter for the sites; towering, forested peaks cover most of the region; elevation 2600´.

Season, Fees & Phone: May to October; $8.00 for a standard site, $10.00 for a "preferred" (lakeside) site; 14 day limit; Sullivan Lake Ranger District ☎(509) 446-7500.

Trip Log: This recreation area—on the shore of a beautiful mountain lake, along a rushing stream, and some distance off the mainstream—is little used by campers from outside the region. Mountainous, evergreen-cloaked, and sparsely populated, Washington's remote northeast corner is one of the state's unheralded scenic sanctuaries.

🏠 *Washington* ▲
Southeast Columbia Basin

⚜ Washington 63 ♿

PLYMOUTH
Lake Umatilla/Corps of Engineers Park

Location: Southern Washington border south of Kennewick.

Access: From Washington State Highway 14 at a point 2 miles west of the Plymouth/Highway 14 Exit on Interstate 82 and 12 miles east of the junction of State Highways 14 & 221 near Paterson, turn south onto a local paved road; continue southerly through the community of Plymouth to Christy Road; turn west onto Christy Road for 0.1 mile to the park entrance; turn south (left) and immediately east into the campground.

Day Use Facilities: Small parking area.

Camping Facilities: 32 campsites with partial hookups; sites are small, level, with minimal separation; parking pads are paved, mostly long pull-throughs; ample space for tents on gravel pads or on the grass; fireplaces; b-y-o firewood; restrooms with showers; holding tank disposal station; paved driveways; limited+ supplies and services are available across the river in Umatilla, Oregon.

Activities & Attractions: Boating; boat launch; designated swimming area; fishing for smallmouth bass, walleye, sturgeon; large day use area nearby; McNary Dam Visitor Center is located across the Columbia River, in Oregon.

Natural Features: Located on the north bank of the Columbia River/Lake Umatilla just west of McNary Dam; vegetation in the campground consists mainly of tall hardwoods, bushes and mown grass; dry, rocky ridges parallel the river on the north and south; the campground is just onshore of Lake Umatilla, created by John Day Dam nearly 100 miles downriver of this point; elevation 300´.

Season, Fees & Phone: May to October, with limited pre- and post- season availability; $12.00; 14 day limit; CoE John Day Project Office, The Dalles, OR, ☎(541) 296-1181.

Trip Log: Plymouth Park is a patch of fertility in this otherwise dry region of southern Washington. Trees and shrubs have been planted to provide each site with a small measure of separation from the driveway and neighboring campers. Broad vistas of the river and surrounding area are available from this riverside location.

⚐ Washington 64 ♿

CHARBONNEAU
Lake Sacajawea/Corps of Engineers Park

Location: Southeast Washington east of Pasco.

Access: From Washington State Highway 124 at milepost 8 +.5 (10 miles east of Pasco, 38 miles west of Waitsburg), turn north onto Sun Harbor Drive; drive 1.7 miles north to the park.

Day Use Facilities: Large picnic area; shelters; drinking water; restrooms; large parking lot.

Camping Facilities: 54 campsites, including 36 with electrical hookups and 18 with full hookups; hookups; sites are medium-sized, with minimal separation; parking pads are paved, fairly level, some are long enough for large rv's; grassy tent areas, many of them on a slight slope; fireplaces and/or barbecue grills; b-y-o firewood; water at several faucets; restrooms with showers; holding tank disposal station; paved driveways; limited supplies at a nearby marina, complete supplies and services are available in the Tri-Cities area.

Activities & Attractions: Boating; fishing; swimming; playground; Ice Harbor Dam Visitor Center is located 2 miles west.

Natural Features: Located just east of Ice Harbor Dam which forms Lake Sacajawea on the Snake River; picnic sites are shaded by tall hardwoods; campsites are all on a hilltop overlooking the water and a natural jetty which protrudes into the lake; some hardwoods dot the manicured lawn, but the camping area is still quite exposed to sun and wind; most sites have views of the lake and bluffs on the opposite shore; elevation 500´.

Season, Fees & Phone: Open all year, with limited services November to March; $12.00 for an electrical hookup site, $12.00 for a full hookup site, $6.00 for overflow camping; 14

day limit; Corps of Engineers Ice Harbor Dam Project Office, Pasco, ☎(509) 547-7781.

Trip Log: Situated on a breezy hill overlooking the Snake River, the park offers vast views of the countryside in all directions. The park is named for Pierre Charbonneau, the French-Canadian member of the Lewis and Clark Expedition and husband of Sacajawea, the Shoshone person who guided the group through Montana and Idaho.

⚐ Washington 65 ♿

FISHHOOK
Lake Sacajawea/Corps of Engineers Park

Location: Southeast Washington east of Pasco.

Access: From Washington State Highway 124 at milepost 16 (18 miles east of Pasco, 30 miles west of Waitsburg), turn north onto Page Road; drive 4.5 miles on this paved road to the park.

Day Use Facilities: Medium-sized picnic area; drinking water; restrooms; parking area.

Camping Facilities: 76 campsites, including 35 tents-only sites and 41 sites with partial hookups, in one long loop; sites are medium-sized, with nominal separation; parking pads are paved and well leveled, considering the terrain; pads are generally medium-length straight-ins, but a few are pull-throughs long enough for very large rv's; large tent spots; barbecue grills and/or fireplaces; b-y-o firewood; water at central faucets; restrooms with showers; holding tank disposal station; paved driveways; complete supplies and services are available in the Richland-Pasco-Kennewick area.

Activities & Attractions: Boating; boat launch; fishing for steelhead, salmon, bass and catfish; designated swimming beach; playground; hiking in adjacent wildlife habitat.

Natural Features: Located on a grassy hillside on the south shore of Lake Sacajawea above Ice Harbor Dam; the dam spans the Snake River to form the lake; park lawns are watered and mown, and dotted with large hardwoods and conifers; rolling, sage-covered hillsides surround the park; dry bluffs border the river; elevation 500´.

Season, Fees & Phone: April to late-September; $10.00 for a tent site, $12.000 for a partial hookup site; 14 day limit; Corps of Engineers Ice Harbor Dam Project Office, Pasco, ☎(509) 547-7781.

Trip Log: Ice Harbor Dam and subsequent irrigation projects have created a welcome recreational refuge here at Fishhook Park. The grassy hillsides, manicured lawns, boat launch and swimming beach stand in distinct contrast to the surrounding sage-and-orchard covered slopes. A railroad line runs along the edge of the park, so be prepared for possible periodic breaks in the tranquil routine here.

♣ Washington 66
FORT WALLA WALLA
Walla Walla City Park

Location: South-central Washington in Walla Walla.

Access: From Washington State Highway 125 at the southwest corner of Walla Walla (on the west side of the highway opposite the fairgrounds and the Plaza Shopping Center), turn west onto Dalles-Military Road; continue west/southwest for 0.8 mile to the park.

Day Use Facilities: Small picnic area; drinking water; restrooms; small parking area.

Camping Facilities: Approximately 30 campsites, some with partial hookups; sites are generally medium-sized, level, with very little separation; parking pads are gravel, and spacious enough to accommodate larger vehicles; lots of large, grassy tent-pitching spots; fire rings; b-y-o firewood; water at several faucets; restrooms with showers; holding tank disposal station; gravel driveways; complete supplies and services are available within 1 mile in Walla Walla.

Activities & Attractions: Old Fort Walla Walla Museum, just north of the park, can be reached via a foot bridge across the creek; county fair held in late August.

Natural Features: Located on watered and mown grass lawns ringed by tall hardwoods; a little creek separates the campground and the day use area; rv sites have somewhat less shelter/shade than tent units; bordered by hilly plains and cropland; elevation 800´.

Season, Fees & Phone: Open all year; principal season is May September; limited services and reduced fees remainder of the year; $8.50 for a standard site, $12.00 for a partial-hookup site; more than 4 people per site, $1.00 each; 7 day limit in season; reservations accepted by mail (call for a reservation form); park office ☎(509) 527-3770.

Trip Log: This is a nicely landscaped and maintained park, somewhat superior to many other municipal campgrounds. Its proximity to

all the services of Walla Walla will be considered an advantage by many campers. The adjacent museum is excellent.

Washington 67 ♿
CHIEF TIMOTHY
Chief Timothy State Park

Location: Southeast corner of Washington west of Clarkston.

Access: From U.S. Highway 12 at milepost 425 +.9 (8 miles west of Clarkston, 21 miles east of Pomeroy), turn north, proceed across the causeway to the park.

Day Use Facilities: Medium-sized picnic area; small shelters; drinking water; restrooms; 2 medium-sized parking lots.

Camping Facilities: 66 campsites, including 33 with full hookups and 16 park 'n walk tent sites; sites are medium-sized, with minimal separation; most parking pads are paved, level, long pull-throughs; excellent, grassy tent sites; fireplaces; firewood is usually for sale, or b-y-o; water at hookups and at several faucets; restrooms with showers; holding tank disposal station; paved driveways; complete supplies and services are available in Lewiston-Clarkston.

Activities & Attractions: Boating; boat launch and docks; really nice playground ("Tot Lot"); pebble and sand swimming beach; Alpowai Interpretive Center.

Natural Features: Located on an island in Lower Granite Lake, an impoundment on the Snake River; planted pines and hardwoods on watered and mown lawns provide very light to light-medium shade; bordered by high, rocky hills and bluffs; elevation 700´.

Season, Fees & Phone: Open all year; please see Appendix for campground fees; park office ☎(509) 758-9580.

Trip Log: The island on which the park stands was formerly a high spot in the Lewis and Clark Valley before the area was flooded by the man-made lake. (Displays and a-v programs in the interpretive center will give you the history of the area which the Indians called *Alpowai*.) All picnic and camp sites have quite a spectacular view. In summer, the park stands in rich green contrast to the rugged, nearly treeless bluffs which border the river. The campground stretches for nearly a half mile along the south shore of the island. Several docks are located along the shore of the island, so you can tie-up to within arm's length of your site.

Oregon *Destinations*

A Western Leader With a Lot of History

Oregon has a reputation to live up to.

From the earliest days of the exploration of the Great American West, Oregon has been sought as the promised land, the fertile, lush, green, territory by the western sea.

Today, Oregon's parks and forests are the promised lands of many recreationers. While much of the highly prized land in the western half of the state has been agriculturalized and populated, thousands of square miles remain in the public domain.

Oregon was one of the early leaders in the establishment of an extensive network of state parks to preserve its natural inheritance. Its state park system is now the envy of dozens of other states.

A trip along the Oregon Coast takes top priority on most visitors' itineraries, and here is where the state park concept has been most completely implemented. While there are a few national forest and county campgrounds along the 360-mile seacoast, numerous state parks provide most of the coastal recreation access.

If you've never been to Oregon, there are a few other practical items which may be of interest to you: Self-service gas has been outlawed; a "bottle law" requires a deposit on most beverage containers, so you may have empties clinking and clanking around in the camper between pit stops; Oregon is one of very few states which does not impose a sales tax; yet it does apply a "lodging tax" to campsite occupancy.

Whether it's along the coast, in the Cascades, or on the eastern plains, your next Oregon recreation destination will be accompanied by outstanding scenery and a lot of history.

Oregon lives up to its reputation.

 Oregon

North Coast

Oregon 1

FORT STEVENS
Fort Stevens State Park

Location: Northwest corner of Oregon southwest of Astoria.

Access: From U.S. Highway 101 (southbound) at milepost 6 +.4 (on the northeast edge of the city of Warrenton near the south end of the bridge/causeway which crosses Youngs Bay, 5 miles southwest of Astoria), turn west onto East Harbor Drive; proceed toward midtown Warrenton, then pick up North Main Avenue and continue generally northwesterly (toward the community of Hammond) as North Main curves and becomes NW Warrenton Drive, and finally Pacific Drive for a total of 4.4 miles from U.S. 101; at the intersection of Pacific Drive and Ridge Road, continue ahead (west) to the historic areas; or turn south (left) onto Ridge Road to the day use areas and the campground.

Alternate Access: From U.S. 101 (northbound) at milepost 9 +.2 on the north edge of the Camp Rilea Military Reservation, turn west, then immediately north and proceed (on what should be a well-signed route to the park) northwesterly on Ridge Road for a total of 4.6 miles to the campground entrance, on the west (left) side of the road; or continue ahead for 1 mile to the day use and historical areas, on the west (left) side of Ridge Road.

Day Use Facilities: 2 picnic areas with shelters and large parking lots at Coffenbury Lake; beach access is provided from 4 large parking lots situated just off of the main road which leads to the tip of the point at the mouth of the river.

Camping Facilities: 605 campsites, including 130 with partial hookups and 213 with full hookups, in 15 loops; (8, small group tent camps are also available); sites are generally small, level, with minimal to fair separation; parking pads are paved, short to medium-length straight-ins or medium to long pull-throughs; medium to large tent areas; water at sites and at several faucets in each loop; restrooms with showers; paved driveways; adequate+ supplies and services are available in the Warrenton/Hammond area.

Activities & Attractions: Fort Stevens Historical Center features self-guided tours of the shore batteries which defended the mouth of the Columbia River from the War Between the States to World War II; museum with military items and interpretive exhibits; several miles of ocean beach; 7 miles of paved bicycle trails; 5 miles of hiking trails; wreck of the Peter Iredale, a sailing ship which ran aground in 1906 on what is now the park's beach; 2 swimming areas, fishing for trout and perch, and limited (10 mph) boating on Coffenbury Lake; watching ships cross the Columbia Bar and fishing at the South Jetty on the northwest tip of the park.

Natural Features: Located on 4000 acres on a peninsula near and along the Pacific Ocean at the mouth of the Columbia River; park vegetation consists of dense stands of hardwoods, conifers and shrubbery in the camping and picnicking areas; remaining sections of the park consist mostly of grass-covered dunes and miles of beach; small Coffenbury Lake is adjacent to the picnic areas and campground; sea level.

Season, Fees & Phone: Open all year; please see Appendix for campground fees; ☎(503) 861-1671.

Trip Log: Fort Stevens is the largest piece of real estate in the Oregon State Park System. Detailed park maps are displayed at several points in order to help you get your bearings once you arrive. Chances are, you'll run out of time before you run out of things to see and do here. One of the shore gun emplacements, Battery Russell, which was shelled by a Japanese sub in WWII, is the only installation in the U.S. mainland to have been attacked by a foreign power since the War of 1812.

⚘ Oregon 2

ECOLA
Ecola State Park

Location: Northern Oregon Coast south of Seaside.

Access: From U.S. Highway 101 at milepost 28 +.1 (at the north edge of the community of Cannon Beach) turn west onto North U.S. 101A

and proceed 0.2 mile to the bottom of the hill; turn northwest (right) onto 5th St. for 0.2 mile, then north for 1.6 miles on a narrow, curving and, steep paved access road to the park.

Day Use Facilities: Picnic area, drinking water, restrooms, medium-sized parking area, and beach access at Ecola Point and at Indian Beach.

Camping Facilities: None; nearest public campgrounds are in Oswald West State Park (walk-in tent camping only) and Fort Stevens State Park.

Activities & Attractions: Ocean beaches; hiking trails; Tillamook Head National Recreation Trail passes through the park.

Natural Features: Located on the south side of Tillamook Head on the Pacific Ocean; most of the park is steep, hilly, and densely forested with stands of conifers and hardwoods over steep hillsides carpeted with ferns; rocky headlands frame the beaches; elevation varies from sea level to 200´.

Season, Fees & Phone: Open all year; please see Appendix for entry fee charged on summer weekends and holidays; ☎(503) 436-2844.

Trip Log: Just the drive on the park road along the exquisitely forested hillsides is worth the trip, let alone the views of the beaches, offshore rocks, and headlands! Ecola is one of the best spots on this segment of the North Coast to watch for gray whales during their annual migrations from December to May.

⚘ Oregon 3 ♿

NEHALEM BAY
Nehalem Bay State Park

Location: Northern Oregon Coast south of Manzanita.

Access: From U.S. Highway 101 at milepost 43 +.9 at the south edge of the community of Manzanita, turn south onto Necarney City Road and proceed 0.25 mile to a fork; turn west (right) and continue west, then south, for 1.7 miles to the park.

Day Use Facilities: 3 picnic areas; drinking water; restrooms; large parking lots, (including some pull-along spaces for rv's); recreational/meeting hall available to groups (reservations recommended year 'round, required during the off-season, September to April.)

Camping Facilities: 292 campsites with partial hookups, in 6 loops; sites are small to small+, level, with nominal to fairly good separation; parking pads are paved, short to medium+ straight-ins; medium to large, grassy tent spots; special areas for hiker-biker and equestrian camping; designated "pet loops"; fire rings; firewood is usually for sale, or b-y-o; water at each site; several restrooms with showers; holding tank disposal station; paved driveways; limited supplies and services are available in Manzanita and Nehalem.

Activities & Attractions: Short trails (some paved) up and over the dunes to the beach from day use and camp areas; bike trails; equestrian trails; beachcombing; very good crabbing, clamming, fishing in the bay; boat launch; 2400´ paved airstrip.

Natural Features: Located on 4-mile-long Nehalem Bay Spit, a long, slender, fairly level peninsula which forms the ocean-side landmass of long, narrow Nehalem Bay; picnic and camp areas are lightly shaded and fairly well wind-sheltered by small to medium-height, pines and shrubs; a grass-covered dune separates the picnic and camp areas from the beach which extends the full length of the spit; high, forested coastal mountains nearly surround the bay; sea level.

Season, Fees & Phone: Day use area open all year; campground open April to November; please see Appendix for campground fees; ☎(503) 368-5943.

Trip Log: There are some excellent Coast Range views from the park, particularly from certain camp loops. If you're planning on camping, you might check out Loops D, E, and F for a bit more privacy and better views.

♣ Oregon 4

CAPE MEARES
Cape Meares State Park

Location: Northern Oregon Coast northwest of Tillamook.

Access: From U.S. Highway 101 in midtown Tillamook, turn west onto Third Street and travel 1.8 miles to the west end of the Tillamook River Bridge and a fork; take the right fork onto the Three Capes Scenic Route and follow this road northwesterly for 7.5 miles; (watch for a sharp left turn at a 3-way intersection at the 4.5-mile point); turn north (right) off the highway onto the park access road and continue for a final 0.7 mile to the main section of the park.

Day Use Facilities: Several picnic tables; drinking water; restrooms; large parking lot.

Camping Facilities: None; nearest public campground is in Cape Lookout State Park.

Activities & Attractions: Paved walkway down to Cape Meares Lighthouse, built in 1890; trail to Octopus Tree (a sitka spruce 10´ in diameter); 1-mile trail leads through the forest down to the beach; 6-mile trail to Tillamook Bay South Jetty; Coast Trail.

Natural Features: Located on hilly terrain at Cape Meares; main park vegetation consists of mown lawns bordered by super tall conifers, hardwoods and shrubbery; tall conifers predominate in the natural sections; the rocky Oregon Islands, including Three Arch Rocks, lie a short distance offshore; elevation sea level to 200´.

Season, Fees & Phone: Open all year; ☎(541) 842-3182 or ☎(541) 842-4981.

Trip Log: The islands noted above not only complement the wild and scenic coastline, but also are part of Oregon Islands National Wildlife Refuge and serve as a breeding and resting place for sea birds and marine mammals. Cape Meares is certainly worth the 10-mile excursion off of '101'.

♣ Oregon 5 ♿

CAPE LOOKOUT
Cape Lookout State Park

Location: Northern Oregon Coast southwest of Tillamook.

Access: From U.S. Highway 101 in midtown Tillamook, turn west onto Third Street and travel 1.8 miles to the west end of the Tillamook River Bridge and a fork; take the left fork and continue south/southwest along the river, up and over the mountain, past the turnoff to Netarts (where you'll pick up the Three Capes Scenic Route southwesterly along Netarts Bay) for 10.5 miles; turn west (right) into the park.

Day Use Facilities: Picnic area; large shelter; drinking water; restrooms; large parking lot.

Camping Facilities: 250 campsites, including 53 with full hookups; (4 group camp areas and a hiker-biker camp are also available); sites are generally small to small+, closely spaced and semi-private; parking pads are paved, mostly level, short to long straight-ins; no extra vehicles permitted in campsite; large grassy tent areas; fireplaces; firewood is usually for sale, or b-y-o; water at faucets throughout; restrooms with showers; waste water basins; holding tank disposal station; paved driveways; gas and groceries in Netarts, 5 miles north; adequate+ supplies and services are available in Tillamook.

Activities & Attractions: Short trails from the day use and camp areas to the beach; nature trail; 7 miles of hiking trails in the area; recreational/meeting hall; amphitheater.

Natural Features: Located in a moderately to heavily forested area made up mostly of tall conifers; excellent Pacific Ocean beach; the park is at the juncture of a rugged peninsula which extends nearly 2 miles into the sea, and a spit which serves as a natural, 5-mile-long 'breakwater' for Netarts Bay; the park is bordered by heavily timbered hills and mountains; sea level.

Season, Fees & Phone: Open all year; campsite reservations accepted, recommended for summer weekends and holidays; please see Appendix for campground fees; ☎(541) 842-3182 or ☎(541) 842-4981.

Trip Log: Cape Lookout is one of the most remote coastal parks—and looks the part. There's an outstanding roadside viewpoint of the cape, the spit, and the bay from the top of a hill a mile south of the park.

🔦 Oregon 6 ♿

SAND BEACH
Siuslaw National Forest

Location: Northern Oregon Coast southwest of Tillamook.

Access: From U.S. Highway 101 at a point 11 miles south of Tillamook, 3.2 miles north of Beaver and 6 miles north of Hebo, turn west onto Sandlake Road/Tillamook County Road 871 (paved) and travel west then south for 5.5 miles to the community of Sandlake; turn west (right) onto County Road 872 (paved, might be signed for "Sandlake Park & Dunes") for 2.4 miles (there's a sharp left turn after the first mile) to the recreation area.

Day Use Facilities: Small picnic area; drinking water; restrooms; small parking area.

Camping Facilities: 101 campsites; (camping for about 50 vehicles in each of 2 nearby paved parking lots, with drinking water and restrooms, is also available); sites are medium to large, level, with minimal to fairly good separation; parking pads are paved, medium to long straight-ins, most are extra wide; large tent

areas; fire rings; b-y-o firewood; water at several faucets; restrooms; paved driveways; gas and camper supplies in Sandlake; adequate+ supplies and services are available in Tillamook.

Activities & Attractions: Dune riding/orv driving; (street-legal vehicles or registered orv's only); 600 acres of national forest dunes, plus 300 acres of adjacent state and county land are available for orv use; crabbing.

Natural Features: Located in an area of sand dunes on a point near the Pacific Ocean; sites are lightly shaded/sheltered by small pines, bushes and tall grass; Sand Lake is actually a small, shallow bay off the ocean; bordered by sand dunes, forested hills, bluffs, and mountains; sea level.

Season, Fees & Phone: May to October for standard campground; parking lot camping is open all year; $10.00 for a standard site, $7.00 for a parking lot site; extra $5.00 entry permit is required from the ranger station *prior* to summer holidays or holiday weekends (Memorial Day, Independence Day, Labor Day); 10 day limit; Hebo Ranger District ☎(541) 392-3161.

Trip Log: Sand Beach is most-often used by orv pilots and their pit crews. It also presents a viable option to any camper who can't get a site at Cape Lookout State Park. A designated "Quiet Zone" helps prevent camper-to-camper confrontations. "Quiet" is a relative term on holiday weekends. From 2000 to 4000 recreationers pack this area on summer holidays.

🔦 Oregon 7 ♿

DEVIL'S LAKE
Devil's Lake State Park

Location: Central Oregon Coast in Lincoln City.

Access: From U.S. Highway 101 at milepost 114 +.7 in Lincoln City, turn east onto North 6th Drive and proceed 0.1 mile, then turn south into the park.

Day Use Facilities: None; nearest day use area is in East Devil's Lake State Park.

Camping Facilities: 100 campsites, including 32 with full hookups; sites are small to small+, essentially level, with nominal to fairly good separation; most parking pads are paved, short straight-ins; hookup units generally can accommodate larger rv's; medium-sized, grassy tent areas; hiker-biker camp near the entrance; fireplaces; firewood is usually for sale, or b-y-o; water at faucets throughout; waste water receptacles; restrooms with solar showers; adequate+ supplies and services are available in Lincoln City.

Activities & Attractions: Boating; boat launch and large dock facility nearby; fishing on the lake; wide, paved walkways from the campground to the lake; Pacific Ocean beach, within walking distance, across the main highway.

Natural Features: Located a few yards from Devil's Lake, a sizable body of freshwater connected to the Pacific Ocean by what is promoted as "the world's shortest river"; somewhat densely forested with conifers and some hardwoods within the campground; sea level.

Season, Fees & Phone: Day use area open all year; campground open mid-April to late October; reservations accepted, recommended for summer weekends; please see Appendix for campground fees; ☎(541) 994-2002.

Trip Log: A full-service public campground so close to the tourist center of Lincoln City is certainly a surprise. A surprise, that is, until you take into account that the park's establishment pre-dates Lincoln City's rise to fame (and fortune) by a number of years. (Lincoln City is the econo-center of what is locally called the "Twenty Miracle Miles".) The town's popularity stems in large measure from its proximity to the 50 percent of Oregon's residents who live in the Portland area.

⚕ Oregon 8

YAQUINA BAY
Yaquina Bay State Park

Location: Central Oregon Coast on the south edge of Newport.

Access: From U.S. Highway 101 at the north end of the Yaquina Bay bridge on the south edge of Newport (either at the very north end of the bridge or a few blocks farther north at SW 9th St.), turn west onto the park loop road and proceed 0.3 mile to the parking areas.

Day Use Facilities: Clusters of picnic tables throughout the park; drinking water; restrooms; large parking areas along the park road.

Camping Facilities: None; nearest public campground is in South Beach State Park.

Activities & Attractions: The old Yaquina Bay Lighthouse, which now serves as a museum (open daily in the afternoon in summer, open weekends in the afternoon remainder of the year, hours subject to change).

Natural Features: Located on a bluff above Yaquina Bay; picnic areas receive light to moderate shade/shelter from small pines and bushes; elevation 100´.

Season, Fees & Phone: Open all year; ☎(541) 867-7451 or ☎(541) 867-4715.

Trip Log: The century-and-a-quarter-old, red-and-white lighthouse has been restored to a handsomely authentic condition. It was near here that the first recorded landfall in the Pacific Northwest was made from a British ship commanded by that intrepid explorer of the Pacific Ocean, Captain James Cook, in March of 1778. News of Cook's extraordinary voyage sparked American interest in the Northwest, and subsequently led to the Louisiana Purchase.

⚕ Oregon 9 ♿

TILLICUM BEACH
Siuslaw National Forest

Location: Central Oregon Coast south of Waldport.

Access: From U.S. Highway 101 at milepost 160 + .5 (4 miles south of Waldport, 30 miles north of Florence), turn west into the campground.

Day Use Facilities: None.

Camping Facilities: 57 campsites; sites are medium to medium+, with fair to excellent separation; most sites have paved, straight-in parking pads, a few have pull-throughs or pull-offs; many pads may require some additional leveling; adequate tent-pitching spots; fireplaces; b-y-o firewood; restrooms; paved driveways; adequate supplies and services are available in Waldport.

Activities & Attractions: Tremendous ocean views; beachcombing, particularly productive during the winter; amphitheater; Siuslaw National Forest Visitor Center at Cape Perpetua, 7 miles south.

Natural Features: Located on the side of a bluff at the ocean's edge; very dense high brush and a few tall conifers provide a significant amount of separation between most sites; a rail fence borders the campground on the ocean side; sea level.

Season, Fees & Phone: Open all year; $11.00; 10 day limit; Waldport Ranger District ☎(541) 563-3211.

Trip Log: This is about the only national forest campground in Oregon which provides campers with beachfront property. A few sites have a commanding view of the ocean, many are tucked-away in the thick shrubbery. Tip: It's usually best to avoid Tillicum Beach in summer; if you really want to camp here during the standard vacation season, you may have to arrive at dawn and wait for a camp spot to open up.

⛺ Oregon 10 ♿

CAPE PERPETUA
Siuslaw National Forest

Location: Central Oregon Coast south of Waldport.

Access: From U.S. Highway 101 at milepost 167 + .3 (11 miles south of Waldport, 23 miles north of Florence), turn east into the Cape Perpetua Visitor Center parking lot; or a few yards north of the visitor center turnoff, turn east onto the campground access road, then proceed 0.1 mile to the campground.

Day Use Facilities: Small picnic area; drinking water; restrooms; large parking lot at the visitor center.

Facilities: 37 campsites; (a group area is also available); sites are mostly medium-sized, with nominal to good separation; parking pads are paved, vary considerably in length, but most are in the small to medium-length range; sites are basically level, but a bit of extra leveling may be required on some pads; many good tent spots; fireplaces; some firewood is available for gathering in the vicinity; water at faucets throughout; restrooms; holding tank disposal station; paved driveway; limited supplies in Yachats, 3 miles north; adequate supplies and services are available in Waldport.

Activities & Attractions: Within a short walk of fascinating tidal pools along the ocean shore; Cape Perpetua Visitor Center has interpretive displays and a-v presentations; a nature trail leads off into the forest from the east end of the campground; small amphitheater.

Natural Features: Located along the rugged coast of the Pacific Ocean (day use areas) and along Cape Creek in a long, narrow valley (campground) in a very lush coastal forest environment; sea level to 50´.

Season, Fees & Phone: Visitor center open all year; campground open May to mid-September; $10.00; 10 day limit; Waldport Ranger District ☎(541) 563-3211.

Trip Log: The tidal pools, with their variety of ocean life, and the national forest visitor center are the main attractions here. The visitor center features informative forestry exhibits and an ageless film, *Forces of Nature*, plus a newer production titled *A Discovery at the Edge*. From its hillside location, the ocean panoramas of this rugged stretch of coastline are positively first class. Even on a stormy day its a treat to stop here. (In fact, *especially* on a stormy day…)

 Oregon ⛺
South Coast

⛺ Oregon 11 ♿

JESSIE M. HONEYMAN
Jessie M. Honeyman State Park

Location: Central Oregon Coast south of Florence.

Access: From U.S. Highway 101 near milepost 193 (3 miles south of Florence, 18 miles north of Reedsport), turn west into the main park entrance; go 0.1 mile to a 'Y'; go right to the day use area, or left to the camp.

Day Use Facilities: Large picnic areas; large shelters; drinking water; restrooms and bathhouses; large parking lots.

Camping Facilities: 381 campsites, including 75 with partial hookups and 66 with full hookups; (hiker-biker campsites and a group camp are also available); sites are generally small to small+, with fair separation; parking pads are paved, reasonably level, short to medium-length straight-ins; tent space varies from small to large; fireplaces or fire rings; firewood is usually for sale, or b-y-o; restrooms with showers; paved driveways; holding tank disposal station; camper supplies at a concession; adequate supplies and services are available in Florence.

Activities & Attractions: Paved walkways to the dunes area; fishing; swimming beaches; boat launches on the lakes; Siuslaw Pioneer Museum in Florence.

Natural Features: Located a short distance inland from the coast in moderate to dense stands of tall conifers mixed with low-level hardwoods; portions of Cleawox and Woahink Lakes are within the park; picnic areas are located on the east and south shores of Cleawox Lake (the smaller of the two) in the main part of the park; another picnic area is on the shore of Woahink Lake, on the east side of U.S. 101; bordered on the west by high sand dunes; the park is noted for its wild rhododendrons; elevation 50´.

Season, Fees & Phone: Open all year; campsite reservations accepted; please see Appendix for campground fees; ☎(541) 997-3851 or ☎(541) 997-3641.

Trip Log: Unless you're an orv enthusiast, you may not think that staying in the heavily used campground is a true treat. (Considering that some of the dunes south of the park are almost 500-feet high, the camp's shortcomings may pale in insignificance in relation to the locally available adventures.) However, this well-used park's day use areas seem only to improve with age. The large picnic shelters are *very* welcome on rainy days.

♣ Oregon 12 &

TAHKENITCH
Oregon Dunes National Recreation Area

Location: Central Oregon Coast north of Reedsport.

Access: From U.S. Highway 101 at milepost 203 +.5 (8 miles north of Reedsport, 13 miles south of Florence), turn west into the campground.

Day Use Facilities: None.

Camping Facilities: 34 campsites; sites are small+ to medium-sized, with fair separation; most parking pads are paved, medium-length straight-ins, a few sites have pull-throughs; some pads may require a little additional leveling; small to medium-sized tent areas; there are a couple of walk-in sites suitable for small tents; fireplaces; firewood is available for gathering; water at faucets throughout; restrooms; paved driveway; adequate supplies and services are available in Reedsport.

(Camping is also available in a half dozen other rustic campgrounds in the national recreation area between Florence and North Bend.)

Activities & Attractions: Tahkenitch Trail leads through dense forest to the open dunes area along the coast; fishing and boating on Tahkenitch Lake; Three-Mile Lake, a little less than 3 miles south, is a favorite hike-in fishing spot; like most lakes in the nra, Tahkenitch and

Three-Mile are stocked with species that include trout, perch, and crappie.

Natural Features: Located in a heavily forested area, but with some 'open' campsites; Tahkenitch Lake, one of the larger lakes on this section of the coast, is a short distance from here, on the east side of the highway; elev. 50´.

Season, Fees & Phone: Open all year; $10.00; 10 day limit; Oregon Dunes National Recreation Area Headquarters, Reedsport, ☎(541) 271-3611.

Trip Log: Tahkenitch is quite different from the other Oregon Dunes National Recreation Area campgrounds in this region. It really looks more like a state park campground. While the other camps appeal mainly to recreationers with dune buggies and other orv's, this nice little spot is more of a 'camper's camp'.

♣ Oregon 13

UMPQUA LIGHTHOUSE
Umpqua Lighthouse State Park

Location: Southern Oregon Coast southwest of Reedsport.

Access: From U.S. Highway 101 at milepost 216 +.7, (0.7 mile south of Winchester Bay, 5 miles south of Reedsport, 22 miles north of Coos Bay), turn west and go 0.15 mile up a hill to a fork; take the right fork and continue up the hill for another 0.35 mile; turn left into the campground entrance, or continue down the hill for another 0.2 mile to the day use area.

Day Use Facilities: Medium-sized picnic area; drinking water; restrooms; medium to large parking area.

Camping Facilities: 63 campsites, including 22 with full hookups; (hiker-biker campsites are also available); most hookup units are near the campground entrance in a side-by-side 'parking lot' arrangement, and have long, level, paved, straight-in parking pads; the main part of the campground is located a short distance beyond the hookup area; most sites here are level, with medium to long, paved pads and good-sized, grassy tent areas; site spacing is fairly close throughout the campground; fire rings; firewood is usually for sale, or b-y-o; water at faucets throughout; restrooms with showers; waste water receptacles; limited supplies in Winchester Bay; adequate supplies and services are available in Reedsport.

Activities & Attractions: Umpqua Lighthouse and Visitor Center, just above the day use areas and campground; trails to and around Lake Marie; small swimming beach on the lake; whale-watching station (platform) at the lighthouse; adjacent to Oregon Dunes National Recreation Area.

Natural Features: Located on moderately to densely forested, hilly terrain around and above a small gem of a lake—Lake Marie; picnic area is near the lake shore; campground is above the lake; elevation 100´.

Season, Fees & Phone: Day use area open all year; campground open April to October; 10 day camping limit; please see Appendix for campground fees; ☎(541) 271-4118.

Trip Log: You can walk up to the lighthouse from the camping and picnicking areas. (If you prefer to drive, there is parking up there.) The 200,000-candlepower light's lens is made of 800 hand-cut prisms which direct the beam as much as 19 miles seaward. Spending a night at the park campground could be a very illuminating experience.

♣ Oregon 14 ♿

WILLIAM M. TUGMAN

William M. Tugman State Park

Location: Southern Oregon Coast south of Reedsport.

Access: From U.S. Highway 101 at milepost 221 +.4 (10 miles south of Reedsport, 11 miles north of Coos Bay), turn east/northeast and proceed 0.1 mile to the park.

Day Use Facilities: Large picnic area; large shelter; drinking water; restrooms; large parking lot.

Camping Facilities: 115 campsites, all with partial-hookups; (a hiker-biker camp is also available); sites are small to small+, level, with fair to fairly good separation; parking pads are paved, medium to long straight-ins; tent areas are medium to large and have a grass/sand surface; fireplaces; firewood is usually for sale, or b-y-o; water at each site; restrooms with showers; waste water receptacles throughout the campground; holding tank disposal station; paved driveways; limited supplies in Lakeside, 1 mile south; adequate supplies in Reedsport; complete supplies and services are available in the Coos Bay-North Bend area.

Activities & Attractions: Paved trails; playground; displays with information about local flora and fauna; swimming; fishing; boat launch and dock.

Natural Features: Located on a large flat; day use area has expanses of mown lawns well-dotted with large conifers; campsites are among moderately dense, medium-height conifers; short evergreens have been planted between campsites; Eel Creek flows along the east side of the day use and camp areas; Eel Lake is on the northeast side of the park; elevation 50´.

Season, Fees & Phone: Day use area open all year; campground open April to October; please see Appendix for campground fees; ☎(541) 759-3604.

Trip Log: This is one of those simple, understated (and possibly underrated) parks. If you favor a romp spot with lots of lawn under your feet, try this one.

♣ Oregon 15 ♿

BASTENDORFF BEACH

Coos County Park

Location: Southern Oregon Coast southwest of Coos Bay.

Access: From U.S. Highway 101 in midtown Coos Bay, travel west on Commercial Avenue and follow signs for "Sunset Bay" along a zigzag, winding, generally westerly and southwesterly route on Commercial Avenue, North 7th St., Central Avenue, Ocean Boulevard, Newmark Avenue, South Empire Boulevard, and Cape Arago Highway for 8.7 miles to the village of Charleston; continue southwesterly on Cape Arago Highway for another 1.7 miles; turn northerly (right) onto the paved park access road and proceed 0.3 mile to the park.

Alternate Access: From U.S. 101 in midtown North Bend, turn west onto Virginia Street and follow the signed route west/southwest for 9.5 miles to the park turnoff. (The abbreviated directions above should be adequate under most conditions. An approach from the north, or a night arrival, might warrant taking the route from North Bend, since it is somewhat more straightforward than the way from Coos Bay.)

Day Use Facilities: Small picnic area; drinking water; restrooms; small parking area.

Camping Facilities: 81 campsites, including 43 with partial hookups and 13 with full hookups, in 4 loops; (a group camp area is also available); sites are small+ to medium-sized, with fair to very good separation; parking pads are paved, mostly medium to long straight-ins; a bit of additional leveling may be needed in some hookup sites; small+ to medium+, grassy tent spots; fireplaces; b-y-o firewood; water at faucets throughout; central restrooms with showers, plus auxiliary vaults; waste water receptacles; holding tank disposal station; paved driveways; camper supplies in Charleston; complete supplies and services are available in the Coos Bay-North Bend metro area.

Activities & Attractions: Beachcombing; designated swimming area; dandy playground; horseshoe and basketball courts.

Natural Features: Located in a forested area a few yards from an ocean beach; most sites are well-sheltered by dense conifers and hardwoods; sea level.

Season, Fees & Phone: May to October; $11.00 for a standard site, $13.00 for a hookup site; 10 day limit; park office ☎(541) 888-5353.

Trip Log: Particularly if you have a longer camping outfit, this local park is certainly worth considering as a nice option to the nearby state park (Sunset Bay). Campsites at Bastendorff Beach are somewhat narrow, but they extend deep into the woods. In fact, taking into account the better privacy factor and its closeness to the beach, this park might have the edge over the state unit.

♠ Oregon 16

SHORE ACRES
Shore Acres State Park

Location: Central Oregon Coast southwest of Coos Bay.

Access: From U.S. Highway 101 in midtown Coos Bay, travel west on Commercial Avenue and follow signs for Sunset Bay along a zigzag, winding, generally westerly and southwesterly route on Commercial Avenue, North 7th St., Central Avenue, Ocean Boulevard, Newmark Avenue, South Empire Boulevard, and Cape Arago Highway for 8.7 miles to the village of Charleston; continue southwesterly on Cape Arago Highway for another 3.7 miles to Sunset Bay State Park Campground turnoff; continue past the campground for a final 0.9 mile; turn west for 0.1 mile to the park. **Alternate Access:** See Sunset Bay State Park.

Day Use Facilities: Small picnic area; drinking water; restrooms; large parking lot.

Camping Facilities: None; nearest public campground is in Sunset Bay State Park.

Activities & Attractions: Paved walkways through impeccably manicured Botanical Gardens; ocean observation building.

Natural Features: Located on a high bluff overlooking the Pacific Ocean; landscaping in the day use area includes mown lawns (about three football fields in size), tall conifers, and shrubs; included in the Botanical Gardens are a rose garden, lily pond, formal garden, and Japanese garden; elevation 100´.

Season, Fees & Phone: Open all year; dogs prohibited outside of vehicles; please see Appendix for summer weekend and holiday entrance fee; ☎(541) 888-4902 or ☎(541) 888-3778.

Trip Log: Plain and simple: there is no way to provide you with a proper written, or even photographic, facsimile of these spectacular, spellbinding gardens. You'll just have to see them for yourself.

♠ Oregon 17 ♿

SUNSET BAY
Sunset Bay State Park

Location: Southern Oregon Coast southwest of Coos Bay.

Access: From U.S. Highway 101 in midtown Coos Bay, travel west on Commercial Avenue and follow signs for Sunset Bay along a zigzag, winding, generally westerly and southwesterly route on Commercial Avenue, North 7th St., Central Avenue, Ocean Boulevard, Newmark Avenue, South Empire Boulevard, and Cape Arago Highway for 8.7 miles to the village of Charleston; continue southwesterly on Cape Arago Highway for another 3.7 miles; turn west (right) into the day use areas; or, opposite the second day use area, turn northeast (left) into the campground. **Alternate Access:** From U.S. 101 in midtown North Bend, turn west onto Virginia Street and follow the signed route west/southwest for 11.5 miles to the park.

Day Use Facilities: 2 picnic areas; drinking water; large shelter; restrooms/bathhouses with sand showers; medium to large parking lots.

Camping Facilities: 137 campsites, including 29 with full hookups, in 4 loops; sites are small to small+, level, with nominal to fair separation; parking pads are paved, most are short to medium-length straight-ins; adequate space for medium to large tents; fire rings; firewood is usually for sale, or b-y-o; water at faucets throughout; restrooms with showers;

paved driveways; camper supplies in Charleston, 3 miles northeast; complete supplies and services are available in Coos Bay.

Activities & Attractions: Swimming beach; fishing; boating; boat launch; hiking trail; Cape Arago Lighthouse, just northwest of the park.

Natural Features: Located along and near Sunset Bay; sandstone bluffs shelter the small bay on the north and south; a sandy beach is on the east edge of the bay; picnic sites are located along the bay, and also on a large, grassy flat along Big Creek near the bay; the campground is a few hundred yards east of the bay; picnic and camp sites receive light to medium shade/shelter from medium to tall conifers, hardwoods, and shrubs; a small creek flows through the campground; sea level.

Season, Fees & Phone: Open all year; campsite reservations accepted, recommended for summer weekends and holidays; please see Appendix for reservation information and campground fees; ☎(541) 888-4902 or ☎(541) 888-3778.

Trip Log: The ocean water in Sunset Bay is a bit warmer than at other less protected beaches. The mini bay, with its snug passage to the open ocean, isn't one of those grand, splashy places where the waves boom all day and night long. It's more like a small, quiet cove. The park's various facilities, especially the campground, are quite well sheltered from wind.

🏕 **Oregon 18** ♿

BULLARDS BEACH
Bullards Beach State Park

Location: Southern Oregon Coast north of Bandon.

Access: From U.S. Highway 101 at milepost 259 +.3 (near the north end of the Coquille River bridge, 2 miles north of Bandon, 20 miles south of Coos Bay), turn west into the park.

Day Use Facilities: Large picnic areas; a number of two-person (maybe three), wooden benches (*alfresco* love seats?) throughout the area; drinking water; large shelters; restrooms; several large parking areas adjacent to the picnic zones and also at the beach.

Camping Facilities: 192 campsites, including 100 with partial hookups and 92 with full hookups; (hiker-biker sites and an 8-site equestrian camp are also available); sites are generally small to medium-sized, level, with nominal to fairly good separation; parking pads

are short+ to long, paved straight-ins; large, grassy tent areas; fire rings; firewood is usually for sale, or b-y-o; water at each site; restrooms with showers; waste water receptacles; holding tank disposal station; paved driveways; adequate supplies and services are available in Bandon.

Activities & Attractions: Paved, level walkway (no bikes permitted) leads 1.5 miles through beautifully landscaped, but very natural, parkland to the beach; other minor trails are in the park; abandoned Coquille River Lighthouse (built in 1896); nice playground; boat launch and dock on the river; salmon fishing, clamming and crabbing; amphitheater.

Natural Features: Located on a large flat along the Coquille River estuary, on the north bank of the river; mature conifers and smaller evergreens, shrubbery and what seems like miles of mown grass are in and around the day use and camping areas; long, mown-grass flats border portions of the river; 4 miles of ocean and riverfront beach are within the park; sea level.

Season, Fees & Phone: Open all year; 10 day camping limit; please see Appendix for campground fees; ☎(541) 347-2209 or ☎(541) 347-3501.

Trip Log: It's the day use portion of Bullards beach that really 'makes' the place. The campground is surely very good; but the picnic tables and small benches situated on the grassy flat along the walkway which parallels the wide river out to the beach convey a tone of relaxation that is hard to pass up.

🏕 **Oregon 19** ♿

CAPE BLANCO
Cape Blanco State Park

Location: Southern Oregon Coast north of Port Orford.

Access: From U.S. Highway 101 at milepost 296 +.5 (4.5 miles north of Port Orford, 23 miles south of Bandon), turn west onto Cape Blanco Road and proceed 4 miles to the day use area and boat launch; or bear left and continue for another 1.5 miles to the campground.

Day Use Facilities: Picnic area; restrooms; parking areas; also a small parking lot above the beach, (access is through the campground).

Camping Facilities: 58 campsites with partial hookups; (hiker-biker sites and an equestrian camp are also available); sites are small+ to medium+ in size, generally level, with good to excellent separation; parking pads are paved, medium to long, straight-ins; some sites are designated as trailer units; medium to large, grassy tent areas; fire rings; firewood is usually for sale, or b-y-o; water at each site; restrooms with showers; waste water receptacles at each site; holding tank disposal station; paved driveways; limited+ supplies and services are available in Port Orford.

Activities & Attractions: Absolutely superb views; a first-rate beach; Hughes House, built in the late 1800's by the family which first settled the land which is now the park, (near the day use area, open to park visitors); boat launch for river access in the day use area; reportedly very good fishing for salmon and steelhead on the river; very steep trail down to the beach from the parking lot south of the campground; Cape Blanco Lighthouse; the park is near Port Orford, oldest townsite on the Oregon Coast (established in 1851).

Natural Features: Located on 1880 acres at Cape Blanco, second-westernmost point in the contiguous 48 states; day use area is located along the south bank of the Sixes River, a mile upstream of the ocean; campground is located on a high, windswept bluff overlooking the ocean; some campsites are lightly sheltered, but many are very well sheltered by conifers and tall, dense shrubbery; long, wide, black sand beach below the campground; day use area is near sea level, campground elevation 200´.

Season, Fees & Phone: Day use area open all year; campground open April to October; please see Appendix for campground fees; ☎(541) 332-6774.

Trip Log: Cape Blanco is the most westerly state park in the adjacent 48 states. If you're looking for an easily accessible picnic spot or campsite that maintains an atmosphere of remoteness and seclusion, this is it.

♣ **Oregon 20**

SAMUEL H. BOARDMAN
Samuel H. Boardman State Park

Location: Southern Oregon Coast north of Brookings.

Access: From U.S. Highway 101 between milepost 344 on the north and milepost 353 +.3 on the south, turn west into several day use areas and a half-dozen viewpoints and trailheads; the areas with facilities are Arch Rock at mile 344 +.4, Whalehead Beach at mile 349 +.2, and Lone Ranch Beach at mile 352

+.5; all viewpoints and day use areas are within 0.3 mile of the highway.

Day Use Facilities: Small picnic areas at Arch Rock, Whalehead Beach, and Lone Ranch Beach; drinking water at Whalehead Beach and Lone Ranch Beach; restrooms at Whalehead Beach and Lone Ranch Beach, vault facilities at Arch Rock; small to medium-sized parking areas at all viewpoints and picnic areas.

Camping Facilities: None; nearest public campground is in Harris Beach State Park.

Activities & Attractions: Paved trails to beaches and promontories; highwayside viewpoints.

Natural Features: Located on 10 miles of beaches and headlands along the Pacific Ocean; picnic spots generally are lightly to moderately shaded; sea level to 100´.

Season, Fees & Phone: Open all year; ☎(541) 469-2021.

Trip Log: Just hop-scotching to each of the viewpoints, savoring the scenes, and snapping a few pix could easily consume a couple of hours of travel time. This is the largest day-use-only park on the Oregon Coast.

♣ **Oregon 21** ♿

HARRIS BEACH
Harris Beach State Park

Location: Southern Oregon Coast north of Brookings.

Access: From U.S. Highway 101 at milepost 355 +.7 (1 mile north of midtown Brookings), turn northwest onto the park access road and proceed 0.35 mile to the park.

Day Use Facilities: Several picnic tables; drinking water; restrooms; medium-sized parking lot.

Camping Facilities: 151 campsites, including 51 with partial hookups, and 34 with full hookups, in 4 loops; (hiker-biker sites are also available); sites are small to medium sized, with nominal to fairly good separation; level to sloped; parking pads are paved, short to medium-length straight-ins; some pads will require additional leveling; fireplaces; firewood is usually for sale, or b-y-o; water at faucets throughout; restrooms with showers; holding tank disposal station; paved driveways; adequate supplies and services are available in Brookings.

Activities & Attractions: Trail to the top of Harris Butte; swimming/wading; reportedly excellent beachcombing and fishing.

Natural Features: Located on a hillside overlooking the beach (day use) and on a hillside a short distance east of the beach (campground); Harris Butte rises between the picnic and camp areas; picnic area is basically unsheltered; vegetation in the campground varies from light to rather dense sections of tall hardwoods and conifers with a considerable amount of flowering bushes and underbrush; numerous rock spire and stack formations stand offshore; great ocean views; sea level to 200´.

Season, Fees & Phone: Open all year; campsite reservations accepted, recommended for anytime during the summer; please see Appendix for reservation information and campground fees; ☎(541) 469-2021.

Trip Log: On the many mornings when conditions are favorable, a curious occurrence will unfold right before your eyes. If you get out early and find a vantage on a high point in the park, you can watch the commercial and sport fishing fleet congregate offshore. Starting with a few craft, the assemblage seems to double in size every few minutes until there are sometimes hundreds of boats bobbing in the briny blue sea.

Oregon
North Western

♠ Oregon 22 &

TRYON CREEK
Tryon Creek State Park

Location: Western Oregon in Portland.

Access: From Interstate 5 Exit 297 in the southwest quadrant of Portland, travel southeasterly on SW Terwilliger Boulevard for 2.4 miles; turn west (right) into the park. **Alternate Access:** From Interstate 205 Exit 8 for Lake Oswego/West Linn, travel northwest on Oregon State Highway 43 for 5.5 miles to the north edge of the city of Lake Oswego; turn northwest onto SW Terwilliger Boulevard and continue for 1.4 miles; turn southwest (left) into the park.

Day Use Facilities: Picnic shelter; drinking water; restrooms; parking lots for foot and bike travelers, and for equestrians.

Camping Facilities: None; nearest public campgrounds are in Champoeg and Milo McIver State Parks.

Activities & Attractions: 8 miles of hiking trails; (limited trailhead access, (no parking) can also be gained from SW Boones Ferry Road on the west side of the park); 3.5 miles of horse trails; 3 miles of bicycle trails; 3, half-mile-loop nature trails; Nature House.

Natural Features: Located in a densely forested canyon on 640 acres flanking Tryon Creek; forestation consists of a mixture of hardwoods and conifers; elevation 100´.

Season, Fees & Phone: Open all year; ☎(503) 653-3166 or ☎(503) 636-4550.

Trip Log: No doubt, countless lines of prose (and even poetry) have been written about this elegantly simple island in the city. Let's just say that it is, perhaps, the West's foremost metropolitan refuge.

♠ Oregon 23 &

CHAMPOEG
Champoeg State Park

Location: Western Oregon southwest of Portland.

Access: From Interstate 5 Exit 278 for Aurora/Donald, (midway between Portland and Salem), travel west on Ehlen Road and Champoeg Road following the "Champoeg" signs for a total of 6 miles from the Interstate; turn north (right) into the park.

Day Use Facilities: 2 very large picnic areas (Oak Grove and Riverside); large, open-air pavilion in Riverside (available to groups by reservation only); drinking water; restrooms; 2 large parking lots.

Camping Facilities: 48 campsites with partial hookups; (an rv group camp is also available, by reservation only); sites are small+, level, with minimal to nominal separation; parking pads are paved, medium to long straight-ins; good tent areas on the lawns; separate group area for rv's; fireplaces or fire rings; firewood is usually for sale, or b-y-o; restrooms with showers; holding tank disposal station; paved driveways; adequate supplies and services are available in Aurora, 8 miles east.

Activities & Attractions: Visitor center; historical museum; replica of a pioneer's log cabin and a restored original settler's house, both sponsored by the DAR; paved hikeway/bikeway; a hiking-only trail follows the river; rv group meeting hall in the campground; historical pageant (see Park Notes section).

Natural Features: Located on prairie flatland on the east bank of the Willamette River; one of the oldest groves of white oak trees in Oregon is a prominent feature of the park; most of the park is landscaped with mown lawns, and tall oaks, trimmed by sections of rail fence; elevation 100´.

Season, Fees & Phone: Open all year; day use entry fee on summer weekends and holidays; please see Appendix for day use and campground fees; ☎(503) 678-1251.

Trip Log: Champoeg is steeped in history—it is the site of Oregon's provisional government, established in 1843, which paved the way to statehood. The park's Oak Grove area is the site of the Champoeg Historical Pageant. Held several evenings a week for several weeks during midsummer, the pageant portrays events leading to Oregon's statehood and plays to an audience of as many as 1500 at a sitting. The sizable set includes cabins, teepees and a turreted fort. (This is no small-time medicine show—it's an *event*.) Champoeg (*sham-poo´-ee*) is a French-Indian word which is thought to mean *Prairie of the Blue Flowers*.

✚ Oregon 24

SILVER FALLS
Silver Falls State Park

Location: Western Oregon southeast of Salem.

Access: From Oregon State Highway 214 at milepost 25 (9 miles east of the junction of Oregon State Highways 214 and 22 southeast of Salem, 16 miles south of Silverton), turn northwest into the South Falls (main) day use area, or southeast into the main campground.

Day Use Facilities: 5 separate picnic areas within one very large complex; (2 areas are reservable by groups); shelters; drinking water; restrooms; 4 medium to large parking lots; concession stand.

Camping Facilities: *Campground*: 104 campsites, including 53 with partial hookups; (a 250-camper capacity youth group camp, a standard group camp, and a horse camp are also available—all by reservations); sites are small to medium-sized, with minimal to fairly good separation; parking pads are paved, short to medium-length straight-ins; many good tent spots are located on grassy areas or on a carpet of pine needles; fireplaces; water at faucets throughout; restrooms with solar showers; holding tank disposal station; paved driveways; adequate supplies and services are available in

Silverton. *Conference Center*: 4 lodges, each with 6 private (2-up) bedrooms and 2 common restrooms can accommodate a total of 48 persons; 10 cabins with private and semi-private rooms and common restrooms can house a total of 28 people; dining hall; meeting rooms; (reservations necessary, a brochure is available).

Activities & Attractions: Trail of Ten Falls—a 7-mile loop—passes the number of waterfalls in its name; 4 miles of paved bicycle trails; 3 mile jogging trail; 12 miles of equestrian trails; 150-person lodge/community building with kitchen in the standard group camp is available for day use; swimming area; playground; basic horse-handling facilities (hitch rails and ramp); visitor center features nature talks and displays.

Natural Features: Located in the foothills of the Cascade Range along the banks of the North and South Forks of Silver Creek; park vegetation consists of a moderately dense mixture of conifers and hardwoods with dense undercover, plus some meadows; picnic ground has large sections of lawns; elevation 600´.

Season, Fees & Phone: Open all year; day use entry fee on summer weekends and holidays; please see Appendix for day use and campground fees; ☎(503) 873-8681.

Trip Log: The road to Silver Falls winds through hilly forest and fertile farmland. Once you arrive, you'll see that most of the waterfalls are no mere trickles like those found in some "falls" parks—they're the real McCoys. A park with an address in a place called "Sublimity" *has* to be good.

✚ Oregon 25

HOUSE ROCK
Willamette National Forest

Location: Western Oregon southeast of Albany.

Access: From U.S. Highway 20 at milepost 54 +.3 (9 miles west of the summit of Tombstone Pass, 27 miles east of Sweet Home), turn south (a hard left if you're westbound) onto a gravel access road and proceed 0.3 mile down into the recreation area. (Note: The access road is very narrow, and is signed as "not suitable for trailers or large rv's".)

Day Use Facilities: Small picnic area; drinking water; vault facilities; ; small parking area.

Camping Facilities: 17 campsites; sites are small to small+, acceptably level, with very good to excellent separation; parking pads are gravel, short straight-ins; small to medium-sized tent areas; fire rings; firewood is available for gathering in the vicinity (may be wet); water at hand pumps; vault facilities; waste water receptacles; narrow, gravel driveway; adequate+ supplies and services are available in Sweet Home.

Activities & Attractions: House Rock Loop Trail; footbridge across the stream; possible fishing.

Natural Features: Located on hilly terrain in a canyon along 2 creeks in the Cascade Range; super dense canopy of conifers, hardwoods, moss and undergrowth covers and surrounds the campground; elevation 1700´.

Season, Fees & Phone: May to late October; $8.00 for a single site, $16.00 for double occupancy; 14 day limit; Sweet Home Ranger District ☎(541) 367-5168.

Trip Log: House Rock is probably the nicest of the half-dozen forest camps along this highway. Most of the campsites are in their own little pockets of foliage. About half are streamside, the remainder are just above the streams. This looks like the kind of place where you wouldn't be at all surprised to catch a glimpse of a tiny guy with pointed ears dressed in a green suit, lugging a pot o' gold and a shovel.

 Oregon

South Western

♣ Oregon 26

ELIJAH BRISTOW
Elijah Bristow State Park

Location: Western Oregon southeast of Eugene.

Access: From Oregon State Highway 58 (eastbound) at milepost 8 +.5 (4.5 miles southeast of Pleasant Hill, 0.5 mile northwest of Dexter), turn north onto North Rattlesnake Road and proceed 0.2 mile; turn east (right) onto Wheeler Road for 0.7 mile, then turn north (left) into the park. **Alternate Access:** From Oregon State Highway 58 (westbound) at milepost 9 +.5, turn north onto Wheeler Road and travel 0.3 mile to the park entrance.

Day Use Facilities: Very large picnic area (sections are reservable by groups); drinking water; restrooms; large parking lot.

Camping Facilities: None; nearest public campground is Black Canyon (Willamette National Forest), 8 miles west of Oakridge.

Activities & Attractions: Hiking trails; equestrian trails; canoeing, floating; access to the Willamette River Greenway (see Park Notes) is located at the northwest corner of the park off of Pengra Road).

Natural Features: Located on slightly rolling flatland bordering the banks of the Middle Fork of the Willamette River; park vegetation varies from large, dense stands of hardwoods to fields of mown or unmown grass; day use area is near the south-west riverbank on an enormous, grassy flat dotted with stands of hardwoods and some conifers and bordered by dense woodland; a sizable stream, Lost Creek, also flows through the park and is crossed on the way to the day use area; elevation 500´.

Season, Fees & Phone: Open all year; ☎(541) 686-7592.

Trip Log: It all begins here. Elijah Bristow is considered to be the starting point of the Willamette River Greenway. The highly ambitious plan was established by the Oregon Legislature to "protect, conserve, enhance and maintain the natural, scenic, historical, agricultural, economic and recreational qualities of lands along the Willamette River". The Greenway stretches from Bristow to the Willamette's confluence with the Columbia River. Although much of the land along the Willamette is private, the Greenway provides boating, hiking, picnicking and camping opportunities on pieces of public property along the 255-mile route. Bristow is one of 5 major state parks and more than 40 small public use sites, plus numerous local parks, on the Greenway. (A large, excellent brochure/map covering the Greenway is available from the State Parks Department.)

♣ Oregon 27

VALLEY OF THE ROGUE
Valley of the Rogue State Park

Location: Southwest Oregon east of Grants Pass.

Access: From Interstate 5 Exit 45B (10 miles east of Grants Pass, 15 miles northwest of Medford, turn south into the park. (Note: If you're southbound, the exit leads directly to the park; if you're northbound, from the exit you'll need to take the viaduct to the south side of the Interstate, then west for 0.2 mile on a frontage road to the park; note also that I-5 lies in an east-west direction in this area.)

Day Use Facilities: Large picnic area; large shelter (reservable by groups); drinking water; restrooms; large parking lot.

Camping Facilities: 174 campsites, including 55 with partial hookups and 97 with full hookups, in 6 loops; (small group camping areas are also available); sites are small+ to medium+ in size, essentially level, with minimal to fair separation; parking pads are paved, short to medium+ straight-ins or medium to long pull-throughs; ample space for large tents in most sites; fireplaces or fire rings; firewood is usually for sale, or b-y-o; restrooms with showers; water at faucets throughout; holding tank disposal station; paved driveways; limited supplies and services are available in Rogue River and Gold Hill.

Activities & Attractions: Boating; boat launch; limited fishing; playground; amphitheater for evening programs in summer.

Natural Features: Located on a large, gently rolling flat above the Rogue River; park vegetation consists of several-dozen acres of mown grass well shaded/sheltered by hardwoods and conifers; closely bordered by forested mountains; elevation 1000´.

Season, Fees & Phone: Open all year; please see Appendix for camp fees; ☎(541) 582-1118.

Trip Log: Tall conifers, spreading oaks, and large madrones (attractive trees with a smooth, red bark) shade the picnic area. Nearly three miles of high riverbank are available for strolling or fishing.

⚕ Oregon 28

JOSEPH P. STEWART
Joseph P. Stewart State Park

Location: Southwest Oregon northeast of Medford.

Access: From Oregon State Highway 62 at milepost 33 +.3 (13 miles northeast of Shady Cove, 34 miles northeast of Medford, 2 miles southwest of the bridge which spans the Rogue River at the east end of Lost Creek Lake), turn north onto the main park access road and proceed northwest for 0.5 mile to the day use area; or from milepost 34 +.2 (0.9 mile east of the main access road), turn northwest onto the campground access road and proceed 0.3 mile to the campground.

Day Use Facilities: 2 adjacent, medium-sized picnic areas; 2 shelters in each area; drinking water; restrooms; 2 medium-sized parking lots.

Camping Facilities: 201 campsites, including 151 with partial hookups, in 4 loops; (a reservable group camp is also available); sites are medium to large, typically level or nearly so, with nominal to fair separation; parking pads are paved, medium to very long straight-ins; plenty of space for tents; fire rings and barbecue grills; firewood is usually for sale, or b-y-o; water at faucets throughout; restrooms with showers; disposal station; paved driveways; limited to adequate supplies and services are available in Shady Cove.

Activities & Attractions: Boating; boat launch; fishing for stocked trout and bass (reportedly very good); swimming beach with bathhouse; playground; 3 miles of paved hiking trails; 5 miles of paved bicycle trails; athletic field; CoE hiking trail circumnavigates the lake.

Natural Features: Located on very gently sloping terrain near the south-east shore of 3400-acre Lost Creek Lake (Reservoir), an impoundment on the Rogue River; vegetation in the day use areas and campground consists of dozens of acres of mown lawns well-dotted with small to medium-sized hardwoods and conifers; surrounded by densely forested mountains; elevation 1900´.

Season, Fees & Phone: Day use area open all year; campground open April to October; please see Appendix for campground fees; ☎(541) 560-3334.

Trip Log: This park offers a lot of activities, be they land or water-based, for the money. But you don't *have* to burn off a lot of calories in order to enjoy the place. Just sitting around, looking out across the immense lawns to the lake and the mountains beyond is enough for many people.

⚕ Oregon 29

UNION CREEK
Rogue River National Forest

Location: Southwest Oregon west of Crater Lake.

Access: From Oregon State Highway 62 at milepost 56 +.1 (1 mile south of the junction of State Highways 62 & 230, 15 miles west of the Annie Springs entrance to Crater Lake National Park, 11 miles north of Prospect), turn west into the recreation area.

Day Use Facilities: Small picnic area; shelters; drinking water; vault facilities; parking area.

Camping Facilities: 99 campsites in 5 loops; sites are large, with good to very good separation; parking pads are gravel, fairly level, straight-ins; many pads can accommodate large vehicle combinations; some nice, secluded tent spots; fireplaces; firewood is available for gathering in the area; water at several faucets; vault facilities; waste water receptacles; paved driveways; camper supplies at a resort 0.5 mile north on Highway 62.

Activities & Attractions: Rogue River Gorge viewpoint, 0.5 mile north, overlooks the river where it rushes through a narrow gorge; foot trails follow Union Creek along both banks; Crater Lake National Park, 15 miles east; summer evening nature programs.

Natural Features: Located on a heavily timbered flat along both sides of Union Creek, where Union Creek flows into the Rogue River; campground vegetation consists mainly of tall conifers, fairly dense underbrush and a conifer-needle forest floor; elevation 1000´.

Season, Fees & Phone: May to September; $7.00; 14 day limit; Prospect Ranger District ☎(541) 560-3623.

Trip Log: The campsites at Union Creek are spacious and private—and some are creekside. The campground is neatly divided into two sections by this clear, mountain stream spanned by a picturesque wooden bridge. An excellent alternative the campground at Crater Lake.

⚲ Oregon 30 ♿

CRATER LAKE
Crater Lake National Park

Location: Southwest Oregon south of Crater Lake.

Access: From Oregon State Highway 62 at the Annie Springs entrance station for Crater Lake National Park (14 miles east of the junction of State Highways 62 & 230, 57 miles northwest of Klamath Falls, 71 miles northeast of Medford), drive north for 100 yards, then turn east (right) into Mazama Campground; or continue northerly for another 3.5 miles to the park visitor center and Rim Drive.

Day Use Facilities: Several small picnic and parking areas and pullouts along Rim Drive; drinking water, restrooms; large parking area at the visitor center.

Camping Facilities: *Mazama Campground*: 198 campsites in 7 loops; sites are medium-sized, level, and fairly well separated; parking

pads are paved, many are medium+ pull-throughs; some very nice, spacious tent areas; fireplaces; b-y-o firewood; water at several faucets; restrooms; (showers may be available at a private lodge nearby); holding tank disposal station; paved driveways; gas, camper supplies, laundromat and showers at a nearby store; nearest sources of complete supplies and services are Klamath Falls and Medford.

Activities & Attractions: Visitor center at Rim Village features interpretive displays and a-v programs; Rim Drive completely circles the lake; lake cruises; fishing is permitted on the lake and streams of the park; Annie Creek Nature Trail descends 1.7 miles to Annie Creek, and the Pacific Crest Trail passes near the campground and extends the length of the park; campground nature programs scheduled for summer evenings.

Natural Features: Located around the forested rim of Crater Lake; peaks of the Cascade Range encircle the lake; campground is on a lightly to moderately forested flat; sites are in among tall trees, or on open grassy areas; Annie Creek flows through a chasm several hundred feet below the campground level; elevation 6000´.

Season, Fees & Phone: June to October; $13.00; 14 day limit; park headquarters ☎(541) 594-2211.

Trip Log: Crater Lake, the second deepest lake in the western hemisphere, is a magnificent sight—from the Rim Drive or from a tour boat on the surface of the lake itself. The deep-blue lake was formed within the *caldera* of an ancient volcano. It is unlikely that any photos you may have seen prior to your arrival will have prepared you for this visual feast.

⚲ Oregon 31 ♿

DOE POINT
Rogue River National Forest

Location: Southwest Oregon between Klamath Falls and Medford.

Access: From Oregon State Highway 140 at milepost 30 +.4 (38 miles west of Klamath Falls, 42 miles east of Medford), turn south, then immediately west onto a paved access road which parallels the highway; drive west for 0.2 mile to the recreation area.

Day Use Facilities: Small picnic area; drinking water; restrooms; small parking area.

Camping Facilities: 25 campsites in 2 loops; sites are medium to large and fairly well-separated; some pads are very long, and many are double-wide in order to accommodate a vehicle and trailer side-by-side; a few pads may require additional leveling; most sites have adequately level tent spots; fireplaces; some firewood is available for gathering in the vicinity; water at several faucets; restrooms; paved driveways; limited supplies 1 mile east on Highway 140; complete supplies and services are available in Medford and Klamath Falls.

(Additional camping is available at nearby Fish Lake Campground.)

Activities & Attractions: Nature trail along the lake; fishing; boat ramp and dock at Fish Lake Campground, 0.7 mile east; great views across the lake.

Natural Features: Located on the forested north shore of Fish Lake in the southern Cascades; a number of sites are right along the lake, which is encircled by timbered slopes; vegetation in the campground consists primarily of tall conifers and a considerable amount of underbrush, providing good separation between sites; elevation 4700´.

Season, Fees & Phone: May to September; $9.00; 14 day limit; Butte Falls Ranger District ☎(541) 865-3581.

Trip Log: This campground is located in a mountain setting with hard-to-top scenery and generally excellent fishing near at hand. Extensive lava fields partly surround the general lake area. Fish Lake has earned its title. Fishing here is reportedly in the very good-to-excellent category. An annual stocking program, an abundance of food and nearly ideal environmental conditions are cited as reasons for the good fish production.

🏕 Oregon 32 ♿

ASPEN POINT
Winema National Forest

Location: Southwest Oregon northwest of Klamath Falls.

Access: From Oregon State Highway 140 at milepost 36 +.3 (32 miles west of Klamath Falls, 48 miles east of Medford), turn south onto Forest Road 3704 (paved); drive southerly for 0.6 mile, then turn west (right) into the recreation area.

Day Use Facilities: Small picnic area; drinking water; restrooms; small parking area.

Camping Facilities: 60 campsites in 2 loops; sites are fairly large with good separation for the

most part; parking pads are gravel, mostly level straight-ins, plus several pull-throughs spacious enough to accommodate very large vehicles; adequate space for tents; fireplaces; some firewood is available for gathering in the area; water at faucets throughout; restrooms; disposal station; paved driveways; camper supplies at a nearby resort; complete supplies and services are available in Klamath Falls.

(Additional camping is available at nearby Sunset Campground.)

Activities & Attractions: Fishing; boating; boat launch and dock; swimming beach; Billie Creek Nature Trail is one of several foot trails in the area; Lake of the Woods Visitor Center nearby.

Natural Features: Located in an open forest setting along the northeast shore of Lake of the Woods in the southern Cascades; campground vegetation consists mostly of tall conifers and very little underbrush; Mountain Lakes Wilderness lies to the east, and Sky Lakes Wilderness is to the north; elevation 5000´.

Season, Fees & Phone: May to September; $9.00; 14 day limit; Klamath Ranger District ☎(541) 883-6824.

Trip Log: Aspen Point has been a popular campground since the 1920's. There are huge stone fireplaces and picnic tables here which were built in the 1930's. Mount McLaughlin, rising to 9500´, is visible across the lake to the north. This national forest is named for the Modoc Indian woman Winema (*Wih-nee´-mah*) who served as a liaison between the Modocs and settlers in Southern Oregon and Northern California during the Modoc War of 1872.

🏨 *Oregon* ⛺
Columbia River Gorge

🏕 Oregon 33

CROWN POINT
Crown Point State Park

Location: Northern Oregon border east of Troutdale.

Access: From the Columbia River Scenic Highway/U.S. 30 at a point 12 miles east of Interstate 84 Exit 18 on the east edge of Troutdale, and 11 miles west of I-84 Exit 35 west of Cascade Locks, turn into the parking spaces along the highway.

Day Use Facilities: Roadside parking for several dozen cars; nearest picnic area and restrooms are at Talbot State Park.

Camping Facilities: None; nearest public campground is in Ainsworth State Park.

Activities & Attractions: Information center in Vista House, a 1918, multi-sided, dome-topped, stone-and-glass memorial to the Oregon pioneers; first-rate viewpoint of the Gorge.

Natural Features: Located atop Crown Point above the Columbia River in the Columbia Gorge; vegetation consists of open grassy areas and a variety of windblown bushes and trees; elevation 700´.

Season, Fees & Phone: Open all year; ☎(541) 695-2261.

Trip Log: Crown Point is one of the most windswept spots in Oregon (or so it seems), with some of the finest scenic views in Oregon as well. The incredible panorama extends dozens of miles up and down the Columbia Gorge. This is a winner!

♠ Oregon 34

BRIDAL VEIL FALLS
Bridal Veil Falls State Park

Location: Northern Oregon east of Troutdale.

Access: From the Columbia River Scenic Highway, U.S. 30 at a point 16 miles east of Interstate 84 Exit 18 on the east edge of Troutdale and 7 miles west of I-84 Exit 35 west of Cascade Locks, turn north into the park.

Day Use Facilities: A few picnic tables are scattered around the small day use area; drinking water; restrooms; medium-sized parking lot;

Camping Facilities: None; nearest public campground is in Ainsworth SP, 7 miles east.

Activities & Attractions: 0.5-mile loop trail to an overlook; 0.6-mile loop trail to the falls.

Natural Features: Located on hilly, densely forested terrain along the walls of the Columbia Gorge; most picnic tables are on a small, open, lawn area adjacent to the parking lot; el. 100´.

Season, Fees & Phone: Open all year; ☎(541) 695-2261.

Trip Log: Bridal Veil Falls is certainly one of the most spectacular sights in the northwest. It rushes over the vertical sides of the Gorge and forms a gossamer sheet as it plunges a couple

hundred feet. Most travelers get only a fleeting glimpse of the waterfall as they whiz by on the Interstate, unaware that that they can get a closer, more leisurely look from this little park.

♠ Oregon 35

ROOSTER ROCK
Rooster Rock State Park

Location: Northern Oregon border east of Troutdale.

Access: From Interstate 84 Exit 25 (8 miles east of Troutdale, 19 miles west of Cascade Locks), turn north into the park entrance; picnic and main parking areas are to the east; picnic areas, shelters and boat launch are to the west.

Day Use Facilities: Several medium to large picnic areas; large shelters; drinking water; restrooms; several very large parking lots.

Camping Facilities: None; nearest public campground is in Ainsworth State Park, 10 miles east.

Activities & Attractions: Windsurfing; swimming; boating; well-sheltered boat launch and docks; hiking trail.

Natural Features: Located along a mile-long section of the south bank of the Columbia River in the Columbia Gorge; park vegetation consists primarily of acres of mown lawns generally well-shaded/sheltered by hardwoods and some conifers; elevation 50´.

Season, Fees & Phone: Open all year; please see Appendix for park entry fee charged on summer weekends and holidays; ☎(541) 695-2261.

Trip Log: Prior to the advent of windsurfing in the early 1980's, according to the locals, "the Gorge was a pretty boring place in summer", partly because of the fierce wind often encountered here. Due to windsurfing's steadily increasing popularity, Rooster Rock has become a major rendezvous point for partakers and spectators of this action-packed pastime.

♠ Oregon 36

EAGLE CREEK
Mount Hood National Forest

Location: Northern Oregon border west of Hood River.

Access: From Interstate 84 eastbound, take Exit 41 (3 miles west of Cascade Locks, 24 miles east of Troutdale); proceed east 0.2 mile on the off-ramp to the fish hatchery; turn south (right) into the recreation area entrance, then east (left) on a fairly steep, paved road for 0.4 mile to the campground. (Note: Exit 41 is an eastbound exit only; if westbound, take Exit 44 at Cascade Locks and proceed 3 miles west on a frontage road to the recreation area.)

Day Use Facilities: Small parking area.

Camping Facilities: 19 campsites; most sites are medium-sized and moderately well separated; parking pads are paved, fairly level, medium-length straight-ins; adequate space for medium-sized tents in most sites; fireplaces, plus a few barbecue grills; a small quantity of firewood is available for gathering in the vicinity, b-y-o is suggested; water at several faucets; restrooms; paved driveway; limited supplies and services are available in Cascade Locks.

Activities & Attractions: Shady Glen Interpretive Trail leads off from an associated day use area; suspension bridge over the creek; Eagle Creek Trailhead, 0.5 mile south.

Natural Features: Located on a densely forested hill overlooking the Columbia River; campground vegetation consists of alder, maple, Douglas fir, and ferns; Eagle Creek enters the Columbia River below the campground, a short distance to the north; elevation 200´.

Season, Fees & Phone: Late-May to October; $7.00; 7 day limit; Columbia Gorge Ranger District ☎(541) 695-2276.

Trip Log: Eagle Creek is an historic campground of the first order of magnitude. Set your WayBack™ Time Machine to the year *1915* and you'll see Eagle Creek Campground being built. It is considered to be the *first national forest public campground* constructed in the United States. Want another 'first'? The restrooms here were the first with flusheroos installed in a Forest Service campground. Neat, huh? A number of the campsites have very impressive views of the Columbia Gorge.

⚐ **Oregon 37** ♿

WYETH

Mount Hood National Forest

Location: Northern Oregon border west of Hood River.

Access: From Interstate 84 Exit 51 (13 miles west of Hood River, 6 miles east of Cascade Locks), turn south off the Interstate, then head immediately west (right) onto Herman Creek Road (paved); continue west for 0.1 mile to the campground, on the south (left) side of the road.

Day Use Facilities: Small parking area.

Camping Facilities: 14 campsites; (6 small group sites are also available; most units are spacious, with fair separation; parking pads are paved, long, wide, level straight-ins; generally good areas for tents, but a few spots might be slightly off-level; fire rings; some firewood is available for gathering in the area; water at faucets throughout; restrooms; paved driveways; limited supplies at Cascade Locks; adequate supplies and services are available in Hood River.

Activities & Attractions: Trailhead parking at the south end of the campground; museum and visitor center in Cascade Locks.

Natural Features: Great views of the Columbia River Gorge from the campground area; tall pine and spruce forest, along with big leafy hardwoods; very little low-level vegetation other than ferns; set against the south face of the gorge; elevation 150´.

Season, Fees & Phone: Mid-May to October; $7.00; 7 day limit; Columbia Gorge Ranger District ☎(541) 695-2276.

Trip Log: An extensive landscaping project accomplished by various government and volunteer groups has turned Wyeth into one of the most attractive campgrounds in this part of the country. The rockwork alone is worth a king's ransom. Definitely worth the stop—even if it's just to take a look. Taking a good look just about everywhere in this region is mandatory. Wyeth and the other parks and camps in this vicinity are within the Columbia River Gorge National Scenic Area. This unique, quarter-million-acre scenic entity was established by Act of Congress in 1986 and transcends national, state, local and private boundaries. It is the first creation of its kind in the United States.

⚐ **Oregon 38**

LEPAGE

Lake Umatilla/Corps of Engineers Park

Location: Northern Oregon border east of The Dalles.

Access: From Interstate 84 Exit 114 for Le Page Park/John Day River Recreation Area, (5 miles east of Rufus, 29 miles east of The Dalles, 24 miles west of Arlington), at the south side of the freeway proceed south on a paved access road for 0.3 mile (past the day use area) to the campground.

Day Use Facilities: Medium-sized picnic area with several small shelters; drinking water; restrooms; medium-sized parking lot.

Camping Facilities: Approximately 12 campsites in a string and a loop; sites are small, level, with nominal to fair separation; parking pads are gravel, short+ pull-offs; enough space for a small tent; vault facilities; (drinking water and restrooms with freshwater rinse showers are in the day use area); complete supplies and services are available in The Dalles.

Activities & Attractions: Designated swimming area; boating; boat launch; fishing.

Natural Features: Located near the mouth of a canyon along the bank of the John Day River at its confluence with the Columbia River; this segment of the Columbia has been dammed to form Lake Umatilla; sites are lightly shaded by large hardwoods; about half of the sites are riverside; bordered by dry, rocky hills and bluffs; elevation 200´.

Season, Fees & Phone: Open all year; no fee; 14 day limit; Corps of Engineers John Day Project Office, The Dalles, ☎(541) 296-1181.

Trip Log: Great little freewayside stop (especially for a freebie). The terrific day use area has watered/mown lawns dotted with hardwoods. Golf course grooming there. From near here are commanding views down through the Columbia Gorge and of Mount Hood rising prominently (on a clear day) in the distance.

Oregon

North Central

🔺 Oregon 39 ♿

TRILLIUM LAKE
Mount Hood National Forest

Location: Western Oregon between Portland and Madras.

Access: From U.S. Highway 26 at milepost 56 +.8 (1.8 miles south of Government Camp, 59 miles north of Madras), turn southwest onto a steep access road and proceed 1.5 miles down to the recreation area.

Day Use Facilities: Large picnic area; drinking water; vault facilities; parking lot.

Camping Facilities: 49 campsites, including 5 double units; most sites are small to medium-sized and fairly well separated; parking pads are paved, medium to long straight-ins; a few pads may require a little additional leveling; many nice, secluded tent spots; fireplaces; firewood is available for gathering in the vicinity; water at faucets throughout; vault facilities; waste water receptacles; paved driveways; camper supplies in Government Camp.

Activities & Attractions: Motorless boating; fishing; swimming; a number of forest roads nearby provide access to the surrounding mountains.

Natural Features: Located on the east shore of Trillium Lake in the Cascade Range; a dense conifer forest provides privacy and shelter for the sites; the small mountain lake (roughly 100 acres) is completely surrounded by forested slopes; elevation 3200´.

Season, Fees & Phone: May to September; $10.00 to $12.00 for a single site, $20.00 for a double site; 14 day limit; Zigzag Ranger District ☎(541) 666-0704.

Trip Log: Trillium Lake is a mountain gem! Really superscenic sights in this basin! A few campsites are located close enough to the lake to provide lake views through the trees. Snow-covered Mount Hood, the loftiest peak in Oregon, is visible across the lake as it rises to over 11,000´ just a few miles north.

🔺 Oregon 40 ♿

HOODVIEW
Timothy Lake/Mount Hood National Forest

Location: North Central Oregon south-east of Government Camp.

Access: From U.S. Highway 26 at milepost 66 +.4 (12 miles southeast of Government Camp, 5 miles northwest of the junction of U.S. 26 & Oregon State Highway 216), turn south onto Forest Road 42/Skyline Road (paved) and travel 8 miles to a major fork; take the west fork (right) onto Forest Road 57 (paved) and proceed 2.7 miles; turn north (right) into the campground.

Day Use Facilities: None.

Camping Facilities: 43 campsites including a number of double-occupancy units, in 2 loops; (a small group site is also available); sites are small to medium sized, with nominal to fair separation; parking pads are gravel, short to medium length straight-ins or pull-offs; pads will require additional leveling; medium to large space for tents; fire rings; firewood is available for gathering within a mile; water at several faucets; vault facilities; waste water receptacles; paved driveways; gas and camper supplies in Government Camp.

(Camping is also available at three other similar forest campgrounds on Timothy Lake's south shore.)

Activities & Attractions: Boating (10 mph max); boat launch; fishing for rainbow, brook and cutthroat trout, and kokanee; a 13-mile hiking trail circumnavigates the lake.

Natural Features: Located on a moderately steep slope along the south shore of Timothy Lake in the Cascade Range; sites are well sheltered by tall conifers; elevation 3200´.

Season, Fees & Phone: May to October; $10.00-$12.00 for a single site, $20.00-24.00 for a double site; 14-day limit; Bear Springs Ranger District ☎(541) 328-6211.

Trip Log: Because of the 'stadium' affect provided by the hillside location, your campsite should have a lake view (unless a high vehicle is parked between your site and the lake). As a bonus, this campground offers what are perhaps the best visual shots of majestic Mount Hood rising a dozen miles beyond the opposite shore. Timothy Lake is only 75 miles from downtown Portland, so its fine scenery and excellent recreational opportunities are available to a substantial urban population at a time-and-fuel-efficient distance.

🏕 Oregon 41 ♿

THE COVE PALISADES
The Cove Palisades State Park

Location: Central Oregon north of Bend.

Access: From U.S. Highway 97/Oregon State Highway 26 at Avenue D in midtown Madras, proceed west and south on Avenue D for 2 blocks, then southwest on Culver Highway (through the town of Metolius) for 7.5 miles to a point between the communities of Metolius and Culver; turn west onto Gem Lane, cross the railroad tracks, and follow this paved road west for 1 mile, then south for 0.8 mile to a turnoff signed for the park; turn west (right) onto the paved park access road and continue for 1.5 miles; turn south (left) into Crooked River Campground; or continue past Crooked River Campground down a steep, winding road and across the Crooked River bridge for an

additional 5 miles to the Deschutes River day use areas and campground.

Day Use Facilities: 3 medium-sized picnic areas; drinking water; restrooms and bathhouses; large parking lots.

Camping Facilities: *Crooked River Campground*: 91 campsites with partial hookups; sites are small to small+, generally level, with minimal separation; parking pads are paved, short to medium-length straight-ins; some grassy spots for tents; fire rings; firewood is usually for sale, or b-y-o; water at sites; restrooms with showers; holding tank disposal station; paved driveways; *Deschutes River Campground*: 181 campsites, including 87 with full hookups; (a group camp is also available); sites are small to small+, with minimal to fair separation; parking pads are paved, mostly short to medium-length straight-ins, plus about a dozen pull-throughs; some pads may require a little additional leveling; medium to large tent spots; fire rings or fireplaces; firewood is usually for sale, or b-y-o; water at faucets throughout; restrooms with showers; paved driveways; gas and camper supplies in the park; adequate supplies and services are available in Madras.

Activities & Attractions: Boating; boat launches and docks at each day use area; fishing (reportedly very good for trout, steelhead, salmon); water skiing; 2 swimming beaches; amphitheater in the Deschutes River Campground; the drive along the canyon's east rim provides spectacular views of the area.

Natural Features: *Crooked River*: Located on the east rim above a deep basaltic canyon above Lake Billy Chinook, a reservoir located at the confluence of 3 rivers—Crooked, Deschutes and Metolius; campground vegetation consists of mown lawns and planted hardwoods which provide limited shade. *Deschutes River*: Located deep in a dry, rocky canyon on the Deschutes River Arm of Lake Billy Chinook; picnic and camp sites are lightly to moderately shaded by hardwoods and junipers; the fork at the confluence of the Deschutes and Crooked Rivers is split by an enormous, rocky landmass called "The Island"; surrounded by sage plains on the rim, and sage slopes and sheer-walled escarpments as viewed from the lake shore; elevation 1900´ at the lake shore to 2600´ at the canyon rim.

Season, Fees & Phone: Open all year, with limited services in winter; campsite reservations accepted, recommended for weekends; please see Appendix for reservation information and campground fees; ☎(541) 546-3412.

Trip Log: If you've ever been to the parks on Lake Powell or Lake Mead on the Arizona-Utah border, you'll have a pretty good idea of what The Cove Palisades looks like. If you're camping, take a quick look at the Crooked River Camp on the rim as you pass by—it's breeziness might help make it more tolerable in warm weather. However, take a closer look at the Deschutes River area—although it'll be a bit warmer down on the canyon floor, it has substantially more greenery for shade and general comfort.

♠ Oregon 42 ♿

BIG LAKE
Willamette National Forest

Location: West-central Oregon northwest of Bend.

Access: From U.S. Highway 20 near milepost 80 (8.5 miles east of the junction of U.S. 20 with Oregon State Highway 126, 40 miles northwest of Bend), turn south onto Forest Road 2690 (paved); proceed 0.7 mile south to a fork in the road; take the left fork, and continue for 2 miles to the recreation area.

Day Use Facilities: Medium-sized picnic area; drinking water; restrooms; medium-sized parking area.

Camping Facilities: 49 campsites; sites are average or better in size, with mostly good separation; north shore units may be a bit roomier; parking pads are gravel, and some pads are spacious enough for large vehicles; a few pads may require additional leveling; some very nice, grassy tent spots; fire rings; limited firewood is available for gathering in the vicinity, b-y-o is suggested; water at several faucets; restrooms; paved driveways; limited supplies and services are available in Sisters.

Activities & Attractions: Boating; sailing; boat launch; fishing; swimming area; the Pacific Crest Trail passes within 0.5 mile.

Natural Features: Located on the north and west shores of beautiful Big Lake in Hidden Valley on the upper west slope of the Cascades; all sites are in an open conifer forest, including some right on the shore of the lake; Mount Washington rises commandingly in full view from the south shore of the lake; Three Fingered Jack Peak can be seen to the north; Mount Washington Wilderness is located just a few miles from the southern edge of the lake; elevation 4600´.

Season, Fees & Phone: May to October; $9.00; 10 day limit; McKenzie Ranger District ☎(541) 822-3381.

Trip Log: The sight of razor-backed Mount Washington rising from the south shore of Big Lake is incredibly impressive! Though only a few campsites are right along the lake, most have views of the exceptionally picturesque lake and surrounding mountains. Definitely and decidedly recommended.

♠ Oregon 43

BLUE BAY & SOUTH SHORE
Suttle Lake/Deschutes National Forest

Location: West-central Oregon northwest of Bend.

Access: From U.S. Highway 20/Oregon State Highway 126 at milepost 87 +.3 (10 miles northwest of Sisters, 6 miles east of Santiam Pass), turn southwest onto a paved lake access road and proceed 0.9 mile to Blue Bay; or continue for an additional 0.15 mile to South Shore; turn northwest (right) into the campgrounds.

Day Use Facilities: Small parking areas.

Camping Facilities: 25 campsites in Blue Bay, 39 campsites in South Shore; sites are generally medium to large, with fair to good separation; parking pads are gravel, mostly medium-length straight-ins, plus a number of long pull-throughs or pull-offs; majority of pads will require additional leveling; adequate space for medium to large tents, but generally a little sloped; fireplaces; some firewood may be available for gathering in the surrounding area, b-y-o to be sure; water at several faucets; vault facilities; waste water receptacles; paved driveways; camper supplies at a nearby store; nearest source of limited supplies and services is Sisters.

Activities & Attractions: Lake Shore Trail; boating; boat launch and dock; fishing; fish cleaning station.

Natural Features: Located on a sloping shelf a few feet above the south shore of Suttle Lake; sites are moderately sheltered/shaded by tall conifers and some hardwoods; Both campgrounds have quite a few nice lakefront sites; bordered by the heavily timbered, low hills and mountains of the Cascade Range; elevation 3400´.

Season, Fees & Phone: May to October; $9.00; 14 day limit; Sisters Ranger District ☎(541) 549-2111.

Trip Log: Suttle Lake was hewn by glaciers about 10,000 years ago and is situated in an elongated basin. Consequently, there aren't any really distant views available here except out toward the hills on the far shores of this medium-sized lake. However, there's a good highwayside viewpoint of spectacular Mount Washington, on U.S. 20 just three miles west of the lake road turnoff.

🏠 *Oregon* ⛺

Newberry National Volcanic Monument

Newberry's visitor center is located on U.S. 97, five miles south of Bend. There you'll find numerous exhibits, displays and a-v programs about the extensive lava fields, cinder cones, and other volcanic features that are found throughout this region. The following recreation sites are located within the main park unit, several miles south and east of the visitor center.

🔺 Oregon 44 ♿

PAULINA LAKE
Newberry National Volcanic Monument

Location: West Central Oregon south of Bend.

Access: From U.S. Highway 97 near milepost 162 (6 miles north of La Pine, 24 miles south of Bend), head east on Paulina Lake Road (Deschutes County Road 21, paved) for 13 miles to the park visitor center; continue east on the main park road for 0.25 mile; turn north (left) onto a paved access road and go 0.1 mile to the recreation area.

Day Use Facilities: Small picnic and parking areas.

Camping Facilities: 55 campsites; sites are medium to medium+ in size, acceptably level, with nominal to fair separation; parking pads are gravel, long pull-throughs or medium-length straight-ins; plenty of space for tents; fireplaces; firewood is available for gathering on forest lands along the county road on the way to the park; water at several faucets; restrooms; holding tank disposal station along the main park road across from the campground entrance; paved driveway; camper supplies at a nearby lodge; public laundry and showers, 4 miles east; gas and groceries+ in La Pine.

Activities & Attractions: 120 miles of hiking and horse trails, including 7.5-mile Paulina Lake Loop around the lake; limited boating (10 mph); boat launch; fishing for rainbows, browns and brookies, also kokanee; playground.

Natural Features: Located on a forested flat about 100 yards from the southwest shore of Paulina Lake in Newberry Crater; sites receive light to light-medium shelter from tall conifers; scenic Paulina Peak rises to 7900´ south of the campground; the lake is rimmed by forested ridges; elevation 6400´.

Season, Fees & Phone: May to October; $11.00; 14 day limit; Lava Lands Visitor Center (Deschutes NF), Bend, ☎(541) 593-2421 or Fort Rock Ranger District (541) 388-5664.

Trip Log: The lake, the nearby solitary peak and the campground were named for Chief Paulina, an Indian leader who figured prominently in the region's history. ("Paulina" is pronounced with a long "i".)

🔺 Oregon 45

LITTLE CRATER
Newberry National Volcanic Monument

Location: West Central Oregon south of Bend.

Access: From U.S. Highway 97 near milepost 162 (6 miles north of La Pine, 24 miles south of Bend), head east on Paulina Lake Road (Deschutes County Road 21, paved) for 13 miles to the park visitor center; continue easterly on the main park road for another 2 miles; turn north (left) onto a paved campground access road for 0.2 mile down to the bottom of the hill, then bear right into the recreation area.

Day Use Facilities: Small picnic and parking area.

Camping Facilities: 48 campsites; (Newberry Group Camp, a half mile west, is a sizable area with full facilities available by reservation); sites are medium+ to large, with nominal separation; parking pads are gravel, mostly long pull-throughs; some pads will require additional leveling; medium to large areas for tents; fireplaces; firewood is readily gatherable on forest lands along the county road outside the park; water at several faucets; vault facilities; holding tank disposal station near the park visitor center; paved driveway with turnaround loop at the far east end; public laundry and showers, 3 miles east; camper supplies, 1 mile west; gas and groceries+ in La Pine.

Activities & Attractions: Hiking and equestrian trails, including the 3.5-mile Little Crater Trail between Paulina and East Lakes;

boating (10 mph); boat launch and docks; fishing for stocked rainbow, brown and brook trout, also kokanee.

Natural Features: Located on a pair of coves along the southeast shore of Paulina Lake; sites receive light to light-medium shelter from tall conifers; Paulina Peak and an enormous obsidian flow rise just south of the campground; the lake is rimmed by the forested slopes of Newberry Crater; elevation 6400´.

Season, Fees & Phone: May to October; $11.00; 14 day limit; Lava Lands Visitor Center (Deschutes NF), Bend, ☎(541) 593-2421 or Fort Rock Ranger District (541) 388-5664.

Trip Log: Prominent, picturesque Paulina Peak is in full view from the east half of the campground. The campground stretches for nearly a half mile along the shore. The good-sized lake can be seen from just about every campsite. If you have a boat, it would be really easy to beach your craft within a few yards of your tent or rv. For these and perhaps other reasons, Little Crater seems to be the most popular camp in the national monument. "Little Crater" refers to a small secondary crater near the campground that's within Newberry's primary *caldera*.

♣ Oregon 46 ♿

EAST LAKE
Newberry National Volcanic Monument

Location: West Central Oregon south of Bend.

Access: From U.S. Highway 97 near milepost 162 (6 miles north of La Pine, 24 miles south of Bend), head east on Paulina Lake Road (Deschutes County Road 21, paved) for 13 miles to the park visitor center; continue easterly on the main park road for another 4 miles; turn north (left) into the campground.

Day Use Facilities: Small parking area.

Camping Facilities: 29 campsites; sites are small+ to medium sized, with nominal to fair separation; parking pads are gravel, short to medium-length straight-ins or long pull-throughs; some pads will require additional leveling; medium to large areas for tents; fireplaces; firewood is available for gathering on nearby hillsides; water at many faucets; restrooms; waste water receptacles; holding tank disposal station near the park visitor center; paved driveway; public laundry and showers, 1 mile east; gas and groceries+ in La Pine.

Activities & Attractions: 120 miles of hiking and horse trails, including a main trail along the rim of Newberry Crater; boating (10 mph max.); boat launch and dock; fishing for several stocked species of trout.

Natural Features: Located a few yards above a cove on the southwest shore of East Lake; sites are very lightly to moderately sheltered by tall conifers; a timbered hillside rises behind the campground; the lake is bordered by the forested rim of Newberry Crater; elevation 6400´.

Season, Fees & Phone: May to October; $11.00; 14 day limit; Lava Lands Visitor Center (Deschutes NF), Bend, ☎(541) 593-2421 or Fort Rock Ranger District (541) 388-5664.

Trip Log: East Lake, nearby Paulina Lake, and their attendant recreational facilities, lie wholly within the *caldera* (crater) of ancient Mount Newberry. The six-mile-diameter basin holds a varied assortment of textbook volcanic features. Newberry is one of the very newest of the national monuments. It formerly was a Deschutes National Forest interpretive and recreation area, but was elevated to national monument status in the early 1990's.

♣ Oregon 47

CINDER HILL
Newberry National Volcanic Monument

Location: West Central Oregon south of Bend.

Access: From U.S. Highway 97 near milepost 162 (6 miles north of La Pine, 24 miles south of Bend), travel east on Paulina Lake Road (Deschutes County Road 21, paved) for 13 miles to the park visitor center; continue easterly on the main park road for another 5.5 miles to the recreation area.

Day Use Facilities: Medium-sized picnic area; drinking water; vault facilities; medium-sized parking lot.

Camping Facilities: 110 campsites in a single, huge loop; sites are small to medium sized, with nominal to fair separation; parking pads are gravel, mostly short to medium-length straight-ins, plus a few long pull-throughs; majority of pads will require additional leveling; medium to large, mostly sloped areas for tents; fireplaces; ample firewood is available for gathering nearby; water at many faucets; vault facilities; waste water receptacles; holding tank disposal station near the park visitor center; paved driveway; public laundry and showers nearby; gas and groceries+ in La Pine.

Activities & Attractions: Hiking and horse trails, including a 22-mile main trail along the rim of Newberry Crater; limited boating (10 mph); boat launch; fishing for regularly stocked, good-sized rainbow, brown and brook trout.

Natural Features: Located on a hillside above the northeast shore of East Lake; sites receive very light to light-medium shelter from tall conifers above some new growth; the lake is rimmed by the forested slopes of Newberry Crater; elevation 6400´.

Season, Fees & Phone: May to October; $11.00; 14 day limit; Lava Lands Visitor Center (Deschutes NF), Bend, ☎(541) 593-2421 or Fort Rock Ranger District(541) 388-5664.

Trip Log: Cinder Hill is the 'last' recreation site on the road into the national monument. Its location at the end of the road should help discourage casual drive by traffic past your picnic or camp site. If you're very selective in choosing a camp spot, it could take a half hour to carefully cruise the large loop to find just the right site. Outstanding lake and mountain views, or peeks through the trees, from most picnic and camp sites.

 Oregon

South Central

♠ **Oregon 48** &

CRANE PRAIRIE
Deschutes National Forest

Location: West-central Oregon southwest of Bend.

Access: From U.S. Highway 97 at Wickiup Junction (3 miles north of La Pine, 27 miles south of Bend), travel westerly on Deschutes County Road 43/Burgess Road (paved) for 11.5 miles; pick up Deschutes County Road 42 (paved) and continue west for another 5.6 miles; turn north (right, 1 mile past the Twin Lakes turnoff) onto Forest Road 4270 (paved) and proceed 4 final miles; turn west (left) into the recreation area.

Alternate Access: From U.S. Highway 97 at milepost 153 (15 miles south of Bend), head west on Deschutes County Road 40 (paved) for 18.5 miles to a 4-way intersection; turn south (right) onto Forest Road 4270 and proceed 3.5 miles; turn west (right) into the recreation area.

Day Use Facilities: Small picnic area; drinking water; vault facilities; medium-sized parking lot.

Camping Facilities: 146 campsites, including a number of 2-family units and 6 park 'n walk tent sites, in 5 loops; sites are medium to large, with nominal to fair separation; parking pads are gravel or are partially paved, mostly medium to long straight-ins, plus a few long pull-throughs; a little additional leveling will be needed on some pads; ample space for tents; fireplaces; tons of firewood are available for gathering in the vicinity or along forest roads on the way in; water at central faucets; vault facilities; paved driveways; gas, camper supplies, laundry and showers at a local resort, seasonally; gas and groceries+ in La Pine.

Activities & Attractions: Boating; boat launches and docks; fishing for bass and rainbow trout; fish cleaning station.

Natural Features: Located on a gently rolling slope along a bay on the northeast corner of Crane Prairie Reservoir, an impoundment on the Deschutes and Cultus Rivers; campsites receive light-medium to medium shade/shelter from tall pines above light ground cover; tent sites offer a little more seclusion than standard sites; Crane Prairie itself is a very large meadow along the north side of the lake; bordered by the forested hills and mountains of the lower east slopes of the Cascade Range; elevation 4500´.

Season, Fees & Phone: May to October; $10.00; 14 day limit; Bend Ranger District ☎(541) 388-5664.

Trip Log: Crane Prairie is the largest and best-equipped camp on the four major bodies of water (Crane Prairie and Wickiup Reservoirs, Cultus and Davis Lakes) in the Deschutes River region. In fact, Crane Prairie's campground even has its own boat launch, in addition to the sizable public ramp in the day use area.

♠ **Oregon 49** &

SHADOW BAY
Willamette National Forest

Location: Western Oregon southeast of Eugene.

Access: From Oregon State Highway 58 at milepost 58 +.9 (26 miles east of Oakridge, 3 miles northwest of Willamette Pass, 25 miles west of the junction of Oregon State Highway 58 & U.S. 97), turn north onto Forest Road 5897 (paved); travel northeasterly for 6.5 miles; turn northwest (left) onto Forest Road 5896; continue for an additional 1.8 miles on a fairly steep access road down to the campground.

Day Use Facilities: Small parking area.

Camping Facilities: 103 campsites, including a few walk-in sites, in 6 loops; sites are medium to large, with average to good separation; parking pads are gravel, most are straight-ins, several are long enough for large rv's; some beautiful tent spots; fireplaces; some firewood is available for gathering in the area; water at several faucets; restrooms; holding tank disposal station; paved driveways; adequate supplies and services are available in Oakridge.

(Camping is also available at North Waldo and Islet Campgrounds, 7 miles north.)

Activities & Attractions: Limited boating (10 mph); boat launch; fishing; swimming; foot trails in the area include the Shoreline Trail and the Waldo Lake Trail; the Pacific Crest Trail passes nearby.

Natural Features: Located in the heart of the Cascade Range on the southeast shore of Waldo Lake; sites farthest from the lake shore are on a grassy hilltop, with some trees for shelter and visual separation; sites closer to the lake are on a forested slope; elevation 5500´.

Season, Fees & Phone: May to September; $9.00 for a single unit, $18.00 for a multiple unit; 14 day limit; Oakridge Ranger District ☎(541) 782-2291.

Trip Log: If the proper weather conditions exist, Waldo Lake becomes a mirror that reflects the images of surrounding mountain peaks. Shadow Bay has the easiest access of the three camps along the lake shore, yet is filled to capacity only on weekends. Of the trio of large lakes in this vicinity (also see Lakes Odell and Crescent), Waldo is the largest, and maybe the prettiest too. Worth the nine-mile trip off the highway.

⚐ Oregon 50

TRAPPER CREEK
Deschutes National Forest

Location: Western Oregon north of Crater Lake.

Access: From Oregon State Highway 58 at milepost 62 +.3 (0.4 mile southeast of Willamette Pass, 29 miles east of Oakridge, 22 miles west of the junction of Oregon State Highway 58 with U.S. 97), turn south onto Forest Road 5810 (paved) and follow it as it curves around the northwest tip of the lake for 2 miles; turn north (left) into the campground.

Day Use Facilities: Small parking area.

Camping Facilities: 32 campsites in 2 loops; sites are medium to large, with fair to good separation; parking pads are gravel, acceptably level, mostly short to medium-length straight-ins, plus a few pull-throughs; medium to large, mostly level, areas for tents; fire rings; firewood is available for gathering in the area; water at several faucets; vault facilities; paved driveways; gas and groceries along Highway 58 in Crescent Lake; adequate supplies and services are available in Oakridge.

Activities & Attractions: Boating; boat launch; fishing; footbridge across the creek.

Natural Features: Located on a slightly sloping, streamside/lakeside flat; swift and clear Trapper Creek enters Odell Lake at this point; sites receive light to medium shelter/shade from tall conifers and some brush; bordered by the heavily timbered mountains of the Cascade Range; elevation 4800´.

Season, Fees & Phone: May to October; $9.00 for a single unit, $18.00 for a double unit; 14 day limit; Crescent Ranger District ☎(541) 433-2234.

Trip Log: Camper's choice (if you get here early): Lakeside or streamside. But all sites are at least within a few minutes' stroll of either the lake or the stream. Chances are you'll agree that this is the best of the camps on scenic Odell Lake.

⚐ Oregon 51 ♿

DIAMOND LAKE
Umpqua National Forest

Location: Southwest Oregon north of Crater Lake.

Access: From the junction of Oregon State Highways 138 & 230 (3 miles south of the community of Diamond Lake, 80 miles northeast of Medford), drive northwest on Highway 230 for 0.3 mile; turn north (right) onto Forest Road 4795 (paved); continue for 2.3 miles along the East Shore Road to the campground. **Alternate Access:** From Oregon State Highway 138 in the small community of Diamond Lake, proceed west on a paved connecting road for 0.2 mile to a 'T'; turn south (left) onto East Shore Road and follow this paved road for 1.2 miles to the campground turnoff. (Note: East Shore Road closely parallels Highway 138 for about 4 miles, but the roads aren't in view of each other; the junctions are a bit tricky, so watch for directional signs.)

Day Use Facilities: Small parking area.

Camping Facilities: 240 campsites in a multitude of loops on 3 tiers; sites are rather small and closely spaced; most parking pads are paved straight-ins; additional leveling may be necessary; a few good-sized tent sites, but many are small; fire rings; some firewood is available for gathering on nearby forest lands; water at several faucets; restrooms; waste water receptacles; holding tank disposal station; paved driveways; camper supplies at nearby small stores and resorts.

Activities & Attractions: Boating; boat launches; fishing; swimming; foot and equestrian trails in the area, including access to the Pacific Crest Scenic Trail; information center located near the entrance; evening programs may be scheduled during the summer in the campground amphitheater.

Natural Features: Located on sloping terrain on the middle-east east shore of Diamond Lake in the southern Cascades; campground vegetation consists primarily of tall conifers, moderate underbrush, and a pine needle-and-grass forest floor; the 3000-acre lake is completely surrounded by heavily forested mountains; elevation 5200´.

Season, Fees & Phone: May to October; $9.00 for a single unit, $14.00 for a double unit, $3.00 extra for a lakeside unit; 14 day limit; Diamond Lake Ranger District ☎(541) 498-2531.

Trip Log: As remote as it is, Diamond Lake is still a very popular recreation area. An important attraction here is the fantastic scenery. The campsites are strung out for almost a mile along the campground driveway. All sites have views, across the lake, of Mount Bailey. Sunsets on the lake can be phenomenal!

Oregon

North Eastern & South Eastern

☼ Oregon 52 ♿

WALLOWA LAKE
Wallowa Lake State Park

Location: Northeast corner of Oregon south of Enterprise.

Access: From midtown Enterprise, travel south on Oregon State Highway 82, through the small community of Joseph, then along the east shore of Wallowa Lake to the park (a total of 12 miles from Enterprise) to the park.

Day Use Facilities: 2 picnic areas; drinking water; restrooms; large parking areas.

Camping Facilities: 210 campsites, including 120 with full hookups, in 5 loops; sites are small+ to medium-sized, most are level, with minimal to fair separation; parking pads are paved, mostly short to medium-length straight-ins, plus about 3 dozen long pull-throughs; excellent spots for tents; fireplaces; firewood is usually for sale, or b-y-o; water at faucets throughout; restrooms with showers; holding tank disposal station; paved driveways; gas and groceries in Joseph; adequate supplies and services are available in Enterprise.

Activities & Attractions: Boating; boat launch; marina; fishing; swimming area; nature trail; hiking trails, including trails into the 200,000-acre Eagle Cap Wilderness; amphitheater for scheduled programs in summer; playground; birding (an excellent guide pamphlet/checklist covering about 200 local species is available from the park office).

Natural Features: Located at the south end of 283-foot-deep Wallowa Lake along the Wallowa River in the Wallowa Mountains; park vegetation consists of light to medium-dense, tall conifers, some bushes and other low-level plants, and large grassy areas; glacial moraines tower 1200 feet above the lake surface; elevation 4600´.

Season, Fees & Phone: April to October; campsite reservations accepted; please see Appendix for reservation information and campground fees; ☎(541) 432-8855 or ☎(541) 432-4185.

Trip Log: Although it is in a relatively isolated region, Wallowa Lake is *very* popular. Certainly the area offers scenic pleasures of the first order. (The Wallowa Mountain region is one of several areas in the West which are compared to the Alps by local promoters—in this case it's "The Switzerland of America". Other regions are labeled "The American Alps", "The Western Alps", and "Little Switzerland". Hasn't anyone ever given thought to the notion that our Western mountains can stand tall on their own merits and that just maybe it is the *Swiss* who should be comparing *their* fine geography to *our* outstanding scenery?)

⚛ Oregon 53 ♿

FAREWELL BEND
Farewell Bend State Park

Location: Eastern Oregon northwest of Ontario.

Access: From Interstate 84 Exit 353 (22 miles northwest of Ontario, 50 miles southeast of Baker), drive north on Huntington Road, parallel to I-84, for 1.0 mile; turn east (right) into the park.

Day Use Facilities: Large and medium-sized picnic areas; drinking water; restrooms; large and medium-sized parking lots.

Camping Facilities: 96 campsites, including 53 with partial hookups; (2 small group camping areas are also available); sites are small to small+, level, with minimal to fair separation; parking pads are short to medium-length straight-ins; most pads are paved; adequate space for large tents in most sites; fireplaces or fire rings; b-y-o firewood; water at faucets throughout; restrooms with showers; disposal station; mostly paved driveways; gas and groceries near the freeway; complete supplies and services are available in Ontario.

Activities & Attractions: Boating; excellent, large, boat launch and docks; fishing (said to be very good for bass and catfish); swimming beach; Oregon Trail interpretive exhibits.

Natural Features: Located on a bluff at a wide, sweeping bend on the Snake River; the day use area and primitive camp loop receive light to medium shade from large hardwoods; the hookup camp loop is shaded/sheltered by large hardwoods and shrubs; the desert plains are crowned by virtually treeless hills and high mountains which border the river; typically breezy; elevation 2100´.

Season, Fees & Phone: Open all year, with limited services October to April; please see Appendix for camping fees; ☎(541) 869-2365.

Trip Log: This is the spot where Oregon Trail pioneers bound for the promised land of cool, green Western Oregon said "good-bye" (and possibly "good-riddance") to the Snake River Plain. Leaving behind the Plain and its harsh surroundings, they headed cross-country toward the Columbia River and the Willamette Valley. Below this point, the Snake would be nothing but trouble anyway as it chiseled its way through Hells Canyon. Farewell Bend is now the greenest stop along Interstate 84 between the Blue Mountains and a state park down in Utah.

If you're passing through, enjoy it while you have the opportunity!

⚛ Oregon 54

GOOSE LAKE
Goose Lake State Park

Location: South-central Oregon on the Oregon-California border.

Access: From U.S. Highway 395 in the hamlet of New Pine Creek (15 miles south of Lakeview, 43 miles north of Alturas, California), turn west onto State Line Road; and proceed 1.2 miles to the park.

Day Use Facilities: Medium-sized picnic area; drinking water; restrooms; medium-sized parking area.

Camping Facilities: 48 campsites with partial hookups; sites are narrow and long, level, with minimal to nominal separation; parking pads are paved, medium-length straight-ins; excellent, large, grassy tent spots; fireplaces; firewood is usually for sale, or b-y-o; water at sites; restrooms with showers; paved driveway; gas and groceries in New Pine Creek; adequate supplies and services are available in Lakeview and Alturas.

Activities & Attractions: Fishing for warm-water species (bullhead, perch, etc.); fishing from a boat is suggested; small, simple, boat launch area; also good to excellent fishing in the local mountains.

Natural Features: Located on the northeast shore of Goose Lake; picnic sites are on a grassy flat along the lake shore and are lightly shaded by large hardwoods; campground vegetation consists of watered and mown grass and hardwoods which provide limited to light shade for most campsites; the lake is in a large, high desert valley surrounded by low, rounded, mountains covered by grass, sage, and some trees; elevation 4700´.

Season, Fees & Phone: April to October; please see Appendix for campground fees; ☎(541) 947-3111.

Trip Log: Goose Lake could be described as an enormous, blue puddle that straddles the Oregon-California border. Although it has been sounded to 24 feet, it's average depth is only 8 feet. This is a nice park that's near a primary highway, and yet in many respects it's really somewhat off the beaten path, too.

California Destinations

World Reserve on the West Coast

California is impossible.

Critics argue that no state with a population density as great as California's has any hope of preserving its natural recreational resources. It can't possibly be done, they say.

In counterpoint, study California's state parks, for starters. Many of the Golden State's own parks are larger, better managed, more awe-inspiring, more visited and more *hospitable* than some--nay, <u>many</u>--of our national parks. (In fact, a couple of California's state parks have a greater land area than a number of U.N. member-nations.)

Aside from just the state parks, consider the north half of California's north half. Fantastic country! And at the opposite end of the state are California's desert lands, magnificent in their tranquillity and sense of timelessness. Then, there is the seacoast. No more accolades need be written about California's Inspiring Coast.

If, ever, someplace truly approaches the concept of being a World Reserve, California's collective public lands would almost certainly be the principal candidate.

A lot of bum jokes have been told in recent years about "The Big One", and California's subsequent slide into the sea. Well, should that apocalyptic event ever take place, here are three likely outcomes: (A) With a lot of hard work and ingenuity, inside of a week the state would be re-united with the mainland; or (B) California would become a sovereign nation (which it almost is, anyway), and inside of a week, would be a net-exporting country (which, as a state, it is, anyway); or (C) Californians would use their tremendous technological talent to transport the state's citizenry to the Moon, where they would then designate half of the lunar surface as parkland, and the remainder they would populate, cultivate, irrigate, and be sending vegetables to the rest of us, all inside of a week.

California *does* the impossible.

California
North Coast

ᐃ California 1 ♿

JEDEDIAH SMITH REDWOODS
Redwood National and State Parks

Location: Northwest corner of California northeast of Crescent City.

Access: From U.S. Highway 199 at milepost 5 (0.7 mile east of the junction of U.S. 199 and California State Highway 197, 9 miles northeast of Crescent City, 77 miles southwest of Grants Pass, Oregon), turn south/west (i.e., right if approaching from Crescent City), into the park.

Day Use Facilities: Medium-sized picnic area; drinking water; restrooms; 2 medium-sized parking lots.

Camping Facilities: *Jed Smith Campground*: 108 campsites; (hike-bike sites are also available); sites are small to small+, level, with fair to good visual separation; parking pads are packed gravel, primarily short to medium-length straight-ins; adequate space for a medium to large tent in most sites; storage cabinets; large, barbecue-height fireplaces; firewood is available for gathering on nearby national forest land, or b-y-o; water at several faucets; restrooms with showers; holding tank disposal station; paved driveways; complete supplies and services are available in Crescent City.

Activities & Attractions: Visitor center and museum featuring exhibits related to local flora and fauna; self-guided nature trail; guided nature walks in summer; swimming area; campfire center for scheduled evening programs; fishing.

Natural Features: Located along the banks of the Smith River in a dense forest of lofty redwoods, and an almost uncountable number of other varieties of trees, shrubs, ferns and small plants; picnic and camp sites are well-shaded/sheltered; picnic sites border a sandy river beach, some campsites are along the riverbank; summers are typically sunny and hot, winters are very rainy; elevation 150´.

Season, Fees & Phone: Open all year; please see Appendix for reservation information, park entry and campground fees; ☎(707) 458-3310 or ☎(707) 464-9533.

Trip Log: Jedediah Strong Smith was born in upstate New York in 1799, but he had moved west to join the ranks of the Mountain Men by the time he was 20. Smith's many remarkable journeys included one during which he passed through this region and discovered an overland route from Northern California to the Columbia River. In his brief lifetime he blazed a hundred trails for the rest of us to follow. He died in a Comanche ambush while leading a wagon train to Santa Fe, at the age of 32. Smith once commented that redwoods were the most noble trees he had ever seen. He probably would be honored knowing a place like this uncommonly beautiful spot, the northernmost of the California state parks, was named after him.

⚑ California 2 ♿

DEL NORTE COAST REDWOODS
Redwood National and State Parks

Location: Northern California Coast south of Crescent City.

Access: From U.S. Highway 101 at milepost 20 +.3 (6 miles south of Crescent City, 15 miles north of Klamath), turn east onto a paved park access road; proceed 1.3 miles to the park.

Day Use Facilities: Trailhead parking.

Camping Facilities: *Mill Creek Campground*: 142 campsites in 2 loops; (several walk-in sites are also available); sites are small+ to medium+, reasonably level, with fairly good to excellent separation; parking pads are hard-surfaced, medium to medium+ straight-ins; tent spots are large and generally private; storage cabinets; fireplaces; b-y-o firewood is recommended; water at several faucets; restrooms with showers; holding tank disposal station; paved driveways; complete supplies and services are available in Crescent City.

Activities & Attractions: Hiking trails include several interconnecting routes around the campground, also Last Chance Trail along an ocean bluff, and Damnation Creek Trail to an ocean beach; (trailheads for the latter 2 trails are near milepost 16, 4 miles south of the campground turnoff); nature trail; guided nature walks and campfire programs in summer; limited trout fishing in Mill Creek.

Natural Features: Located along the banks of Mill Creek in a redwood forest, bordered by steep, forested hills (campground); dense undergrowth provides excellent privacy for many campsites; some sites are creekside; a profusion of wildflowers is seen in spring; regional climate is typically temperate and foggy, but the campground's microclimate is fairly sunny and warm in summer; densely forested hills lie throughout much of the park; sea level to 1000´.

Season, Fees & Phone: April to October, with limited availability other times; please see Appendix for reservation information, park entry and campground fees; ☎(707) 464-9533.

Trip Log: The park's lands are along a seven-mile corridor on both sides of the main highway, roughly between mileposts 15 and 22, and border portions of Redwood National Park. Mill Creek is one of the finest camps in the state park system. If the Enchanted Forest had a campground, it might look like this.

⚑ California 3 ♿

PRAIRIE CREEK REDWOODS
Redwood National and State Parks

Location: Northern California Coast south of Crescent City.

Access: (Northbound) From U.S. Highway 101 at a point 4 miles north of Orick, turn northerly onto Drury Scenic Parkway and proceed 2 miles; turn west onto a park access road and proceed 0.15 mile west then south to the visitor center; continue for 0.4 mile south to the picnic area, or another 0.1 mile to the main campground; or continue northerly on the Scenic Parkway for an additional 9 miles of redwood scenery. **Alternate Access:** (Southbound) From U.S. Highway 101 at a point 4 miles south of Klamath, turn southerly onto Drury Scenic Drive and reverse the above directions.

Day Use Facilities: Medium-sized picnic area; drinking water; restrooms; several small parking areas.

Camping Facilities: *Elk Prairie Campground*: 75 campsites in 3 loops; (hike-bike sites are also available); a dozen sites along the edge of the prairie are medium-sized, level, with nominal separation; remaining sites are level, and vary from small to spacious, with fairly good to very good separation; parking pads are paved, short to medium-length straight-ins; large tent spots; fireplaces or fire rings; firewood is usually for sale, or b-y-o; water at several faucets; restrooms with showers; holding tank disposal station; paved driveways; (primitive campsites are also available at Gold Bluffs Beach); gas and groceries in Orick and Klamath.

Activities & Attractions: 70 miles of hiking trails within the park, including the 4.2 mile James Irvine Trail which leads from the main park area to the beach; self-guided nature trail; visitor center with extensive exhibits; campfire circle; guided nature walks and evening programs in summer; stream fishing.

Natural Features: Located in a forested area along the Pacific Coast; the visitor facilities are along the edge of a small prairie/meadow; most sites are shaded/sheltered by tall trees and considerable undergrowth; some sites are creekside; sea level to 300´.

Season, Fees & Phone: Open all year; please see Appendix for reservation information, park entry and campground fees; ☎(707) 488-2171.

Trip Log: The Scenic Drive formerly was U.S. 101. The highway was re-routed to the east and widened into a four-laner. Now the former numbered blacktop provides an outstanding opportunity for visitors to become 'intimate' with the towering trees along its route. Prairie Creek is also well-known for its several resident herds totaling about 200 Roosevelt elk. Elk are commonly seen browsing in the meadow near the visitor center and picnic and camp grounds.

♣ California 4 ♿

REDWOOD
Redwood National and State Parks

Location: Northwest California north of Eureka-Arcata.

Access: From U.S. Highway 101 near milepost 120 (1 mile south of Orick) turn west into the visitor center parking lot, or the day use area, 200 yards south of the visitor center; or between mileposts 118 and 119 , pull off onto the west shoulder of the highway to the campsites.

Day Use Facilities: Medium-sized picnic area; drinking water; restrooms; large parking lot.

Facilities: *Freshwater Lagoon Spit Campground*: Enough room for a hundred+ rv's, plus space for perhaps a couple dozen tents; rv areas consist of tightly spaced parallel parking on what amounts to the level, extra-wide, gravel highway shoulder on the west side of U.S. 101, (vehicles must be at least 30 feet off the pavement); a large, designated tent area is at the south end of the long beach; several dozen picnic tables and fire rings are scattered along the highway shoulder and in the tent area; b-y-o firewood; no drinking water; vault facilities; (drinking water and restrooms are available at the visitor center, 1 mile north); gas and groceries+ in Orick; complete supplies and services are available in Arcata.

Activities & Attractions: Redwood National and State Parks Visitor Center, 1 mile north, has interpretive displays and audio-visual presentations; beach access trails; whale watching.

Natural Features: Located along a Pacific Ocean beach and in the forested hills east of the beach; picnic area is beachside; rv spaces are on the highway shoulder just shoreside of a long sandy beach; tent sites are on the beach; a rocky promontory at the south end of the beach rises above the tent sites; Redding Rock rises from the surf at the north end of the beach; to the east, across the highway, is 2-mile-long Freshwater Lagoon, and densely forested hills and mountains; sea level.

Season, Fees & Phone: Open all year; suggested donation $5.00; 15 day limit; Redwood National and State Parks Visitor Center ☎(707) 464-6101, ext. 5265.

Trip Log: A 'memorandum of understanding' between the state park and national park offices established the collective Redwood National and State Parks in the early 1990's. The consortium consists of the original territory of Redwood NP, plus the trio of major state parks along this section of coastline: Prairie Creek Redwoods, Del Norte Coast Redwoods, and Jedediah Smith Redwoods. Under the agreement, the three state parks and the national park haven't lost their individual identities; but it specifies that the agencies will cooperate in managing this entire area of redwood coastline in accordance with common goals. Most of Redwood National Park is inland, accessible via Bald Hill Road, on the northeast edge of Orick. Trails from the road lead into the old growth redwood forest protected in the park. Possibly the best approach to seeing Redwood might be to stop at the visitor center to obtain the park handouts and maps, and perhaps talk with an info specialist.

♣ California 5 ♿

HUMBOLDT REDWOODS
Humboldt Redwoods State Park

Location: Northwest California southeast of Eureka.

Access: From U.S. Highway 101 at milepost 33 +.2 at the Weott Exit, (22 miles north of Garberville, 3 miles south of Dyerville, 25 miles south of Fortuna), turn west onto Newton Road; proceed west 0.2 mile to a 'T' intersection; turn south (left) onto Avenue of the Giants (Road 254) and proceed south for 1.5 miles to the visitor center and Burlington Campground.

Day Use Facilities: Small picnic area, drinking water, restrooms, medium sized parking lot at the visitor center.

Camping Facilities: *Burlington Campground*: 58 campsites; (hike-bike sites are available 1.7 miles north at the Marin Garden Club Grove, check in at Burlington first); sites are small, level, with minimal separation; parking pads are paved, short straight-ins; tent spots are moderately large; storage cabinets; fire rings; firewood is usually for sale, or b-y-o; water at several faucets; restrooms with showers; holding tank disposal station nearby at Williams Grove; paved driveways; gas and groceries in Weott.

(Camping is also available in the park's Albee Creek and Hidden Springs Campgrounds, north and south of here, respectively.)

Activities & Attractions: Large visitor center with flora, fauna, and historical exhibits, an audio-visual program, and an interpretive garden; nature walks and other interpretive programs, marathons and campfire programs are scheduled throughout the summer (a current calendar is available from the park office); over 100 miles of hiking and horse trails, including the strenuous Grasshopper Trail which leads to Grasshopper Peak at 3379´; (a detailed brochure/map with contour lines is available).

Natural Features: Located on a forested flat in a narrow valley across the Avenue from the South Fork of the Eel River (campground); the entire valley has huge redwoods towering over a forest floor of hardwoods and ferns; very little light filters down through the 'giants', and the campground generally remains heavily shaded, with a unique atmosphere; the entire park encompasses some 51,000 acres; park elevation ranges from 100´ along the river to 3400´ in the highlands.

Season, Fees & Phone: Open all year; please see Appendix for reservation information, park entry and campground fees; ☎ (707) 946-2311.

Trip Log: As California's premier sanctuary for *Sequoia sempervirens*, the regal coast redwood, Humboldt Redwoods has an atmosphere—a mystique if you will—that gives it a unique status among the Northern California redwood parks. Spearheaded by the Save-the-Redwoods League, an ongoing movement to purchase and set aside the redwood forests has reinstated over 500 memorial redwood groves to the public domain, including more than a hundred parcels just in Humboldt Redwoods alone. The foregoing sections describe the park's main area; several other groves, picnic and camp areas are along the Avenue of the Giants for several miles north and south of here.

♣ California 6 ♿

MACKERRICHER
MacKerricher State Park

Location: Northern California Coast north of Fort Bragg.

Access: From California State Highway 1 at milepost 64 +.9 (3 miles north of Fort Bragg, 12 miles south of Westport), turn west onto a paved access road; proceed 0.2 mile to the park.

Day Use Facilities: Medium-sized picnic area; drinking water; restrooms; medium-sized parking lot.

Camping Facilities: 143 campsites, including 12 walk-in sites, in 3 loops; sites are small to medium-sized, mostly level, with nominal to very good separation; parking pads are short to medium-length, gravel/sand or paved, straight-ins or pull-offs; tent spots are generally large; fireplaces; firewood is usually for sale, or b-y-o; water at several faucets; restrooms with showers; holding tank disposal station; paved driveways; adequate supplies and services are available in Fort Bragg.

Activities & Attractions: Surf fishing and abalone hunting; designated scuba areas; fishing for stocked trout on Lake Cleone; hand-propelled boating and small boat launch on the lake; beach hiking trail from Ten Mile River at the north tip of the park to Pudding Creek Beach south of the main park area; trail around Lake Cleone; seal and whale watching at Laguna Point (accessible via a local road underpass from near the picnic area); equestrian trails; guided nature walks and campfire programs in summer.

Natural Features: Located along the Pacific Ocean just south of Laguna Point; Mill Creek flows westward into small, freshwater Lake Cleone and then continues on to the sea; picnic sites are on the shore of Lake Cleone; many of the campsites are in dense vegetation of tall conifers and underbrush, other sites are more in the open; sea level.

Season, Fees & Phone: Open all year; please see Appendix for reservation information, park entry and campground fees; ☎(707) 937-5804.

Trip Log: Most people probably see only the developed area of the park. But there are seven miles of beach and dunes to be explored as well, most of it north of the main park zone. The relatively mild climate (usually cool, sometimes foggy in summer, chilly but not cold, though occasionally rainy in winter), contributes to the excellent picnicking, camping and beach walking opportunities during most of the year.

 California ⚑
North Bay

⚑ California 7

GERSTLE COVE
Salt Point State Park

Location: Northern California Coast northwest of Bodega Bay.

Access: From California State Highway 1 at milepost 39 +.9 (7 miles north of the community of Fort Ross, 9 miles south of Stewarts Point), turn west into the park area.

Day Use Facilities: Small picnic area, vault facilities and small parking areas at South Gerstle Cove and Stump Beach; medium-sized picnic area, vault facilities and 2 medium-sized lots at Fisk Mill Cove.

Camping Facilities: 30 campsites; (a group camp is also available, by reservation); sites are small, with nominal to fairly good separation; parking pads are paved, mostly short to short+ straight-ins; some will probably require a little additional leveling; medium to large areas for tents; fire rings; firewood is usually for sale, or b-y-o; water at several faucets; restrooms; holding tank disposal station; paved driveways; camper supplies in Stewarts Point.

(Camping is also available in the park's Woodside area, east of the highway.)

Activities & Attractions: Gerstle Cove Marine Reserve; designated scuba and skin diving areas; trails to the beach from most day use areas; hiking/horse trails east of the highway.

Natural Features: Located on a hillside above the Pacific Ocean; conifers provide very light shade/shelter for most picnic sites; campsites are generally well sheltered by tall conifers; elevation at Gerstle Cove and other areas west of the highway, sea level to 100´.

Season, Fees & Phone: Open all year; please see Appendix for reservation information, park entry and campground fees; ☎(707) 847-3221.

Trip Log: This stretch of the coast is a bit rockier and more heavily forested than many of the other Northern California coastal access points. (But what or who is 'Gerstle'; is it anything like *gestalt*?) Gerstle Cove Marine Reserve in the well-sheltered waters at the north end of the Cove was one of the first underwater parks to be designated in California.

⚑ California 8 ♿

FORT ROSS
Fort Ross State Historic Park

Location: Northern California north of Bodega Bay.

Access: From California State Highway 1 at milepost 33 (12 miles northwest of Jenner, 2 miles south of the hamlet of Fort Ross), turn west onto the park access road and proceed 0.25 mile to the park.

Day Use Facilities: Small picnic area; drinking water; restrooms; large parking lot.

Camping Facilities: None; nearest standard public campground is in Salt Point State Park; (a 25-site primitive campground with limited availability is located 1.7 miles south of Fort Ross SP, at the bottom of a ravine off the west side of the highway.)

Activities & Attractions: Paved trail (0.3 mile) from the parking lot to a restoration of Fort Ross; (ask at the visitor center for handicapped access arrangements); visitor center with exhibits and audio-visual programs.

Natural Features: Located on a bluff above the ocean; park vegetation consists of large, open grassy tracts and stands of conifers; elevation 100´.

Season, Fees & Phone: Open all year; please see Appendix for entry fees; ☎(707) 847-3286.

Trip Log: The village and fortress of Ross, several houses and a stout wooden fort, was founded in 1812 by Russian and Alaskan Indian seal fur hunters. The extensive reconstruction allows you to see Fort Ross somewhat as it was when the Russians set up housekeeping here. One original building, the commandant's residence, still stands inside the stockade and was restored to its original appearance. The stockade and the twin-domed chapel crowned by a Saint Cyril's Cross also have been authentically rebuilt.

♣ California 9 ♿
GUALALA POINT
Sonoma County Regional Park

Location: Northern California Coast northwest of Bodega Bay.

Access: From California State Highway 1 at milepost 58 +.3 (0.2 mile south of the Sonoma-Mendocino county line, 2 miles south of Gualala, 10 miles north of Stewarts Point), turn east onto a paved access road; proceed 0.3 mile to the park.

Day Use Facilities: Small picnic area; drinking water; restrooms; medium-sized parking area.

Camping Facilities: 25 campsites, including 7 walk-ins; sites are small to medium-sized, with very good to excellent separation; parking pads are paved, mostly level, short to medium-length straight-ins; tent spots are very private, many are grassy, and most are level; fire rings; firewood is usually for sale, or b-y-o; water at several faucets; restrooms; holding tank disposal station; narrow, paved driveways; gas and groceries+ are available in Gualala.

Activities & Attractions: Hiking and bicycle paths, including a beach trail; visitor center has interpretive exhibits and natural displays; fishing (especially for steelhead); abalone hunting; beachcombing; nature study; whale watching.

Natural Features: Located along the south bank of the Gualala River just east of where it flows into the Pacific Ocean; the river is very wide, and normally deep and slow-moving through this section; very dense vegetation in the park consists of a mixture of hardwoods, conifers, ferns and smaller plants; sea level.

Season, Fees & Phone: Open all year; $15.00; 14 day limit; park office ☎ (707) 785-2377.

Trip Log: The lush vegetation at Gualala Point provides tunnels of greenery for the roads, trails and campsites. All the campsites are really secluded and, as a rule, the park's atmosphere is serene.

♣ California 10 ♿
BODEGA BAY
Sonoma Coast State Beach

Location: Northern California Coast near Bodega Bay.

Access: From California State Highway 1 at milepost 11 +.7 (1 mile north of the town of Bodega Bay), turn west onto a park access road and proceed 0.4 mile to the entrance station; just past the entrance, turn west (left) and proceed 0.8 mile out to South Salmon Creek Beach; or continue ahead past the entrance for 0.3 mile to the Bodega Dunes main camp loops. **Additional Access** (for Bodega Head): From Highway 1 at milepost 11 +.1 on the north edge of Bodega Bay, (0.6 mile south of the Bodega Dunes turnoff above), turn west onto Bay Shore Road and go 0.3 mile west and south to a 3-way intersection at the bottom of the hill; turn west (right) onto Bay Flat Road and proceed 3.5 miles to the headland.

Day Use Facilities: Small picnic area, vaults, medium-sized parking lot at South Salmon Creek Beach; vault facilities and 3 small parking lots at and near Bodega Head.

Camping Facilities: *Bodega Dunes Campground*: 98 campsites; (hike-bike sites are also available); sites are small, level, with nominal to fairly good separation; parking pads are hard-surfaced, mostly short straight-ins; adequate space for medium to large tents in most sites; fire rings; firewood is usually for sale, or b-y-o; water at several faucets; restrooms with showers; holding tank disposal station; paved driveways; gas and groceries in Bodega Bay.

Activities & Attractions: Trails to the beach and out to Bodega Head from Bodega Dunes; campfire center.

Natural Features: Located in a dunes area on Bodega Bay (campground), on a 2-mile-long beach along the northwest side of the peninsula (South Salmon Creek Beach) and on a rocky point (Bodega Head); campsites are very lightly to lightly shaded but well-sheltered from wind by large, full evergreens and dense bushes; most other areas are covered with tall grass plus a few small evergreens; sea level to 50´.

Season, Fees & Phone: Open all year; please see Appendix for reservation information, park entry and campground fees; ☎(707) 875-3483 or☎(707) 875-3382.

Trip Log: Only a few Bodega Dunes campsites overlook the bay, but the sea's edge is only a short walk from any campsite. There is much more dense, low-level vegetation in this campground than in most other state beach campgrounds on the North Coast. The views from Bodega Head are worth the cost of a couple of miles off the highway.

♣ **California 11** ♿

BU-SHAY
Lake Mendocino/Corps of Engineers Park

Location: Northwest California north of San Francisco.

Access: From California State Highway 20 at milepost 36 +.6 (3.3 miles east of the junction of Highway 20 & U.S. Highway 101, 27 miles west of Lakeport), turn west onto a paved access road, then go south (under the highway overpass and along the river) for 1.1 miles to the campground entrance; continue for 0.25 mile, then turn right into the campground.

Day Use Facilities: Medium-sized picnic area; drinking water, restrooms, large parking area in the nearby Pomo day use area.

Camping Facilities: 168 campsites in 2 loops; sites are mostly medium-sized, with reasonable separation; parking pads are paved, medium to long straight-ins; some pads may require additional leveling; most sites have excellent, large, grassy tent spots; fireplaces and fire rings; b-y-o firewood is recommended; water at several faucets; restrooms with showers; holding tank disposal station; narrow paved driveways; complete supplies and services are available in Ukiah, 10 miles southwest.

(Camping is also available at the lake's Kyen Campground, 1 mile west.)

Activities & Attractions: Boating; boat launch nearby at Oak Grove; sailing; fishing for striped bass, largemouth and smallmouth bass, crappie and catfish; swimming at Pomo day use area; 14 miles of hiking trails in the park; playground; visitor center.

Natural Features: Located on the northeast shore of Lake Mendocino in Coyote Valley in the Coast Range; vegetation consists predominantly of large oaks and light underbrush on grassy slopes; bordered by hills covered with oaks and madrones; Lake Mendocino is a flood-control and storage reservoir on the East Fork of the Russian River; elevation 800´.

Season, Fees & Phone: April to September; $11.00; 14 day limit; Lake Mendocino CoE Project Office ☎ (707) 462-7581.

Trip Log: Lake Mendocino is an attractive blue jewel amid rolling golden hills and tree-dotted low mountains. The access is quite convenient, since it's within a few miles of U.S. 101, and a couple hours' drive from San Francisco. Though oaks are the predominant vegetation in this park, the great redwood forests are within a few miles to the west.

♣ **California 12** ♿

CLEAR LAKE
Clear Lake State Park

Location: Northwest California north of Santa Rosa.

Access: From California State Highway 29 at milepost 34.2 at the east edge of Kelseyville, (9 miles southeast of Lakeport), turn north onto Main Street; follow a well-signed, zigzag route (or just follow the traffic) along Main Street, Gaddy Lane and Soda Bay Road for 4.1 miles to the park; turn north (left) onto the park access road and proceed 0.2 mile to the park. (Note: this is the simplest routing of at least 5 accesses from State Highways 29, 175 and 281; they all eventually lead to Soda Bay Road.)

Day Use Facilities: Large picnic area; large group picnic area (reservable); drinking water; restrooms; medium-sized and large parking lots.

Camping Facilities: *Cole Creek Campground*: 26 campsites; (hike-bike sites are also available); *Kelsey Creek Campground*: 65 sites; sites in both campgrounds are medium to large, level, with nominal to fair separation; parking pads are paved, medium to medium+ straight-ins; excellent, grassy tent spots; *Upper and Lower Bayview Campgrounds*: 31 campsites in Lower Bayview and 35 sites in Upper Bayview; sites are mostly medium-sized, with nominal to fair separation; parking pads are paved, short to medium-length straight-ins; many pads may require additional leveling; medium to large tent spots, some may be sloped; *all campgrounds*: storage cabinets; fireplaces; b-y-o firewood is recommended; water at faucets throughout; restrooms with showers; holding tank disposal station near the visitor center; paved driveways;

adequate supplies and services are available in the Kelseyville-Lakeport area.

Activities & Attractions: Boating; boat launch; fishing for largemouth bass, crappie, bluegill and catfish; swimming beach; visitor center; campfire circle; Indian Nature Trail; hiking trails; interpretive programs in summer.

Natural Features: *Kelsey Creek*: located on the south shore of Clear Lake, between the lake and the Kelsey Creek bayou; most sites have lake views; *Cole Creek*: located along Cole Creek a few hundred yards from the lake shore; large hardwoods provide light to medium shade in both areas, with some open grassy sections in Kelsey Creek; *Upper and Lower Bayview*: located on a hill above Soda Bay; large oak trees and sparse grass are the predominant forms of vegetation; some sites have lake views through the trees; the lake is ringed by wooded hills and mountains; summer temperatures commonly exceed 90º F; elevation 1300´.

Season, Fees & Phone: Open all year; please see Appendix for reservation information, park entry and campground fees; ☎(707) 279-2267 or ☎(707) 279-8650.

Trip Log: For such a relatively small park (it covers less than a square mile), this place is loaded with a variety of natural settings and facilities, hence the rather involved descriptions above. Choosing a campsite at Clear Lake is difficult: to camp on top, with more commanding views; or to stay at lake level, closer to the park's activities. Clear Lake is the largest natural lake totally within California. Yes, Tahoe is larger; but the key words here are *totally within* California.

⚑ **California 13** ♿

SPRING LAKE
Sonoma County Regional Park

Location: Northern California in Santa Rosa.

Access: From California State Highway 12 at milepost 18 +.6 on the east side of Santa Rosa, turn south onto Mission Boulevard and go 0.2 mile; swing west (right) onto Montgomery Drive and proceed 0.15 mile; turn south (left) onto Summerfield Road and travel 1 mile; turn east (left) onto Hoen Avenue, go 100 yards, then jog left onto Newanga Avenue and continue east for another 0.6 mile to the park.

Day Use Facilities: Several small and medium-sized picnic areas with drinking water, restrooms and various-sized parking areas are throughout the park.

Camping Facilities: 31 campsites; (a group camp is also available, by reservation); sites are small to medium-sized, tolerably level, with nominal to fairly good separation; parking pads are paved, predominantly medium-length straight-ins; large tent areas, some are a bit sloped; fire rings; b-y-o firewood; water at several faucets; restrooms with showers; holding tank disposal station; paved driveway; complete supplies and services are available in Santa Rosa.

Activities & Attractions: Fishing; limited boating; boat launch; short hiking trail down to the lake; swimming lagoon.

Natural Features: Located on a rocky, rolling hilltop above Spring Lake; sites receive light to light-medium shade from large oaks, plus some madrones and conifers on sparse grass; bordered by forested hills and mountains; elevation 200´.

Season, Fees & Phone: Open all year, but open only on weekends and holidays from mid-September to mid-May; $15.00; 14 day limit; reservations accepted, contact the park office ☎(707) 539-8082.

Trip Log: Good scenery, both near and distant. Glimpses of the lake, through the trees, from some sites. The small lake is dotted with several islands, and a high peak rises to the south.

⚑ **California 14** ♿

BOTHE-NAPA VALLEY
Bothe Napa Valley State Park

Location: Northern California northwest of Napa.

Access: From California State Highways 29/128 at milepost 33 +.5 (3 miles southeast of Calistoga, 4 miles northwest of St. Helena), swing south/west onto the park access road and proceed 0.2 mile to the park.

Day Use Facilities: Large picnic area; group picnic area with ramada; drinking water; restrooms; parking along the park road; horse trailer parking lot.

Camping Facilities: 50 campsites, including 9 walk-in units; (a group camp is also available); sites are small, with nominal to fairly good separation; parking pads are packed/oiled gravel, short to short+ straight-ins; some pads may require a little additional leveling; small to medium-sized areas for tents; storage cabinets; fire rings or fireplaces; firewood is usually for sale, or b-y-o; water at several faucets;

restrooms with showers; adequate supplies and services are available in Calistoga.

Activities & Attractions: 7 miles of hiking trails; history trail to Bale Grist Mill (see separate info); small (motel-size), creek-fed swimming pool (in the day use area, a few feet from the highway); visitor center with interpretive displays and a 3D map of the region; (a park brochure/map showing contour lines and the locations of many Napa Valley wineries is available).

Natural Features: Located on the northwest edge of Napa Valley; picnic area is on a grassy flat, with light to medium shade provided by tall conifers; campsites are moderately shaded/sheltered by hardwoods and some conifers; bordered by forested hills; elevation 350´.

Season, Fees & Phone: Open all year; please see Appendix for reservation information, park entry and campground fees; (camping is limited to one night only); ☎(707) 942-4575.

Trip Log: Adjacent Bale Grist Mill State Historic Park provides a neat opportunity to see one of the few, fully functioning water wheels available to the public. (Champion Lake State Park near Imperial, Nebraska has one too, if you're ever in that neighborhood.) The mill is complete with a 36´ wooden, flume-fed wheel, gearworks, and massive millstones. Especially if you have kids, grandchildren, friends who are kids, or students, this place is worth a visit.

⚑ **California 15** ♿

JACK LONDON
Jack London State Historic Park

Location: Northern California southeast of Santa Rosa.

Access: From California State Highway 12 at milepost 30 +.7 near the town of Glen Ellen (9 miles north of Sonoma, 13 miles south of Santa Rosa) turn southwest onto Arnold Drive and proceed 1 mile into midtown Glen Ellen; turn west onto London Ranch Road and go 0.9 mile to the park.

Day Use Facilities: 2 small picnic areas; drinking water; restrooms; 2 large parking lots.

Camping Facilities: None; nearest public campground is in Sugarloaf Ridge State Park.

Activities & Attractions: Beauty Ranch, home of the early twentieth century fiction writer Jack London; working ranch exhibits;

trails to London's grave (0.5 mile) and Wolf House (0.6 mile), 0.5 self-guiding loop trail through Beauty Ranch; museum in the 'House of Happy Walls', built in 1919 by London's widow, Charmian, includes many of his works and the collection of objects gathered in their travels around the world.

Natural Features: Located in the foothills of Sonoma Mountain above Sonoma Valley; (one of London's best-known books, *Valley of the Moon*, is descriptive of this valley); much of the park is moderately to densely wooded with oaks, eucalyptus, madrones, other hardwoods and some conifers; elevation 700´.

Season, Fees & Phone: Open all year; please see Appendix for park entry fees; ☎(707) 938-5216.

Trip Log: Jack London was born in San Francisco in 1876, but Oakland is generally considered to be his home town. As a young man, he worked his way around the Oakland waterfront, around California and around the world. His adventures eventually led to his becoming one of the most popular and prolific novelists and short story writers of the twentieth century. Known best for *Call of the Wild*, *White Fang* and *The Sea Wolf*, London drew on first-hand experience in the Far North and at sea.

The park highlights the life London led here at Beauty Ranch between 1905 until his death in 1916. He established the ranch in order to experiment with and perfect new agricultural techniques. He raised fine horses, livestock, fruit and vegetable crops. London continued his adventurous, hard-working, hard-spending, hard-drinking lifestyle until his death here in 1916 at the age of 40. Jack London once wrote: "Everything I build is for the years to come".

⚑ **California 16** ♿

SONOMA
Sonoma State Historic Park

Location: Northern California north of San Francisco.

Access: From California State Highway 12 in midtown Sonoma at the town plaza, go east then north around the plaza to Spain Street; most park buildings are situated on the north side of Spain Street, east and west of 1st Street East. **Additional Access** (for the Vallejo Home): From California State Highway 12 at a point 0.3 mile west of the town plaza in midtown Sonoma, turn north onto 3rd Street West and proceed 0.4 mile to the park. (If you have the time, it would be a pleasant, 15 minute walk from the main park downtown on Spain Street to the Vallejo Home, or vice versa.)

Day Use Facilities: Small picnic area in the mission courtyard; picnic tables and drinking water in the plaza; restrooms at the mission and near the barracks; large, city parking lot between 1st East & 1st West, north of the historic area; streetside parking is also available; also small (very nice) picnic area; drinking water; restrooms; medium-sized parking lot at the Vallejo Home.

Camping Facilities: None; nearest public campground is in Sugarloaf Ridge State Park.

Activities & Attractions: Restored and renovated Mission San Francisco Solano, Toscano Hotel, Blue Wing Inn and Army barracks, complete with period furniture; Restored, Gothic-Victorian style home of General M.G. Vallejo.

Natural Features: Located in-town and on the edge of town in the Sonoma Valley; park contains several gardens/courtyards; elev. 100´.

Season, Fees & Phone: Open all year; please see Appendix for park entry fees; ☎(707) 938-1519 (district office); ☎(707) 938-0151 (mission); ☎(707) 938-1215 (Vallejo Home).

Trip Log: Sonoma's history dates back to 1823 when the Mission San Francisco Solano, the most northerly of the Franciscan missions was founded. The present chapel was constructed in the 1840's by General Mariano Guadalupe Vallejo. Sonoma was the headquarters for the Bear Flag Revolt in 1846, which was the impetus for California's independence, and California's famous grizzly bear flag was designed here. The barracks served the Mexican and American military, then it was turned into a winery by the good general. The Blue Wing Inn was a gambling hall and saloon, and now holds concessionaires'' shops. And the Toscano Hotel, with its authentic furnishings right down to the bottle of Red Eye on the bar, goes back to the late 1800's. All of the buildings in this section of the park are within a block of the plaza, so the sidewalk tour method works very well here. The Vallejo Home unit of the park features the house owned by General Vallejo, the Mexican general who eventually became an important player in early California politics.

♠ California 17 ♿

MOUNT TAMALPAIS
Mount Tamalpais State Park

Location: Northern California northwest of San Francisco.

Access: From California State Highway 1 (northbound) at milepost 3 +.4 (3 miles west of the junction of Highway 1 & U.S. 101 near Mill Valley), head northwest on Panoramic Highway for 5.1 miles to the Bootjack picnic area, or another 0.3 mile to a 3-way junction and the Pantoll campground; continue southwest on Panoramic Highway for another 3.6 miles to Stinson Beach; from Highway 1 (southbound) in Stinson Beach, proceed northeast on Panoramic Highway and reverse the above directions. (Note: the above routing via the park's main road, Panoramic Highway, will serve the majority of travelers; short, paved roads are available for local exploration.)

Day Use Facilities: Small picnic area, small group picnic area, drinking water, restrooms and large parking lot at Bootjack; small picnic area, drinking water, restrooms and parking lot at the visitor center; Mountain Theater.

Camping Facilities: *Pantoll Campground*: 16 park 'n walk campsites, plus approximately 25 enroute sites for self-contained vehicles, and a hike-bike site; park 'n walk sites are small, sloped, with fair separation; parking is in a fairly level, paved lot; tent areas are medium to large and somewhat level; storage cabinets; fireplaces; firewood is usually for sale, or b-y-o; water at several faucets; restrooms. *Steep Ravine Environmental Campground*: 6 primitive campsites and 10 small cabins; campsites have small to medium-sized tent areas, table, fireplace, storage cabinet; cabins have a 'sleeping platform', table, inside wood stove and outdoor fireplace; firewood is available; water at faucets; vault facilities; (2 group camps, and a small backpack camp for individuals and groups are also available, in other areas in the park); complete supplies and services are available in Mill Valley.

Activities & Attractions: More than 50 miles of trails within the park, connecting to a 200-mile system of trails on adjacent public land; (a brochure/map with contour lines is available); horses are allowed on fire roads and designated trails; bicycles are allowed on designated fire roads and paved roads; 3 designated hang glider launch points; visitor center at East Peak; "Mountain Theater", with room for about 3,000 individuals, (via a 0.7 mile trail from the

Bootjack parking lot, or 0.2 mile trail from the Ridgecrest Boulevard parking lot).

Natural Features: Located on and around Mount Tamalpais; the park's vegetation consists of dense sections of hardwoods and conifers, open meadows, and brushy hillsides; most picnic and camp sites (except enroute sites) are well-shaded/sheltered by tall conifers and/or hardwoods; sea level to 2586´.

Season, Fees & Phone: Open all year; please see Appendix for reservation information and campground fees; ☎(415) 388-2070.

Trip Log: "Mount Tam" itself is a triple-peaked ridge with a difference of a few feet between its highest points. *Tamalpais* is said to mean "Land of the Tamal (Indians)". The Cushing Memorial Theater ("Mountain Theater") is a large, outdoor amphitheater of native stone which was built by the CCC during the 1930's. Its serves as the stage for the long-run, annual "Mountain Play" and is sometimes used for weddings and other special occasions.

🏕 **California 18** ♿

MOUNT DIABLO
Mount Diablo State Park

Location: Western California northeast of Oakland.

Access: From Interstate 680 in Walnut Creek (*northbound*) take the Ygnacio Valley Road Exit, travel northeast on Ygnacio Valley Road for 2.2 miles; turn southeast (right) onto Walnut Avenue and go 1.6 miles, then jog right onto Oak Grove for 100 yards, then left onto North Gate Road for 1.7 miles to the northwest park. From I-680 in Walnut Creek (*southbound*) take the North Main Exit and go south on North Main for 0.6 mile, then turn left onto Ygnacio Valley Road and continue as above.

Alternate Access: From Interstate 680 in Danville at the Diablo Road Exit, head easterly on Diablo Road for 2.9 miles; turn north (left) onto Mount Diablo Scenic Road and proceed 3.7 miles to the park's south entrance station. (Note: The north road climbs/descends more gradually and has fewer switchbacks than the south road.)

Day Use Facilities: Rock City/Artist Point/Horseshoe picnic areas combined have a number of tables scattered over a wide area, also drinking water, central restrooms, vaults, scattered parking; Summit Road picnic areas are small, scattered, with vault facilities nearby.

Camping Facilities: 58 campsites in 3 major areas (*Junction, Live Oak, Juniper*); (4 standard group camps and 2 group horse camps are also available, by reservation); sites are small to small+, with minimal to nominal separation; parking pads are gravel, mostly short straight-ins, plus some medium+ pull-throughs in Juniper; many pads will require additional leveling; small to medium-sized tent areas; assorted fire appliances; b-y-o firewood; water at faucets; vault facilities; (restrooms nearby at Junction); complete supplies and services are available in Walnut Creek.

Activities & Attractions: Observation deck at the summit; miles of hiking trails (a detailed brochure/map is available); small interpretive center.

Natural Features: Located on the summit and sides of Mount Diablo; the mountain is cloaked with large, open grassy areas and stands of oaks, plus a few tall conifers; most picnic and camp sites receive very light to light-medium shade; elevation 300´ to 3849´.

Season, Fees & Phone: Open all year; please see Appendix for reservation information, park entry and campground fees; ☎(415) 837-2525.

Trip Log: From Mount Diablo's summit you can see about half of California (or so it might seem). Actually, on a clear day you can see portions of nearly two-thirds of the state's 58 counties, or roughly one-fourth of its land area (about 40,000 square miles). It is claimed that the view is excelled only by the panorama from Africa's 19,000´ Mount Kilimanjaro. To get a good visual effect from this solitary peak, you don't *have* to drive all the way to the top—but just about everyone does.

🏠 *California* ⛺
South Bay

🏕 **California 19** ♿

AÑO NUEVO
Año Nuevo State Reserve

Location: Central California Coast northwest of Santa Cruz.

Access: From California State Highway 1 at milepost 1 +.6 (10 miles north of Davenport, 15 miles south of Pescadero), turn west into the park access road and proceed 0.3 mile to the visitor center. (An additional day use access point is located near milepost 6.)

Day Use Facilities: Drinking water; restrooms and vault facilities; medium-sized parking lot.

Camping Facilities: None; nearest public campground is in Butano State Park.

Activities & Attractions: Guided tours during the elephant seal breeding season, December to April, reservations required; several hiking trails; visitor center.

Natural Features: Located on a beach and a bushy coastal plain; the forested Santa Cruz Mountains rise to the east; sea level.

Season, Fees & Phone: Open all year; no dogs allowed; please see Appendix for reservation information and park entry fees; ☎(415) 879-0595 or ☎(415) 879-0852 or ☎(415) 979-0227.

Trip Log: "Northern Elephant Seal breeding season is always an exciting event", say the park's promotional posters. To visit Año Nuevo State Reserve during this season you must be on a guided walk led by a trained volunteer naturalist. The bulls (which commonly are the length and weight of a compact car, but can be as long and hefty as a loaded mini-pickup) make their grand appearances beginning in early December and continue arriving through February. By mid-March, though, mom and pop have left on the honeymoon, leaving behind the weaned pups who hang around through April. The three-mile round-trip on the guided walk takes about 2.5 hours.

⚑ California 20 ⅋

HENRY COWELL REDWOODS
Henry Cowell Redwoods State Park

Location: Central California coastal area north of Santa Cruz.

Access: From California State Highway 1 at milepost 17 +.5 in midtown Santa Cruz, take the State Highway 9/River Street Exit and travel north on Highway 9 for 4.8 miles; turn east (right) onto a park access road and proceed 0.4 mile to the day use area. **Additional Access (campground):** From Highway 1 at the Ocean Street-Felton Exit in Santa Cruz at milepost 17 +.3, turn north onto Ocean Street and proceed 0.2 mile; bear right onto Graham Hill Road, go northerly for 3 miles, then turn west (left) onto a park access road for 0.2 to the campground entrance station. **Alternate Access:** From the intersection of California State Highway 9 and Graham Hill Road in midtown Felton, travel south on Highway 9 for 0.6 mile to the day use area turnoff; or from that same intersection in Felton, travel southeast on Graham Hill Road for 2 miles to the campground access road.

Day Use Facilities: Large picnic area; drinking water; restrooms; several parking lots; concession stand.

Camping Facilities: *Graham Hill Campground*: 113 campsites; (bike sites are also available); sites are medium to medium+ in size, with good separation; parking pads are gravel/dirt, medium-length straight-ins; good to excellent tent-pitching opportunities; at least half of the parking pads and tent areas are essentially level, others are a touch sloped; storage cabinets; fireplaces or fire rings; b-y-o firewood; water at faucets throughout; restrooms with showers; paved driveways; groceries on Graham Hill Road within 2 miles north and south; complete supplies and services are available in Santa Cruz.

Activities & Attractions: 15 miles of hiking and horse trails; redwood groves; trail from the campground to an observation deck; steelhead and salmon fishing in winter.

Natural Features: Located in the western foothills of the Santa Cruz Mountains; the picnic area overlooks the banks of the San Lorenzo River, which winds southerly through the center of the park; most picnic and camp sites are well sheltered/shaded; elevation 100´ to 500´.

Season, Fees & Phone: Open all year; please see Appendix for reservation information, park entry and campground fees; ☎(408) 335-4598 (office) or ☎(408) 438-2396 (campground).

Trip Log: Think of the park as being shaped like a drinking gourd. The day use area is in the 'handle'; the campground is on the rim of the 'bowl'. Except for service roads and trails, the remaining 90 percent of the dipper is semi-wilderness. It's a really nice place.

⚑ California 21 ⅋

SUNSET
Sunset State Beach

Location: Central California Coast southeast of Santa Cruz.

Access: From California State Highway 1 (southbound) near milepost 8, at the San Andreas Road/Seascape Exit (1 mile east of Aptos), head south on San Andreas Road for 5.2 miles to Sunset Beach Road; turn west onto Sunset Beach Road and proceed 0.8 mile to the park. **Alternate Access:** From Highway 1 (northbound) at milepost 0.9 (just north of the Santa Cruz-Monterey county line) take the Watsonville/State Highway 129 Exit, go to the west side of the freeway, then north on a frontage road for 0.3 mile to a 'T' intersection; turn southwest (left) onto Beach Road and proceed 1.4 miles; turn northwest (right) onto San Andreas Road and travel 2 miles; turn west onto Sunset Beach Road and continue as above.

Day Use Facilities: Medium-sized picnic area; drinking water; restrooms; large parking lot; concession stand.

Camping Facilities: 90 campsites in 3 loops; (hike-bike sites and a medium-sized group camp are also available); sites are small, with minimal to nominal separation; parking pads are paved, mostly short to short+ straight-ins, plus a few pull-offs; many pads will require a little additional leveling; adequate space for large tents in most sites; fire rings; firewood is usually for sale, or b-y-o; water at several faucets; restrooms with showers; paved driveways; complete supplies and services are available in Watsonville.

Activities & Attractions: Beach trails over the dune; campfire center.

Natural Features: Located along an ocean beach and in slightly hilly/rolling terrain just east of a long dune; vegetation consists of short grass, some small bushes, and large, full conifers that provide a fairly generous amount of shelter/shade in many sites; bordered by farm fields to the east; sea level.

Season, Fees & Phone: Open all year; please see Appendix for reservation information, park entry and campground fees; ☎(408) 724-1266.

Trip Log: Sunset is located about midway along the sweeping arc of Monterey Bay's shoreline. It is one of the nicer looking and more tranquil of the dozen local state beaches, and thus was selected to represent this important recreational region. A dune separates the camp loops from the ocean, so there are no ocean views. Don't let that stop you. The campground is in a very nice 'piney' setting.

♠ California 22 &

MONTEREY
Monterey State Historic Park

Location: Central California Coast in Monterey.

Access: From California State Highway 1 (southbound) at the north end of Monterey, take the Del Monte Avenue Exit and travel southwesterly on Del Monte Avenue for 1.8 miles; turn north (right) onto Washington Street to the parking lots closest to the center of the park and the park office. **Alternate Access:** From State Highway 1 (northbound) at the south city limit of Monterey, take the Munras Avenue Exit and proceed 1.7 miles, first on Munras, then pick up Abrego, which shortly merges with Washington, in downtown Monterey and Washington's intersection with Del Monte Avenue; continue straight across Del Monte Avenue to the parking lots.

Day Use Facilities: Sitting benches and picnic tables in several local parks/plazas; drinking water; restrooms; metered streetside parking, plus several large city parking lots and garages within 5 blocks of the waterfront.

Camping Facilities: None; nearest public campground is in Laguna Seca county park, 11 miles east on State Highway 68.

Activities & Attractions: Self-guided walking or driving tour of historic homes, businesses and government buildings.

Natural Features: Located along and near Monterey Bay; nicely landscaped gardens and courtyards are scattered throughout the historic area; (you might even get to see that silly seal who likes to catch some sun on the decks of sailboats berthed along the wharf); sea level.

Season, Fees & Phone: Open all year; (no fee); ☎(408) 649-7118.

Trip Log: The easiest approach to finding your way around is to (a) get here before noon on a weekday; (b) park your vehicle as close to the wharf as you can; and (c) find one of the large maps on display at key locations in the historic district. As an alternative to (b) and (c), you can just cruise the entire downtown neighborhood looking for historic buildings, all of which should be signed and most of which are in modern use. If you enjoy viewing beautiful, century-old, traditional Spanish and colonial American buildings preserved in first-class condition, with tastefully landscaped gardens, courtyards, plazas, parks, and tree-lined walks, near an historic waterfront, look no farther.

♠ California 23 &

ASILOMAR
Asilomar State Beach and Conference Grounds

Location: Central California Coast northwest of Monterey.

Access: From California State Highway 1 at its junction with State Highway 68 (at the north edge of Carmel, 3 miles southwest of Monterey), travel northwest on Highway 68 for 3.1 miles to the intersection of Sunset Drive and Asilomar Boulevard; continue ahead on Sunset for 0.1 mile to the beach, or turn right onto Asilomar into the conference grounds. (Note: '68 starts out as Holman, curves and becomes Sunset, then finally becomes Asilomar.)

Day Use Facilities: Parallel parking along Sunset Drive.

Camping Facilities: Meeting rooms and lodging for individuals or "almost any size convention or conference" on the grounds. (And when you see this setup, you'll believe it. Ed.)

Activities & Attractions: Boardwalks and numerous paths to the beach.

Natural Features: Located adjacent to a mile-long section of ocean beach and on a short bluff above the beach; the rocky shoreline is backdropped by grass-covered dunes; conference grounds are fully landscaped; sea level.

Season, Fees & Phone: Open all year; Conference Grounds operated by a concessionaire; it is suggested that you contact the concessionaire for current brochures, rate cards, and reservation information; ☎(408) 372-8016; beach info only ☎(408) 372-4076.

Trip Log: A long time ago, this complex started out as a YMCA summer camp. Well, sort of. The 'Y' reportedly began building this retreat back in the early 1900's and expanded it beyond the point of no return. (From a fiscal standpoint, it was mostly outflow, and no net return.) In the mid 1950's, the property was sold to the state and subsequently turned into a unit of the state park system. The buildings and grounds are fully in keeping with what could be termed an atmosphere of "maintained naturalness" of the Monterey Peninsula. *Asilomar* is a Spanish phrase for "seaside refuge".

⚘ California 24 ♿

POINT LOBOS
Point Lobos State Reserve

Location: Central California Coast south of Monterey.

Access: From California State Highway 1 at milepost 70 +.5 (4 miles south of Carmel, 22 miles north of Big Sur), turn west into the park.

Day Use Facilities: Several small picnic areas; drinking water; restrooms; several small parking areas.

Camping Facilities: None; nearest public campground is in Pfeiffer-Big Sur State Park.

Activities & Attractions: Foot trails crisscross the reserve; designated scuba diving area can be used by certified pairs or teams of divers, (park permit required); (a detailed brochure/map, a walker's guide, flower and bird booklets, etc. are available).

Natural Features: Located along and under the Pacific Ocean; vegetation consists of tall conifers, hardwoods and brush, cypress, and open meadows; watching for gray whales during their annual December to May migration, best in mid-winter; sea otters, harbor seals, sea lions and deer are among the resident critters; sea level.

Season, Fees & Phone: Open all year; no motorhomes, trailers or dogs (especially Greyhounds) allowed; please see Appendix for park entry fees; ☎(408) 624-4909.

Trip Log: More than a quarter-million visitors come here each year to reflect on what has been hyperbolically described as "the greatest meeting of land and water in the world". (That same verbal sketch has also been used to illustrate Monterey's world-renowned 17-Mile Drive.) With less than a square mile of area, the number of people allowed in the reserve at any given time during busy periods is tightly regulated, so you might have a bit of a wait outside the gate on a sunny Saturday in August.

⚘ California 25 ♿

PFEIFFER BIG SUR
Pfeiffer Big Sur State Park

Location: Central California Coast south of Monterey.

Access: From California State Highway 1 at milepost 46 +.8 in Big Sur (27 miles south of Carmel, 67 miles north of San Simeon), turn east into the park.

Day Use Facilities: Several small or medium-sized picnic areas; 3 reservable group picnic areas with shelters; drinking water; restrooms; several medium to large parking lots.

Camping Facilities: 218 campsites; (bike sites and 2 hike-in group camps are also available); sites are small to small+, level, with separation varying from none to good; parking pads are gravel/dirt, short to medium-length straight-ins; excellent tent-pitching possibilities; fireplaces; b-y-o firewood; water at several faucets; restrooms with showers; holding tank disposal station; paved driveways; Big Sur Lodge has cabin rentals and a restaurant (operated by concessionaire); small store and laundry in the park; gas and groceries along the highway; nearest source of complete supplies and services is in Monterey.

Activities & Attractions: Nature trails; hiking trails; fishing; ball field; small nature center; campfire center; the 165,000-acre Ventana Wilderness in Los Padres National Forest, lies just east of the park.

Natural Features: Located on a large, densely forested flat along the Big Sur River and on bordering slopes near the west edge of the Santa Lucia Mountains; park vegetation consists of a wide variety of hardwoods, conifers, including some 1200-year-old redwoods, brush and ferns; some picnic and camp sites are in dense forest, others are in more open sections; the picnic and camp grounds stretch for a mile along the river, picnics on one bank, camps on the other; elevation 200´.

Season, Fees & Phone: Open all year; please see Appendix for reservation information, park entry and campground fees; ☎(408) 667-2315.

Trip Log: Named *El Pais Grande del Sur* by the Spanish, "The Big Country of the South" is just "Big Sur" to everybody now. The dense, rain forest-like environment along the river makes the park appear as if it were actually hundreds of miles to the north—in Northwest California, or even Oregon or Washington. Life in Big Sur is a flashback to the 60's. There probably are more vintage VW bugs and vans, with appropriately attired, suitably hirsute occupants to match, than in any other region in the West, with the possible exception of Boulder, Colorado.

♣ **California 26** ♿

LAGUNA SECA
Monterey County Park

Location: Central California coastal area southeast of Monterey.

Access: From California State Highway 68 at milepost 10 +.9 (7 miles southeast of Monterey, 11 miles southwest of Salinas), turn north onto a steep, winding, paved road and continue for 0.9 mile to the park.

Day Use Facilities: Large picnic area; drinking water; restrooms; large parking lot.

Camping Facilities: 177 campsites, including 110 with partial hookups, in 2 major areas; sites are basically small, with little separation; parking pads are gravel/dirt, mainly short to medium-length straight-ins; most pads will probably require additional leveling; tent-pitching areas are moderately sized, and vary in state of levelness; fire rings; firewood is usually for sale, or b-y-o; water at central faucets and in hookup units; restrooms with showers; holding tank disposal station; paved roadways; complete supplies and services are available in Monterey and Salinas.

Activities & Attractions: Overlooks the Laguna Seca motor sports racetrack; shooting range; nature preserve; sweeping, 360° views from most sites.

Natural Features: Located on a group of hilltops on the west slope of the Coast Range; campground vegetation consists of well-worn grass and some short to medium-height trees; some sites are partially sheltered, most are in the open; surrounded by grass-and-tree-covered hills; elevation 800´.

Season, Fees & Phone: Open all year; $12.00 for a standard site, $17.00 for a partial hookup site; 15 day limit; park office ☎ (408) 755-4899.

Trip Log: If you're a camper and a racing enthusiast, this one's for you. Only a comparatively few world-class courses offer on-premises camping, and this is one of the better ones. Even if you're not a race fan, the magnificent panoramas (especially when the fog either rolls-in or lifts) from this hilltop spot are well worth the stay.

♣ **California 27** ♿

PINNACLES
Pinnacles National Monument

Location: Western California south of Salinas.

Access: From U.S. Highway 101 near milepost 61 at the exit for Soledad/California State Highway 146 (25 miles south of Salinas, 19 miles north of King City), proceed northeasterly on Highway 146 for 1 mile into Soledad; then head southeast (watch for the signs), continuing on Highway 146 for 13 miles as the road gradually winds northeasterly to the Chaparral Ranger Station, picnic area and campground, just beyond. (Note: the last half-dozen miles are steep and curvy and are "not

recommended for cars with trailers".)
Additional Access: From the junction of California State Highways 25 & 146 at a point 16 miles southeast of Paicines, head southwest on Highway 146 for 7 miles to the Bear Gulch Visitor Center and day use areas. (Note that the two main areas are connected by trail only.)

Day Use Facilities: Medium-sized picnic/camp area with shared facilities at Chaparral; small picnic areas, drinking water, restrooms, small parking area at Bear Gulch.

Camping Facilities: *Chaparral Campground*: 18 park 'n walk or walk-in campsites; (group camping is also available, by reservation only); sites are small to medium-sized, fairly level, with nominal separation; parking is in a paved lot; small to medium-sized areas for tents on a sandy surface; b-y-o shade; barbecue grills; charcoal fires only; water at central faucets; restrooms; paved driveway; adequate supplies and services are available in Soledad.

Activities & Attractions: Foot trails cross rugged hills from Chaparral to Bear Gulch and to other areas on the east side of the park (about a two-hour trip).

Natural Features: Located on hilly terrain in the Gabilan Range; sites are unshaded to lightly shaded by a few large hardwoods on a surface of crunchgrass and brush; very rugged surroundings, including spired and cragged rock formations; elevation 1400´.

Season, Fees & Phone: Open all year; camping is limited to Monday through Thursday (i.e., no weekend camping), February to June; $11.00; park headquarters ☎(408) 389-4485.

Trip Log: The Pinnacles are the eroded, last remnants of an ancient volcano. The twisty road up to the park's Chaparral area is more suitable for Volvos and 'Vettes than for Winnebagos and other wonder wagons. February to Memorial Day is the busiest time here. If you're looking for an uncrowded midsummer picnic or camp spot when all of the waterfront parks are overflowing, you might consider Pinnacles' Chaparral area. Summer daytime temps often reach 100°F, but nighttime lows can dip into the 40's. It may be h-o-t, but you'll probably have only the rangers and the rattlers for company.

⚕ **California 28** ⛿

SAN LORENZO
Monterey County Regional Park

Location: Western California south of Salinas.

Access: From U.S. Highway 101 at the Broadway Exit in King City near milepost 41, proceed east for 0.4 mile to the park.

Day Use Facilities: Large picnic area; shelters; drinking water; restrooms; large parking area.

Camping Facilities: 125 assorted campsites, including nearly 100 with partial or full hookups; (a nice group camp area is also available); sites are small to medium-sized, level, with minimal to nominal separation; parking pads are grass, packed gravel, or hard-surfaced, long straight-ins or long parallel pull-throughs; large, sandy pads for tents in standard sites; fire rings or barbecue grills; water at central faucets and at hookup sites; restrooms with showers; holding tank disposal station; paved driveways; adequate+ supplies and services are available in King City.

Activities & Attractions: Agriculture and Rural Life Museum features exhibits of antique farm equipment; day use area; playground.

Natural Features: Located on a large flat in the Salinas River Valley; sites receive very light to light-medium shade from very large hardwoods and some evergreens on watered and mown grass; bordered by agricultural land; the valley is flanked by hills and mountains in the medium distance; elevation 300´.

Season, Fees & Phone: Open all year; $11.00 for a standard site, $15.00 for a partial hookup site, $17.00 for a full hookup site, $1.00 for a pooch; weekly rates available; park office ☎(408) 755-4899.

Trip Log: Good mountain views east and west, particularly west toward the Coast Range. San Lorenzo is probably one of the best freeway stops in the state.

⚕ **California 29** ⛿

BIG BASIN REDWOODS
Big Basin Redwoods State Park

Location: Western California northwest of Santa Cruz.

Access: From California State Highway 236: the northeast park boundary crosses near milepost 13, the southeast boundary is near milepost 7 +.5; visitor center is 9 miles northwest of the city of Boulder Creek. Individual access points: visitor center and a picnic area are at milepost 9 +.3; a paved side road leads north from the visitor center for 0.3 mile to 2 other picnic areas; campground turnoffs are within 0.9 mile south of the visitor center, along either side of the main highway.

Day Use Facilities: 3 medium-sized picnic areas; drinking water; restrooms; small or medium-sized parking lots for picnic areas and trailheads; snack bar and small store.

Camping Facilities: *Standard campsites*: 152 sites in 3 major sections; sites are generally small, with nominal to fairly good separation; parking pads are gravel, short to medium-length straight-ins; most pads in hillside loops will require additional leveling; small to medium+ areas for tents; storage cabinets; fire rings; firewood is usually for sale or b-y-o; water at several faucets; restrooms with showers; holding tank disposal station; paved driveways; (6 trail camps are also available). *Tent cabins*: 36 cabins in the Huckleberry section; cabins are small, woodframed, with wood siding to about 4´ above ground level and all-around window screening; peaked, open-frame roof is covered by canvas, with a storm flap to enclose the screening; 2 bunks with foam pads in each unit (i.e., cozily sleeps four if they're on really good terms); each cabin has a parking pad, table, fire ring, plus a small table and wood stove inside; adequate supplies and services are available in Boulder Creek.

Activities & Attractions: 100 miles of trails for hiking or for hiking/equestrian use; (a detailed brochure/map with contour lines is available); Redwood Nature Trail leads to one of the most impressive stands of redwoods in the park (a guide booklet is available).

Natural Features: Located in a densely forested, deep and steep region of the Santa Cruz Mountains; picnic areas, Sempervirens and Blooms Creek camp areas are located along the creek bottoms, other camp areas are on hillsides; all picnic and camp sites are moderately shaded/sheltered by redwoods and hardwoods; sea level to 1600´ (1000´ at the visitor center).

Season, Fees & Phone: Open all year; please see Appendix for reservation information, park entry and campground fees; ☎(408) 338-6132.

Trip Log: The highway winds through just the southeast corner of the park, so autobound visitors catch only a narrow glimpse of the park's total majesty, but it's still an exceptionally nice drive. But most people who've been here agree that the true way to see the park is to get out onto a trail. Big Basin Redwoods is the grandparent of all California state parks. It was established in 1901 as California Redwood Park in the Big Basin, the first park created by the citizens of California.

 **California** Δ

Northwest Inland

Δ **California 30**

TREE OF HEAVEN
Klamath National Forest

Location: Northern California north of Yreka.

Access: From California State Highway 96 at milepost 99 +.1 (12 miles east of Klamath River, 13 miles north of Yreka), turn south onto a paved, steep access road; proceed down for 0.3 mile to the campground.

Day Use Facilities: None.

Camping Facilities: 21 campsites in 2 loops; sites vary in size, with nominal to fair separation; parking pads are gravel, level, short to medium-length straight-ins; most sites have excellent tent spots; assorted fire appliances; b-y-o firewood is recommended; water at several faucets; vault facilities; paved driveways; gas and groceries in Klamath River; adequate supplies and services are available in Yreka.

Activities & Attractions: River access at a small, hand-launch ramp; floating the Wild and Scenic Klamath River; scenic drive along the river.

Natural Features: Located between the Coast Range and the Cascade Range along the bank of the Klamath River; sites are on a grassy, tree-covered flat along this swiftly flowing river; the Tree of Heaven and other planted hardwoods and big, bushy pines shelter the campground; most sites have a river view; tree-dotted hills border the canyon; summer temperatures reach or exceed 100°F; elevation 2100´.

Season, Fees & Phone: Open all year, with limited services October to April; $8.00; 14 day limit; Oak Knoll Ranger District, Klamath River, ☎(916) 465-2241.

Trip Log: Tree of Heaven, a native of China, commonly came West into the wilderness with resourceful pioneers. Many settlers planted this variety because its rapid growth and coarse foliage made the Tree of Heaven excellent for shade and windbreaks. Prime examples of the large hardwood flourish in the campground area. They help make Tree of Heaven a topnotch forest camp. Camping would be a pleasure in this region no matter what the facilities were like, though. The Klamath River Highway ('96) passes through some of the best country in the West.

⚐ California 31 ⚐

CASTLE CRAGS
Castle Crags State Park

Location: North-central California north of Redding.

Access: From Interstate 5 near milepost 63 +.5 (6 miles south of Dunsmuir, 50 miles north of Redding), turn west onto Castle Creek Road; go 0.3 mile; turn north (right) into the park.

Day Use Facilities: Medium-sized picnic area, drinking water, restrooms and medium-sized parking lot along the river; small picnic area and small parking lot at the vista point.

Camping Facilities: 64 campsites in 3 loops; (3 environmental camps and enroute/overflow sites are also available); sites are small to medium-sized, with fair to fairly good separation; parking pads are paved, short to medium-length straight-ins; many pads will require a strong dose of additional leveling; tent spots are mostly sloped; large, stone fireplaces; firewood is usually for sale, or b-y-o; water at several faucets; restrooms with showers; paved driveways; gas and groceries at the freeway interchange.

Activities & Attractions: Terrific views from the vista point; 18 miles of hiking and equestrian trails, including 7 miles of the Pacific Crest Trail along the base of the Crags; self-guided nature trail; guided nature walks; campfire center for scheduled summer evening programs; trout fishing (said to be good); swimming/wading in the river and in Castle Creek.

Natural Features: Located between the Coast Range and the Cascades a few miles north of the Sacramento Valley, at the base of an unusual geological feature, Castle Crags; another prominent volcanic feature, Mt. Shasta, is clearly visible from points in the park; the Sacramento River flows through a canyon past the day use area and is within a short walk of most campsites; tall pines, oaks and light underbrush predominate; elevation ranges from 2000´ to 6000´.

Season, Fees & Phone: Open all year; please see Appendix for reservation information, park entry and campground fees; ☎(916) 235-2684.

Trip Log: On a reasonably clear day, not only are the comely Castle Crags visible from the vista point, but 14,100 foot Mount Shasta can be viewed in all its glory from the same advantageous perch hundreds of feet above the canyon floor.

⚐ California 32 ⚐

DOUGLAS CITY
Public Lands/BLM Recreation Site

Location: Northwest California west of Redding.

Access: From California State Highway 299 at milepost 57 +.9 (6 miles south of Weaverville, 36 miles west of Redding), turn west onto Steiner Flat Road; follow a well-signed route through Douglas City for 0.5 mile and turn south (left) onto a paved access road; proceed 0.25 mile down to the campground.

Day Use Facilities: None.

Camping Facilities: 19 campsites; sites are mostly medium-sized, with fairly good to very good separation; parking pads are paved, level, medium to long straight-ins; some very nice, level, roomy tent spots; fireplaces; some firewood is usually available for gathering in the area; water at several faucets; flush & vault facilities; paved driveways; gas and groceries in Douglas City; adequate supplies and services are available in Weaverville.

Activities & Attractions: Fishing; floating; beach access; Clair Engle Lake (Trinity Lake) and Lewiston Lake are both within an hour's drive.

Natural Features: Located along the bank of the Trinity River in a deep valley in the Coast Range; campsites are all on a narrow flat within a few yards of the riverbank; tall pines, cedars and considerable underbrush provide very good shelter/separation for the sites; views of the river and surrounding green hills and mountains from many sites; elevation 1600´.

Season, Fees & Phone: May to October; $9.00; 14 day limit; U.S. Bureau of Land Management Redding Resource Area Office ☎(916) 224-2100.

Trip Log: This is not your typical BLM campground. It's one of their super specials. It has water, lots of trees, and, as a bonus, it's just a (paved) mile off the main thoroughfare.

♠ California 33 ♿

OAK BOTTOM
Whiskeytown-Shasta-Trinity
National Recreation Area

Location: Northwest California west of Redding.

Access: From California State Highway 299 at milepost 11 +.4 (10 miles west of Redding, 25 miles east of Douglas City), turn southeast onto the Oak Bottom access road; proceed 1.1 miles to the recreation area.

Day Use Facilities: Large picnic area; drinking water; restrooms; large parking lot.

Camping Facilities: 100 tent campsites and 50 rv sites; spaces in the rv lot are paved, mostly level, with zilch separation, adequate for long vehicles; tent sites are all park 'n walk units, small, with nominal separation; tent spots are a bit sloped, and most are on bare earth; fireplaces; b-y-o firewood is recommended; restrooms; (freshwater rinse showers are available near the swimming beach); holding tank disposal station in the rv lot; paved driveways; complete supplies and services are available in Redding.

Activities & Attractions: Boating; boat launch; marina near the rv lot; sailing; fishing for trout and salmon; swimming; gold-panning; hiking and jogging trails; ranger-guided interpretive activities; visitor center, 5 miles east; Shasta State Historic Park, 7 miles east.

Natural Features: Located on the northwest shore of Whiskeytown Lake on the east edge of the Coast Range; tent sites are situated on a series of small hills overlooking the lake; tent campground vegetation consists of a variety of scattered trees and small bushes; a number of sites have views of the lake through the trees; tall peaks of the Trinity Mountains rise to the west; the lake is virtually surrounded by green hills and mountains; elevation 1200´.

Season, Fees & Phone: Open all year, with limited services September to May; $10.00 for an rv spot, $12.00 for a tent site; 14 day limit; please see Appendix for reservation information; Whiskeytown Unit Headquarters ☎(916) 241-6584.

Trip Log: Lots of people come to Whiskeytown for water recreation, and, possibly, because of its colorful history. Unlike the other three lakes that make up this national rec area, Whiskeytown is maintained at a stable level in summer. Also unlike the other units in the nra operated by the Forest Service, this one is run by the National Park Service. You can tell.

♠ California 34 ♿

ANTLERS
Whiskeytown-Shasta-Trinity
National Recreation Area

Location: North-central California north of Redding.

Access: From Interstate 5 at milepost 41, at the Lakeshore Drive-Antlers Road Exit, (26 miles north of Redding, 29 miles south of Dunsmuir), turn south onto Antlers Road (parallels the Interstate on the east); proceed south, east and north for 0.7 mile; turn east (right) into the campground.

Day Use Facilities: Small picnic area, drinking water, restrooms, and medium-sized parking area, nearby.

Camping Facilities: 59 campsites, including 18 multiple-occupancy units, in 2 loops, plus overflow sites; sites are medium to large with good to excellent separation; parking pads are level, paved, medium to long straight-ins; some excellent tent spots; fire rings; firewood is usually available for gathering in the surrounding area; water at several faucets; restrooms, plus auxiliary vaults; gas and groceries at the Lakeshore exit; complete supplies and services are available in Redding.

Activities & Attractions: Boating; boat launch nearby; fishing; amphitheater for scheduled interpretive programs; many remote areas of Shasta Lake are accessible only by boat.

Natural Features: Located between the Coast Range and the Cascade Range near the north end of Shasta Lake, on the Sacramento River Arm; the lake was created in 1948 by the damming of the Sacramento, McCloud, and Pit Rivers; moderately dense forest of tall pines, oaks and manzanitas; elevation 1100´.

Season, Fees & Phone: Open all year, with limited services in winter; $10.00 for a single site, $14.00 for a multiple site; 14 day limit; Forest Service Information Center ☎(916) 275-1587.

Trip Log: When all factors are considered, Antlers is perhaps one of the best public campgrounds in this area. Sites here are comfortable and private, a boat ramp is nearby for lake access, commercial outlets for basic supplies are within a few miles, and access from I-5 is quite easy. Because of the possibilities of deep drawdown in order to fulfill Shasta's irrigation and electrical power responsibilities, best times of the year for taking full advantage of its recreational opportunities are spring and early summer. If you're planning on boating, particularly in the upper reaches of the lake, it might be helpful to request a 'tide table' from the information center.

♠ California 35

BAILEY CANYON
Six Rivers National Forest

Location: Northwest California southwest of Weaverville.

Access: From California State Highway 36 at milepost 3 +.3 (2 miles east of the settlement of Mad River, 20 miles west of the junction of State Highways 36 & 3 east of Forest Glen), proceed southeast on Lower Mad River Road (paved) for 11 miles; turn south (right) and go down 0.1 mile to the campground.

Day Use Facilities: Small picnic area, drinking water, vault facilities, and medium-sized parking area, 3 miles east.

Camping Facilities: 25 campsites; sites are small to small+, with nominal separation; parking pads are gravel, primarily short straight-ins, plus a few medium-length straight-ins; additional leveling will be needed on most pads; medium to large tent areas, though most are sloped; fire rings; b-y-o firewood; water at several faucets; vault facilities; paved driveway; gas and camper supplies at the marina, 2 miles west, and in Mad River.

(Camping is also available on weekends at Fir Cove Campground, 0.5 mile west.)

Activities & Attractions: Fishing for trout, large and small mouth bass, crappie; boating; carry-in boat launching at the beach; public boat launch and docks at Sheriffs Cove, 4 miles west.

Natural Features: Located in a deep ravine on a steep slope above the north shore of Ruth Lake in the Coast Range; sites are very well sheltered by tall conifers and scattered hardwoods; a seasonal stream flows down through the campground; sandy gravel beach; the reservoir is bordered by the high, miles-long ridges; elevation 2700´.

Season, Fees & Phone: May to October; $6.00; 14 day limit; Mad River Ranger District ☎(707) 574-6233.

Trip Log: Excellent panoramas from the camp's beach as well as from along the main road. The lake's brilliant turquoise waters beautifully complement the deep green blanket on Mad River Ridge that rises as much as a thousand feet above the opposite shore.

 California ♠
Northeast Inland

♠ California 36

HEMLOCK
Medicine Lake/Modoc National Forest

Location: Northeast California northwest of Alturas, southwest of Lava Beds National Monument.

Access: From California State Highway 89 at milepost 8 (1 mile east of Bartle, 16 miles east of McCloud), turn north onto Forest Road 15; travel northerly for 4.5 miles to a major 3-way intersection; turn northeasterly (right) onto Forest Road 49 and head northeast for 26.5 miles to the Medicine Lake Recreation Area turnoff; turn westerly (left) onto the recreation area road and proceed 0.3 mile to a 'T'; turn south (left) and go 0.2 mile to the day use area; or turn northwest (right), proceed 0.15 mile, then turn south (left) into the campground.

Alternate Access: From California State Highway 139 at milepost 27 +.9 (28 miles northwest of Canby, 24 miles south of Tulelake), turn west onto Tionesta Road/Forest Road 97; head generally southwesterly on Forest Road 97 for 24 miles to a major 'T' intersection; turn north (right) onto Forest Road 49 and proceed 1.6 miles to the Medicine Lake Recreation Area turnoff and continue as above. (All roads via either of the two principal routes to the recreation area are paved.)

Day Use Facilities: Large picnic area; drinking water; vault facilities; large parking lot.

Camping Facilities: 19 campsites; sites are small, quite sloped, with nominal separation; parking pads are gravel, medium-length straight-ins; small to medium-sized tent areas; fire rings and some barbecue grills; b-y-o firewood, or pick up some wood on forest lands on the way in; water at central faucets; vault facilities; paved driveway; camper supplies are in Tionesta, 22 miles east; limited+ supplies and services are available in Tulelake, 51 miles northeast or McCloud, 46 miles southwest.

(A.H. Hogue Campground, very similar in size, surroundings and facilities, is located just west of Hemlock Campground.)

Activities & Attractions: Designated swimming beach in the day use area; fishing for stocked trout; limited boating (see posted speed limits at the boat ramp); hiking trail.

Natural Features: Located along the shores of Medicine Lake; day use area is on the east shore; campground is on a steep slope above the northeast shore; picnic sites are very lightly shaded; campsites receive medium shelter from tall conifers; several nice campsites are on a shoreline shelf; the lake is rimmed by the forested hills and low mountains of the Medicine Lake Highlands; elevation 6700´.

Season, Fees & Phone: June to October; $7.00; 15 day limit; Doublehead Ranger District, Tulelake, ☎(916) 667-2246.

Trip Log: Medicine Lake is in the center of a *caldera*, the "cauldron" or crater, as it were, of an extinct volcano. The lake covers about a square mile, and has been measured to a depth of 150 feet, but it may be deeper. Although it has no known outlets, the lake level remains constant, and its water is clear and cold. It is likely that subterranean passages through the lava flow carry away excess water which would normally flow through an outlet stream on any other lake. You don't have to be a camper to enjoy this recreation area. The large picnic ground is just above the long, sandy swimming beach. You can watch your kids dip into the lake's cool waters or curl their toes in the warm sand. Fishing is said to be good either from the shore or from a boat. Rainbow and brook trout are regularly stocked throughout the summer.

🔺 **California 37**

MEDICINE
Medicine Lake/Modoc National Forest

Location: Northeast California northwest of Alturas, southwest of Lava Beds National Monument.

Access: From California State Highway 89 at milepost 8 (1 mile east of Bartle, 16 miles east of McCloud), turn north onto Forest Road 15; travel northerly for 4.5 miles to a major 3-way intersection; turn northeasterly (right) onto Forest Road 49 and head northeast for 26.5 miles to the Medicine Lake Recreation Area turnoff; turn westerly (left) onto the recreation area road and proceed 0.3 mile to a 'T'; turn northwest (right), go 0.6 mile, then turn south (left) into the campground. **Alternate Access:** (See the *Alternate Access* for Hemlock Campground, above.)

Day Use Facilities: Large picnic area, drinking water, vault facilities; large parking area, nearby; (see *Hemlock* information).

Camping Facilities: 22 campsites; sites are small+, level, with nominal separation; parking pads are gravel, medium-length straight-ins; medium to large tent spots; fire rings and many barbecue grills; b-y-o firewood is suggested, or gather firewood on forest lands before reaching the recreation area; water at several faucets; vault facilities; paved driveway; nearest camper supplies are in Tionesta, 22 miles east; limited+ to adequate supplies and services are available in Tulelake, 51 miles northeast or McCloud, 46 miles southwest.

Activities & Attractions: Sandy swimming beach, 0.8 mile east; fishing for stocked trout; limited boating (see posted speed limits at the boat ramp); hiking trail.

Natural Features: Located on a flat on the middle north shore of Medicine Lake; campsites receive medium shelter from tall conifers; a wide beach borders the lakeside edge of the campground; the lake is in a basin encircled by the timber-cloaked hills and low mountains of the Medicine Lake Highlands; elevation 6700´.

Season, Fees & Phone: June to October; $7.00; 15 day limit; Doublehead Ranger District, Tulelake, ☎(916) 667-2246.

Trip Log: Medicine Lake was formerly the site of a centuries-old Modoc summer village. The lake's pristine location and its crystal-clear waters were held in high spiritual respect as well as aesthetic esteem by the Modocs. Solemn "medicine" ceremonies took place along its shore. The hundreds of square miles of lava fields throughout this vast region were "The land of mountains of glass and rocks that float on water".

🔺 **California 38** ♿

LAVA BEDS
Lava Beds National Monument

Location: Northeast California northwest of Alturas.

Access: From California State Highway 139 at milepost 27+.9 (28 miles northwest of the intersection of Highways 139 and 299 near Canby, 28 miles southeast of the California-Oregon border), turn westerly onto County Road 97/Forest Road 97 (paved) and proceed 2.5 miles; turn north onto Lava Beds National Monument Road/Forest Road 10 (paved), and travel 14 miles to the visitor center and the campground turnoff (opposite the center).

Alternate Access: From California State Highway 139 at a point 2 miles northwest of Newell, 7 miles southeast of the California-Oregon border, head south, west, then south again on Forest Road 10 (paved) for 21 miles to the visitor center. (Note: The *Access* is best if you're northbound on '139 from Alturas and other points south; the *Alternate Access* works well if you're inbound from Oregon and also like roundabout, but scenic, drives.)

Day Use Facilities: Medium-sized picnic area; drinking water; restrooms; large parking area.

Camping Facilities: *Indian Well Campground*: 42 campsites; sites are about average in size, with little to some separation; parking pads are paved, mostly level, short to medium-length straight-ins or pull-offs; tent areas are small to medium sized, and somewhat level; fireplaces, plus many barbecue grills; b-y-o firewood; water at several faucets; restrooms; paved driveways; gas and groceries are available on County Road 97.

Activities & Attractions: Lava cave exploration, either self-guided or ranger-guided; outdoor nature walks; 35 miles of scenic drives; amphitheater for evening programs.

Natural Features: Located on hilly or rolling terrain amid dozens of square miles of lava fields; campground is on a slightly sloping, rocky sage flat (or is it a mostly flat, rocky, sage slope?); the visitor center and campground overlook a vast valley-basin to the northeast; a sparse population of junipers/cedars provides some shade and shelter; the region is dotted with cinder cones; elevation 4500´.

Season, Fees & Phone: Open all year, with limited services mid-September to May; $8.00; 14 day limit; Lava Beds National Monument Headquarters ☎(916) 667-2282.

Trip Log: This is an intriguing, off-the-beaten-path park. The regional landscape isn't quite as starkly forbidding as the name suggests, (but close). The campground rarely fills. Bring warm clothing, even in midsummer. Also bring a flashlight, good shoes, and a water bottle if you're planning to take the underground tour.

♣ California 39 ♿

BLUE LAKE
Modoc National Forest

Location: Northeast California southeast of Alturas.

Access: From U.S. Highway 395 in midtown Likely (18 miles south of Alturas), head east onto Jess Valley Road (Forest Road 64/Modoc County Road 64, paved) for 9.5 miles to a major fork; bear southerly (right), continuing on Forest Road 64 for another 6.7 miles south and east (to the end of the pavement); turn southerly onto the recreation area access road (paved, 1-lane in sections) and go 1 mile to the day use turnoff, then along the east end of the lake) for another 0.5 mile to the campground.

Day Use Facilities: Drinking water; vault facilities; small parking lot.

Camping Facilities: 48 campsites; sites are small+ to medium sized, with nominal to fair separation; parking pads are gravel, short to medium-length straight-ins; additional leveling will be needed on most pads; large tent spots, but most are a bit sloped; fire rings; some firewood may be available for gathering in the surrounding area, b-y-o is suggested; water at several faucets; vault facilities; paved driveways; gas and groceries in Likely, adequate supplies and services are available in Alturas.

Activities & Attractions: Blue Lake National Recreation Trail (foot travel); trout fishing; limited boating; boat ramp; small dock; handicapped-access fishing pier.

Natural Features: Located on the shore of Blue Lake in the south Warner Mountains; day use area is along the north shore, campground is on a hillside above the south shore; campsites are lightly to moderately shaded by tall conifers; a large open meadow borders the campground on the southeast; the 260-acre lake is in a basin encircled by timbered slopes; elevation 6000´.

Season, Fees & Phone: May to November; $7.00; 14 day limit; Warner Mountain Ranger District, Cedarville, ☎(916) 279-6116.

Trip Log: Nice little lake. The well-shaded Blue Lake Trail skirts the west shore of the lake and winds 1.5 miles between the day use and camp areas. Most days you'll see more deer tracks than people prints on the trail. Some campsites are on a narrow shelf overlooking the timbered lake shore. Big chunks of igneous (lava) rocks are scattered around the hillside.

♣ California 40 ♿

EAGLE
Eagle Lake/Lassen National Forest

Location: Northeast California northwest of Susanville.

Access: From California State Highway 36 at milepost 21 (3 miles west of Susanville, 2.8 miles east of the junction of State Highways 36 & 44), turn north onto Eagle Lake Road/Lassen County Road A1 (paved) and proceed 13.4 miles to an intersection right by the California Department of Forestry fire station; turn east (right) onto a paved road (Road 231) and continue for 0.75 mile to recreation area. (Access is also possible from the north, around the west side of Eagle Lake, from California State Highway 139.)

Day Use Facilities: Large picnic area; drinking water; restrooms; large parking lot.

Camping Facilities: 50 campsites; sites are small to medium+ in size, level, with minimal separation; parking pads are paved, medium to long straight-ins; excellent tent spots; gathering of firewood prior to arrival from local forest lands, or b-y-o is recommended; water at several faucets; restrooms; holding tank disposal station 1 mile west at Merrill Campground; paved driveways; security patrols; camper supplies at the marina, 0.5 mile east; adequate+ supplies and services are available in Susanville.

Activities & Attractions: Boating; boat launch; marina nearby; fishing for the elusive Eagle Lake trout.

Natural Features: Located on a flat near the south shore of Eagle Lake; vegetation consists primarily of medium-dense, very tall conifers on a surface of grass and evergreen needles; forested hills and low mountains surround the lake; elevation 5100´.

Season, Fees & Phone: May to October; $13.00-$17.00; 14 day limit; Eagle Lake Ranger District, Susanville, ☎(916) 257-2151.

Trip Log: Eagle Lake has a well-deserved, and also widespread, reputation for excellent scenery, boating and fishing. Consequently, weekend sites are typically reserved well in advance. If this campground is full (likely), campsites may be available at Christie Campground, 4 miles northwest, or at 20-site Aspen Grove Campground, 0.3 mile east.

♣ California 41 ♿

MERRILL
Eagle Lake/Lassen National Forest

Location: Northeast California northwest of Susanville.

Access: From California State Highway 36 at milepost 21 (3 miles west of Susanville, 2.8 miles east of the intersection of State Highways 36 and 44), turn north onto Eagle Lake Road/Lassen County Road A1 (paved) and travel 14.3 miles to milepost 14 +.3; turn northeast (right) into the campground.

Day Use Facilities: None.

Camping Facilities: 182 campsites in 5 loops; sites are small to average in size, essentially level, with minimal separation; parking pads are earth/gravel, medium-length straight-ins; some pads may require additional leveling; medium to large tent areas; fire rings; some firewood may be available for gathering in the surrounding area; gathering firewood prior to arrival, or b-y-o, is suggested; water at several faucets; restrooms; holding tank disposal station; paved driveways; security patrols; camper supplies at the marina, 2 miles east; adequate+ supplies and services are available in Susanville.

Activities & Attractions: Boating; fishing for Eagle Lake trout; amphitheater.

Natural Features: Located on the south shore of Eagle Lake; campground vegetation primarily consists of grass, and medium-dense, very tall conifers; the lake is surrounded by forested hills and low mountains; elevation 5100´.

Season, Fees & Phone: May to October; $13.00-$17.00; 14 day limit; Eagle Lake Ranger District, Susanville, ☎(916) 257-2151.

Trip Log: This campground might almost remind you of many oceanside campgrounds. Most of the sites are tucked in among the trees, but there is a line of sites situated along an open, grass and gravel beach. (For the price of admission, maybe they also host an afternoon hospitality hour. Ed.)

♣ California 42 ♿

CHRISTIE
Eagle Lake/Lassen National Forest

Location: Northeast California northwest of Susanville.

Access: From California State Highway 36 at milepost 21 (3 miles west of Susanville, 2.8

miles east of the junction of State Highways 36 and 44), turn north onto Eagle Lake Road/Lassen County Road A1 (paved) and proceed 16.5 miles to the campground (at milepost 16 +.5). (Access is also possible from the north, from California State Highway 139, via Eagle Lake Road.)

Day Use Facilities: None.

Camping Facilities: 69 campsites in 3 loops; sites are medium-sized, level, with some separation; parking pads are paved, medium to long straight-ins or pull-throughs; large tent areas; fire rings; some firewood may be available for gathering in the surrounding area; gathering firewood prior to arrival, or b-y-o, is suggested; water at several faucets; restrooms; holding tank disposal station at Merrill Campground, 2 miles southeast; paved driveways; camper supplies at the marina, 3 miles east; adequate+ supplies and services are available in Susanville.

Activities & Attractions: Boating; fishing; activities such as junior ranger programs may be scheduled.

Natural Features: Located on the southwest shore of Eagle Lake; campground vegetation consists of medium-dense, medium to tall conifers on a needle-covered, reddish earth, forest floor; forested hills and low mountains surround the lake; elevation 5100´.

Season, Fees & Phone: May to October; $12.00-$16.00; 14 day limit; Eagle Lake Ranger District, Susanville, ☎(916) 257-2151.

Trip Log: A few campsites have views of the lake through the forest, but it's only a short walk from any of the sites to the shoreline. It costs a bit less to camp at Christie than at the other forest camps near here.

⋀ California 43 ♿

MCARTHUR-BURNEY FALLS

McArthur Burney Falls Memorial State Park

Location: Northeast California northeast of Redding.

Access: From California State Highway 89 at milepost 27 +.55 (5.8 miles north of the junction of State Highways 89 and 299 near Burney, 52 miles southeast of the junction of Highway 89 and Interstate 5 near Dunsmuir), turn north/west; proceed 0.1 mile to the park.

Day Use Facilities: Small picnic areas; drinking water; restrooms nearby; several medium-sized parking lots; concession stand.

Camping Facilities: 118 campsites in 2 sections; (a small environmental/walk-in camp is also available); overall, sites are medium to large, essentially level, with fair to good separation; parking pads are paved or earth/gravel, short to medium-length straight-ins, many are extra wide; large tent areas; storage cabinets; fireplaces or fire rings; b-y-o firewood; water at several faucets; restrooms with showers; holding tank disposal station; paved driveways; gas and groceries 1 mile south.

Activities & Attractions: Hiking trails, including a 1-mile Falls Trail and a 1.5-mile Rim Trail from the falls/camping area to Lake Britton; amphitheater for evening campfire programs; museum; fishing for warm water species, boating, boat launch and sandy beach at Lake Britton; good to excellent trout fishing in local streams, especially wide, deep, fast, beautiful (and world-famous) Hat Creek.

Natural Features: Located on a large, forested flat along the rim of Burney Creek Gorge, at the southern end of the Cascade Range; Burney Falls is within the gorge; picnic and camp sites are sheltered/shaded by moderately dense, tall conifers and some smaller hardwoods; elevation 3000´.

Season, Fees & Phone: Open all year; please see Appendix for reservation information, park entry and campground fees; ☎(916) 335-2777.

Trip Log: A fascinating feature of the falls, which is the focal point of the park, is that its water supply originates in an aquifer (underground lake), and the falls flows all year, even when the creek is bone dry a half-mile upstream. Because it is some distance from Northern California's major metro areas, and because of its cool (but relatively dry) weather during much of the year, the park doesn't see a lot of use except in summer. But both spring and fall are superb times to visit here.

⋀ California 44

BRIDGE

Hat Creek/Lassen National Forest

Location: Northeast California north of Lassen Volcanic National Park.

Access: From California State Highway 89 at milepost 4 (4 miles north of the junction of State Highways 89 & 44 near Old Station, 19 miles north of Lassen Park, 18 miles south of the junction of State Highways 89 & 299 near Burney), turn west into the campground.

Day Use Facilities: None.

Camping Facilities: 25 campsites; sites are medium to large, essentially level, with fair to very good separation; parking pads are paved, medium to long straight-ins, plus a couple of pull-throughs; large tent areas; fire rings and barbecue grills; some firewood is available for gathering in the area; gathering firewood on nearby forest lands prior to arrival, or b-y-o, is suggested; water at several faucets; vault facilities; paved driveways; gas and groceries are available 5 miles south.

Activities & Attractions: Hat Creek Trail; trout fishing; self-guided exploration of Subway Cave, 4 miles south (free).

Natural Features: Located on a slightly rolling flat along Hat Creek; vegetation consists primarily of medium-dense, tall conifers, plus small timber and small hardwoods; surrounding terrain is comprised of partially timbered hills and low mountains; excellent views of distant Mount Shasta from near the campground; situated on a major lava bed; elevation 4000´.

Season, Fees & Phone: May to October; $10.00; 14 day limit; Hat Creek Ranger District, Fall River Mills, ☎(916) 336-5521.

Trip Log: As it flows past this campground, Hat Creek is a beautiful, deep, clear, swiftly moving stream in summer. In terms of environment, Bridge is probably near the top of the list of campgrounds along this highway.

♣ California 45 ♿

CAVE
Hat Creek/Lassen National Forest

Location: Northeast California north of Lassen Volcanic National Park.

Access: From California State Highway 89 at a point 0.3 mile north of the junction of State Highways 89 & 44 near Old Station (15 miles north of Lassen Park, 22 miles south of the junction of State Highways 89 & 299 near Burney), turn east into the day use area or west into the campground.

Day Use Facilities: Small picnic area; drinking water; restrooms; medium-sized parking lot.

Camping Facilities: 46 campsites in 2 areas; sites are small to medium-sized, basically level, with fair to good separation; parking pads are paved, medium to long, straight-ins; excellent tent-pitching opportunities; fire rings and barbecue grills; gathering firewood on nearby

forest lands prior to arrival, or b-y-o, is recommended; water at several faucets; restrooms; paved driveways; gas and groceries are available less than a mile south.

Activities & Attractions: Self-guided venturing into Subway Cave, accessed from the day use area; trout fishing on Hat Creek; handicapped-access fishing platform; foot bridge across the creek.

Natural Features: Located in a valley on a flat along and near Hat Creek; light to medium-dense, tall conifers provide adequate shelter and shade for most sites; surrounding terrain is comprised of partially timbered hills and low mountains; situated on a major lava bed; elevation 4200´.

Season, Fees & Phone: May to October; $10.00; 14 day limit; Hat Creek Ranger District, Fall River Mills, ☎(916) 336-5521.

Trip Log: Subway Cave, a lava tube with a trail about a third of a mile long, is certainly worth looking into (so to speak), as long as you're not claustrophobic. (Parents and kids have a particularly good time exploring the tunnel—especially when the leader douses the flashlight!) The campground is larger than it looks from the entrance. It might pay to thoroughly check it out before checking-in, since the limits extend to nearly 0.4 mile south of the gate.

♣ California 46 ♿

HAT CREEK
Hat Creek/Lassen National Forest

Location: Northeast California north of Lassen Volcanic National Park.

Access: From California State Highway 89 at milepost 61 +.1 (1.4 miles south of the junction of State Highways 89 & 44 near Old Station, 14 miles north of Lassen National Park), turn west into the campground.

Day Use Facilities: Small parking area.

Camping Facilities: 55 campsites; sites are medium-sized, with minimal to fair separation; parking pads are paved, medium-length, reasonably level, straight-ins; good tent areas; fire rings, plus some barbecue grills; limited firewood is available for gathering in the general vicinity; firewood-gathering prior to arrival, or b-y-o, is suggested; water at several faucets; restrooms, plus auxiliary vaults; holding tank disposal station at a day use facility across the highway; paved driveways; gas and groceries within 1.5 miles, north and south.

Activities & Attractions: Trout fishing; handicapped access fishing platform; foot bridge across the creek; Spatter Cone Nature Trail (1.5 miles) passes volcanic features; Subway Cave, (national forest site, no charge) 2 miles north.

Natural Features: Located on a sloping, rolling flat in light forest of short to medium-tall pines; the campground area is dotted with lava rock; Hat Creek flows along the western perimeter of the campground; low, partially timbered hills lie in the surrounding area; elevation 4400´.

Season, Fees & Phone: May to October; $10.00; 14 day limit; Hat Creek Ranger District, Fall River Mills, ☎(916) 336-5521.

Trip Log: Excellent access to the campground's namesake, a world famous trout stream. This area is believed to be the origin of a massive lava flow that spread northward through Hat Creek Valley for more than 20 miles. The fiery event took place in geologically modern times, less than two millennia ago.

⚕ California 47 ♿

MANZANITA LAKE
Lassen Volcanic National Park

Location: Northeast California at the northwest corner of Lassen Volcanic National Park.

Access: From California State Highway 89 (the main park road) at a point 0.55 mile from the northwest entrance station and 29 miles from the southwest entrance station, turn south onto a paved access road and proceed 0.45 mile to the campground.

Day Use Facilities: Small picnic area, drinking water, restrooms, small parking area, nearby.

Camping Facilities: 181 campsites in 4 loops; sites are small to medium in size, with fair to good separation; parking pads are gravel/sand, mostly short to medium-length straight-ins or pull-throughs; many pads may require some additional leveling; tent areas are generally medium-sized, but many are large, and most are tolerably level; fire rings; firewood is usually for sale, or b-y-o; water at several faucets; restrooms; holding tank disposal station; paved driveways; ranger station; gas, groceries, ice and showers are available at nearby stores.

Activities & Attractions: Several trails; amphitheater for evening campfire programs; limited boating.

Natural Features: Located on the slightly sloping shore of Manzanita Lake, (but no lake views from campsites); campground vegetation consists primarily of light to medium-dense, tall conifers and manzanitas; a good-sized stream flows near the campground area; bordered by high mountains; elevation 5900´.

Season, Fees & Phone: Late-May to mid-September; $11.00; 14 day limit; park headquarters ☎(916) 595-4444.

Trip Log: You'll find some good shots of Lassen Peak from the campground area. Many campsites are actually quite spacious (by national park standards). The other camp in the park's northwest corner, Crags Campground, five miles northeast and just off the main park road, is open during peak periods.

⚕ California 48 ♿

SUMMIT LAKE
Lassen Volcanic National Park

Location: Northeast California near the center of Lassen Volcanic National Park.

Access: From California State Highway 89 (the main park road) at a point 12.5 miles southeast of the northwest entrance station and 16 miles northeast of the southwest entrance station, turn east into the North or South units, 0.15 mile apart.

Day Use Facilities: Small picnic area; drinking water; restrooms; small parking area.

Camping Facilities: 49 campsites in the North unit and 52 campsites in the South unit; sites are rather small, with minimal to fair separation; parking pads are paved, short to medium-length straight-ins or pull-throughs; adequate space for a medium-sized tent in most sites; fire rings; b-y-o firewood; water at several faucets; restrooms in the North unit, vault facilities in the South unit; gas and groceries are available at Manzanita Lake, 12 miles northwest.

Activities & Attractions: Trails; motorless boating; amphitheater.

Natural Features: Located along the lake shore (picnic area) and on slightly hilly terrain near the north and south shores (campground) of small Summit Lake in the Cascade Range; vegetation consists of light to medium-dense conifers, and very little grass or underbrush; timbered hills and mountains in the surrounding area; elevation 6800´.

Season, Fees & Phone: Late-May to mid-September; $11.00 in the North unit, $9.00 in the South unit; 14 day limit; park headquarters ☎(916) 595-4444.

Trip Log: All picnic sites and some campsites have lake views, a few more in the North unit than in the South unit. But the view from the south end may be a little more interesting. It probably would be a good idea to check both sides before settling in. Because of its popularity (it's a nice lake), this recreation site is a bit frayed around the edges.

⚘ California 49 ♿

SOUTHWEST
Lassen Volcanic National Park

Location: Northeast California at the southwest corner of Lassen Volcanic National Park.

Access: From California State Highway 89 (the main park road) at a point 0.1 mile north of the park's southwest entrance station and 30 miles south of the northwest entrance station, turn east into the campground.

Day Use Facilities: Small picnic and parking area.

Camping Facilities: 21 park 'n walk campsites; sites are small, with nominal to fair separation; enough space for a small tent on a sloped surface; paved parking is available nearby; paved walkways to the sites from the parking area; water at central faucets; restrooms; gas and groceries in Mineral, 10 miles south.

Activities & Attractions: Good views of Lassen Peak and its surroundings.

Natural Features: Located on a boulder-strewn hillside above a ravine near the southern tip of the Cascade Range; sites are lightly sheltered-shaded by tall conifers; elevation 6000´.

Season, Fees & Phone: Late-May to mid-September; $9.00; 14 day limit; park headquarters ☎(916) 595-4444.

Trip Log: For a campsite with fewer neighbors than you'll have in the other areas along the park's main road, check out this one if you're a tent camper. Southwest has also been known as Sulphur Works, after a local geological feature. Good mountain views here. This and the foregoing two sections describe the major developed visitor areas in the park. In addition to these recreation sites along the main park road, two other park camps are available in the boonies. Juniper Lake in the southeast corner of

the park, and Warner Valley in the south-central area, are small tent camps accessed from State Highway 89 in Chester. From Chester head north for 13 miles on Juniper Lake Road, or 17 miles via Chester-Warner Valley Road, respectively, to the small, primitive camps.

⚘ California 50

ALMANOR
Lake Almanor/Lassen National Forest

Location: Northeast California southeast of Lassen Volcanic National Park.

Access: From California State Highway 89 at milepost 36 +.7 (10 miles southeast of Chester, 17 miles northwest of Greenville, directly opposite the Almanor Rest Area), turn north onto a paved access road and proceed 0.75 mile to the South unit, or 0.1 mile farther to the North unit.

Day Use Facilities: Small picnic area, drinking water, restrooms, medium-sized parking lot in the highway rest area.

Camping Facilities: 52 campsites in the South unit, 49 campsites in the North unit; sites are medium to large, with fair to good separation; parking pads are paved or gravel, short to long straight-ins; most pads are level or nearly so; good to excellent tent-pitching possibilities; fire rings; some firewood is available for gathering in the vicinity; water at several faucets; vault facilities; paved driveways; gas and groceries in Almanor, 0.5 mile, or Canyon Dam, 7 miles southeast; limited to adequate supplies and services are available in Chester or Greenville.

Activities & Attractions: Fishing; boating; boat launch; amphitheater.

Natural Features: Located on level to slightly rolling terrain within walking distance of the southwest shore of Lake Almanor; vegetation consists of tall grass, tall pines and light underbrush; some sites are in the open, others are sheltered; the lake area is surrounded by forested hills and mountains; elevation 4500´.

Season, Fees & Phone: May to October; $9.00; 14 day limit; Almanor Ranger District, Chester, ☎(916) 258-2141.

Trip Log: Ahhh, this is a nice place to camp. A little busy, perhaps, but still nice. The campground covers a huge area. Although there are beaten paths throughout the camp, it's satisfying to just wander through the tall grass. Incidentally, the softly aristocratic name for the lake was derived from the names of Alice

Martha and Eleanor Earl, the daughters of Guy Earl, an early pioneer.

⚑ California 51 ♿

LONG POINT
Antelope Lake/Lassen National Forest

Location: Northeast California south of Susanville.

Access: From U.S. Highway 395 at milepost 52 +.7 in Janesville (13 miles south of Susanville, 11 miles north of Milford), turn west onto Janesville Grade (Lassen County Road 208, winding, with some *very* steep sections); proceed 14.5 miles to a 3-way intersection; turn northwesterly (right) onto Forest Road 03 and continue for another 1.7 miles to a 'T' intersection; turn northerly (right) onto Forest Road 53 and go 0.7 mile; turn west (left) onto the campground access road for a final 0.7 mile to the campground. (Note: All roads are paved; allow about 45 minutes to reach the camp from the main highway, more if you're driving a large outfit; road signs state that Janesville Grade is "impassable in inclement weather".)

Day Use Facilities: Small picnic area, drinking water, vault facilities, small parking lot, 2 miles west along the lake's north shore.

Camping Facilities: 38 campsites, including many double units; (a nearby group camp area is also available); sites are small+ to medium-sized, with nominal separation; parking pads are paved, medium-length straight-ins, plus some long pull-throughs; additional leveling will be needed on many pads; medium to large areas for tents, though most are somewhat sloped; fire rings; b-y-o firewood; water at several faucets; vault facilities; (holding tank disposal station at the Boulder Creek Ranger Station, 5 miles northwest); paved driveways; complete supplies and services are available in Susanville.

Activities & Attractions: Boating; boat launch, 2 miles northwest; fishing; handicapped-access fishing area.

Natural Features: Located on hilly terrain on a point of land extending from the southeast shore of Antelope Lake; campsites receive medium to dense shelter from tall conifers; the lake is bordered by the wooded hills and low mountains of the northern tip of the Sierra Nevada; elevation 5000´.

Season, Fees & Phone: $12.00 for a standard site, $14.00 for a "prime lakeside" unit; April to November; 14 day limit; (all campsites must have someone 18 years or older to register);

Mount Hough Ranger District, Quincy, ☎(916) 283-0555.

Trip Log: Families with lots of children seem to favor Long Point, so it would be prudent to cruise the loop extra carefully while looking for a campsite. When you first see the timbered setting here, you may wonder how Antelope Lake was named, since this mile-high mountain valley environment looks much more like prime elk habitat than it does antelope country. According to local legend, a small band of 'lost' antelope were seen in the valley by explorers long before the lake was formed. Antelope Valley, Antelope Creek and Little Antelope Creek, all on the east side of the present lake, were thus named for the sprightly open plains critters.

⚑ California 52

LONE ROCK
Antelope Lake/Lassen National Forest

Location: Northeast California south of Susanville.

Access: From U.S. Highway 395 at milepost 52 +.7 in Janesville (13 miles south of Susanville, 11 miles north of Milford), turn west onto Janesville Grade (Lassen County Road 208, winding, with some *very* steep sections); travel 14.5 miles to a 3-way intersection; turn northwesterly (right) onto Forest Road 03 and continue for another 1.7 miles to a 'T' intersection; turn northerly (right) onto Forest Road 53 and follow the lake loop road around the north side of the lake for 5.7 miles (to the Boulder Creek Ranger Station); turn southeast (left) onto the campground access road for 0.15 mile to a fork; take the left fork for 0.15 mile to the campground.

Day Use Facilities: Small picnic area, drinking water, vault facilities, small parking lot, 4 miles east along the lake's north shore.

Camping Facilities: 87 campsites, including a few double units, in 2 loops; sites are medium sized, most are reasonably level, with minimal to nominal separation; parking pads are paved, short to medium+ straight-ins; plenty of space for large tents; fire rings or fireplaces; b-y-o firewood; water at several faucets; vault facilities; holding tank disposal station at the ranger station; paved driveways; camper supplies at a camp store (summer); complete supplies and services are available in Susanville.

(Camping is also available in adjacent Boulder Creek Campground.)

Activities & Attractions: Antelope Lake Nature Trail (paved); amphitheater for campfire programs on summer weekends; boating; boat launch, 2 miles east; fishing.

Natural Features: Located on a large, gently sloping forested flat along or near the northwest shore of Antelope Lake, a reservoir on Antelope Creek and several other streams; campsites are moderately sheltered by tall conifers above light sparse tall grass and a carpet of pine needles; a few sites are lakeside or have lake views through the trees; the lake is bordered by the wooded hills and low mountains of the northern Sierra Nevada; elevation 5000´.

Season, Fees & Phone: $12.00 for a standard site, $14.00 for a prime lakeside site; April to November; 14 day limit; (campsites must have someone 18 years or older to register); Mount Hough Ranger District, Quincy, ☎(916) 283-0555.

Trip Log: Although many of the campsites are closely spaced, they extend quite a distance rearward, so they're somewhat larger than they may first appear. Unlike so many California reservoirs, Antelope Lake wasn't primarily intended to be a source of irrigation water. It is a recreation project of several cooperating state and federal agencies. Hence, also unlike many Golden State impoundments, the midsummer water level of the 930-acre lake remains reasonably constant.

🏕 California 53 ♿

GRIZZLY
Lake Davis/Plumas National Forest

Location: North-eastern California northwest of Reno, Nevada.

Access: From California State Highway 70 at milepost 78 +.8 (3 miles east of Portola, 2 miles west of Beckwourth), travel north on Grizzly Road (paved) for 6.5 miles; turn west (left) into the campground. (Alternate access note: Lake Davis can also be reached via a paved road from West Street in midtown Portola; the access is a bit longer and slightly more complicated than the principal Access above.)

Day Use Facilities: Small picnic area, drinking water, restrooms, small parking area nearby.

Camping Facilities: 55 campsites in 2 loops; sites are medium to medium+ in size, with fair to good separation; parking pads are paved, mostly medium to long straight-ins; most pads will require a little additional leveling; large,

somewhat sloped tent spots; fireplaces and fire rings; some gatherable firewood is available in the general area; water at several faucets; restrooms; paved driveways; holding tank disposal station nearby on Grizzly Road; camper supplies near the dam; limited+ supplies and services are available in Portola.

Activities & Attractions: Fishing for several varieties of trout; boating; three boat launches along the lake's east shore.

Natural Features: Located on a slope above the southeast shore of Lake Davis; sites receive moderate shade/shelter from tall conifers above flowering plants, tall grass and a thick coating of pine needles; some sites are near the lake shore; the lake is bordered by well-timbered hills and low mountains; elevation 5900´.

Season, Fees & Phone: May to October; $13.00; 14 day limit; Beckwourth Ranger District, Mohawk, ☎(916) 836-2575.

Trip Log: If you consider site size and levelness to be important campsite characteristics, you need travel no farther up the road than Grizzly. Even though the lake really isn't within view of most sites, there are nonetheless some excellent camp spots here. The forest floor in the camp area, especially in the draws and coulees, is liberally coated with leafy flowering plants of an uncommon variety.

🏕 California 54 ♿

GRASSHOPPER FLAT
Lake Davis/Plumas National Forest

Location: North-eastern California northwest of Reno, Nevada.

Access: From California State Highway 70 at milepost 78 +.8 (3 miles east of Portola, 2 miles west of Beckwourth), head north on Grizzly Road (paved) for 7 miles; turn west (left) into the campground.

Day Use Facilities: Small picnic area, drinking water, restrooms, small parking area nearby.

Camping Facilities: 70 campsites in 3 loops; sites are small+ to medium-sized, with nominal to fair separation; parking pads are paved, mostly medium-length straight-ins; majority of pads will require a little additional leveling; large, generally sloped tent spots; fireplaces and fire rings; some firewood is available for gathering in the general vicinity; water at several faucets; restrooms; paved driveways; holding tank disposal station nearby on Grizzly

Road; camper supplies near the dam; limited+ supplies and services are available in Portola.

Activities & Attractions: Fishing for native and stocked trout, including a rainbow-kamloops crossbreed; also bass and catfish; boating; three boat launches along the lake's east shore.

Natural Features: Located on a rolling slope above the southeast shore of Lake Davis; sites are moderately sheltered by tall, slim conifers above patches of tall grass and a thick carpet of pine needles; some sites are near the lake shore; the lake is encircled by forested hills and mountains; elevation 5900´.

Season, Fees & Phone: May to October; $13.00; 14 day limit; Beckwourth Ranger District, Mohawk, ☎(916) 836-2575.

Trip Log: Campsites in the uppermost loop (i.e., those closest to the entrance) are farthest from the lake but are also the most level in the place. Following Grizzly Road up the east shore of the lake for another three miles will take you to Lightening Tree Campground, a rustic area for self-contained camping.

♣ California 55

SPRING CREEK

Frenchman Lake/Plumas National Forest

Location: North-eastern California northwest of Reno, Nevada.

Access: From the junction of California State Highways 70 & 284 in the town of Chilcoot, travel north on Highway 284 for 8 miles to the dam; turn east (right) continuing on a paved local road for another mile, then turn north (left) onto a paved access road and proceed 0.1 mile down into the campground.

Day Use Facilities: None.

Camping Facilities: 35 campsites in 2 loops; (a group camp near the dam is also available); sites are medium-sized, with nominal to fair separation; parking pads are paved, mostly medium to long straight-ins, plus a couple of pull-offs; most pads will require a little additional leveling; large, generally sloped tent areas; fireplaces; b-y-o firewood is suggested; water at several faucets; vault facilities; paved driveways; gas and groceries in Chilcoot.

(Also available: Frenchman Campground, which you'll pass on the way into Spring Creek, has 3 dozen sites ona steep slope a couple hundred yards above the lake shore.)

Activities & Attractions: Fishing; boating; boat launch nearby; lake trail.

Natural Features: Located on a steep slope above the south tip of Frenchman Lake; sites receive light-medium shade from tall conifers above some sagebrush; Spring Creek enters the lake at this spot; the lake is bordered by lightly forested hills; elevation 5600´.

Season, Fees & Phone: May to October; $12.00; 14 day limit; Milford Ranger District ☎(916) 253-2223.

Trip Log: Nearly all sites here have lake views: either full views or views through the trees. Considering the slope, the parking, table and tent areas have been reasonably well leveled. A very pleasantly scenic lake. Whoever named the lake's natural features (perhaps it was the "Frenchman"?) may have had fishing on his mind when he handed out the 'handles'. Included on the list of notable spots along the shoreline are Nightcrawler Bay, Lunker Point, and Salmon Egg Shoal. (The origin of "Snallygaster Point" is uncertain.)

♣ California 56 ♿

BIG COVE

Frenchman Lake/Plumas National Forest

Location: North-eastern California northwest of Reno, Nevada.

Access: From the junction of California State Highways 70 & 284 in the town of Chilcoot, travel north on Highway 284 for 8 miles to the dam; turn east (right), continuing on a paved road for another 1.8 miles, then swing sharply north (left) for a final 0.5 mile; turn northwest (left) into the campground.

Day Use Facilities: None.

Camping Facilities: 38 campsites in 2 loops; sites are medium to medium+, level or nearly so, with zip to fair separation; parking pads are paved, short to medium-length straight-ins or pull-throughs; medium to large areas for tents; fireplaces; b-y-o firewood is recommended; water at several faucets; restrooms; paved driveways; gas and groceries in Chilcoot.

Activities & Attractions: Fishing for rainbow, brook and kamloops trout; boating; boat launch nearby.

Natural Features: Located near the shore of a cove at the southeast end of Frenchman Lake (Reservoir) on the east slope of the Sierra Nevada; sites are on a sage flat dotted with some conifers; bordered by lightly timbered hills; elevation 5600´.

Season, Fees & Phone: May to October; $12.00; 14 day limit; Milford Ranger District ☎(916) 253-2223.

Trip Log: There are a dozen nice sites along the edge of a low bluff about 20 feet above the lake shore. If you need a level site, this camp would probably be your best choice of the trio of campgrounds on Frenchman Lake. The relatively small lake (1600 acres) has 21 miles of shoreline, courtesy of numerous bays, inlets and coves.

⁂ California 57 ♿

EMPIRE MINE
Empire Mine State Historic Park

Location: East-central California northeast of Sacramento.

Access: From the junction of California State Highways 49 & 20 near the south end of the city of Grass Valley, proceed east on Empire Street for 0.6 mile to the park boundary; continue ahead for another 0.7 mile to the visitor center and the center of the park. (Note: from Highway 49 take the Empire Street Exit, then go east on Empire; from Highway 20 eastbound, just continue straight ahead over the freeway and onto Empire Street East.)

Day Use Facilities: 2 small picnic areas; drinking water; restrooms; several small and medium-sized parking lots.

Camping Facilities: None; nearest public campground is White Cloud (Tahoe National Forest) 10 miles east of Nevada City on State Highway 20.

Activities & Attractions: Self-guiding or guided tours of the building and grounds of a gold mine dating back to 1850; visitor center with exhibits and a-v programs.

Natural Features: Located high in the foothills on the west slope of the Sierra Nevada; park vegetation consists mostly of grassy hills moderately forested with tall conifers; picnic sites are tucked in among the trees off the parking lots; elevation 2600´.

Season, Fees & Phone: Open all year, subject to weather conditions; please see Appendix for park entry fees; ☎(916) 273-8522.

Trip Log: Hardrock mining lacks much of the 'glamour' and aesthetic appeal of the classic picture of the old prospector wearing a turned-up hat, panning for gold in a nugget-flecked creek. Hardrock is just plain hard work. Nearly all of the men who worked the depths of the Empire Mine from the late 1800's until the mine folded in the mid-1950's came from Cornwall in England. You can get a good idea of what it must have been like to work the Empire by taking a few hours to investigate the couple-dozen major buildings and displays here. There's a *lot* to look at. The many old stone buildings and walls, mine shaft, giant ore bin, shops, and yard full of heavy equipment are all in remarkably good condition.

⁂ Special Section

THE GOLD CAMPS OF '49
Tahoe National Forest

The area in and around Nevada City and the Yuba River Valley is popular not only for recreation but for its historical significance. The territory is rich in ghost towns, old diggings, and stories of gold miners who came here to seek their fortunes. Adventurers still flock to the area to try their luck at finding the precious metal. The information for "The Gold Camps of '49" has been listed in an abbreviated form because so much of the information is repetitive. Unless otherwise noted, *all have the following features in common*:

Common Elements of the Gold Camps:

Location: Northeast California northeast of Sacramento. (Of the 12 campgrounds listed here, 11 of them are in Sierra County, and 1 is in Yuba County.)

Access: From California State Highway 49 from a point 20 miles north of Nevada City to a point 11.5 miles west of Sierraville; all campgrounds are along or near California State Highway 49.

Sources of Supplies: Limited to adequate supplies and services are available in Nevada City and Truckee; gas & groceries are available in North San Juan (3 miles south of the Nevada/Yuba county line); Downieville (Sierra milepost 16.7); Sierra City (Sierra milepost 28.9); and Sierraville (6 miles east of Sierra County milepost 47.5).

Season & Phone: Generally, the campgrounds are available May to September; 14 day limit of stay; Downieville Ranger District Information ☎(916) 288-3231.

Natural Features: In general, the campgrounds are situated along or near the North Yuba River in a forested canyon bordered by timbered ridges.

Activities & Attractions: Fishing; hiking; Wild Plum Loop Trail provides access to the Pacific Crest Trail; Kentucky Park Mine and Museum east of Sierra City; gold dredging or panning.

"There's gold in them thar hills!"

⚑ California 58 ♿

SCHOOLHOUSE

Access: From milepost 3 +.65 (Yuba County), turn west onto Marysville Road (E20); proceed 3.25 miles; turn north (right) onto a paved access road and proceed 0.15 mile to the campground.

Camping Facilities: 67 campsites; sites are small to medium-sized, and most are well separated; pads are paved, mostly short straight-ins; some pads may require additional leveling; some sites have large tent areas; fireplaces and fire rings; firewood is available for gathering in the area; water at several faucets; restrooms, plus auxiliary vaults; paved driveways; $9.00.

Natural Features: Located on a rolling, forested hilltop above Bullards Bar Reservoir (on the North Yuba River); elevation 2200´.

Trip Log: This is the most easily accessible of five campgrounds situated along the shore of Bullards Bar Reservoir. The season usually extends from April to October.

⚑ California 59

FIDDLE CREEK

Access: From milepost 4 +.9, turn south and immediately west into the campground.

Camping Facilities: 13 campsites; sites are small, with very little separation; dirt parking pads; no room for trailers or large camping vehicles; fireplaces; limited firewood is available for gathering in the area; no drinking water; vault facilities; hard-surfaced driveway; $9.00.

Natural Features: Located on a flat along the river; elevation 2200´.

Trip Log: This is a miners' and fishermen's 'tent city'. Gold dredging is permitted under certain conditions.

⚑ California 60

INDIAN VALLEY

Access: From milepost 5 +.35, turn south onto a paved access road; proceed 0.15 mile to the campground.

Camping Facilities: 17 campsites; sites are small to medium in size, with nominal to fair separation; parking pads are gravel/dirt, level, short to medium-length straight-ins; some good tent spots; fireplaces and fire rings; firewood is available for gathering in the vicinity; water at several faucets; vault facilities; paved driveways; $9.00.

Natural Features: Located on a rocky flat along the river; elev. 2200´.

Trip Log: There are many riverside sites where you can toss a line out into one of the rocky river's deep pools where some good-sized trout lurk. These rather small sites are commonly jammed to capacity.

⚑ California 61

RAMSHORN

Access: From milepost 10 +.8, turn north into the lower loop of the campground; proceed 0.25 mile east and up to the upper loop.

Camping Facilities: 16 campsites in 2 loops; sites are small to medium-sized, with very little separation; parking pads are dirt, fairly level, short to medium-length straight-ins; some tent spots are adequate for large tents; fireplaces; firewood is available for gathering in the vicinity; water at several faucets; vault facilities; gravel/dirt driveways; $9.00.

Natural Features: Located just across and above the highway from the river; some tall pines, cedars and open grassy areas in the campground; elevation 2600´.

Trip Log: The upper loop is not recommended for trailers since it's tight, and there's no turnaround. Some sites, though very close to the highway, have nice views across the river and up the canyon.

⚑ California 62

UNION FLAT

Access: From milepost 22 +.65, turn south into the campground.

Camping Facilities: 14 campsites; sites are small and close together, for the most part;

parking pads are gravel/dirt, short to medium-length straight-ins; some pads may require additional leveling; some tent spots are spacious enough for large tents; fireplaces; firewood is available for gathering in the vicinity; water at faucets; vault facilities; gravel driveways; $9.00.

Natural Features: Located on a hilly riverbank; elevation 3400´.

Trip Log: This is another popular gold dredging camp. Because most sites are streamside or nearly streamside, the campground is often filled to capacity.

♣ California 63

LOGANVILLE

Access: From milepost 27 +.1, turn south, then bear left for 0.1 mile to the upper loop; or bear right and proceed 0.2 mile to the lower loop.

Camping Facilities: 18 campsites in 2 loops; sites in the lower loop are a bit roomier than the small sites in the upper loop; separation ranges from fair to good; parking pads are dirt, fairly level, short to medium-length straight-ins; some tent spots are adequate for large tents; fire rings; firewood is available for gathering in the area; water at central faucets; vault facilities; dirt driveway; $9.00.

Natural Features: Located on a forested hilltop (upper loop); or on a forested flat a few yards from the river (lower loop); elevation 3800´.

Trip Log: There are no river views from the sites, but unlike most other campgrounds in this area, there is a moderate amount of privacy provided by the fairly tall, dense conifers.

♣ California 64

WILD PLUM

Access: From milepost 29 +.8, turn south onto Wild Plum Road; bear right; proceed 1.35 miles (paved for 0.6 mile), and over a 1-lane bridge to the campground's lower section; upper section is 0.1 mile farther.

Camping Facilities: 47 campsites in 3 loops; sites are small to medium in size, with nominal to average separation; parking pads are gravel/dirt, short to medium-length straight-ins; some pads may require additional leveling; some tent spots are a bit sloped or rocky; fire rings and fireplaces; firewood is available for

gathering in the area; water at several faucets; vault facilities; gravel/dirt driveways; $9.00.

Natural Features: Located along Haypress Creek; 2 loops are on a boulder-strewn, forested flat along the creek; the third loop is above the creek on a forested bluff; elevation 4400´.

Trip Log: Some sites in the lower loop are creekside and some in the upper loop have a view of the creek through the trees. Sites at Wild Plum are away from the mainstream of activity, so the atmosphere is somewhat more relaxed.

♣ California 65

SARDINE

Access: From milepost 34 +.3, turn northwest onto Gold Lake Road (signed for "Sierra Buttes Recreation Area"), drive 1.4 miles; turn southwest (left) and go 0.5 mile down to the campground.

Camping Facilities: 29 campsites; sites are small to medium-sized, with fair separation for most sites; parking pads are mostly small to medium-length straight-ins; some good tent spots; fireplaces; some firewood may be available for gathering, but b-y-o is recommended; water at several faucets; vault facilities; June to October; $9.00.

Natural Features: Located on a sage slope with tall forested peaks and the Sierra Buttes visible from nearby; elevation 5800´.

Trip Log: Because of nearby boating and swimming areas, Sardine Campground tends to become packed during much of the summer. (The name then befits the camping circumstances.) Jackcamping isn't permitted around here.

♣ California 66

SALMON CREEK

Access: From milepost 34 +.3, turn northwest onto Gold Lake Highway (signed for "Sierra Buttes Recreation Area"), proceed 1.6 miles; turn southwest (left) into the campground.

Camping Facilities: 33 campsites in 2 loops connected by a string; sites are mostly medium-sized, with nominal to fair separation; parking pads are hard-surfaced/gravel, short to medium-length straight-ins; some pads may require additional leveling; some good tent spots; fireplaces; firewood is usually available for gathering in the vicinity; water at several faucets; vault facilities; hard-surfaced driveways; June to October; $9.00.

Natural Features: Located on a sage and grass flat along Salmon Creek; more vegetation in sites along the creek and less vegetation (mostly sage) in sites out in the open; elevation 5800´.

Trip Log: The vistas from here are much more expansive than the views from down in the Yuba River Canyon along the highway. To the west, Sierra Buttes are prominent amid forested hills and mountains. There are a dozen small mountain lakes within a dozen miles of Salmon Creek Campground. Virtually all of them are easily accessible.

⚶ California 67

SIERRA

Access: From milepost 36 +.5, turn south into the campground.

Camping Facilities: 16 campsites; sites are fairly good-sized, with average or better separation; parking pads are gravel, medium to long straight-ins; some pads may require additional leveling; some spacious tent spots; fireplaces; firewood is available for gathering in the area; no drinking water; vault facilities; gravel driveways; $7.00.

Natural Features: Located on a forested slope along Sierra Creek; elevation 5600´.

Trip Log: There are some vast scenic views from along the highway in this area.

⚶ California 68

CHAPMAN CREEK

Access: From milepost 37 +.3, turn north into the campground.

Camping Facilities: 29 campsites; sites are large, with good separation; parking pads are gravel, medium to long straight-ins; large mostly level, tent spots; fireplaces; firewood is available for gathering in the area; no drinking water; vault facilities; paved driveways; $9.00.

Natural Features: Located on a rolling flat; lightly forested with very tall timber and large grassy areas; elevation 6000´.

Trip Log: This is a really nice camp—with some of the most spacious and private sites along this stretch. If you can bring your own drinking water, you're all set.

⚶ California 69

YUBA PASS

Access: From milepost 40 +.88, turn south and proceed 0.1 mile to the campground.

Camping Facilities: 20 campsites; most sites are large, with fair to good separation; parking pads are gravel, fairly level, medium to long straight-ins; some very good tent spots; fire rings and fireplaces; firewood is available for gathering in the area; no drinking water; vault facilities; gravel driveways; $9.00.

Natural Features: Located in a semi-open forest setting very near the summit of Yuba Pass; elevation 6700´.

Trip Log: This campground is just over the rise from some steep grades on the slopes bordering the great Sierra Valley. Because it's far from the mainstream of activity along the Yuba River, Yuba Pass Campground is seldom filled to capacity.

End of *Gold Camps of '49* Special Section

 California
North Central Inland

⚶ California 70 ♿

BUCKHORN
Black Butte Lake/Corps of Engineers Park

Location: North-central California northwest of Sacramento.

Access: From Interstate 5 at the northernmost of the two Orland exits (signed for Highway 32), turn west onto Newville Road (Road 200); head northwest for 12 miles (past the park HQ and around the north end of the lake) to Buckhorn Road; turn east (left) onto Buckhorn Road for a final mile to the campground.

Day Use Facilities: Small picnic area, drinking water, restrooms, small parking area in Orland Butte Park, on the lake's southeast shore.

Camping Facilities: 65 campsites in 4 loops; (a couple dozen primitive sites and a group camp area are also available); sites vary from small+ to large, with nominal separation; parking pads are paved, medium to long straight-ins, plus a few super-long pull-throughs; many pads will require a little additional leveling; large tent areas, most are fairly level; barbecue grills; b-y-o firewood; water at several faucets; restrooms with showers; holding tank disposal station;

paved driveways; gas and groceries on Road 200, near the freeway, and in Orland.

(Camping is also available in Orland Butte Park, on the southeast shore of the lake.)

Natural Features: Located on a rolling hill on a point on the northwest shore of Black Butte Lake; park vegetation consists of short grass and large oaks; majority of the sites have some shade/shelter; many deer often pass through the campground on their way to get a sip at the lake, particularly in summer; surrounded by grassland, hills and buttes; the Coast Range lies several miles to the west; elevation 500´.

Activities & Attractions: Boating; boat launches; fishing for bass, crappie and Florida bluegill; Buckhorn Interpretive Trail (a good guide booklet is available from the park office); playground.

Season, Fees & Phone: Open all year; $13.00 for a standard site, $7.00 for a primitive site; 14 day limit; CoE Black Butte Lake Project Office ☎(916) 865-4781.

Trip Log: This park is a winner! The facilities are excellent and the views are terrific. It's a real deal. The lake's other park, Orland Butte, has similar facilities, the views are also good, but Buckhorn is still a bit nicer. The so-called "Florida bluegill" is a prolific, good-sized, scrappy critter that's one of the most popular fish on the lake. In spring, it is caught in tremendous numbers.

⚐ California 71 ♿

OLD SACRAMENTO
Old Sacramento State Historic Park

Location: Central California in Sacramento.

Access: From Interstate 5 (northbound) near milepost 23 on the west edge of downtown Sacramento, take the J Street/Downtown Exit onto Third Street (Third St. parallels the freeway on the east side of I-5); go down Third for a few yards to Capitol Avenue, then west (left) over the Interstate; get in the right lane and just after crossing over I-5, hang a right into the park. **Alternate Access:** From Interstate 5 (southbound) take the J Street Exit, pass under the freeway (west to east) to Third Street; turn south (right) onto Third, go 0.1 mile to Capitol, then turn west (right), and continue as above.

(Note: Old Sacramento is sandwiched between I-5 and the river; there are a number of parking lots in the area; considering the traffic and parking congestion inside Old Sacramento

during busy periods, you might save time and fuel in the long run by just quickly finding an open spot soon after exiting the freeway and walking a couple of blocks into the park.)

Day Use Facilities: Several benches along the river; drinking water; restrooms inside the railroad museum and near the parking garage; parking lots (including a designated rv lot north of the railroad museum), parking garage, limited streetside parking.

Camping Facilities: None; nearest public campgrounds are in Folsom Lake State Recreation Area.

Activities & Attractions: Reconstructions, renovations and replications of the original downtown Sacramento waterfront district; California State Railroad Museum has restored railroad cars and more than 40 exhibits about railroading; Sacramento History Center; Pony Express monument (Sacramento was the western terminus of the 2000-mile Pony Express route which originated in St. Joseph, Missouri.)

Natural Features: Located along the east bank of the Sacramento River; riverside day use area is landscaped with small sections of grass and a few trees; elevation 20´.

Season, Fees & Phone: Open all year; please see Appendix for park entry fees; ☎(916) 445-7373 (railroad museum).

Trip Log: There are dozens of interesting historical buildings and sites here, as well as the many tourist-oriented shops, pubs, restaurants and cafes inside them. The local visitor information center on Front Street can provide you with a free map and "walking tour" guide. But the park's *primo* attraction is the railroad museum. Inside the 100,000-square foot brick building are more than 20 locomotives and cars—each of them restored to a spit-shine level of perfection. The exhibits—all from the Golden State's Golden Age of Railroading—collectively constitute what is billed as "the finest railroad museum in North America". They're probably right. Old Sacramento is the place where the Pony Express and the Iron Horse meet on common ground.

⚐ California 72 ♿

SUTTER'S FORT
Sutter's Fort State Historic Park

Location: East-central California in Sacramento.

Access: From Interstate 80 Business Route (eastbound) in downtown Sacramento (0.7 mile north of the junction of Business I-80 & U.S. Highway 50), take the N Street Exit; at the bottom of the ramp, continue ahead (north, parallel to the freeway) for 0.2 mile to L Street; turn west (left) onto L Street, and proceed 0.2 mile; the park is located on the north side of L Street, between 28th & 26th Streets. **Alternate Access:** From Biz I-80 (westbound) in downtown Sacramento (1 mile south of the American River), take the J Street Exit; at the bottom of the ramp, continue south on 29th Street (parallel to the freeway) for 0.2 mile; turn west (right) onto L Street and continue as above.

Day Use Facilities: Small picnic area; drinking water; restrooms; metered streetside parking in the surrounding area.

Camping Facilities: None; nearest public campgrounds are in Folsom Lake State Recreation Area.

Activities & Attractions: Restoration of an adobe fort originally built in the 1840's by Swiss-German adventurer and entrepreneur John Augustus Sutter; extensive and impressive exhibits depict pioneer life in early California; self-guided tours of the fort for individuals; guided tours for groups and special presentations, including an "Environmental Living" program, for elementary school children by reservation; costumed staff and volunteers demonstrate pioneer baking, spinning, weaving, blacksmithing, candle-making, etc.; activities include re-enactments of events in the history of the fort and the Sacramento Valley; State Indian Museum, next door to this park.

Natural Features: Located in the Sacramento Valley; park vegetation consists of mown lawns lightly shaded in some areas by large hardwoods; a pair of ponds add an aquatic touch to the grounds and attract small wildlife; elevation 20´.

Season, Fees & Phone: Open all year; please see Appendix for park entry fees; ☎(916) 445-4422; for group reservations ☎(916) 445-4209.

Trip Log: John Sutter figured prominently in the history of Mexican California and in early American California. He built this 50,000-square-foot fort to serve as the headquarters for his agricultural and commercial empire. Few other historic parks in California equal or surpass the extensiveness of displays, scope of programs and level of community involvement as this one.

⚑ **California 73** ♿

MARSHALL GOLD DISCOVERY

Marshall Gold Discovery State Historic Park

Location: East-central California northeast of Sacramento.

Access: From California State Highway 49 at milepost 23 +.2 in Coloma (8 miles northwest of Placerville, 19 miles southeast of Auburn), turn west onto Bridge Street and go 0.1 mile to the visitor center.

Day Use Facilities: Medium-large picnic areas, drinking water, restrooms, large parking lots at North Beach and Sutter's Mill (picnic area at the Mill is on the west side of the highway, across from the parking lot); small picnic area, restrooms and small parking area near the Marshall Monument; group picnic area in the Beer Garden, a few yards off the highway, just south of the visitor center (available by reservation).

Camping Facilities: None; nearest public campgrounds are in Auburn State Recreation Area, 17 miles north.

Activities & Attractions: Replication of Sutter's Mill, site of the discovery which touched-off the California Gold Rush; hiking and interpretive trails; visitor center with interpretive displays (small parking lot at the v.c., so be prepared to park 'n walk from one of the other lots); mining exhibit contains examples of equipment used in different types of mining operations; grave site topped by a statue of James W. Marshall overlooks the valley from a hilltop; site of the celebrated Metropolitan Saloon and Bowling Alley (location of one of California's first 'strikes' of a different sort), and other historic buildings and sites in and around Coloma; interpretive and hiking trails; rafting/floating; recreational gold panning area.

Natural Features: Located in a narrow valley along the banks of the South Fork of the American River; park vegetation consists of conifer-and-hardwood-dotted, grassy flats along and near the river and lightly forested hills; elevation 800´.

Season, Fees & Phone: Open all year; please see Appendix for reservation information and park entry fees; ☎(916) 622-3470.

Trip Log: Little did James Marshall realize when he first glimpsed those flecks of 'something' glittering in the sunshine of the Sierra foothills that fateful January day in 1848 that his discovery was about to precipitate one of most extraordinary events in Western history. Marshall had been building a small sawmill on the bank of the South Fork of the American River for California entrepreneur John Sutter when he spotted what soon proved to be gold in the mill's tailrace. Word of the 'find' spread slowly at first; but by 1849 the rush was running full tilt as thousands of fortune hunters from around the world walked, rode, sailed, begged, borrowed, bought and fought their way to the gold fields of the Sierra. But Marshall was left far behind in this race to riches and he never achieved the wealth which might have been expected from his singularly significant revelation. Marshall spent his remaining days embittered and lonely, living in a simple log cabin a few yards from the spot where the second history of California began.

⁂ California 74 ♿

BEAL'S POINT
Folsom Lake State Recreation Area

Location: East-central California northeast of Sacramento.

Access: From U.S. Highway 50 near milepost 15 +.7 at the Hazel Avenue/Sacramento County Highway E3 Exit southwest of Folsom, travel north on Hazel Avenue for 2.4 miles; turn east (right) onto Madison Avenue and proceed 2 miles, then pick up Greenback Lane and continue east for another mile to a 3-way intersection at Greenback Lane and Folsom-Auburn Road; turn north (left) onto Folsom-Auburn Road and proceed 2.6 miles; turn east (right) onto the park access road and go 0.2 mile to the park. **Alternate Access:** From Interstate 80 at the Greenback Lane/Elkhorn Boulevard/Sacramento County Highway E14 Exit (13 miles northeast of Sacramento, 4 miles southwest of Roseville) travel east on Greenback Lane/E14 for 8 miles to the intersection of Greenback Lane & Folsom-Auburn Road and continue as above.

Day Use Facilities: Large picnic area; about a dozen small to medium-sized ramadas (sun shelters); drinking water; restrooms; large parking lot; (another day use area with a medium-sized picnic area, vault facilities, a boat ramp and parking lot is located on the lake's south shore, 5 miles northeast of Folsom, then 0.4 mile north off of Green Valley Road).

Camping Facilities: 49 campsites, including a number of park 'n walk units; sites are small to medium-sized, with nominal to fairly good separation; parking surfaces are paved, short to

short+ straight-ins, some are double-wide and some will require a little additional leveling; adequate space for mostly small to medium-sized tents; fire rings; b-y-o firewood; water at several faucets; restrooms with showers; paved driveway; adequate+ supplies and services are available in the Folsom area.

Activities & Attractions: Large, sandy swimming beach; boating; boat launch; (another boat launch is located on the east side of Hazel Avenue near U.S. 50); American River Bikeway begins near here and ends at Old Town Sacramento, 32.8 miles downstream; state park staff-guided tours of the historic Folsom Powerhouse (groups by reservation only, contact the park office for info).

Natural Features: Located near the base of the foothills of the Sierra Nevada; day use area is along the shore and has large tracts of lawns lightly dotted with hardwoods; campground is on and around a grassy, lightly forested knoll; elevation 300´-450´.

Season, Fees & Phone: Day use area open all year, campground open April to October; please see Appendix for reservation information, park entry and campground fees; ☎(916) 988-0205.

Trip Log: Much of the lake and its surrounding hills can be viewed from the day use area and beach. If you're camping ... no campfire sing-along would be complete without a soulful rendition of the ol' Country favorite "Folsom Prison Blues". (The slammer that's the song's namesake is near the lake's south shore.)

⁂ California 75 ♿

INDIAN GRINDING ROCK
Indian Grinding Rock State Historic Park

Location: East-central California east of Sacramento.

Access: From California State Highway 88 at milepost 23 +.4 (in the small community of Pine Grove, 9 miles east of Jackson, 3.4 miles west of the junction of State Highways 88 & 26), turn north onto Pine Grove-Volcano Road (paved); proceed 1.3 miles northeast, then turn west (left) into the park.

Day Use Facilities: Small picnic area; drinking water and restrooms nearby; small parking lot.

Camping Facilities: 21 campsites; (primitive sites with shelters are also available); sites are small to medium-sized, with generally good separation; parking pads are gravel, medium-length, mostly straight-ins, plus a few pull-throughs; some additional leveling may be necessary in many sites; good, private tent spots, adequate for medium to large tents; fire rings, plus a few barbecue grills; b-y-o firewood; storage cabinets; water at several faucets; restrooms; paved driveway; gas and groceries in Pine Grove; limited supplies and services are available in Jackson.

Activities & Attractions: Reconstructed Indian village with petroglyphs, displays and exhibits; interpretive programs; nature trail; museum with exhibits and Indian crafts demonstrations; guided group tours, available by reservation.

Natural Features: Located on forested flats and slopes in the western foothills of the Sierra Nevada; tall conifers, oaks, and a considerable amount of underbrush separate most of the campsites nicely; the park has some open meadows as well; elevation 2400´.

Season, Fees & Phone: Open all year; please see Appendix for reservation information, park entry and campground fees; ☎(209) 296-7488.

Trip Log: The main grinding rock is a massive limestone table measuring about 25 yards by 60 yards. The rock contains nearly 1200 small holes, "mortar cups", which were worn into the soft stone by enthusiastic Miwok Indians grinding acorns and other seeds to make hot cereal or cake flour. The rock also is randomly marked with more than 350 petroglyphs. Within the reconstructed village are small, bark teepees used as family residences and a *hun'ge* or roundhouse, a domed, multi-sided, wooden structure that serves as a community center. The roundhouse is actively used by local Indians for dances and ceremonials.

♣ **California 76**

CAPLES LAKE
Eldorado National Forest

Location: East-central California east of Sacramento.

Access: From California State Highway 88 at milepost 1 +.1 (in Alpine County) (60 miles east of Jackson, 5 miles west of Carson Pass, 12 miles west of Pickett's Junction), turn south into the day use area or north into the campground.

Day Use Facilities: Small picnic area; drinking water; restrooms; small parking area.

Camping Facilities: 39 campsites in 2 loops and a connecting string; sites are small to

medium-sized, with average separation; parking pads are paved, mostly medium-length straight-ins; some additional leveling may be required; some fairly good-sized tent spots, but many are rather small and rocky; fireplaces or fire rings; firewood is usually for sale, or b-y-o; water at several faucets; vault facilities; paved driveways; camper supplies at a small resort nearby; limited supplies and services are available in Jackson.

Activities & Attractions: Boating, boat launch and fishing on Caples Lake; hiking trails in the vicinity; the drive along Highway 88 offers some super scenery.

Natural Features: Located high in the Sierra Nevada; day use area is along the north shore of Caples Lake; camp is across the highway from the north shore; short to medium-height conifers and moderate underbrush are interspersed with large boulders in the recreation area; a steep rock ridge borders the camping area on both sides; elevation 7800´.

Season, Fees & Phone: May to September; $10.00; 14 day limit; Amador Ranger District, Pioneer, ☎(209) 295-4251.

Trip Log: Caples Lake is a beautiful mountain lake in a sub-alpine setting just below the tree line. There is lake access within a short walk of any of the campsites. Unfortunately, some of these sites are rather close to the highway. But look at the bright side: A few of the roadside sites also have lake views through the trees.

♣ **California 77** ♿

COLUMBIA
Columbia State Historic Park

Location: East-central California east of Stockton.

Access: From California State Highway 49 at milepost 20 +.3 (2.5 miles north of Sonora, 15 miles south of Angels Camp), turn northeast onto Parrotts Ferry Road/Tuolumne County Road E18 (paved) and proceed 1.6 miles to the park; the main parking lot is east (right) off the main road just as you enter the park; most of the midtown streets are closed to motor vehicles.

Day Use Facilities: Medium-sized picnic area (in and around the parking lot); drinking water; restrooms adjacent to the parking lot and at several other locations in town; large parking lot; limited streetside parking is also available.

Camping Facilities: Restored 20-room City Hotel (operated by the local junior college, reservations suggested); nearest public campgrounds are in Stanislaus National Forest, northeast of Sonora.

Activities & Attractions: Well-preserved and/or renovated Gold Rush-era town, including more than 40 buildings within the historic district; 'living history' programs, festivals, parades, theater performances, contests and fly-ins are scheduled throughout the year; mining machinery exhibit; nature trail; concessioned or leased businesses provide food service, gifts, etc.; (also, a swimming pool at the local elementary school is open to the public in summer).

Natural Features: Located in the Sierra Nevada, closely bordered by forested hills and mountains; elevation 2100´.

Season, Fees & Phone: Open all year; (no fee); ☎(209) 532-4301.

Trip Log: It is somewhat possible to take a motor tour of Columbia by skirting the edge of downtown and glancing up the streets and alleys; but the fun starts when you get out from behind the dashboard and wander around. There are large signboards with detailed maps of the historic area posted at strategic points around town, so you should be able to find your way OK. Gold was discovered in Columbia in the aftermath of an 1850 cloudburst and the population grew to over 6,000 in 6 weeks. In its heyday, the town was known as the "Gem of Southern Mines". Some $87 million (in nineteenth-century, non-inflated dollars) of gold was drawn from its veins. Columbia, which resembles the famous copper-mining boomtown of Jerome, Arizona in many respects, is also now one of the West's most lively ghost towns.

♣ California 78 ♿

RAILTOWN 1897
Railtown 1897 State Historic Park

Location: East-central California east of Stockton.

Access: From California State Highways 49 & 108 at the northeast edge of Jamestown (3 miles southwest of Sonora) turn east onto Fifth Avenue and proceed 0.4 mile to the park.

Day Use Facilities: Medium-sized picnic area; drinking water; restrooms; medium-large parking area; refreshment stand.

Camping Facilities: None; nearest public campgrounds are in Stanislaus National Forest, northeast of Sonora.

Activities & Attractions: Restored depot, railyard, roundhouse, and car barns of the Sierra Railway of California; steam train excursions include 1-hour "Mother Lode Cannonball" round trip to Chinese Station, plus several 2.5-hour "specials", e.g., "Keystone Special" round-trip to the town of Keystone, "Twilight Limited" evening train with a bbq at the end of the run, and a "New Year's Eve Party Train" (to who knows where?).

Natural Features: Located in the Sierra Nevada, bordered by forested hills and mountains; picnic sites are on a lightly shaded lawn; elevation 1400´.

Season, Fees & Phone: Open all year, with limited hours in winter; 1-hour excursions scheduled Saturdays, Sundays and holidays from April through November, "Specials" scheduled mostly June through September; passenger tickets for adults start at about $9.00 for the 1-hour rides and go to $34.00+ for certain "Specials"; children's tickets are 50-60 percent of the adult fare; "family plan" tickets are also available; reservations are highly recommended well in advance for the "Specials"; (it is suggested that you contact the park for current rates and a timetable); ☎(209) 984-3953 or ☎(209) 984-3115.

Trip Log: Steam trains hauled the nation's passengers and freight from the 1830's to the 1950's when they were retired in favor of more efficient diesel-electric locomotion. Nowadays, the classic "choo-choos" run only in places like this park. (Railtown 1897 has a 'sister park' in a very different Western region: Rusk-Palestine State Park in the pine forest of East Texas operates half-day trips on the gleaming yellow Texas State Railroad.) All of the 'old timers' who lend a hand at Railtown help make this a special park.

♣ California 79 ♿

CALAVERAS BIG TREES
Calaveras Big Trees State Park

Location: East-central California northeast of Stockton.

Access: From California State Highway 4 at milepost 44 +.4 (23 miles east of Angels Camp, 27 miles southwest of Lake Alpine), turn south and go 0.1 mile to the park entrance.

Day Use Facilities: 5 small or medium-sized picnic areas; group picnic area at North Grove;

drinking water; restrooms; medium to large parking lots.

Camping Facilities: *North Grove Campground*: 74 campsites; (group camp area is also available nearby, by reservation); sites are small to medium-sized, with minimal to fair separation; parking pads are reasonably level, dirt/gravel straight-ins, plus a few pull-throughs; medium to large tent areas; some designated tent sites; *Oak Hollow Campground*: 55 sites; (3 environmental camp areas are located within several miles north and south of Oak Hollow); sites are small to medium-sized, with minimal to fair separation; parking pads are dirt/gravel, mostly short straight-ins, plus some extra-wide straight-ins and a few medium-length pull-offs; medium to large tent areas; *both campgrounds*: fireplaces; firewood is usually for sale, or b-y-o; water at several faucets; restrooms with showers; paved driveways; disposal station at North Grove; adequate supplies and services are available in Arnold, 3 miles west.

Activities & Attractions: Self-guided nature trail through North Grove; special Three Senses Trail; loop trail through a section of South Grove; several other, longer hiking trails through the park (a detailed brochure/map with contour lines is available); visitor center; rustic community building; campfire circle; trout fishing in the Stanislaus River.

Natural Features: Located in a conifer forest on the west slope of the Sierra Nevada; North Grove holds about 150 giant sequoias; much larger South Grove Natural Preserve protects a primeval sequoia forest; the North Fork of the Stanislaus River flows through the center of the park; elevation 3500´ to 5400´.

Season, Fees & Phone: Open all year, subject to brief closures during periods of heavy snow, with limited services October to May; please see Appendix for reservation information, park entry and campground fees; ☎(209) 795-2334.

Trip Log: *Sequoiadendron giganteum* is the largest (though not quite the tallest) of the three species of redwoods left on the planet. Suddenly encountering these trees while merely driving past the park is startling.

⚲ California 80 ♿

LAKE ALPINE
Lake Alpine/Stanislaus National Forest

Location: Eastern California northeast of Stockton and south of Lake Tahoe.

Access: From California State Highway 4 at the east end of Lake Alpine near milepost 4 (4 miles east of the Alpine-Calaveras county line, 49 miles northeast of Angels Camp, 28 miles southwest of the junction of State Highways 4 & 89 south of Markleeville), turn south and continue a short 0.1 mile to the campground.

Day Use Facilities: None.

Camping Facilities: 25 campsites; sites are small to medium in size, with nominal separation; parking pads are paved, mostly level, short to medium-length straight-ins; medium to large, level tent spots; fireplaces; firewood is available for gathering in the vicinity; water at several faucets; restrooms; paved driveways; gas, general store, laundromat and showers at a lodge, 0.2 mile east.

Activities & Attractions: Fishing; boating; boat launch nearby.

Natural Features: Located on the gently sloping west shore of Lake Alpine in Bear Valley in the Sierra Nevada; a light to medium dense forest of tall conifers provides adequate shelter/shade in most campsites; the lake is surrounded by low, heavily timbered ridges and hills; elevation 7400´.

Season, Fees & Phone: June to October; $12.00; 14 day limit; Calaveras Ranger District, Hathaway Pines, ☎(209) 795-1381.

Trip Log: This is an interesting location. The classic, High Sierra panoramas are absent. Instead, the terrain immediately around the lake is more, well, call it "gentle", rather than "grand".

⚲ California 81 ♿

PINE MARTEN & SILVER VALLEY
Lake Alpine/Stanislaus National Forest

Location: Eastern California northeast of Stockton and south of Lake Tahoe.

Access: From California State Highway 4 at the east end of Lake Alpine near milepost 5 (5 miles east of the Alpine-Calaveras county line, 27 miles southwest of the junction of State Highways 4 & 89 south of Markleeville, 50 miles northeast of Angels Camp), turn south onto the campground access road; proceed 0.1 mile to Pine Marten Campground; or continue past Pine Marten to Silver Valley Campground.

Day Use Facilities: None.

Camping Facilities: *Pine Marten*: 32 campsites; sites are small to medium-sized, closely spaced, but with some visual separation; parking pads are gravel/paved, short to medium-length straight-ins; medium to large tent areas; about half of the sites are reasonably level, remainder are slightly sloped; fireplaces or fire rings; firewood is available for gathering in the area; water at several faucets; restrooms; paved driveways; *Silver Valley*: 21 campsites; sites are small to medium-sized, with fair separation; parking pads are gravel/paved, mostly short to medium-length straight-ins; additional leveling may be needed on many pads; enough space for medium to large tents in most sites, but areas are generally a bit sloped; fireplaces or fire rings; firewood is available for gathering in the area; water at several faucets; restrooms; paved driveways; gas, general store, laundromat and showers at a lodge, 1 mile west.

Activities & Attractions: Fishing; limited boating; trails to the lake; Highland Creek Trailhead.

Natural Features: Located on a slight to moderate slope above the east end of Lake Alpine in the Sierra Nevada; a medium to dense forest of tall conifers provides ample shelter for campsites; elevation 7400´.

Season, Fees & Phone: June to October; $12.00; Calaveras Ranger District, Hathaway Pines, ☎ (209) 795-1381.

Trip Log: Trout fishing is said to be reasonably good on the lake. Alpine is also becoming a popular lake with windsurfers and other small-boat sailors. A glimpse of the lake through the forest can be had from some sites here. There is also a small, no fee, backpackers campground nearby, a few yards off the highway.

⚕ **California 82**

SILVER CREEK
Toiyabe National Forest

Location: Eastern California northeast of Stockton and south of Lake Tahoe.

Access: From California State Highway 4 at milepost 24 +.4 (8 miles southwest of the junction of State Highways 4 & 89 south of Markleeville, 69 miles northeast of Angels Camp), turn north or south into either of the 2 campground loops.

Day Use Facilities: None.

Camping Facilities: 22 campsites in 2 loops; sites are about average in size, with minimal to fairly good visual separation; parking pads are mostly paved straight-ins, plus a few longer

pull-throughs; some additional leveling may be necessary on many pads; medium to large, slightly sloped tent areas; fire rings; firewood is available for gathering in the area; water at several faucets; vault facilities; paved driveways; gas and groceries+ are available in Markleeville, 12 miles north.

Activities & Attractions: Scenic views; stream fishing.

Natural Features: Located along Silver Creek, high on the east slope of the Sierra Nevada; campground vegetation is primarily mixed, tall conifers and tall grass; lofty, rugged, gray peaks and timbered slopes surround the campground; elevation 6800´.

Season, Fees & Phone: June to October; $8.00; 14 day limit; Carson Ranger District, Carson City NV, ☎ (702) 882-2766 (office) or (702) 882-9211 (recorded information).

Trip Log: This is a dandy spot. There's a lot of scenery in the Sierra, and some of the best is around here. It's not the easiest roadside campground to reach, particularly from the west. Highway signs advise against trailer-towing west of here through the Ebbetts Pass area. There are several miles of steep, sharp switchbacks and very narrow roads that start (or end) near the campground. (They must have used a helicopter to haul the asphalt.) But, wow! The near-wilderness environment in this region is really something.

⚕ **California 83** ♿

PINECREST
Stanislaus National Forest

Location: Eastern California east of Stockton.

Access: From California State Highway 108 at milepost 30 +.2 (30 miles east of Sonora, 51 miles west of U.S. 395), turn east (i.e., an easy right turn off the highway if eastbound) onto Pinecrest Lake Road (paved) and proceed 0.6 mile to the recreation area.

Day Use Facilities: Large picnic area; drinking water; restrooms; large parking lot.

Camping Facilities: 200 campsites in 5 loops; sites are average-sized, mostly level, with minimal to fair separation; parking pads are paved, medium to long straight-ins; large tent spots in most units; fireplaces; firewood is available for gathering in the general vicinity; gathering firewood on national forest lands prior to arrival is recommended; water at several faucets; restrooms; holding tank disposal station on Highway 108, 0.3 mile west of the Pinecrest Lake Road turnoff; paved driveways; ranger station, 0.7 mile; small store nearby; complete supplies and services are available in Sonora.

Activities & Attractions: Boating; boat launch and dock; fishing; designated swimming area with sand/pebble beach; amphitheater.

Natural Features: Located on a timbered flat along (day use) or a few yards from (camp) the southwest shore of Pinecrest Lake, on the west slope of the Sierra Nevada; vegetation consists of light to medium-dense tall conifers, plus some second growth timber and a small amount of undercover; elevation 5600´.

Season, Fees & Phone: May to October; camping $13.00; picnicking $5.00; Summit Ranger District, Pinecrest, ☎(209) 965-3434.

Trip Log: A camp or picnic site here is one of the more expensive pieces of national forest rental real estate in California. Although the lake is certainly beautiful, and the campsites are nice, it might be worth considering staying in one of the many other, less expensive, campgrounds along this highway. (Pocket the difference, and spend it on that Alaska trip.)

California
Lake Tahoe

⚕ California 84 ⚹

DONNER MEMORIAL
Donner Memorial State Park

Location: Eastern California west of Reno, Nevada.

Access: From Interstate 80 near milepost 13 at the Donner Lake/Donner State Park Exit, 1 mile west of Truckee, from the south side of the freeway proceed west on Donner Pass Road for 0.3 mile; turn south (left) into the park.

Day Use Facilities: Large picnic area; drinking water; restrooms; a half-dozen medium-sized parking lots.

Camping Facilities: 154 campsites in 3 loops; sites are small to medium-sized, with nominal to fair separation; parking pads are sand/gravel, short to medium-length straight-ins; some pads may require a little additional leveling; most tent spots are reasonably level and will accommodate good-sized tents; storage cabinets; fireplaces and fire rings; firewood may be available for gathering on national forest land in the vicinity, or b-y-o; water at several faucets; restrooms

with showers; paved driveways; adequate supplies and services are available in Truckee.

Activities & Attractions: Swimming and wading; short hiking trails; nature trail; (guide pamphlet available); cross-country skiing; campfire center for scheduled programs in summer; guided nature walks; Emigrant Trail Museum has information about building the railroad through Donner Pass, and about the Donner party's winter in the Sierra, including a slide presentation; boating (public boat launch at the northwest corner of the lake); lake and stream fishing (reportedly fair) for stocked trout and kokanee salmon.

Natural Features: Located in the Sierra Nevada along the northeast shore of Donner Lake in an open, conifer forest; tall pines, scattered underbrush and sparse grass are the predominant forms of vegetation; picnic sites are along the lake shore; elevation 6000´.

Season, Fees & Phone: Museum and limited day use facilities open all year; campground open May to October; please see Appendix for reservation information, park entry and campground fees; ☎(916) 587-3841.

Trip Log: Of all the Sierra's lakes, Donner Lake's beauty may be second only to Lake Tahoe's. Many travelers would say that, in some ways, it's the other way around. The park is surprisingly busy in winter because of the typically good x-c skiing conditions found here and the Sierra's beautiful winter scenery.

⚕ California 85 ⚹

WILLIAM KENT
Lake Tahoe Basin Management Unit

Location: Eastern California on the west shore of Lake Tahoe.

Access: From California State Highway 89 at milepost 6 + .3 (6 miles north of the El Dorado-Placer County line, 2 miles south of Tahoe City, 16 miles south of Truckee), turn east into the day use area or west into the campground.

Day Use Facilities: Small picnic area; drinking water; restrooms; small parking area.

Camping Facilities: 95 campsites in a complex loop; sites are small to medium-sized, with nominal separation; parking pads are paved, short to medium-length straight-ins; some pads may require additional leveling; most sites have good tent spots for medium-sized tents, but many are a bit sloped; fireplaces; b-y-o firewood; water at several faucets; restrooms;

paved driveways; adequate supplies and services are available in Tahoe City.

Activities & Attractions: Swimming beach; boating; (boat launch at Meeks Bay); fishing; great scenic drive along Lake Tahoe's shore.

Natural Features: Located in the Sierra Nevada just across the highway from the west shore of Lake Tahoe; campground vegetation consists mainly of tall conifers, very little underbrush, and a small, open, interior grassy area; elevation 6300´.

Season, Fees & Phone: May to October; $13.00; 7 day limit; Lake Tahoe Basin Management Unit, South Lake Tahoe, ☎(916) 573-2600 or (916) 544-5994.

Trip Log: The west shore of Lake Tahoe is a highly developed area with numerous resorts, commercial establishments and summer homes. The campgrounds along the shore of the lake are commonly filled early in the day during most of the summer. Kaspian Campground, 2 miles south and managed by the same federal agency, offers sites principally for hikers/bikers.

♣ **California 86** ♿

SUGAR PINE POINT
Sugar Pine Point State Park

Location: Eastern California on the west shore of Lake Tahoe.

Access: From California State Highway 89 near milepost 26 (1 mile south of the El Dorado/Placer County line, 2 miles south of Tahoma, 18 miles north of South Lake Tahoe), turn east to the day use area and the visitor center; or near milepost 26 +.5, turn west onto the campground access road and proceed 0.1 mile to the camping area.

Day Use Facilities: Small picnic area; drinking water; restrooms; medium-sized parking area.

Camping Facilities: *General Creek Campground*: 175 campsites in 4 loops; (group camps are also available, by reservation); sites are small to medium-sized, essentially level, with nominal to fairly good separation; many units are situated in clusters; parking pads are hard-surfaced, short to medium+ straight-ins; tent spots vary from small to large; assorted fire appliances; firewood is usually for sale, or b-y-o; storage cabinets; water at several faucets; restrooms with showers; (showers available in summer only); holding tank disposal station; paved driveways; groceries in Tahoma;

adequate+ supplies and services are available in South Lake Tahoe.

Activities & Attractions: Fishing; fishing pier; day use area has a half-mile-long sandy beach; hiking trails; nature trail; amphitheater; visitor center; early settler's cabin.

Natural Features: Located in the Sierra Nevada, along and above the west shore of Lake Tahoe, where General Creek flows into the lake; vegetation consists of tall conifers, a small amount of underbrush, and some new growth timber; elevation 6300´.

Season, Fees & Phone: Open all year, with limited services September to May; please see Appendix for reservation information, park entry and campground fees; ☎(916) 525-7982.

Trip Log: Visitors who come here in summer miss three of Lake Tahoe's four best seasons. Sugar Pine Point is the only state park on Lake Tahoe with winter camping. Winter campers can expect to find deep snow pack, snow storms, and nighttime lows near zero. However, it should also be noted that seeing Lake Tahoe and its snow-cloaked mountains in the crisp, clear, cold air following a frontal passage is one of the outdoors' most memorable occasions.

♣ **California 87** ♿

MEEKS BAY
Lake Tahoe Basin Management Unit

Location: Eastern California on the west shore of Lake Tahoe.

Access: From California State Highway 89 at milepost 24 +.8 (16 miles north of the South Lake Tahoe area, 2.4 miles south of the El Dorado-Placer County line), turn east into the recreation area.

Day Use Facilities: Small picnic area; drinking water; restrooms; small parking area.

Camping Facilities: 40 campsites in 4 loops; sites are small to average-sized, with little to fair separation; parking pads are paved, level, short to medium-length straight-ins; tent spots are quite level and large enough to accommodate good-sized tents; fire rings and barbecue grills; b-y-o firewood is recommended; water at several faucets; restrooms; paved driveways; camper supplies nearby; complete supplies and services are available in South Lake Tahoe.

Activities & Attractions: Boating; windsurfing; boat launch; fishing; designated swimming beach.

Natural Features: Located in the Sierra Nevada on Meeks Bay along the west shore of Lake Tahoe; campground vegetation consists of sparse grass and underbrush, and some tall conifers; limited views through the trees of the lake; elevation 6300´.

Season, Fees & Phone: May to October; $13.00; 7 day limit; Lake Tahoe Basin Management Unit, South Lake Tahoe, ☎(916) 573-2600 or (916) 544-5994.

Trip Log: Meeks Bay has one of the few public boat launches along the west shore of Lake Tahoe. All campsites at Meeks Bay are quite close to the highway. The Lake Tahoe Basin Management Unit operates several public campgrounds in the area. It's a special division of the Forest Service that manages public lands on three national forests around Lake Tahoe. The sub-agency was set up to provide a unified approach to management of Tahoe's exceptionally important natural resources.

♣ California 88

D.L. BLISS
D.L. Bliss State Park

Location: Eastern California on the west shore of Lake Tahoe.

Access: From California State Highway 89 at milepost 19 +.5 (7 miles south of the El Dorado/Placer county line, 11 miles north of the South Lake Tahoe area), turn northeast onto the park access road; proceed 1 mile down a curvy, narrow roadway to the park entrance station; campsites are in 3 sections within 1.3 miles of the entrance station; day use area is at the far north end of the park road, just beyond the last camp loop, 2.4 miles from the highway. (Note: there is limited maneuvering room in the park; only very short trailers are welcome.)

Day Use Facilities: Medium-sized picnic area; drinking water; restrooms; 2 medium-sized parking lots.

Camping Facilities: 168 campsites in 3 sections; (a group camp is also available, by reservation); most sites are small, quite sloped, with fair to good separation; parking areas are mostly dirt, short to short+ straight-ins; many pads will require additional leveling; fairly good sized, sloped tent spots; storage cabinets; assorted fire appliances; b-y-o firewood; water at several faucets; restrooms with showers; paved driveways; adequate+ supplies and services are available in South Lake Tahoe.

Activities & Attractions: Swimming beach in the day use area; hiking (Rubicon Trail leads to Vikingsholm and to Eagle Creek Falls in adjacent Emerald Bay State Park); Lighthouse Trail to an old lighthouse; Balancing Rock Nature Trail; campfire center.

Natural Features: Located along and above the west shore of Lake Tahoe just north of Emerald Bay; day use area is adjacent to Lester Beach and Calawee Cove Beach; campsites are all situated on a forested slope; vegetation consists of light to medium-dense, tall conifers, including gnarled and stunted sugar pines, and a considerable amount of undergrowth; some campsites are near the lake shore; elevation 6300´ to 7000´.

Season, Fees & Phone: May to September; please see Appendix for reservation information, park entry and campground fees; ☎(916) 525-7277.

Trip Log: D. L. Bliss has what is considered to be one of the two best beaches on the lake. The area is named for a lumberman whose family donated the original tract for the park. This is one of the few state parks where a campsite might be available late in the day during the week without a reservation.

♣ California 89

EMERALD BAY
Emerald Bay State Park

Location: Eastern California on the west shore of Lake Tahoe.

Access: From U.S. 89 at milepost 15 +.3 (7 miles northwest of the South Lake Tahoe area, 12 miles south of the El Dorado/Placer County line), turn northeast into the main park area; or from near milepost 17 +.5, turn east into the Emerald Bay Overlook parking lot.

Day Use Facilities: Small picnic area at Vikingsholm; drinking water; restrooms; Vikingsholm Trail parking in the Emerald Bay Overlook parking lot

Camping Facilities: *Eagle Point Campground*: 100 campsites; (20 primitive, walk-in or boat-in campsites on the middle north/west shore of the bay are also available); sites are small to small+, with minimal to nominal separation; parking pads are mostly short straight-ins, and many will require additional leveling; some parking pads are hard-surfaced, others are gravel/sand; tent spots are small to medium-sized and may be a bit sloped or rocky; storage cabinets; fire rings and barbecue grills; b-y-o firewood is recommended; water at several faucets; restrooms with showers; paved driveways; gas and groceries on Highway 89, 4 miles south; adequate+ supplies and services are available in the South Lake Tahoe area.

Activities & Attractions: Guided tours of Vikingsholm, a 38-room castle built in 1929; steep, 1 mile trail from the parking lot down to Vikingsholm; swimming beach and a short trail to Eagle Falls from Vikingsholm; trail to the beach from the lower camp loop; boating; sailing; dock and mooring buoys at the boat-in camp; (public boat launch in Camp Richardson, 5 miles southeast); shoreline fishing for small trout; boat fishing for Mackinaw trout and kokanee salmon; campfire center; Rubicon Trail leads 3.5 miles from near Vikingsholm to D.L. Bliss State Park.

Natural Features: Located around Emerald Bay on the southwest shore of Lake Tahoe; upper campsites are on a forested slope; lower sites are situated out on tree-dotted Eagle Point; vegetation includes tall conifers, moderate underbrush and sparse grass; Lake Tahoe's only isle, Fannette Island, lies near the southwest tip of the bay; elevation 6300´ to 7000´.

Season, Fees & Phone: June to September; please see Appendix for reservation information, entry and campground fees; extra fee for Vikingsholm tour; ☎(916) 541-3030.

Trip Log: Emerald Bay is shaped like an elongated 'U' with a narrow harbor entrance. The half-mile wide, 1.5-mile long bay is one of the best-sheltered spots on the lake. This part of Lake Tahoe's shoreline is indeed naturally beautiful. Vikingsholm is considered by some to be the foremost example of Scandinavian architecture west of the North Sea. The granite castle, replete with towers and turrets and an authentic sod roof, was designed to replicate a Norse fortress of the ninth century A.D. It is said to have been built without disturbing a single tree on Lake Tahoe's shore. The Indians called Lake Tahoe "Lake of the Sky", and someone has yet to improve on that title.

⚑ California 90 ♿

GROVER HOT SPRINGS
Grover Hot Springs State Park

Location: Eastern California south of Carson City, Nevada.

Access: From California State Highways 89 & 4 at milepost 14 +.8 in midtown Markleeville,

turn west onto Montgomery Street which becomes Hot Springs Road; proceed 3.5 miles; turn north (right) into the park.

Day Use Facilities: Medium-sized picnic area; drinking water; restrooms; medium-sized parking area; large parking lot at the pools.

Camping Facilities: 76 campsites in 2 sections; sites are medium to large with minimal to fair separation; parking pads are paved, short to medium-length, most are straight-ins, many pads may require additional leveling; tent spots are on grass or pine needle surfaces, some are sloped, many are spacious enough for large tents; storage cabinets; fireplaces; firewood is usually for sale, or b-y-o; water at several faucets; restrooms with showers; paved driveways; gas and groceries+ in Markleeville.

Activities & Attractions: Hot springs pools; nature trail; 3 hiking trails; stream fishing for small trout (stocked periodically as stream conditions permit); amphitheater for scheduled programs in summer; Nordic skiing.

Natural Features: Located in a valley on the east side of the Sierra Nevada, with mountains rising sharply on 3 sides; grassy slopes and meadows are interspersed with stands of aspens and conifers; elevation 5800´.

Season, Fees & Phone: Open all year, with limited services (i.e., camping only in the picnic area, with no showers) October to May; pool hours vary seasonally; please see Appendix for reservation information, park entry and campground fees; extra fee for pool use; ☎(916) 694-2248.

Trip Log: Grover's mineral-rich waters leave the ground at 148º, but the temps in the water of the park's two pools run 102º to 105º. Unlike the water of most hot springs, the sulphur content of the water here is quite low. (A breakdown of the mineral content is available from the park office.) Many people believe that these waters, which percolate up from thousands of feet below the surface, are good for just about whatever ails you. You don't have to come here to use the pools, though. The alpine scenery is worth the trip.

⚑ California 91

TWIN LAKES
Toiyabe National Forest

Location: Eastern California southwest of Bridgeport.

Access: From U.S. Highway 395 at milepost 76 +.8 in Bridgeport, turn south onto Kirkwood

Street/Twin Lakes Road (paved) and travel south and southwest for 10 miles; about 100 yards before reaching the lake (just past a resort) turn easterly (left) onto a gravel access road and proceed 0.15 mile; turn left and go 200 yards to *Sawmill* Campground; or continue for another 0.1 mile to *Lower Twin Lakes* Campground.

Day Use Facilities: Small picnic area; vault facilities; small parking area.

Camping Facilities: *Lower Twin Lakes*: 17 campsites in 2 loops; sites are small to medium-sized, basically level, closely spaced, with fair visual separation; parking pads are gravel, medium-length straight-ins; *Sawmill*: 8 campsites; sites are quite small and closely spaced; parking pads are gravel, short straight-ins; *both camps*: medium to large tent areas; fire rings or fireplaces; b-y-o firewood; water at faucets; vaults; gravel driveways; laundry and showers at local resorts; adequate supplies and services are available in Bridgeport.

Activities & Attractions: Boating; fishing on the lake and on the stream; hiking trails.

Natural Features: Located lakeside (picnic area) and just above the lakes' outlet stream, Robinson Creek (campgrounds) in a valley near the northeast tip of Lower Twin Lakes; tall conifers and some short aspens provide moderate shelter/shade for most campsites; bordered by sage slopes and a sage flat, with views of the high peaks of the Sierra Nevada in the distance; elevation 7000´.

Season, Fees & Phone: May to October; $10.00 in Lower Twin Lakes, $7.00 in Sawmill; 14 day limit; Bridgeport Ranger District ☎(619) 932-7070.

Trip Log: Terrific vistas in this area, which is the principal reason for venturing up here. Facilities, however, are so-so. Lower Twin Lakes has some very nice streamside sites in one loop. Sawmill is off the principal gravel road, so drive-by traffic is minimized. (Along the forest road on the way to this pair of camps is Robinson Creek Campground; it has 54 sites, water and vaults along a nice stream that offers good trout fishing.

⩗ California 92 ♿

BODIE

Bodie State Historic Park

Location: Eastern California southeast of Bridgeport.

Access: From U.S. Highway 395 at milepost 69 + .9 at the junction of U.S. 395 & California State Highway 270 (7 miles south of Bridgeport, 19 miles north of Lee Vining), travel east on Highway 270 for 13 miles (paved most of the way) to the park. (It is suggested that you check on road conditions prior to venturing out to the park from September through May.)

Day Use Facilities: Small picnic area; drinking water; restrooms; large parking lot.

Camping Facilities: None; nearest public campgrounds are 3 Toiyabe National Forest camps on Twin Lakes Road (paved), 8 to 11 miles west of Bridgeport.

Activities & Attractions: Self-guided walking tour along the streets of the well-preserved remains of more than 100 buildings of the gold mining town of Bodie.

Natural Features: Located on treeless, brushy, grassy, high desert terrain in the Bodie Hills near the east slopes of the Sierra Nevada; elevation 8400´.

Season, Fees & Phone: Open all year, subject to weather conditions, principal season is May to October; please see Appendix for park entry fees; ☎(619) 647-6445.

Trip Log: In its prime, Bodie had a population of more than 10,000, including a cross-section of gold miners, saloon keepers, merchants, tavern tramps, swindlers, hooligans, and outlaws determined to cash in on the gold rush of the mid-1800's. Bodie survived a lengthy economic decline as the gold supply dwindled by the early 1880's, only to meet a swift and tragic death when a fire storm destroyed half of the town in the Depression year of 1932. The entire population escaped the blaze, leaving everything behind. No one returned after the fire, and Bodie became locked in time. Because of its remote, high-altitude location near the California-Nevada border, Bodie has remained virtually untouched for more than half a century. There are still tables set with dishes, schoolhouse desks piled with books, and bourbon on the bar—as if waiting for the specters of the owners to reclaim their belongings. As you turn off the main highway and head east across the seemingly limitless high desert, your mind may echo the words of the little pioneer girl who wrote in her diary: "Goodbye God, I'm going to Bodie".

California ⚕

Yosemite National Park

Yosemite's scenic wonders have been lauded in literally tens of thousands of books, periodicals, and picture captions. So you probably already know, in general, what visual treats await you. What follows are details of most of the developed recreational facilities within the park's major visitor areas. Access to Yosemite is becoming increasingly restricted during the burdensome summer season. Hopefully, the information will help you make 'efficient' plans to get the most out of your all-too-brief, perhaps once-in-a-lifetime visit.

⚕ California 93 ♿

HODGDON MEADOW
Yosemite National Park

Location: Eastern California in western Yosemite National Park.

Access: From California State Highway 120/Big Oak Flat Road at a point 100 yards southeast of the Big Oak Flat Entrance Station of Yosemite National Park (8 miles northwest of Crane Flat Junction, 28 miles east of the town of Big Oak Flat), turn north onto a paved campground access road and proceed 0.5 mile, then swing right into the campground.

Day Use Facilities: None.

Camping Facilities: 105 campsites, including many park 'n walk sites; (several small group sites are also available); sites are small, generally a little sloped, closely spaced, with nominal to fair visual separation; parking surfaces are sandy gravel/earth, primarily short straight-ins, plus some medium+ pull-throughs; medium to large areas for tents; storage lockers (bear boxes); fireplaces; b-y-o firewood is recommended; water at central faucets; restrooms; paved driveways; limited supplies and services are available in Yosemite Village.

Activities & Attractions: Forest setting.

Natural Features: Located on a rolling slope in the Sierra Nevada; campsites are lightly to moderately sheltered/shaded by tall conifers above an 'open' forest floor with some low hardwoods that provide limited visual separation; a meadow is a short distance east of the campground; elevation 4900´.

Season, Fees & Phone: March to October; $13.00; 14 day limit; reservations mandatory June-October; please see Appendix for additional reservation information; park information ☎(209) 372-0265 (live) or (209) 372-0264 (comprehensive recorded message).

Trip Log: Although there are a couple dozen sites which can accommodate small motorhomes and short trailer combinations, Hodgdon Meadow is really a 'tent campers' special'. A number of park 'n walk campsites are on small 'shelves' below their parking spaces. Pleasant atmosphere here.

⚕ California 94 ♿

CRANE FLAT
Yosemite National Park

Location: Eastern California in western Yosemite National Park.

Access: From Big Oak Flat Road (California State Highway 120) at a point 0.15 mile west of the junction of Big Oak Flat Road & Tioga Pass Road (8 miles east of the Big Oak Flat entrance, 16 miles west of Yosemite Village and 32 miles west of the Tioga Pass entrance), turn south onto the paved campground access road and proceed 0.15 mile to the campground entrance.

Day Use Facilities: None.

Camping Facilities: 165 campsites in 5 loops; sites are typically small, sloped, with minimal to fair separation; parking pads are short pull-offs or straight-ins; adequate space for a medium to large tent in most sites; special sections for campers with pets; firewood is available for gathering in the park; gathering firewood prior to reaching the campground is recommended; fireplaces; water at several faucets; restrooms; paved driveways; gas and snacks at a service station 0.15 mile west; limited supplies and services are available in Yosemite Village.

Activities & Attractions: Tuolumne and Merced Groves of Giant Sequoias are both within a few miles; nature walks, campfire programs in summer.

Natural Features: Located on a rolling slope in a dense forest of super tall conifers, plus some young timber; a small meadow is adjacent to the campground; elevation 6200´.

Season, Fees & Phone: May to October; $13.00; 14 day limit; park information ☎(209) 372-0265 (live) or (209) 372-0264 (comprehensive recorded message).

Trip Log: If Crane Flat and nearby Hodgdon Meadow (described elsewhere) are both filled when you arrive, you may be able to secure a spot in one of several small national forest and BLM camps along Highway 120 and Highway 140 west of the park. Also, Tamarack Flat, a 52-site, no-water, Yosemite camp area, may be available. It's located 4 miles east of Crane Flat on Tioga Pass Road, then 3 miles south on a rough park road.

⚕ California 95 ♿

YOSEMITE VALLEY
Yosemite National Park

Location: Eastern California in south-central Yosemite National Park.

Access: From any of the park entrances, follow the signs to Yosemite Valley/Yosemite Village to the one-way road (Southside Drive) through the valley, eastbound; at a point just opposite the turnoff to Curry Village, turn northerly (left) for 0.2 mile to *Upper River* on the right and *Lower River* on the left; or continue past the turnoff to River Campground for 0.5 mile to *Upper Pines* on the right, *Lower Pines* on the left, and *North Pines* straight ahead, across the river.

Day Use Facilities: Several picnic areas, drinking water, restrooms, and small to medium-sized parking areas are scattered throughout Yosemite Valley.

Camping Facilities: *River Campground*: 263 campsites in 2 major sections; sites are small, basically level, and closely spaced; parking pads are paved, mostly short or short+ straight-ins; adequate space for a large tent in most sites; *Pines Campground*: 499 campsites in 3 major sections; (a group camp is also available in this vicinity); sites are small+, essentially level, with nominal separation; parking pads are paved, mostly short+ straight-ins; adequate space for a large tent in most sites; *all camps*: fireplaces; gathering firewood outside the Valley prior to arrival in the campgrounds is recommended; water at central faucets; restrooms; holding tank disposal stations; paved driveways; limited+ supplies and services for campers are available in Yosemite Village.

(Substantial visitor services, including concessionaire-operated food and lodging, are available in Yosemite Valley; contact park headquarters for brochures & current rates.)

Natural Features: Located in a moderately dense conifer forest along the banks of the Merced River in Yosemite Valley; closely bordered by forested slopes; elevation 4000´.

Activities & Attractions: Trails; visitor center; nature center; nature walks; campfire programs; free shuttle buses.

Season, Fees & Phone: Most day use areas and visitor services are open all year; certain camp sections are open all year, subject to weather conditions; $15.00; 7 day limit; campsite reservations required year 'round; please see Appendix for additional reservation information; park information ☎(209) 372-0265 (live); or (209) 372-0264 (comprehensive recorded message).

Trip Log: Many of Yosemite's most notable natural features are in and around Yosemite Valley. The classic natural architecture, for which Yosemite is world-renowned, is no more evident than it is here in this narrow valley. River Campground and its bigger twin, Pines, are so comparable that it really comes down to which one you're able to obtain reservations for. However, sites in Pines do seem to be slightly larger or farther apart than those in its near-twin camp, River Campground. North Pines is adjacent to a large horse/mule stable complex. In addition to Yosemite Valley's huge, standard campgrounds at Pines and River, a walk-in tent camp is available at the far west end of the Valley complex. Sunnyside Campground has three dozen tent sites, water, restrooms, and is generally available all year. A 25-site backpackers' camp for campers without vehicles is located in the Valley as well. A two-night limit is imposed in the backpackers' camp. The shuttles are a good deal.

⚕ California 96 ♿

WAWONA
Yosemite National Park

Location: Eastern California in the southwest corner of Yosemite National Park.

Access: From Wawona Road (a continuation of California State Highway 41) at a point 1 mile north of Wawona, 6 miles north of the South Entrance Station, and 26 miles south of Yosemite Village, turn east into the History Center or west into the campground.

Day Use Facilities: Small picnic area; drinking water; restrooms; small parking area.

Camping Facilities: 100 campsites in 3 loops; (a group camp is also available); sites are small, close together and somewhat sloped; parking pads are gravel, mostly short straight-ins or pull-offs; adequate space for a large tent in most sites; fireplaces; firewood is available for gathering in the park; water at faucets; restrooms; paved driveways; gas and camper supplies in Wawona; limited supplies and services in Yosemite Village; adequate supplies and services are available in Oakhurst, 22 miles south.

Activities & Attractions: Pioneer Yosemite History Center; trails; fishing; campfire programs; Mariposa Grove, largest of 3 sequoia groves in the park, lies several miles south.

Natural Features: Located on the east bank of the South Fork of the Merced River; campground vegetation consists primarily of light to medium dense tall conifers; sites in the A and C sections tend to be more in the open than those in the middle B Loop; many sites are along the river or have a river view; heavily timbered hills and ridges flank the river; elevation 4000´.

Season, Fees & Phone: Open all year; $11.00; 14 day limit; park information ☎(209) 372-0265 (live) or (209) 372-0264 (recorded message).

Trip Log: The campground stretches along the river for almost a mile. Toward the north end, the sites are pretty tightly packed and the driveway is narrow. As an option, Summerdale, a national forest camp just outside the park, has larger and more level sites in a creekside setting, but costs a little more as well.

⚐ California 97 ♿

WHITE WOLF
Yosemite National Park

Location: Eastern California in central Yosemite National Park.

Access: From Tioga Pass Road (California State Highway 120) at a point 22 miles east of the Big Oak Flat entrance and 32 miles west of the Tioga Pass entrance, turn north onto a paved access road and proceed 1.2 miles to the campground entrance, on the right side of the road, just past the lodge.

Day Use Facilities: None.

Camping Facilities: 87 campsites; sites are small and closely spaced, and vary from fairly level in most sites, to a little sloped in some; parking pads are gravel, mainly short straight-ins; large tent areas; fireplaces; some firewood is available for gathering in the surrounding area; water at several faucets; restrooms; paved

driveways; showers at the lodge; gas and camper supplies at Tuolumne Meadows, 25 miles east.

Activities & Attractions: Trails; campfire programs and nature walks in summer.

Natural Features: Located in a moderately dense stand of tall conifers; a small creek flows past a number of sites; a meadow lies just south of the camping area; elevation 8000´.

Season, Fees & Phone: June to October; $11.00; 14 day limit; park information ☎(209) 372-0265 (live) or (209) 372-0264 (recorded message).

Trip Log: Since the parking spots here are a little snug, this campground seems to be favored mostly by tenters and tent trailer campers. Another park campground that's accessible from near White Wolf is Yosemite Creek. From Tioga Pass Road at a point 0.4 mile east of the White Wolf turnoff, head south on a rough road for five miles to the campground. Yosemite Creek has 75 basically primitive sites, vaults, no drinking water and a nominal fee, near a stream. Neither the rugged road into Yosemite Creek nor the small campsites are really compatible with large vehicles or vehicles with trailers.

⚐ California 98

PORCUPINE FLAT
Yosemite National Park

Location: Eastern California in central Yosemite National Park.

Access: From Tioga Pass Road (California State Highway 120) at a point 31 miles east of the Big Oak Flat entrance and 23 miles west of the Tioga Pass entrance, turn north into the campground.

Day Use Facilities: None.

Camping Facilities: 52 campsites; sites are small, tolerably level, with nominal to fair separation; parking surfaces are earth/gravel, mostly short to short+ straight-ins or pull-offs; small to medium-sized tent areas; fireplaces; some firewood is available for gathering in the area; no drinking water; vault facilities; narrow, gravel/earth driveways; gas and camper supplies at Tuolumne Meadows, 25 miles east.

Activities & Attractions: Forest atmosphere; roadside convenience.

Natural Features: Located on a forested flat; sites are moderately sheltered by tall conifers; elevation 8100´.

Season, Fees & Phone: May to October; $7.00; 14 day limit; park info ☎(209) 372-0265 (live) or (209) 372-0264 (comprehensive recorded message).

Trip Log: There's a hushed, tall timber environment here. The vehicle paths are narrow and prone to be rutty, and most of the campground can only handle smaller vehicles. The campsites are scattered throughout the forest in a complex of strings and loops, so it would pay to take your time to find all of the isolated sites here. (Finding a vacant site after dark could be a challenge.) Regardless, or because of, its undeveloped state, Porcupine Flat fills early every night in midsummer, as do all of Yosemite's campgrounds.

⚐ California 99 ♿

TUOLUMNE MEADOWS
Yosemite National Park

Location: Eastern California near the east boundary of Yosemite National Park.

Access: From Tioga Pass Road (California State Highway 120) at a point 7 miles west of the Tioga Pass entrance and 48 miles east of the Big Oak Flat entrance, turn south, proceed 0.15 mile to the campground.

Day Use Facilities: Small picnic area; drinking water; restrooms; medium-sized parking area.

Camping Facilities: 325 campsites, including about 25 backpacker sites; sites are small and closely spaced, with minimal visual separation, and slightly sloped; parking pads are short, dirt straight-ins; adequate space for a large tent in most sites; separate section for campers with pets; fireplaces or fire rings; firewood is available for gathering in the park; gathering firewood from outside the campground area, or b-y-o, is suggested; water at several faucets; restrooms; narrow, roughly paved driveway; gas, camper supplies, and showers nearby.

Activities & Attractions: Elizabeth Lake Trail leads off from the south end of the campground; numerous other trails in the area; campfire circles; limited fishing.

Natural Features: Located on a rolling, rocky flat in a moderately dense stand of tall conifers on the edge of Tuolumne Meadows; the Tuolumne River flows past the east end of the camp; a timbered ridge lies to the north, high peaks rise to the east and south; elev. 8600´.

Season, Fees & Phone: June to October; $13.00 for a standard site, $4.00 per person for backpackers or others without vehicles; reservations required July-August; 14 day limit; please see Appendix for additional reservation information; park information ☎(209) 372-0265 (live) or (209) 372-0264 (comprehensive recorded message).

Trip Log: This ancient, venerable, simple campground is a favorite with tent campers. It's a bit far to commute between here and dazzling Yosemite Valley (55 miles). Quite candidly, though, you may discover that you don't *have* to stay within striking distance of the Valley, and that Tuolumne's own natural luster is very gratifying indeed. Just east of the park's Tioga Pass entrance (about 8 miles from Tuolumne Meadows) is an Inyo National Forest recreation area, Tioga Lake. This highwayside spot has a small camp that's mainly suitable for tent campers, and a small parking area. The alpine lake views are superlative and worth at least a short stop.

 California
South Central Coast

⚐ California 100 ♿

KIRK CREEK
Los Padres National Forest

Location: Central California Coast south of Monterey.

Access: From California State Highway 1 at milepost 19 (29 miles south of Big Sur, 39 miles north of San Simeon), turn west into the campground.

Day Use Facilities: None.

Camping Facilities: 33 campsites in 2 loops; (a hike-bike site is also available); sites are generously medium-sized, and most are quite private; parking pads are gravel, medium-length straight-ins; most pads will probably require additional leveling; large, slightly sloped tent areas; fire rings; b-y-o firewood is recommended; water at several faucets; restrooms; paved driveways; gas and groceries, 3 miles south and 4 miles north; nearest sources of limited or better supplies and services are 60 miles, north or south.

Activities & Attractions: Terrific views; trailhead on the east side of the highway.

Natural Features: Located on a moderately steep, open slope just above the Pacific Ocean; campground vegetation consists of dense, ceiling-height shrubbery around most sites, plus some tall conifers; steep, brushy hills and mountains form the backdrop to the east; a coastal promontory lies a short distance to the north; elevation 100´.

Season, Fees & Phone: Open all year; $11.00; 14 day limit; Monterey Ranger District, King City, ☎ (408) 385-5434.

Trip Log: Kirk Creek is undoubtedly a popular spot. It reportedly fills up on most nights during summer. But it might be worth a wait to get a campsite. The views up and down the coast are quite impressive. This is one of only a handful of national forest campgrounds along the entire Pacific Coast.

⚐ **California 101** ♿

PLASKETT CREEK
Los Padres National Forest

Location: Central California Coast south of Monterey.

Access: From California State Highway 1 at milepost 13 +.6 (34 miles north of San Simeon, 34 miles south of Big Sur), turn west into the day use area, or east into Plaskett Creek Campground.

Day Use Facilities: Small picnic area; drinking water; restrooms; medium-sized parking lot.

Camping Facilities: 43 campsites in a main loop plus a small side loop; sites are generally medium-sized, with minimal separation; parking pads are paved, short to medium-length straight-ins, and many will require a little additional leveling; plenty of room for tents, though spaces are generally slightly sloped; fire rings and barbecue grills; limited firewood is available for gathering, b-y-o is recommended; water at faucets; restrooms; paved driveways; gas and groceries, 2 miles north.

Activities & Attractions: Sand Dollar Beach, adjacent to the day use area.

Natural Features: Located on a tree-dotted bluff between the highway and the ocean (day use area), and on a slight to moderate slope at the base of a forested hill several hundred yards from the Pacific Ocean (campground); camp vegetation consists of a spacious, grassy infield ringed by large evergreens; elevation 200´.

Season, Fees & Phone: Open all year; $11.00; 14 day limit; Monterey Ranger District, King City, ☎ (408) 385-5434.

Trip Log: Plaskett Creek almost has the appearance of a state park—it has a 'landscaped' look. The campsites are of typical width and spacing; but they are quite long or 'deep', and consequently tents can be pitched on the expansive infield 'lawn' quite a distance from the loop driveway. The sites in the small loop just to the north of the primary camping area are smaller, but a little more private. Plaskett Creek might have spaces available a little later in the day than Kirk Creek (described above), since it isn't right at the ocean's edge. Supplies are really scarce along this stretch of the coast. Morro Bay and Monterey, each about 60 miles south and north, respectively, are the only real supply points, other than a few snack and gas stops, on this section of the Coast.

⚐ **California 102** ♿

HEARST SAN SIMEON
Hearst San Simeon State Historical Monument

Location: Central California Coast northwest of San Luis Obispo.

Access: From California State Highway 1 at milepost 57 +.7 (in the community of San Simeon, 8 miles north of Cambria) turn northeast onto the park access road and proceed 0.5 mile to the parking lot; tour ticket sales windows are inside the visitor center.

Day Use Facilities: Small picnic area; drinking water and restrooms inside the visitor center; huge parking lot, including designated rv, bus and motorcycle parking sections; snack bar.

Camping Facilities: None; nearest public campground is in San Simeon State Beach.

Activities & Attractions: Guided tours of "Hearst Castle", which includes a 130-room main residence "La Casa Grande", plus guest houses, pools, and 125 acres of formal gardens; four tours (each about 1 hour 45 minutes) are available; Tour 1 is the suggested first-time tour; elaborate visitor center features displays and audio-visual presentations about Hearst and the construction of this truly palatial estate.

Natural Features: Located on a hill 2 miles east of the Pacific Ocean; landscaping defies description; sea level to 200´.

Season, Fees & Phone: Open all year, daily except certain major holidays; for guided tours, $14.00 for adults and teens, $8.00 for children

6-12; (price includes a $2.00 "service fee" if you purchase the tickets on-site, or a $2.00 "reservation fee" for tickets reserved through MISTIX, so the cost is the same whether you reserve or walk-in unannounced); (parking lot and visitor center are free of charge, subject to change); please see Appendix for additional reservation information; ☎(805) 927-2000.

Trip Log: Communications magnate William Randolph Hearst began building *La Cuesta Encantata* ("The Enchanted Hill") in 1919. It was designed to be a kingly residence for one of the wealthiest and most influential private citizens of the period. The only way to see the "Castle" (except at a distance) is to take a guided tour. Reservations are strongly recommended. (About a million tourists come here each year, and the park is busy even on rainy Monday mornings in February.) One of many shuttle buses will take you up the hill from what must be the largest visitor center of any park in the country. Really, the place rivals Grand Central Station. You can look at countless photographs of this place, but until you actually walk the magnificently landscaped grounds and grand hallways of this humble abode, you'll still not believe it.

⚑ California 103 ♿

MORRO BAY
Morro Bay State Park

Location: Central California Coast northwest of San Luis Obispo.

Access: From California State Highway 1 at milepost 27 +.8 (11 miles northwest of San Luis Obispo, 1 mile south of the city of Morro Bay), turn south onto South Bay Boulevard; proceed 0.8 mile, then bear southwest (right) onto State Park Road for 0.75 mile to the park.

Day Use Facilities: Medium-sized picnic area, drinking water, restrooms and parking area adjacent to the campground; a few picnic tables, drinking water, restrooms, medium-sized parking lot at the museum.

Camping Facilities: 135 campsites, including 20 with partial hookups; (hike/bike sites and a reservable group camp are also available); sites are small to small+, level, with nominal to fair separation; parking pads are medium-length, gravel/dirt straight-ins in most of the sites; hookup units have paved pull-throughs; good-sized, level tent areas; storage cabinets; fireplaces or fire rings; firewood is usually for sale, or b-y-o; water at hookups and at several

faucets; restrooms with showers; holding tank disposal station; paved driveways; adequate supplies and services are available in Morro Bay.

Activities & Attractions: Museum of Natural History features displays and audio-visual programs; guided nature walks and interpretive programs; 1.5 mile fitness trail; hiking trails, including trails to viewpoints on Black Hill; fishing; boating; public boat launch just north of the park; 18-hole public golf course and marina, operated by concessionaires.

Natural Features: Located primarily on a large wooded flat on the east shore of Morro Bay; tall conifers and some hardwoods provide a substantial amount of shelter/shade in most camp and picnic sites; Black Hill rises to 661´ east of the bayside section, another hill tops 900´; sea level to 911´.

Season, Fees & Phone: Open all year; museum fee $2.00 for adults, $1.00 for children under 18 (subject to change); please see Appendix for reservation information, park entry and campground fees; ☎(805) 772-2560 or 772-9723 (office), or 772-2694 (museum).

Trip Log: There's little doubt that this is one of the nicer coastal parks. The natural history museum has an observation room from which you can look out to haystack-shaped Morro Rock and across Morro Bay through an array of large windows (bay windows, so to speak). Excellent picture-taking possibilities here.

⚑ California 104 ♿

EL CHORRO
San Luis Obispo County Regional Park

Location: Central California coastal area northwest of San Luis Obispo.

Access: From California State Highway 1 at milepost 22 +.2 (5 miles northwest of San Luis Obispo, 6 miles southeast of Morro Bay, opposite the main entrance to the Camp San Luis Obispo National Guard facility), turn north onto a paved access road, and proceed 0.3 mile to the park.

Day Use Facilities: Large picnic area; drinking water; restrooms; large parking lot.

Camping Facilities: 25 campsites; sites are mostly small, tolerably level considering the slope, with nominal separation; parking pads are paved, medium-length straight-ins; large areas for tents; fire rings; b-y-o firewood; water at several faucets; restrooms with coin-op showers;

adequate supplies in Morro Bay; complete supplies and services are available in San Luis Obispo.

Activities & Attractions: Sports field; just a few miles from/to the ocean.

Natural Features: Located on a gentle slope in a valley surrounded by low, grassy hills; landscaping consists of small hardwoods and some conifers on a grassy surface; elev. 150´.

Season, Fees & Phone: Open all year; $12.00; 15 day limit; San Luis Obispo County Parks Department ☎(805) 549-5219.

Trip Log: If a picnic spot or campsite is tough to find at the area's seaside parks (Pismo and Morro Bay), as is often the case, El Chorro might be a welcome alternative. It's only a few minutes' drive from here to the sand and the surf. Superior views of neighboring hills and rugged mountains from up here.

♣ **California 105**

OCEANO
Pismo State Beach

Location: Southern California Coast south of San Luis Obispo.

Access: From California State Highway 1 in Oceano at a point 1.1 miles south of the intersection of Highway 1 and Grand Avenue in Grover City, turn west onto Pier Avenue and proceed 0.2 mile; turn north (right) into the campground entrance; or continue west for another 0.2 mile to the day use/beach access area.

Day Use Facilities: Restrooms; medium-sized parking lot.

Camping Facilities: 82 campsites, including 42 with partial hookups, in 2 sections; sites are small to small+, level, with minimal to fair separation; hookup pads are paved, medium to long, parallel pull-throughs; standard pads are mostly short to medium-length straight-ins; excellent tent-pitching possibilities in the standard section; fire rings; firewood is usually for sale, or b-y-o; water at several faucets; restrooms with showers; paved driveways; groceries nearby; adequate+ supplies and services are available within 3 miles.

Activities & Attractions: Trails from the campground along the lagoon and to the beach; lagoon interpretive trail (a guide pamphlet is available); nature programs; beach access; park golf course; Pismo Dunes SVRA, adjacent.

Natural Features: Located on a moderately to densely wooded flat (campground) or on an open beach (day use); campsites are lightly to moderately shaded/sheltered by large hardwoods, tall conifers, and bushes; Oceano Lagoon, adjacent to the campground, and high dunes provide added natural interest; sea level.

Season, Fees & Phone: Open all year; please see Appendix for reservation information, park entry and campground fees; ☎(805) 489-2684.

Trip Log: When the tide is out, there are several square miles of sand that you can wander out onto. The beach is world famous for its Pismo clams and you might bag a 'keeper'. Camping and picnicking are also available in Pismo's nearby North Beach area. North Beach has 103 lightly sheltered campsites, restrooms, and a medium-sized picnic area. If you want to camp or picnic at Pismo Beach, it's a tough choice between Oceano and North Beach. Both are quite nice. North Beach is in a more open setting, with less tall vegetation, but with large, grassy areas. Oceano's environment is perhaps somewhat more interesting, however.

♣ **California 106** ♿

LA PURISIMA MISSION
La Purisima Mission State Historic Park

Location: Southern California northwest of Santa Barbara.

Access: From California State Highway 246 at a point 12.5 miles west of U.S. 101 at Buellton and 4.5 miles northeast of Lompoc, proceed northwest on Purisima Road for 0.8 mile, then turn north (right) into the park. **Alternate Access:** From California State Highway 1 at its junction with Santa Barbara County Road S20 (3 miles north of Lompoc) proceed southeast on Purisima Road for 2 miles to the park turnoff.

Day Use Facilities: Medium-sized picnic area; drinking water; restrooms; medium-large parking lot.

Camping Facilities: None; nearest public campground is in Gaviota State Park.

Activities & Attractions: Complete reconstruction of an Early California Spanish mission; paved walkways throughout the grounds; visitor center with historical exhibits, including dioramas; historical and natural interpretive programs and guided tours scheduled regularly throughout the year (a calendar is available upon request).

Natural Features: Located in *La Canada de los Berros* (Canyon of the Watercress) in the Purisima Hills on the north edge of the Santa Ynez Valley; park vegetation consists of immense tracts of grass, and stands of hardwoods; picnic sites are nicely shaded; elevation 100´.

Season, Fees & Phone: Open all year; please see Appendix for park entry fees; ☎(805) 733-3713 or ☎(805) 733-1303.

Trip Log: *Mission la Purisima Concepcion de Maria Santisima* was founded in 1787 by Franciscan Padre Fermin De Lasuen, as the eleventh of the twenty-one California missions. The mission served the Chumash Indians and taught them not only religion but agricultural and industrial arts as well. But a 'secularization' (i.e., land grab) of the California missions by the Mexican governors in the 1830's led to the Franciscans' withdrawal from this mission in 1834. Exactly 100 years later, a consortium of private and religious organizations, plus local and state agencies, donated or purchased land for La Purisima's renewal; the CCC excavated the site and began to rebuild the structures as authentically as possible. The tens of thousands of square feet of church, courtyards, living quarters, workshops, gardens and orchards now make up what is said to be the only completely restored mission in the Western United States.

♣ California 107 ᵹ

REFUGIO
Refugio State Beach

Location: Southern California Coast west of Santa Barbara.

Access: From U.S. Highway 101 near milepost 36 +.5 (9 miles east of Gaviota, 22 miles west of Santa Barbara), take the Refugio Road Exit, then from the south side of the freeway, go southwest on Refugio Road for 0.4 mile to the park. (If you're northbound on U.S. 101, you'll need to take a freeway underpass to get onto the park road.)

Day Use Facilities: Large picnic area; drinking water; restrooms; large parking lot; concession stand

Camping Facilities: 85 campsites in 2 sections; (hike-bike sites and a large group camp are also available); sites are very small to small, level, with minimal to fair separation; sites in the south section are perhaps a little larger and better-separated than those in the other loop; parking pads are gravel/dirt, mostly short

straight-ins; small tent areas; fire rings; firewood is usually for sale, or b-y-o; water at several faucets; restrooms with showers; paved driveways; complete supplies and services are available in Santa Barbara.

(Day use areas and campgrounds are also available in nearby El Capitan State Beach and Gaviota State Park.)

Activities & Attractions: Swimming beach; surf fishing.

Natural Features: Located along and near a small cove on the Santa Barbara Channel; the park has lots of short and tall palms, big hardwoods, shrubbery, and open, expansive lawns; picnic sites are minimally to very lightly shaded, most campsites are well shaded and sheltered; bordered by the Santa Ynez Mountains to the north; sea level.

Season, Fees & Phone: Open all year; please see Appendix for reservation information, park entry and campground fees; ☎(805) 968-3294.

Trip Log: Refugio is one of the best state beaches in terms of landscaping. On an off-season weekend, it would be a very nice place to spend some leisure time. It benefits from direct southerly exposure and is fairly well sheltered from heavy seas when a norther' blows down the coast. The Channel Islands provide a measure of protection from southerly seas as well.

♣ California 108 ᵹ

CACHUMA LAKE
Santa Barbara County Recreation Area

Location: Southwest California north of Santa Barbara.

Access: From California State Highway 154 at milepost 14 +.7 (24 miles northwest of Santa Barbara, 7 miles southeast of Santa Ynez), turn northeast onto a paved access road and continue 0.2 mile to the park entrance.

Day Use Facilities: Large picnic area; drinking water; restrooms; large parking lot.

Camping Facilities: 530 campsites (+/- a dozen or so), including a few with hookups, in 6 major areas; (hike-bike sites are also available; group camp areas are available by reservation); sites vary from small to medium+ in size, with minimal to very good separation; most parking pads are gravel/dirt, short to medium-length straight-ins; hookup pads are gravel, long straight-ins which may require additional leveling; most tent areas are large and generally level; fireplaces or fire rings; b-y-o firewood; water at several faucets; restrooms with showers; holding tank disposal station; paved driveways; gas and camper supplies and laundry in the park; limited supplies and services are available in Santa Ynez.

Activities & Attractions: Boating; fishing for bass, panfish, trout and catfish; nature trails; swimming pool; playground.

Natural Features: Located on a peninsula on the northwest shore of man-made Cachuma Lake, on the north slope of the Santa Ynez Mountains; vegetation consists of lots of oaks and a few pines throughout the park, plus sections of lawns; elevation 800´.

Season, Fees & Phone: Open all year; $12.00 for a standard site, $16.00 for a hookup site; park office ☎(805) 688-4658.

Trip Log: A description of this BIG park with its BIG campground is difficult to encapsulate. The largest and most private sites are in the Mohawk area, 0.5 mile east (right) of the entrance station. The hookup units are in the Apache area, near the entrance. The best views (and there are some really great lake/mountain views here) may be from the camping areas out along a peninsula, directly north (straight ahead) of the entrance station. Then, too, there's a small cluster of hike-bike-tent sites on Teepee Island, accessible via a footbridge adjacent to a parking area. Good luck!

♣ California 109 ♿

LOS PIETROS
Santa Ynez Canyon/Los Padres National Forest

Location: Southwest California north of Santa Barbara.

Access: From California State Highway 154 at milepost 21 +.6 (17 miles north of Santa Barbara, 14 miles southeast of Santa Ynez), turn east onto Paradise Road and drive 4.7 miles; turn south (right) into the campground.

Day Use Facilities: None.

Camping Facilities: 37 campsites; sites are average-sized, with nominal separation; parking pads are paved, short to medium-length straight-ins, and many will require a little additional leveling; large, but slightly sloped, tent areas; fire rings and barbecue grills; b-y-o firewood is recommended; water at several faucets; restrooms; paved driveway; ranger station 0.8 mile east; limited supplies in Santa Ynez;

complete supplies and services are available in Santa Barbara.

(Camping is also available at Paradise and Fremont Campgrounds, both with about 15 campsites, which you'll pass on the way up to Los Pietros.)

Activities & Attractions: Trails; early spring trout fishing on the Santa Ynez River.

Natural Features: Located on a rolling slope on the south side of Santa Ynez Canyon; most sites are quite well sheltered by large oak trees; some views of the canyon and nearby mountains from the campground area; elevation 1000´.

Season, Fees & Phone: Open all year; $8.00; 14 day limit; Santa Barbara Ranger District ☎(805) 967-3481.

Trip Log: Interestingly, even though this area is only 10 miles from the ocean, summer days often experience temperatures well into the 90's. The high temps are due to a regional phenomenon known as the Santa Ana, a hot, dry, easterly wind. This campground might be an excellent choice for a warm-day camp, since it has more shade than any of the other campgrounds in Santa Ynez Canyon.

♣ California 110

SANTA YNEZ
Santa Ynez Canyon/Los Padres National Forest

Location: Southwest California north of Santa Barbara.

Access: From California State Highway 154 at milepost 21 +.6 (17 miles north of Santa Barbara, 14 miles southeast of Santa Ynez), turn east onto Paradise Road and travel 8.8 miles to the campground, on the south (right) side of the road.

Day Use Facilities: None.

Camping Facilities: 34 campsites; sites are medium to medium+ in size, level, with minimal separation; parking pads are gravel, medium-length straight-ins; plenty of room for tents; fire rings and barbecue grills; limited firewood is available for gathering, b-y-o is suggested; water at several faucets; vault facilities; narrow, paved driveway; limited supplies in Santa Ynez; complete supplies and services are available in Santa Barbara.

Activities & Attractions: Fishing; hiking trails; several orv roads and trails.

Natural Features: Located near the bank of the Santa Ynez River in Santa Ynez Canyon along the north slope of the Santa Ynez Mountains; campground vegetation consists of grass and some low brush, plus tall, full oak trees which provide a considerable amount of shade/shelter; dryish, tree-and-brush-covered hills and high mountains surround the area; elevation 1100´.

Season, Fees & Phone: Open all year; $8.00; 14 day limit; Santa Barbara Ranger District ☎(805) 967-3481.

Trip Log: This is the farthest east of the major camps in Santa Ynez Recreation Area. It might be helpful for you to stop at the ranger station at Los Prietos, 4 miles west of here, on the way into the canyon. Maps and detailed information about local foot trails and areas designated for orv (off-road vehicle) use are available there.

 California ⛺

Los Angeles Basin

⛺ **California 111**

WHEELER GORGE
Los Padres National Forest

Location: Southwest California northeast of Ventura.

Access: From California State Highway 33 (Maricopa Highway) at milepost 19 +.2 (9 miles north of Ojai, 60 miles south of Maricopa) turn west into the campground.

Day Use Facilities: None.

Camping Facilities: 72 campsites; sites are generally medium-sized, level, with good visual separation; most parking pads are paved, short to medium-length straight-ins; some pads are gravel, and a handful are long, paved pull-throughs; medium-sized tent areas; fire rings and barbecue grills; b-y-o firewood is recommended; water at several faucets; vault facilities; paved driveways; adequate+ supplies and services are available in Ojai.

Activities & Attractions: Fishing; many trails in the area; Matilija Hot Springs and Matilija Reservoir, 4 miles southwest.

Natural Features: Located on a roadside flat along the North Fork of Matilija Creek in Wheeler Gorge; vegetation in the campground consists primarily of dense, medium-high oaks and willows which provide a considerable amount of shade/shelter; small side streams flow through the campground; surrounded by dry, brushy hills and mountains; elevation 2000´.

Season, Fees & Phone: April to November; $10.00; 14 day limit; Ojai Ranger District ☎(805) 646-4348.

Trip Log: If you're coming from Ojai (which, chances are, you will be), you'll have to pass through several low, narrow tunnels and a slim section of road to get here. The highway is really snakey coming in from the north, as well. Information and sketched maps about the trails in the area may be available at the campground's info station, or from the ranger station in Ojai. Another local public campground is Camp Comfort County Park, on the southwest corner of Ojai. It has close to a hundred small tent and rv sites (some with electrical-hookups), and showers.

⛺ **California 112** ♿

MCGRATH
McGrath State Beach

Location: Southern California Coast west of Oxnard.

Access: From U.S. Highway 101 near milepost 28 +.5 in Ventura, take the Seaward Avenue Exit, then from the south/west side of the freeway, turn southeast (left) onto Harbor Boulevard and go southeast and south for 3 miles; turn west (right) onto the park access road and go 0.15 mile to the park. **Alternate Access:** From California State Highway 1 (Oxnard Boulevard) in Oxnard, at a point 1 mile south of the junction of State Highway 1 & U.S. Highway 101 turn west onto Gonzales Road and travel 4.5 miles; turn north (right) onto Harbor Boulevard and proceed 0.6 mile; turn west (left) onto the park access road; continue as above.

Day Use Facilities: Medium-sized parking lot.

Camping Facilities: 174 campsites; (a hike/bike site is also available); sites are small to small+, level, with nominal to fairly good separation; parking pads are paved, short to medium-length straight-ins; large, grassy areas for tents; fire rings; b-y-o firewood; water at central faucets; restrooms with showers; disposal station; paved driveways; complete supplies and services are available in Ventura and Oxnard.

Activities & Attractions: Beachcombing; trail to the beach; Santa Clara River Nature Trail; small visitor center; campfire center; Channel Islands NP visitor center, 1 mile north.

Natural Features: Located along and near an ocean beach; campground is on the lee side of a dune and has large expanses of grass bordered by dense bushes and medium-height trees; Santa Clara Estuary Natural Preserve, adjacent; sea level.

Season, Fees & Phone: Open all year; please see Appendix for reservation information, park entry and campground fees; ☎(805) 654-4744

Trip Log: McGrath's campground is unique among California camps. The sites are situated in six clusters or pods, with three perfectly circular cul-de-sacs within each pod. The parking pads radiate outward at an angle from each cul-de-sac. The entire campground, therefore, if you were to view it from above (or on the campground map), would resemble an assemblage of gears—for an 18-speed transmission, a Rube Goldberg contraption, or maybe a cuckoo clock.

♠ California 113 &

MALIBU CREEK
Malibu Creek State Park

Location: Southern California northwest of Los Angeles.

Access: From U.S. Highway 101 (Ventura Freeway) at the Las Virgenes Road/Malibu Canyon Exit (7 miles east of Thousand Oaks, 6 miles west of Woodland Hills), travel south on Las Virgenes Road/L.A. County Road N1 for 3.5 miles; turn west (right) onto the park access road; go 0.1 mile to the park. **Alternate Access:** From California State Highway 1 at a point 2 miles west of Malibu, head north on Malibu Canyon Road for 6 miles to the park access road and continue as above.

Day Use Facilities: Medium-sized picnic area; group picnic area; drinking water; restrooms; large parking lots for day users, visitor center and trail users.

Camping Facilities: 63 campsites; (hike/bike campsites and 2 group camps are also available); sites are small+, with nominal separation; parking pads are hard-surfaced, short straight-ins; additional leveling will be required in some sites; enough space for just about any-size tent; fireplaces; charcoal fires only; water at several faucets; restrooms with showers; disposal station; paved driveways; complete supplies and services are available in Thousand Oaks and Woodland Hills.

Activities & Attractions: More than 15 miles of hike/horse trails and 15 miles of fire roads; mountain bikes are limited to designated fire roads; (a large, detailed park brochure/map with contour lines is available from the park office); nature trail for visually handicapped individuals; fishing for rainbow trout (stocked in cooler seasons), bass, bluegill, sunfish, bullheads; visitor center (accessible via a trail); campfire center.

Natural Features: Located in Malibu Canyon and in the craggy Santa Monica Mountains west of the canyon; the park land and its associated natural preserves lie along the banks of Malibu Creek (and one or both sides of Road N1) from near the Pacific Ocean to a point 2 miles north of the main park entrance, as well as extensively west of the creek; picnic sites are unshaded, campsites are unshaded to very lightly shaded; elevation 100´ to 2300´.

Season, Fees & Phone: Open all year; please see Appendix for reservation information, park entry and campground fees; ☎(818) 706-1310 or ☎(805) 987-3303.

Trip Log: Malibu Creek prides itself as being "on the boundary of two worlds...the freeways, people and pressures of the Los Angeles Basin...and within an easy walk are rugged cliffs and shady canyons, brushy fields and bedrock pools, solitude and silence". And that, in a nutshell, is what the park is all about.

♠ California 114 &

WILL ROGERS
Will Rogers State Historic Park

Location: Southern California west of Los Angeles.

Access: From Interstate 405 at the Sunset Boulevard Exit in the Brentwood-Bel Air area west of Los Angeles (6 miles south of the junction of I-405 & U.S. 101, 3 miles north of the junction of I-405 & I-10) travel southwest on Sunset Boulevard for 4.5 miles; turn northerly (a hairpin right) onto Will Rogers State Park Road and proceed 0.6 mile to the park entrance.

Alternate Access: From California State Highway 1 near Pacific Palisades (2 miles northwest of the junction of State Highway 1 & I-10 in Santa Monica), proceed northerly on Chautauqua Boulevard for 1 mile, then turn northeast (right) onto Sunset Boulevard and continue for another mile to the park access road and continue as above. (Note: Sunset Boulevard is narrow, curvy, steep, with fast traffic; if you're pulling a trailer, an early Sunday morning visit might be your best bet.)

Day Use Facilities: Small picnic area; drinking water; restrooms; large parking lot.

Camping Facilities: None; nearest public campground is in Malibu Creek State Park.

Activities & Attractions: Home of the early 20th century entertainer, film star and home-spun philosopher, Will Rogers; biographical film; self-guided tours of the main house and grounds (audio tour of the grounds); group tours (by reservation, contact the park office); Inspiration Point Trail (2-mile loop); nature trail; nature center; visitor center; occasional matches are held on the ranch's polo grounds.

Natural Features: Located on hilly terrain on the south slope of the Santa Monica Mountains above Santa Monica Canyon; the park is landscaped with large sections of lawns, tall hardwoods, conifers, evergreens and shrubs; elevation 700´.

Season, Fees & Phone: Open all year; please see Appendix for park entry fees; ☎(213) 454-8212.

Trip Log: Born in a small house near Oologah in Northeast Oklahoma in 1879, Will Rogers first earned a living as a cowboy on ranches in the green and gold hills of the Cherokee. He started into show business early in life as a trick roper, and by the 1930's had risen to the top of his profession as a humorist, film star, newspaper columnist and radio commentator. In line with his unassuming personality, Rogers referred to this property as a "ranch"; just about anyone else might call it an "estate". He died in an airplane crash in Alaska in 1935 and is buried in Claremore, Oklahoma. Rogers' unembroidered philosophy "I never met a man I didn't like" is one of twentieth century America's most-often quoted principles.

♠ California 115

TABLE MOUNTAIN
Angeles National Forest

Location: Southwest California northwest of San Bernardino.

Access: From California State Highway 2 at milepost 79 +.9, just west of the national forest visitor center at Big Pines, (4 miles northwest of Wrightwood, 61 miles northeast of Glendale) turn north onto Table Mountain Road (paved) and continue up the hill for 1.1 miles; turn left onto the campground access road, and go a final 0.15 mile to the campground.

Day Use Facilities: None.

Camping Facilities: 118 campsites in 6 loops; sites are medium to a generous medium in size, with nominal separation; parking pads are gravel/sand, medium-length straight-ins; large tent areas; about half the sites are reasonably level, the remainder are quite sloped; fire rings, plus a few barbecue grills; some firewood may be available in the general vicinity, gather some wood before arriving to be sure; water at several faucets; vault facilities; limited supplies and services are available in Wrightwood.

Activities & Attractions: Nature trail; Big Pines Visitor Center; Sheep Mountain Wilderness lies due south of here.

Natural Features: Located on a westward-facing slope on Table Mountain, on the northwest edge of Blue Ridge, northeast of the San Gabriel Mountains; campground vegetation consists of tall pines and other conifers, some oaks, and a small amount of young growth and low-level brush; the campground lies almost directly in line with the San Andreas Rift; elevation 7000´.

Season, Fees & Phone: May to October; $11.00; Valyermo R.D. ☎(805) 944-2187.

Trip Log: On a reasonably clear night, the brilliant lights in the valleys below and the dazzling galactic display overhead compete for your undivided attention. For views, you might check the Zuni Loop first.

♠ California 116 ♿

PRADO
San Bernardino County Regional Park

Location: Southwest California west of Riverside.

Access: From California State Highway 83 at a point 1.2 miles northeast of the junction of Highway 83 & State Highway 71 northwest of Corona and 7 miles south of the junction of Highway 83 & State Highway 60 (Pomona Freeway) at Ontario, turn southeast onto the paved park access road; proceed 0.1 mile to the park entrance station, then 0.5 mile to 1 mile farther to the day use areas and campground.

Day Use Facilities: Immense day use area; shelters; group picnic areas; drinking water; restrooms; plenty of parking.

Camping Facilities: 50 campsites with full-hookups; (rv group camping and youth group camping areas are also available, by reservation); site size is slightly above average, with little separation; parking pads are paved, level, mostly long pull-thoughs; tent areas are large and level; fireplaces, plus some barbecue grills; firewood is usually for sale, or b-y-o; water at sites; restrooms with showers; paved driveway; complete supplies and services are available within 10 miles in just about any direction.

Activities & Attractions: Fishing (extra fee); boating (no gasoline motors, 18´ limit); boat ramp and courtesy dock; equestrian trail; playground; sports fields, golf course and shooting range close by.

Natural Features: Located on a slightly rolling, grassy hill planted with shade trees; the park is surrounded primarily by flat to gently rolling agricultural land; the park's 56-acre lake is within view of many of the campsites; elevation 900´.

Season, Fees & Phone: Open all year; $17.00; 14 day limit; park office ☎(714) 597-4260.

Trip Log: Combine the grassy slopes dotted with hardwoods, the lake, and a couple of adjacent large-scale livestock operations, and you have a true pastoral setting for this park. For a camp spot, it is suggested that you arrive by noon Friday for a weekend spot in summer.

♠ California 117 &

YUCAIPA
San Bernardino County Regional Park

Location: Southwest California southeast of San Bernardino.

Access: From Interstate 10 at the Yucaipa Boulevard Exit near milepost 36 (4 miles east of Redlands, 15 miles northeast of Beaumont), from the north side of the freeway, travel east on Yucaipa Boulevard for 2.7 miles to Oak Glen Road; turn northeast (left) onto Oak Glen Road, and continue for 1.85 miles, then turn left into the park.

Day Use Facilities: Large picnic area; shelters; group picnic area; drinking water; restrooms; large parking lot.

Camping Facilities: 35 campsites, including 26 rv sites and 9 individual tent/small group units, in two areas; sites in the rv section are large, mostly level, with some separation; parking pads are paved, mostly long pull-throughs, some spacious enough for the longest rv's, plus a few long straight-ins; sites in the tent/group area are park 'n walk units, situated on a level, sandy gravel pavilion; tent units have ramadas (sun

shelters); barbecue grills; b-y-o firewood; water at several faucets; restrooms with showers in both areas; complete supplies and services are available in Yucaipa.

Activities & Attractions: Fishing (extra fee); playgrounds; swimming lagoon, waterslide (extra fee).

Natural Features: Located on a pair of hillsides which flank a chain of 3 lakes; watered, mown lawns planted with hardwoods surround most of the sites; the entire area is bordered by dry hills and mountains; elevation 2900´.

Season, Fees & Phone: Open all year; $12.00; 14 day limit; reservations accepted, advisable for weekends, contact the park office ☎ (714) 790-1818.

Trip Log: There are golf courses and there are campgrounds, and then there are campgrounds that resemble golf courses. And this is one of them. You could slip a freight train into some of the rv sites (or, more likely, a Presidential Special.) A very nice park.

♠ California 118 &

LAKE PERRIS
Lake Perris State Recreation Area

Location: Southern California southeast of Riverside.

Access: From California State Highway 60 near milepost 19 (11 miles west of the junction of Highway 60 & Interstate 10 near Beaumont, 6 miles east of the junction of Highway 60 & Interstate 215 east of Riverside) take the Moreno Beach Drive Exit and travel south on Moreno Beach Drive for 3.2 miles, then southwest (right) on Via Del Lago for 1.2 miles to the Moreno (north) park entrance.

Alternate Access: From California State Highway 215 (Escondido Freeway) in Val Verde (4 miles northwest of the city of Perris, 4 miles southeast of the junction of Highway 215 & California State Highway 60 east of Riverside), head east on Pomona Expressway for 2.3 miles; turn north (left) onto Lake Perris Drive and proceed 1.2 miles to the Perris (southwest) entrance. (There are at least a dozen other possible routes to the park, but the above accesses should serve the majority of visitors.)

Day Use Facilities: Large picnic areas with ramadas (sun shelters); group picnic areas with ramadas (reservable by groups, contact the park office); drinking water; restrooms; more than a dozen medium to large parking lots; concession stand.

Camping Facilities: 431 campsites, including 264 with partial hookups; (several group camp areas and a primitive equestrian camp are also available); sites are small- to small+, with minimal to nominal separation; hookup sites are clustered in small 'parking lot' arrangements; most parking pads are paved, short straight-ins; about half of the pads will require a little additional leveling; enough space for medium to large tents in most sites; fireplaces and/or fire rings; b-y-o firewood; storage cabinets (bear boxes); water at several faucets; restrooms with showers; waste water receptacles; holding tank disposal station; paved driveways; complete supplies and services are available within 5 miles west/northwest.

Activities & Attractions: Boating; several boat launches; marina; designated sailing area; fishing for bass, also stocked trout, catfish, bluegill, sunfish; fishing piers; designated swimming beaches; water slide; playground; 9-mile-long (mostly paved) hiking/biking trail around the lake; hiking trails to overlook points; equestrian trail around the lake and into natural lands on the east/northeast corner of the park; designated rock-climbing area on the south side of the lake; designated upland game hunting areas; Regional Indian Museum has interpretive displays related to the history and culture of Mojave Desert Indians; campfire circle and interpretive center; nature walks, evening campfire programs, fishing clinics and other outdoor-related activities, scheduled seasonally.

Natural Features: Located on rolling, sloping terrain around the shore of Lake Perris; picnic and camp sites are on the north shore and are very lightly to lightly shaded by scattered hardwoods and conifers on a surface of sparse grass; sandy beach; bordered by dry, boulder-strewn rolling hills and low mountains; elevation 1600´.

Season, Fees & Phone: Open all year; Moreno entrance open 24 hours, Perris entrance open daytime hours (subject to change); campsite reservations are "definitely recommended" for weekends, spring through fall; please see Appendix for reservation information, park entry and campground fees; ☎(714) 657-0676.

Trip Log: All picnic sites and just about all camp spots have good lake and mountain views. Alessandro Island, a massive, solitary mound, rises from the lake just offshore of the campground and one of the two day use areas. Tent campers have much better sites than rv'ers

here. Lake Perris has the largest developed campground in the California state park system.

 # California
Southwest Corner

⚑ California 119 ♿

DOHENY
Doheny State Beach

Location: Southern California Coast northwest of San Clemente.

Access: From Interstate 5 in Dana Point at the Beach Cities/Pacific Coast Highway/ California Highway 1 Exit (near milepost 7, 3 miles south of San Juan Capistrano, 7 miles north of San Clemente) proceed westerly on a viaduct for 1 mile and onto Pacific Coast Highway; at Del Obispo Street, turn southerly (left) onto Dana Point Harbor Drive, go 0.1 mile to Park Lantern, then swing east (left again) onto the park access road for 0.1 mile to the park.

Day Use Facilities: Medium-large picnic areas; group picnic areas; drinking water; restrooms and freshwater rinse showers; very large parking lots; concession stand.

Camping Facilities: 120 campsites; (hike/bike sites are also available); sites are small+, level, with minimal to nominal separation; parking pads are paved, short to short+ straight-ins plus some medium to long pull-throughs; generally enough room for small tents; fire rings; firewood is usually for sale, or b-y-o; water at several faucets; restrooms with showers; holding tank disposal station; paved driveways; complete supplies and services are available within 3 miles.

Activities & Attractions: Swimming; volleyball courts; hiking trail; fishing; interpretive center.

Natural Features: Located at the edge of the sand, with large hardwoods, palms and large shrubs that provide very light to light-medium shade/shelter in the day use and camp areas; acres of mown lawns; ocean views from many picnic and camp sites; sea level.

Season, Fees & Phone: Open all year; please see Appendix for reservation information, park entry and campground fees; ☎(714) 496-6172.

Trip Log: Getting off the Interstate might involve a minute or two of perspiration (especially if the traffic is heavy and you're hauling a big rig), but it's worth the effort. Of the trio of beach parks in the area (also see San Clemente and San Onofre), Doheny would be the one to show to your friends.

⚐ California 120 ♿

SAN CLEMENTE
San Clemente State Beach

Location: Southern California Coast in San Clemente.

Access: From Interstate 5 (northbound) in San Clemente, take the Cristianitos Road/Avenida del Presidente Exit to the west side of the freeway, then north for 0.9 mile on Avenida del Presidente; turn west onto Avenida Calafia and proceed 0.2 mile; turn south (left) onto the park access road for 0.2 mile to the park. **Alternate Access:** From Interstate 5 (southbound) take the Avenida Calafia Exit west onto Avenida Calafia and continue as above.

Day Use Facilities: Medium-sized picnic area with ramadas (sun shelters); drinking water; restrooms; large parking lot.

Camping Facilities: 157 campsites, including 72 with full hookups; (several hike/bike sites and a reservable group camp are also available); sites are small to small+, essentially level, with minimal to nominal separation; parking pads are paved, short to medium-length straight-ins or long pull-throughs; some sites have small ramadas for the table area; plenty of tent space; fire rings; firewood is usually for sale, or b-y-o; water at several faucets; restrooms with showers; paved driveways; complete supplies and services are available in San Clemente.

Activities & Attractions: Swimming; fishing; trail down to the beach campfire center.

Natural Features: Located on a bluff on a large, grassy flat dotted with hardwoods; picnic area is on a shelf just below the blufftop and overlooks the ocean, most campsites are some distance from the edge of the bluff; some campsites receive very light to light shade from large hardwoods; elevation 100´.

Season, Fees & Phone: Open all year; please see Appendix for reservation information, park entry and campground fees; ☎(714) 492-3156.

Trip Log: San Clemente was the site of a former Western White House. (No, it wasn't the actor's local address; it was the home of the *other* President from California.) The facilities at the state beach are quite good. Lots of grass and a fair number of trees. Most picnic sites and only a few campsites have ocean views.

⚐ California 121 ♿

GUAJOME
San Diego County Park

Location: Southwest corner of California northeast of Oceanside.

Access: From California State Highway 76 at milepost 7 +.1 (7 miles northeast of Oceanside, 11 miles southeast of the California 76 Exit on Interstate 15 near Bonsall), turn south onto Guajome Lakes Road, and proceed 0.1 mile to the park. (If you're traveling Interstate 5, take the Mission Road-Highway 76 Exit at Oceanside, then northeast on '76.)

Day Use Facilities: Large picnic area; drinking water; restrooms; large parking lot.

Camping Facilities: 17 campsites with partial hookups; sites are slightly above-average in size, with fairly good visual separation; parking pads are paved straight-ins, some are double-wide, and most are long and level; tent areas are medium to large and level; fire rings; firewood is usually for sale, or b-y-o; water at sites; restrooms with showers; holding tank disposal station; paved driveway; complete supplies and services are available in Oceanside.

Activities & Attractions: Children's play area; fishing; hiking and equestrian trails; Rancho Guajome Adobe historical site nearby; famous, and very photogenic, Mission San Luis Rey, just west of the park.

Natural Features: Located on a hilltop, with short conifers, bushes, palms, and watered and mown lawns, overlooking a valley; small Guajome Lake, a pond complete with an island, is near the campground; elevation 600´.

Season, Fees & Phone: $12.00 for a site, $2.00 for an extra vehicle, $1.00 for dogs; Open all year; 14 day limit; reservations available, contact the San Diego County Parks and Recreation Department Office, 21 to 90 days in advance, at ☎(619) 565-3600; for general information(619) 565-5928.

Trip Log: Nice park. Subjectively speaking, this is one of the nicest-looking parks in this part of California. It fits in well with the surrounding suburban/semi-rural community. If you don't *have* to picnic, play and stay on the beach, this park is well worth a look.

♠ California 122 ♿

OLD TOWN SAN DIEGO
Old Town San Diego State Historic Park

Location: Southwest California in San Diego.

Access: From Interstate 5 at the Old Town Avenue Exit, (3 miles northwest of downtown San Diego), proceed to the northeast side of the freeway then northeast on Old Town Avenue for 1 block; turn northerly (left) onto San Diego Avenue and go 0.35 mile through the commercial district to a 'T' intersection; turn southwest (left) onto Twiggs Street for 1 block, then northwest (right) on Congress Street for a few yards to the main parking lot.

Day Use Facilities: Picnicking/sitting area in the plaza; drinking water; restrooms; large main parking lot; additional parking is available in lots at or near the 3 other corners of the historic district as well as in several lots and parking garages in the vicinity.

Camping Facilities: None; nearest public campground is in Silver Strand State Beach.

Activities & Attractions: Restorations or reconstructions of nearly 20 homes, commercial establishments and government buildings dating back to 1821-1872; several museums; guided tours each afternoon; self-guided tour (an excellent guide booklet is available at the park office).

Natural Features: Located principally in an area bordered by Wallace Street on the northwest and Twiggs Street on the southeast, Congress Street on the southwest and Juan Street on the northeast; the Plaza has a large mown lawn dotted with huge hardwoods; several courtyards and gardens are also landscaped appropriately; sea level.

Season, Fees & Phone: Open all year; (no fee); ☎(619) 237-6770.

Trip Log: San Diego is the location of the first permanent Spanish settlement in California. On the hill east of the park, the Founding Father of California's missions, Junipero Serra, established Mission San Diego in July 1769. In the 1820's a small village sprung up at the base of the hill below the initial site of the mission. 'Old Town' was the original section of the city and it has been known by that name for more than a century. The park re-creates a 50-year period in the mid-nineteenth century which saw a transition from Mexican to American rule. The park and surrounding commercial district are first-rate in just about every respect. You could easily spend a day here and not see it all.

♠ California 123

OBSERVATORY
Cleveland National Forest

Location: Southeast corner of California northeast of San Diego.

Access: From the junction of San Diego County Highways S6 & S7 (8 steep, twisty, scenic miles via Highway S6 from the junction of S6 and California State Highway 79 near Rincon Springs, or 12 easier miles via Highway S7 from the junction of S7 and Highway 79 near Lake Henshaw), proceed northeast on S6 for 2.4 miles to milepost 50 +.2; turn southeast (right), and go 0.1 mile to the campground.

Day Use Facilities: Large parking lot at the observatory.

Camping Facilities: 42 campsites; sites are medium to large, with some separation; parking pads are paved, medium-length straight-ins, most of which will require some additional leveling; tent areas are large and somewhat level; fire rings and barbecue grills in most sites; some firewood is available for gathering in the vicinity; water at several faucets; vault facilities; camper supplies at a small store at the junction of Highways S6 & S7, 2 miles south.

Activities & Attractions: Renowned Palomar Observatory (open for limited visitation by the public during daytime hours) can be reached via a 2.3 mile trail from the campground, or by continuing up Highway S6.

Natural Features: Located on a sloping flat just below the summit of Mount Palomar; campground vegetation consists of a wide variety of hardwoods and conifers on a grass-and-needle-covered forest floor; large, open, grassy areas within the camp; elevation 4800´.

Season, Fees & Phone: May to November, but occasionally open as late as the end of December; $8.00; 14 day limit; Palomar Ranger District, Ramona, ☎(619) 788-0250.

Trip Log: Cal-Tech's famous scientific institution to which the campground's name eludes is impressive enough in photographs. But to personally view that gleaming white dome encircled by rich green grass and trees, against the backdrop of a deep blue sky, is an experience. This campground is a bit of a surprise, considering it's in Cleveland National Forest (which is about 80 percent chaparral).

♣ California 124 &

GREEN VALLEY
Cuyamaca Rancho State Park

Location: Southwest corner of California northeast of San Diego.

Access: From California State Highway 79 at milepost 4 +.2 (7 miles north of Interstate 8 Julian/Japatul Road Exit, 16 miles south of Julian), turn west into the Green Valley entrance. **Additional Access** (for the museum): From Highway 79 at milepost 6 +.25 (2 miles north of the Green Valley area) turn east onto a paved access road and proceed 0.35 mile to the museum parking lot.

Day Use Facilities: Medium-sized picnic area at Arroyo Seco, large picnic area at Falls/River; drinking water and restrooms in both areas; 3 medium-sized parking lots; small picnic spot, small parking lot and restrooms at the museum.

Camping Facilities: 81 campsites in 2 loops, plus an extension; (hike/bike campsites and a primitive camp, accessible by trail, are available nearby); sites are small+, quite sloped, with nominal to fair separation; parking pads are mostly paved, short to medium-length straight-ins; additional leveling would be needed in virtually all sites; medium to large tent areas; fire rings; b-y-o firewood; water at most sites; restrooms with showers; paved driveways; gas and groceries in Julian; nearest source of complete supplies is El Cajon, 30 miles southwest.

(Picnicking and camping are also available in the park's Paso Picacho area, 5 miles north.)

Activities & Attractions: Trails, trails, trails—the park has more than a hundred miles of equestrian and foot trails, several of which lead off from this area; short trail from the day use area to the falls (but don't get your expectations up too high about the drop of these tumbling waters); interpretive displays; campfire center; museum houses exhibits and artifacts about the local Kumeya-ay Indians and the early Spanish explorers.

Natural Features: Located on rolling slopes near the edge of a ravine in a densely forested river valley; the Sweetwater River flows past the day use areas and campground loops; some of the state's largest canyon live oaks are within the park; surrounding mountainous areas have moderately dense forestation interspersed with meadows; elevation at Green Valley 4000´.

Season, Fees & Phone: Open all year, subject to winter weather conditions; please see Appendix for reservation information, park entry and campground fees; ☎(619) 765-0755.

Trip Log: The park museum is in an old, attractive two-story building with walls made of local stone which was the home of the previous owner of Cuyamaca Rancho. (The state bought this sizable spread in 1933 at reportedly half its appraised value.) The handiwork of the Civilian Conservation Corps can still be identified in certain places around the park—the CCC built the park's first trails and campgrounds during the Great Depression. (Incidentally, *Cuyamca* is pronounced like *Coo-yah-mah´-kah*.)

🏠 *California* ⛺
Kings Canyon & Sequoia National Parks

From an administrative standpoint, Kings Canyon and Sequoia are operated as one park. Most visitors don't perceive them that way, however. While Kings Canyon offers immense horizontal views of rugged mountains and valleys, Sequoia features neck-craning, closeup, vertical perspectives of the regal, giant conifers which are its namesake.

♣ California 125 &

AZALEA, CRYSTAL SPRINGS, SUNSET
Kings Canyon National Park

Location: East-central California east of Fresno.

Access: From California State Highway 180/Kings Canyon Road in Grant Grove Village in Kings Canyon National Park (58 miles east of Fresno, turn west into the park visitor center; or 0.2 mile past the visitor center, turn west into *Sunset*; or at a point 0.3 mile north of the visitor center, turn west into *Azalea* or east into *Crystal Springs*. (Note that the road follows a north-south line is this section.)

Day Use Facilities: Small picnic area; drinking water; restrooms; medium-sized parking area.

Camping Facilities: *Azalea*: 118 campsites; *Crystal Springs*: 67 campsites; *Sunset*: 192 campsites; *all camps*: sites are generally small+ to medium-sized, with nominal to fair separation; parking pads are paved or gravel/dirt, short to medium-length straight-ins; although pads have been fairly well leveled, additional leveling will be needed in many sites; large, well-cleared, but sloped tent areas; fireplaces or fire rings; b-y-o firewood; water at several faucets; restrooms; holding tank disposal station in Azalea; paved driveways; gas and groceries are available in Grant Grove Village.

Activities & Attractions: Several trails in the area; national park visitor center; naturalist-guided programs; ski touring.

Natural Features: Located on moderately steep, rolling terrain in the Sierra Nevada; campground vegetation consists of a variety of moderately dense, tall conifers, plus a small amount of young growth and brush; overall, Sunset probably has the most shelter/shade, Azalea the least; some of the sites in Sunset have valley views, most other sites have limited views; elevation 6500´.

Season, Fees & Phone: One of the campgrounds is open all year, with limited services in winter; other camps are open May to October; $8.00; 14 day limit; Sequoia & Kings Canyon NPs Headquarters, Three Rivers, ☎(209) 565-3456 (info office) or (209) 565-3351 (24-hour recording).

Trip Log: These three campgrounds are similar enough to describe them as if they were just three sections of the same huge campground. Any one of the threesome should serve well for someone passing between Sequoia and Kings Canyon, or who desires a high, cool campsite. But the park's other visitor area, 30 long but scenic miles east of here at Cedar Grove (see Sheep Creek, et. al.), is certainly worth going the extra mileage to visit and explore. One of the best mountain/canyon panoramas in the Sierra—of Kings Canyon and Monarch Wilderness, to the east—is available along the road on the way to Cedar Grove.

⚘ California 126 ♿

SHEEP CREEK
Kings Canyon National Park

Location: East-central California east of Fresno.

Access: From California State Highway 180/Kings Canyon Road in Grant Grove Village in Kings Canyon National Park (4 miles northeast of the park's Big Stump Entrance Station, 58 miles east of Fresno) head easterly on Highway 180 for 29 miles to the end of Highway 180 at the park's Cedar Grove area; continue east on a paved park road for 1.3 miles; turn north (left), into the campground.

Day Use Facilities: Several small picnic areas, drinking water, restrooms, and small parking areas are in the vicinity.

Camping Facilities: 111 campsites; sites are small to medium-sized, with fair to fairly good separation; parking pads are paved, mostly short straight-ins, plus a few longer long pull-throughs; additional leveling will be needed on many pads; large, generally sloped tent areas; fireplaces; some firewood may be available for gathering in the general area; lockable storage cabinets (bear boxes); water at several faucets; restrooms; paved driveways; holding tank disposal station; gas, groceries, showers and coin-op laundry are available in Cedar Grove.

Activities & Attractions: Hiking trails to falls viewpoints and into the back country; motor nature trail; amphitheater for scheduled nature programs; short foot trails in the campground area; Boyden Caverns (Sequoia National Forest) 3 miles west.

Natural Features: Located on a slope above the South Fork of the Kings River in Kings Canyon; Sheep Creek enters the river from the south near the campground; majority of campsites are quite well sheltered/shaded by tall conifers; closely bordered by high, steep hills and mountains; elevation 4600´.

Season, Fees & Phone: May to November; $8.00; 14 day limit; Sequoia & Kings Canyon NPs Headquarters, Three Rivers, ☎(209) 565-3456 (info office) or (209) 565-3351 (24-hour recording).

Trip Log: It may be difficult to decide (if a decision can even be made) which is the better of the two totally different perspectives of Kings Canyon you'll encounter on your trip to this remote spot. On one hand are the commanding panoramas of the canyon you'll see from highwayside overlooks (or *outlooks*) on the way to and from the inner canyon. And then there are the very pleasing river vistas and spectacular vertical views from the canyon floor. Kings Canyon is one of the neatest places in the Sierra.

⚘ California 127 ♿

SENTINEL
Kings Canyon National Park

Location: East-central California east of Fresno.

Access: From California State Highway 180/Kings Canyon Road in Grant Grove Village in Kings Canyon National Park (4 miles northeast of the park's Big Stump Entrance Station, 58 miles east of Fresno) head easterly on Highway 180 for 29 miles to the end of Highway 180 at the park's Cedar Grove area; continue east on a paved park road for 1.7 miles; turn north (left), go 0.1 mile, then swing west (left) into the campground.

Day Use Facilities: Several small picnic areas, drinking water, restrooms, and small parking areas are in the vicinity.

Camping Facilities: 83 campsites; sites are small to small+, with nominal to fair separation; parking pads are hard-surfaced, mostly short straight-ins, plus a few longer long pull-throughs; a little additional leveling may be needed in some sites; large tent areas, some are a bit sloped or bumpy; fireplaces; some firewood may be available for gathering in the general vicinity; bear boxes; water at several faucets; restrooms; paved driveways; ranger station; gas and groceries in Cedar Grove.

Activities & Attractions: Hiking trails to falls viewpoints and into the back country; motor nature trail; amphitheater for scheduled nature programs.

Natural Features: Located on a rolling, gentle slope in Kings Canyon above the South Fork of the Kings River in the Sierra Nevada; campsites receive ample shelter/shade from moderately dense tall conifers; closely bordered by high, steep mountains; elevation 4600´.

Season, Fees & Phone: May to November; $8.00; 14 day limit; Sequoia & Kings Canyon NPs Headquarters, Three Rivers, ☎(209) 565-3456 (info office) or (209) 565-3351 (24-hour recording).

Trip Log: All things considered, Sentinel may offer best compromise of site size, separation and levelness of the trio of camps in Cedar Grove. The river is just a short walk down the slope from any campsite in all three campgrounds.

♣ California 128 &

MORAINE
Kings Canyon National Park

Location: East-central California east of Fresno.

Access: From California State Highway 180/Kings Canyon Road in Grant Grove Village in Kings Canyon National Park (4 miles northeast of the park's Big Stump Entrance Station, 58 miles east of Fresno) head easterly

on Highway 180 for 29 miles to the end of Highway 180 at the park's Cedar Grove area; continue east on a paved park road for a final 2.4 miles to the campground, on the north (left) side of the road.

Day Use Facilities: Several small picnic areas, drinking water, restrooms, and small parking areas are in the vicinity.

Camping Facilities: 120 campsites; (Canyon View Group Campground, 0.4 mile west, is also available, by reservation only); sites are good-sized, with nominal to fair separation; parking pads are sandy gravel, mostly medium to long pull-offs or pull-throughs, plus some straight-ins; a little additional leveling may be needed in many sites; large, generally sloped tent areas; bear boxes; fire rings; some firewood may be available for gathering in the area; water at several faucets; restrooms; paved driveways; gas and groceries in Cedar Grove.

Activities & Attractions: Hiking trails to falls viewpoints and into the high country; motor nature trail.

Natural Features: Located on a northward-facing, forested slope deep in Kings Canyon near the South Fork of the Kings River; campsites are lightly to moderately sheltered/shaded by tall conifers and a few hardwoods on a surface of evergreen needles; closely flanked by the high, rocky, steep mountains of the west slope of the Sierra Nevada; elevation 4600´.

Season, Fees & Phone: May to November (or as needed); $8.00; 14 day limit; Sequoia & Kings Canyon NPs Headquarters, Three Rivers, ☎(209) 565-3456 (info office) or (209) 565-3351 (24-hour recording).

Trip Log: Once you get settled in at the campground, be sure to take the five-mile trip easterly for another four miles to the turnaround loop and parking area at Road's End. Scenic high drama unfolds from there.

♣ California 129 &

DORST
Sequoia National Park

Location: East-central California east of Fresno.

Access: From the Generals Highway (the main north-south road between Kings Canyon and Sequoia National Parks) at a point 3.5 miles south of the north park boundary near Stony Creek Village, 18 miles south of Grant Grove

Village, and 26 miles north of Lodgepole Village, turn west onto a paved access road and go down 0.2 mile into the campground.

Day Use Facilities: None.

Camping Facilities: 238 campsites in a maze of loops; sites are small to medium-sized, with minimal to nominal separation; parking pads are gravel or paved, mostly short straight-ins; additional leveling may be needed on many pads; medium to large, generally sloped areas for tents; storage lockers; fire rings; gathering firewood on national forest lands prior to arrival is suggested; water at several faucets; restrooms; holding tank disposal station; paved driveway; gas and groceries at Stony Creek Village, 4 miles north, and at Grant Grove and Lodgepole.

Activities & Attractions: Muir Grove Trail; amphitheater.

Natural Features: Located on steep, hilly terrain near Dorst Creek on the west slope of the Sierra Nevada; sites are very well-sheltered by medium-dense, tall conifers; surrounded by dense forest; a meadow is south of the campground; elevation 6500´.

Season, Fees & Phone: May to October; $9.00; 14 day limit; Sequoia & Kings Canyon NPs Headquarters, Three Rivers, ☎(209) 565-3456 (info office) or (209) 565-3351 (24-hour recording).

Trip Log: Super tall trees here—some as tall as you'd ever hope to see. Some rockwork lends engineering assistance and a touch of trim to the campground.

♣ California 130 ♿

LODGEPOLE
Sequoia National Park

Location: East-central California east of Fresno.

Access: From the Generals Highway (the main north-south road between Kings Canyon and Sequoia National Parks) at Lodgepole (14 miles south of the north park boundary near Stony Creek Village, 15 miles north of the south park boundary at Ash Mountain), turn east (i.e., right, if northbound), to the visitor center and the campground.

Day Use Facilities: Large picnic area; drinking water; restrooms; large parking lot.

Camping Facilities: 266 campsites in 3 major complex loops; sites are typically small, with

separation ranging from nil to minimal; sites in the section closest to the entrance (#'s 1-67) are the largest and most level, followed by those in the next-closest section (#'s 189-266), then the upper section (#'s 76-187, no trailers); parking pads are paved or gravel, mainly short to medium-length straight-ins, which are level, or reasonably level considering the terrain; most spaces can accommodate a large tent on a fairly level surface; storage lockers (bear boxes); fire rings; b-y-o firewood; water at several faucets; restrooms; holding tank disposal station; paved driveways; ranger station; showers, gas, coin-op laundry and a large market are available near the visitor center.

(Concessionaire-operated lodging is available at Lodgepole, please contact park headquarters for brochures & current rates.)

Activities & Attractions: Stands of giant sequoias; visitor center; several trails; nature center.

Natural Features: Located in a canyon along the Marble Fork of the Kaweah River; the first camp section is located on a riverside flat, the middle section is on a hilltop, and the upper section is along a rather steep, boulder-strewn hillside; moderately dense conifer forest provides ample shelter/shade in most sites; elevation 6700´.

Season, Fees & Phone: Open all year, subject to weather conditions, with limited services October to May; $9.00-$11.00; 14 day limit; reservations recommended July-August, please see Appendix for additional reservation information; Sequoia & Kings Canyon NPs Headquarters, Three Rivers, ☎(209) 565-3456 (info office) or (209) 565-3351 (recording).

Trip Log: Lodgepole is the hub of park activity, mainly because nearly all of the park's visitor services are here. This area might remind you a little of Yosemite—both in the shape and color of the rock, and in the state of activity. (Bring your waffle-stompers and climbing gear if there's a chance you'll get a campsite in the upper section.)

♣ California 131 ♿

BUCKEYE FLAT
Sequoia National Park

Location: East-central California east of Fresno.

Access: From the Generals Highway (the main north-south road between Kings Canyon and Sequoia National Parks) at a point 6 miles north of the Ash Mountain entrance station (northeast of Three Rivers) and 10 miles south of Giant Forest Village, turn east (i.e., right, if northbound) onto a narrow, paved access road and proceed 0.4 mile to the campground.

Day Use Facilities: None.

Camping Facilities: 28 campsites; sites are small and closely spaced; parking pads are paved, short, sloped straight-ins; (no motorhomes or trailers permitted); tent areas are medium to large, and as level as can be expected under the local circumstances; storage lockers; fire rings; b-y-o firewood; water at central faucets; restrooms; paved driveway; gas and groceries near Ash Mountain; limited supplies and services are available in Three Rivers.

Activities & Attractions: Several hiking trails (a map and info sheet are available at visitor center at Ash Mountain); stream fishing.

Natural Features: Located on a sloping flat in a narrow canyon along the Middle Fork of the Kaweah River; a dense stand of hardwoods forms a leafy canopy over much of the campground and provides some visual separation between sites; surrounded by hills covered with grass, brush, and some trees; high mountains to the east; elevation 2800´.

Season, Fees & Phone: April to October; $9.00; 14 day limit; Sequoia & Kings Canyon NPs Headquarters, Three Rivers, ☎(209) 565-3456 (info office) or (209) 565-3351 (24-hour recording).

Trip Log: At first sight, this campground seems strangely out of place, after all the things you've heard about Sequoia National Park. It's not in the high country with the lofty cone-bearers for which the park is named. Rather, it's in the lowlands, engulfed in hardwoods. Buckeye Flat is a neat, almost cozy, little place.

⚑ California 132 ᕯ

POTWISHA
Sequoia National Park

Location: East-central California east of Fresno.

Access: From the Generals Highway (the main north-south road between Kings Canyon and Sequoia National Parks) at a point 4 miles north of the Ash Mountain entrance station (northeast of Three Rivers) and 12 miles south of Giant Forest Village, turn west (i.e., left, if northbound) into the campground.

Day Use Facilities: None.

Camping Facilities: 44 campsites; sites are medium-sized, with nominal separation; parking pads are paved, medium-length, and most are pull-offs or pull-throughs which probably could accommodate most rv's; additional leveling will probably be needed on most pads; tent spaces are large but a little sloped; fire rings; b-y-o firewood; water at central faucets; restrooms; holding tank disposal station nearby; gas and groceries are available near Ash Mountain; limited supplies and services are available in Three Rivers.

Activities & Attractions: Fishing; visitor center at Ash Mountain; several hiking trails (a map is available at the visitor center).

Natural Features: Located in a canyon on a flat along the Marble Fork of the Kaweah River near its confluence with the Kaweah's Middle Fork; campsites are situated in a light to moderately dense stand of hardwoods; brushy hillsides and mountainsides border the campground; high mountains are visible from many sites; elevation 2100´.

Season, Fees & Phone: Open all year; $9.00; 14 day limit; Sequoia & Kings Canyon NPs Headquarters, Three Rivers, ☎(209) 565-3456 (info office) or (209) 565-3351 (24-hour recording).

Trip Log: If you're entering Sequoia from the south on California Highway 198, this would be the first campground inside the park. It's a good spot to ponder the road ahead: the next dozen miles are pretty snakey, steep and slow-going. A lot of rv travelers park their trailers or motorhomes here, and take the towing or towed vehicle (whatever works) into the high country. If you're coming down out of Sequoia from the north, it's a good place to stop and let your brakes and emotions cool.

🏚 *California* ⚑
Southern Sierra Nevada: West Slopes

⚑ California 133 ᕯ

FORKS
Bass Lake/Sierra National Forest

Location: East-central California north of Fresno.

Access: From California State Highway 41 (Southern Yosemite Highway) at milepost 39 (3.5 miles north of Oakhurst, 10 miles south of Fish Camp), turn southeast onto Road 222 (Bass

Lake Road, paved, begins as a 4-lane road) and travel 3.5 miles to a major fork; take the right fork and go 0.3 mile to a second major fork; bear right again and continue along the south-west lake shore on Road 222 for another 1.8 miles; turn southwest (right) into the campground, or easterly into the day use area.

Day Use Facilities: Medium-sized picnic area; drinking water; restrooms; parking area.

Camping Facilities: 31 campsites; sites vary from small to large, with fair separation; parking pads are hard-surfaced, mostly short straight-ins; small to large, sloped tent spots; fire rings, plus some barbecue grills; b-y-o firewood is recommended; water at several faucets; restrooms; paved driveways; disposal station nearby on Road 222; adequate supplies and services are available in Oakhurst.

Activities & Attractions: Goat Mountain Trail (watch out for poison oak); designated swimming beach nearby; boating; windsurfing; fishing; South Entrance of Yosemite NP, 12 miles north of the Bass Lake Road turnoff.

Natural Features: Located on sloping terrain above a bay on the south-west shore of Bass Lake; dense oaks and tall conifers provide ample shelter for most campsites; the lake is encircled by forested hills and mountains; elevation 3400´.

Season, Fees & Phone: April to November; (Forks or one of the other Bass Lake camps may be available with limited services in winter); $11.00; 10 day limit; Mariposa Ranger District, Oakhurst, ☎ (209) 683-4665 or Bass Lake Recreation Office (209) 642-3212 (summer).

Trip Log: Bass Lake is one of the more popular water recreation spots in this region. The forested shore line and surrounding higher terrain make it so. Another area, Lupine-Cedar Bluff Campground, 2 miles south of here (midway between Forks and Spring Cove, described below), consists of a pair of adjacent, formerly independent camps rolled into one 113-site campground. The forest atmosphere there is a little more 'open' than in the other Bass Lake camps. Forks and Spring Cove have been selected to represent Bass Lake because of their more interesting locations and facilites.

🏕 California 134 ♿

SPRING COVE
Bass Lake/Sierra National Forest

Location: East-central California north of Fresno.

Access: From California State Highway 41 at milepost 39 (3.5 miles north of Oakhurst, 10 miles south of Fish Camp), turn southeast onto Road 222 (Bass Lake Road, paved) and travel 3.5 miles to a fork; take the right fork and go 0.3 mile to a second fork; bear right again and continue on Road 222 for another 4.2 miles; turn east into the day use area or west into the campground.

Day Use Facilities: Small picnic area; drinking water; restrooms; small parking area.

Camping Facilities: 63 campsites; sites are very small to small, sloped, with slight to fair separation; parking pads are packed gravel or hard-surfaced, majority are short straight-ins; small to medium-sized tent areas; fireplaces; b-y-o firewood is recommended; water at several faucets; restrooms; paved driveways; adequate supplies and services are available in Oakhurst.

(Additional, small campsites are available in the Wishon Point camp area, 1 mile farther up the main lake road.)

Activities & Attractions: Spring Cove Trail (watch for poison oak); windsurfing; fishing.

Natural Features: Located on a moderate slope above the south-west shore of Bass Lake; campsites receive moderate shade/shelter from tall conifers; the lake lies in a basin ringed by forested hills and low mountains; elevation 3400´.

Season, Fees & Phone: April to November; $11.00; 10 day limit; Mariposa Ranger District, Oakhurst, ☎(209) 683-4665 or Bass Lake Recreation Office (209) 642-3212 (summer).

Trip Log: Some nice lakeshore picnic sites are within walking distance of this campground. For a longer walk, you could head up the Spring Cove Trail to the Goat Mountain Trail, then down that route to Forks Campground (see info above). The 8.5 mile trip is along moderate grades through the forest. Be sure to remember to fill your canteen at the campground before you embark.

🏕 California 135 ♿

KERN RIVER
Kern County Park

Location: South-central California northeast of Bakersfield.

Access: From California State Highway 178 near milepost 11 (11 miles northeast of Bakersfield, 32 miles southeast of Lake Isabella), turn north onto Alfred Harrell

Highway and proceed 1.9 miles; turn right (at the fire station) onto Lake Ming Road and continue for 0.75 to the park.

Day Use Facilities: Large picnic area; shelters; group picnic area with shelters; drinking water; restrooms; large parking lot.

Camping Facilities: 50 campsites in a single, large, oval loop; sites are medium to large, with a fair amount of spacing and visual separation between sites; parking pads are paved, quite long, basically level, pull-throughs; large, level, grassy areas for tents; fire rings and barbecue grills; b-y-o firewood; water at several faucets; restrooms with showers; holding tank disposal station; paved driveway; complete supplies and services are available in Bakersfield.

Activities & Attractions: Boating; fishing.

Natural Features: Located on the south bank of the Kern River; park vegetation consists of watered, mown lawns and numerous hardwoods which provide some shade/shelter in virtually every campsite; many flowering trees and bushes decorate the grounds; surrounded by low hills and barren bluffs; a local high point known as Ant Hill rises to about 950´ just south of the park; elevation 450´.

Season, Fees & Phone: Open all year; $9.00-$13.00 (depending upon the season; reservations accepted; Kern County Parks Department, Bakersfield, ☎(805) 861-2345.

Trip Log: There are a number of nice county parks in Southern California, and this is one of them. It's landscaping stands out in quite marked contrast to the stark local terrain.

⚕ California 136 &

HUNGRY GULCH & BOULDER GULCH
Isabella Lake/Sequoia National Forest

Location: South-central California northeast of Bakersfield.

Access: From California State Highway 155 at milepost 67 +.2 (2.5 miles south of Wofford Heights, 5 miles north of the community of Lake Isabella), turn west into Hungry Gulch or east into Boulder Gulch.

Day Use Facilities: None.

Camping Facilities: 78 campsites in each of the 2 areas; sites are medium-sized, with fair to good separation; parking pads are paved, mostly medium-length straight-ins, plus some medium to long pull-throughs; most pads will require a

little additional leveling; large, slightly sloped, tent areas; fire rings; b-y-o firewood; water at several faucets; restrooms with showers; paved driveways; limited to adequate supplies and services are available in the Wofford Heights-Kernville, and Lake Isabella areas.

(An additional 78 campsites with similar facilities are available at Pioneer Point Campground, 2 miles south.)

Activities & Attractions: Boating; fishing; Coso Mine Loop and Isabella Peak Vista Trail; playground.

Natural Features: Located along the west shore (Hungry Gulch) or on genetly sloping terrain above the west shore (Boulder Gulch) of Isabella Lake in the semi-arid Kern River Valley; campground vegetation consists largely of conifers plus some hardwoods; most sites have some shelter/shade; elevation 2700´.

Season, Fees & Phone: April to October; $13.00; Cannell Meadow Ranger District, Kernville, ☎(619) 379-5646.

Trip Log: Camper's Choice: a little closer to the lake (but not actually on the shore) here in Boulder Gulch; better views from up above in Hungry Gulch, just across the road. A lot of campers come here to fish, so here are a few tips from knowledgeable locals which might contribute to making your campout more successful: Salmon eggs and spinners seem to work consistently well on trout, but you'll need to fish the deepest holes in summer. Bassers should normally stick to the coves and use lures. (Reportedly, Isabella Lake produces good bass catches.) Bluegill and crappie can be caught in smaller coves on worms and jigs. Catnappers have found that clams, anchovies and worms work well just about anywhere on the lake.

⚕ California 137 &

LIVE OAK
Isabella Lake/Sequoia National Forest

Location: South-central California northeast of Bakersfield.

Access: From California State Highway 155 at milepost 64 +.9 (0.2 mile south of Wofford Heights, 7 miles north of the community of Lake Isabella), turn west into the campground.

Day Use Facilities: None.

Camping Facilities: 199 campsites in 2 main sections (called Live Oak North and Live Oak South), including some sites designated for small group use; sites are small to medium-sized, with some visual separation; parking pads are paved, short to medium-length straight-ins or pull-throughs; most pads will require additional leveling; medium-sized tent areas; fire rings; b-y-o firewood; water at several faucets; restrooms with showers; holding tank disposal station across the highway at Tillie Creek Campground; limited to adequate supplies and services are available in the Wofford Heights-Kernville, and Lake Isabella areas.

Activities & Attractions: Boating; boat launch nearby; fishing for bass, panfish, catfish; trout stocked in the fall.

Natural Features: Located on a gently sloping hillside above the west shore of Isabella Lake; numerous medium to large oak trees, plus a few other small hardwoods and conifers, provide ample to good shelter/shade in most sites; the entire area is encircled by fairly dry hills and high, partially forested mountains; some of the uppermost sites overlook the lake; elevation 2700´.

Season, Fees & Phone: May to October; $13.00; Cannell Meadow Ranger District, Kernville, ☎ (619) 379-5646.

Trip Log: Some of the sites here are quite nice. Since Live Oak isn't exactly within easy walking distance of the lake, it sees less use than some of the other campgrounds near it, notably Tillie Creek, just across the highway. Residential areas are adjacent to this campground.

♣ California 138 &

TILLIE CREEK
Isabella Lake/Sequoia National Forest

Location: South-central California northeast of Bakersfield.

Access: From California State Highway 155 at milepost 64 +.9 (0.2 mile south of Wofford Heights, 7 miles north of the community of Lake Isabella), turn east into the campground.

Day Use Facilities: None.

Camping Facilities: 159 campsites; (4 large group camp areas are also available); sites are generally medium-sized, with fair to very good separation; parking pads are paved, reasonably level, primarily medium to medium+ straight-ins, plus some longer pull-throughs or pull-offs; adequate level space for a large tent in most sites; fire rings; b-y-o firewood; water at several faucets; restrooms with showers; holding tank disposal station; limited to adequate supplies and

services are available in the Wofford Heights-Kernville, and Lake Isabella areas.

Activities & Attractions: Boating; boat launch nearby; fishing for bass, panfish, catfish; trout stocked in the fall; playground; fish cleaning station; amphitheater.

Natural Features: Located on the west shore of Isabella Lake in the semi-arid Kern River Valley; campground vegetation consists of oaks and other hardwoods, plus some conifers; sites closest to the lake shore are quite 'open'; sites farther from the lake are situated in more dense vegetation; the Greenhorn Mountains and the Piute Mountains lie to the west and southeast, respectively; the Sierra Nevada rises several miles to the east; elevation 2600´.

Season, Fees & Phone: Open all year, with limited services in winter; $7.00 (charged March to September only); Cannell Meadow Ranger District, Kernville, ☎ (619) 379-5646.

Trip Log: This is the largest, best-equipped and most-frequented of the half-dozen campgrounds on this side of the lake. All sites are within a few minutes' easy walk of the lake shore.

♣ California 139

HEADQUARTERS
Sequoia National Forest

Location: South-central California northeast of Bakersfield.

Access: From the intersection of Kernville Road and Sierra Way at the east end of Kernville (11 miles northeast of the community of Lake Isabella, 54 miles northeast of Bakersfield), turn north onto Sierra Way and proceed 2.9 miles to the campground, on the west (left) side of the highway.

Day Use Facilities: None.

Camping Facilities: 37 campsites; sites are small to medium-sized, level, with separation varying from very little to very good; parking pads are paved/gravel, short to medium straight-ins; large areas for tents on a sandy base; fire rings; a scant amount of firewood is available for gathering in the vicinity, b-y-o is recommended; water at several faucets; vault facilities; paved driveways; limited to adequate supplies and services are available in the Kernville-Wofford Heights metropolitan area.

(Additional riverside national forest camping is available at Camp 3, 1 mile north of here.)

Activities & Attractions: Stream fishing for regularly stocked trout; Isabella Lake recreation area, a few miles south.

Natural Features: Located on a flat along the east bank of the Kern River; campground vegetation consists of a mixture of pines and large, full hardwoods which provide adequate to very good shelter/shade in most campsites; rocky hills and ridges border the river east and west; views of high, rocky mountains to the north; elevation 2700´.

Season, Fees & Phone: $9.00; open all year (on an alternate basis in winter with a neighboring campground, Camp 3); 14 day limit; Cannell Meadow Ranger District, Kernville, ☎(619) 376-3781.

Trip Log: This is one of the nicer campgrounds in the Kern River-Lake Isabella area. Its variety of mature vegetation provides welcome shelter, plus an interesting contrast to the rocky surroundings. The Kern River is unique among the Sierra's major streams. Beginning high in the northeast tip of Sequoia National Park, it flows north to south, rather than east to west, along most of its 165-mile length. Also unlike its sister streams, the Kern no longer has a link with the sea.

🏕 California 140 ♿

RED ROCK CANYON
Red Rock Canyon State Park

Location: South-east California east of Bakersfield.

Access: From California State Highway 14 near milepost 40 +.5 (17 miles south of the junction of California State Highways 14 and 178 at Freeman Junction near Inyokern, 25 miles north of Mojave) turn west, then immediately north onto Abbott Drive (paved); continue for 0.75 mile, then turn southwest (left) onto a gravel access road to the park visitor center; the picnic area is just west of the v.c.; the campground is 0.5 mile farther west; or from near milepost 40 (0.5 mile south of the v.c. turnoff) turn east into the Red Cliffs area.

Day Use Facilities: Small picnic area with ramada, drinking water, vault facilities and small parking area at the visitor center; vault facilities and large parking lot at Red Cliffs.

Camping Facilities: *Ricardo Campground*: 50 campsites; sites are generally small to medium in size, with nominal to fairly good separation; parking pads are gravel, medium to long, level straight-ins; tent areas are large, somewhat level; fire rings; definitely b-y-o firewood; water at central faucets; vault facilities; gravel driveway; gas and camper supplies, 6 miles south; limited supplies in Inyokern; adequate supplies and services are available in Mojave.

Activities & Attractions: Red Cliffs Natural Preserve (open only to hiking); several miles of hiking trails; (vehicle travel permitted only on designated roads); campfire center near the visitor center/ranger station.

Natural Features: Located on a Mojave Desert plain; Red Cliffs area has high, red and white cliffs shaped into columns; campground is partly encircled by eroded, low, white cliffs (locally called "White House Cliffs"); park vegetation consists of small Joshua trees and short, desert brush; the Sierra Nevada rises a few miles to the west; elevation 2600´.

Season, Fees & Phone: Open all year; please see Appendix for reservation information, park entry and campground fees; ☎(805) 942-0662.

Trip Log: Red Rock Canyon itself flanks about a four-mile stretch of highway within the park, so you can enjoy the area to a limited extent just by taking a few extra minutes to stop at one or more of the several roadside pull-outs. Probably the most spectacular of the easily accessible viewpoints is at the large Red Cliffs parking lot. Although some visitors do take advantage of the desert tranquillity here in summer, it makes a much better fall through spring park. Skywatching can be highly gratifying in these clear desert skies.

 California ⛺
Southern Sierra Nevada: East Slopes

🏕 California 141 ♿

OH! RIDGE
Inyo National Forest

Location: Eastern California south of Lee Vining.

Access: From U.S. Highway 395 at milepost 40 +.3 (at June Lake Junction, 11 miles south of Lee Vining, 15 miles north of Mammoth Lakes Junction, 54 miles northwest of Bishop), turn southwest onto California State Highway 158 (June Lake Loop Road) and proceed 1.1 miles; turn west onto a paved access road and continue for another 1.1 miles, around the west end of the campground, to the entrance. **Alternate Access:** From the junction of U.S. 395 & State Highway 158 (at U.S. 395 milepost 46 +.4, 6 miles south of Lee Vining) travel southwest then northeast on Highway 158 for 14 miles to the campground turnoff.

Day Use Facilities: Small parking area.

Camping Facilities: 148 campsites; (small group camps are also available); sites are small, with very little separation; parking pads are paved, short, basically level straight-ins; framed-and-graveled pads for table and tent areas; adequate level space for a large tent in most sites; barbecue grills; a limited amount of gatherable firewood may be available some distance from the campground, b-y-o is recommended; water at several faucets; restrooms; paved driveways; small store near the campground entrance.

Activities & Attractions: Boating; fishing; designated swimming area.

Natural Features: Located on a sage flat on a bench above the north end of June Lake; a few conifers dot the flat; timbered ridges and rugged, gray mountains surround the area; elevation 7700´.

Season, Fees & Phone: May to November; $11.00; 14 day limit; Mono Lake Ranger District, Lee Vining, ☎(619) 647-6525.

Trip Log: Are there some views here, or what! If there isn't a view from any given site, there certainly would be one from a short walk away. (OH! Ridge was dubbed the "Animal Cracker Campground" by a young 'field editor' because of the names given to each of the multitude of small loops—Dove, Squirrel, Rabbit, Deer—well, you get the picture.)

⚕ California 142 ♿

JUNE LAKE
Inyo National Forest

Location: Eastern California south of Lee Vining.

Access: From the junction of U.S. Highway 395 & California State Highway 158 at U.S. 395 milepost 40 +.3 (15 miles north of Mammoth Lake Junction, 11 miles south of Lee Vining) proceed southwest on Highway 158 (June Lake Loop Road) for 2.5 miles to milepost 2 +.55 on the north edge of the town of June Lake; turn west (right) into the campground. **Alternate Access:** From the junction of U.S. 395 & State Highway 158 (at U.S. 395 milepost 46 +.4, 6 miles south of Lee Vining) travel southwest then northeast on Highway 158 for 13 miles to the campground turnoff.

Day Use Facilities: Small parking area.

Camping Facilities: 28 campsites, including 6 tents-only sites; sites are small to medium-sized, with nominal to good separation; parking pads are gravel, tolerably level, mostly short straight-ins; tent space varies from small to large; fire rings; b-y-o firewood is recommended; water at central faucets; restrooms; paved driveway; gas and groceries in June Lake.

Activities & Attractions: Fishing; boating; boat launch; hiking trails in the area.

Natural Features: Located on a slope above the south-east shore of June Lake; most sites receive light-medium shade from aspens and a few conifers; tent spots are in the open; bordered by hills and mountains; elev. 7600´.

Season, Fees & Phone: May to November; $11.00; 14 day limit; Mono Lake Ranger District, Lee Vining, ☎(619) 647-6525.

Trip Log: Most campsites, except for those in the tent section, are in their own little cubby holes notched into the stand of aspens that encircles the camp's grass-and-sage infield.

⚕ California 143 ♿

SILVER LAKE
Inyo National Forest

Location: Eastern California south of Lee Vining.

Access: From the junction of U.S. Highway 395 & California State Highway 158 at U.S. 395 milepost 40 +.3 (15 miles north of Mammoth Lake Junction, 12 miles south of Lee Vining) travel southwest then northwest on Highway 158 (June Lake Loop Road) for 7 miles to milepost 7 +.2; turn west (right) into the campground. **Alternate Access:** From the junction of U.S. 395 & State Highway 158 (at U.S. 395 milepost 46 +.4, 6 miles south of Lee Vining) proceed southwest on Highway 158 for 8.5 miles to the campground.

Day Use Facilities: Small parking area.

Camping Facilities: 65 campsites; sites are small to medium-sized and level; most sites have minimal to nominal separation, some sites have very good visual separation; parking pads are paved, medium to long straight-ins; large, grassy tent areas; fire rings; b-y-o firewood; water at several faucets; restrooms; paved driveways; gas and camper supplies at a nearby resort; adequate supplies and services are available in Lee Vining.

Activities & Attractions: Rush Creek Trail; access to hiking trails that lead into the Ansel Adams Wilderness; stream and lake fishing; limited boating; boat launch.

Natural Features: Located in a valley on a grassy, creekside flat along Rush Creek at the north tip of Silver Lake; sites are minimally sheltered by a few small conifers and some high bushes on a thick carpet of grass; a waterfall is just downstream (north) of the campground; the campground is closely bordered by rocky hills and rugged mountains along its east side, the peaks of the Sierra Nevada rise to 13,000´ a few miles to the west; elevation 7200´.

Season, Fees & Phone: May to November; $11.00; 14 day limit; Mono Lake Ranger District, Lee Vining, ☎(619) 647-6525.

Trip Log: Stupendous scenery near here! Sage slopes rise many hundreds of feet above the valley to meet the high, craggy, peaks of the Eastern Sierra. You might expect to wake up to a fresh dusting of snow on the high ridgetops even in early July. The highway passes through a very scenic canyon about two miles north of the campground. Sure, you can see most of your neighbors here; but just look at the stunning views instead!

♣ California 144 ♿

TWIN LAKES
Mammoth Lakes/Inyo National Forest

Location: Eastern California southeast of Lee Vining.

Access: From the junction of U.S. Highway 395 & California State Highway 203 at Mammoth Lakes Junction (milepost 25 on U.S. 395, 26 miles south of Lee Vining, 39 miles north of Bishop), travel west on Highway 203 for 4 miles (through Mammoth Lakes Village) to a major junction; continue straight ahead ('203 takes off to the right) on Lake Mary Road (Forest Road 10) for 2 miles to Tamarack Road (just after the creek bridge); turn right, and continue for 0.4 mile to the first camping area, (upper section) or to the right, for another 0.3 mile, to the main camping area.

Day Use Facilities: Small parking area.

Camping Facilities: 97 campsites in 2 main areas; sites are small to medium-sized, basically level, with minimal to nominal separation; some sites in the upper section are sloped; parking pads are gravel or paved, short to medium-length straight-ins; adequate space for a large tent in most sites; fireplaces; some firewood

may be available for gathering locally, b-y-o is suggested; water at several faucets; restrooms; holding tank disposal station; paved driveways; gas and camper supplies at a small local store; adequate supplies and services are available in Mammoth Lakes Village.

Activities & Attractions: Super scenery; national forest visitor center in Mammoth Village; fishing; limited boating.

Natural Features: Located on a moderately timbered flat (main section) and on a forested hillside (upper section) along the shore of Twin Lakes in the eastern Sierra Nevada; elevation 8700´.

Season, Fees & Phone: June to October; $11.00; 7 day limit; Mammoth Ranger District ☎(619) 934-2505.

Trip Log: Fantastic! Rugged mountains, clear, blue lakes, cascading waterfalls. Mammoth Lakes lives up to its reputation for scenic excellence. Twin Lakes is the largest of the campgrounds around the lakes. It also has some of the best (maybe *the* best) scenery. Incidentally, the name Mammoth Lakes refers to the district in which the lakes are located, rather than to the names of the lakes themselves.

♣ California 145 ♿

LAKE MARY
Mammoth Lakes/Inyo National Forest

Location: Eastern California southeast of Lee Vining.

Access: From the junction of U.S. Highway 395 & California State Highway 203 at Mammoth Lakes Junction (milepost 25 on U.S. 395, 26 miles south of Lee Vining, 39 miles north of Bishop), travel west on Highway 203 for 4 miles (through Mammoth Lakes Village) to a major junction; continue straight ahead ('203 takes off to the right) on Lake Mary Road (Forest Road 10) southerly for another 3.3 miles (to a point 1.2 miles beyond the Twin Lakes turnoff); bear right at fork, go 0.3 mile, then swing left for a final 0.1 mile to the campground.

Day Use Facilities: Small picnic area, drinking water, restrooms, small parking area at the visitor center; several small picnic and parking areas are along the shores of the lakes.

Camping Facilities: 51 campsites in 2 sections; sites are small and closely spaced; parking pads are paved, sloped, short to medium-length straight-ins; adequate, but sloped, space for a medium to large tents in most sites; fireplaces or fire rings; limited firewood is available for gathering in the area, b-y-o to be sure; water at several faucets; restrooms; camper supplies at a store within walking distance; adequate supplies and services are available in Mammoth Lakes Village.

Activities & Attractions: Hiking trails; national forest visitor center near Mammoth Village; guided walks and evening programs in summer; fishing.

Natural Features: Located on a terraced slope near the shore of Lake Mary; the lake is ringed with tall conifers and closely encircled by the rocky peaks of the Sierra Nevada; elevation 8900´.

Season, Fees & Phone: June to mid-September; $11.00; 14 day limit; Mammoth Ranger District ☎(619) 934-2505.

Trip Log: The lake-mountain views from near the campground are really excellent. Lake Mary's camping arrangements may be a little nicer, but adjacent Lake George has slightly better views.

⩔ California 146 ♿

LAKE GEORGE
Mammoth Lakes/Inyo National Forest

Location: Eastern California southeast of Lee Vining.

Access: From the junction of U.S. Highway 395 & California State Highway 203 at Mammoth Lakes Junction (milepost 25 on U.S. 395, 26 miles south of Lee Vining, 39 miles north of Bishop), travel west on Highway 203 for 4 miles (through Mammoth Lakes Village) to a major junction; continue straight ahead ('203 takes off to the right) on Lake Mary Road (Forest Road 10) southerly for another 3.3 miles (to a point 1.2 miles beyond the Twin Lakes turnoff); bear right at fork, go 0.3 mile, then swing left for a final 0.7 mile, crossing the bridge over St. Mary Lake outlet, to the campground.

Day Use Facilities: Small picnic area, drinking water, restrooms, small parking area at the visitor center; several small picnic and parking areas are along the shores of the lakes.

Camping Facilities: 18 campsites, including a number of walk-ins; sites are small and tightly spaced; parking pads are paved, short straight-ins; additional leveling will probably be needed on most pads; enough space for a medium to

large tent in most sites, but it may be sloped; fireplaces or fire rings; limited firewood is available for gathering in the area, b-y-o is recommended; water at several faucets; restrooms; camper supplies at a store within walking distance; adequate supplies and services are available in Mammoth Lakes Village.

(Camping is also available in Coldwater Campground, 0.8 mile beyond the turnoff to Lake George; Coldwater is on a forested, creekside slope several hundred yards above the lake; it has 79 campsites, drinking water and restrooms.)

Activities & Attractions: Hiking trails; guided nature walks and evening programs in summer; fishing; national forest visitor center near Mammoth Village.

Natural Features: Located on a hill above the shore of Lake George in the eastern Sierra Nevada; campsites are moderately sheltered by tall conifers; elevation 8900´.

Season, Fees & Phone: June to mid-September; $11.00; 7 day limit; Mammoth Ranger District ☎(619) 934-2505.

Trip Log: Lake George is tucked away in a pocket at the south end of the chain of lakes. There are some stunningly beautiful lake-mountain vistas from here. You may need pitons instead of tent pegs to batten down the canvas on the steep, rocky slope in Lake George. But it's sure worth the view.

⩔ California 147 ♿

EAST FORK
Rock Creek/Inyo National Forest

Location: Eastern California northwest of Bishop.

Access: From U.S. Highway 395 at milepost 10 +.3 in Toms Place (24 miles north of Bishop, 41 miles south of Lee Vining), turn south onto Rock Creek Road (Forest Road 12, paved) and proceed 0.1 mile to the Rock Creek Recreation Area Entrance Station; obtain a camping permit, then head southerly on Rock Creek Road for 6 miles; turn east (left) into the campground.

Day Use Facilities: None.

Camping Facilities: 133 campsites; sites are very small to small+, slightly sloped, with fair to good separation; parking pads are sandy gravel, short to medium-length straight-ins; many pads may require a little additional leveling; small to medium-sized areas for tents;

fire rings and/or barbecue grills; limited firewood is available for gathering in the area, b-y-o is recommended; water at several faucets; restrooms; paved driveway; camper supplies at nearby resorts; gas and groceries in Toms Place.

(Camping is available in July & August at 14-site Iris Meadow Campground, 2 miles north, which you'll pass on the way to East Fork.)

Activities & Attractions: Trail along the creek; several other hiking trails in and around the canyon; John Muir Wilderness.

Natural Features: Located in Rock Creek Canyon along the banks of Rock Creek about a half mile downstream of the creek's confluence with its East Fork; sites are very lightly to moderately sheltered/shaded by short aspens and tall conifers; bordered by sage slopes and lightly timbered canyon walls that steeply rise from the canyon floor; elevation 9000´.

Season, Fees & Phone: June to September; $9.00; 14 day limit; White Mountain Ranger Dist., Bishop, ☎(619) 873-4207 or Rock Creek Entrance Station(619) 935-4253 (summer only).

Trip Log: The campground strrrretches for three-quarters of a mile along the creek. As you progress through the campground up the canyon, you'll encounter sites nestled in their own private little aspen-cordoned nooks; then there's a large group of sites on an open sage slope; finally, at the upper end, are sites which offer limited overhead shade but do provide shelter from wind and early/late sun. Other forest camps along Rock Creek Road include Holiday Campground, a half mile up Rock Creek Road from the main highway. Holiday has 33 sites, drinking water and vaults, situated on a lightly forested slope. Also French Camp, just 0.2 mile south of the entrance station. It has 86 lightly sheltered sites along or near the creek, restrooms, and a disposal station. French Camp, because of its comparatively low altitude and proximity to the highway, potentially has one of the longer seasons and heaviest use of all the Rock Creek camps.

♠ California 148 ♿

ROCK CREEK LAKE
Rock Creek/Inyo National Forest

Location: Eastern California northwest of Bishop.

Access: From U.S. Highway 395 at milepost 10 +.3 in Toms Place (24 miles north of Bishop, 41 miles south of Lee Vining), turn

south onto Rock Creek Road (Forest Road 12, paved) and proceed 0.1 mile to the Rock Creek Recreation Area Entrance Station; obtain a camping permit, then head southerly on Rock Creek Road for 8.6 miles; turn southeasterly (left, at the resort) onto a paved access road and proceed 0.3 to the recreation area.

Day Use Facilities: Small picnic area; drinking water; restrooms; small and medium-sized parking areas.

Camping Facilities: 28 campsites, including a number of park 'n walk or walk-in tent sites, in 2 areas; (a group camp is available in a separate area); sites are small- to small+ in size; separation varies from none to nominal; parking surfaces are paved, short straight-ins or pull-offs; enough space for small tents in most sites, medium-sized tents in some sites; several sites have framed tent pads; fire rings; some firewood is available for gathering in the vicinity, (may have to do some clambering to get to it); b-y-o firewood to be sure; water at several faucets; restrooms; paved driveways; gas and camper supplies at nearby resorts.

(Camping is available during July & August at 11-site Pine Grove Campground, 0.1 mile north, which you'll pass on the way up.)

Activities & Attractions: Several hiking/horse trails lead into the adjacent wilderness areas; trout fishing; limited boating.

Natural Features: Located above the shore of Rock Creek Lake in a high-rimmed, sub-alpine basin at the head of a canyon in the Sierra Nevada; sites are unsheltered, or lightly sheltered, by some conifers and hardwoods; elevation 9600´.

Season, Fees & Phone: May to November; $9.00; 7 day limit; White Mountain Ranger Dist., Bishop, ☎(619) 873-4207 or Rock Creek Entrance Station(619) 935-4253 (summer only).

Trip Log: Being a Rock Creek Lake day-tripper should be an entirely tolerable role to assume. If you're into hiking, more than a dozen alpine lakes can be reached via an interconnecting network of trails. Many are within a five-mile walk of here. (A trail description/map handout is available from the ranger station.) The deep lake has a noticeable 'drop-off' just offshore which may be favorable to fishing from shore. On-site observations reveal that fishing for small trout can be productive.

♠ California 149 ♿

FOUR JEFFREY
Bishop Creek/Inyo National Forest

Location: Eastern California southwest of Bishop.

Access: From the junction of U.S. Highway 395 & California State Highway 168 in midtown Bishop, head west and southwest on Highway 168 (West Line Street) for 10 miles to the Bishop Creek Canyon Entrance Station; obtain a camping permit, then continue for another 5 miles to a major fork near milepost 3+.3; hang a left onto a paved road and proceed southeast for 1 mile; turn easterly (left) and go 0.1 mile to the campground.

Day Use Facilities: None.

Camping Facilities: 106 campsites; sites are small to medium-sized, with minimal to good separation; parking pads are sandy gravel, short to medium-length straight-ins; most pads will require additional leveling; small to medium-sized, generally somewhat sloped areas for tents; b-y-o shade; fire rings and barbecue grills; b-y-o firewood is recommended; water at several faucets; restrooms; holding tank disposal station; hard-surfaced driveways; camper supplies in Aspendell, on Highway 168 near mp 1; complete supplies and services are available in Bishop.

(Camping is also available at 9-site Forks Campground, along the access road just after you angle off the main Bishop Creek Road.)

Activities & Attractions: Super Sierra Scenery.

Natural Features: Located on steeply sloped terrain in a narrow valley on the east slope of the Sierra Nevada; most sites are on an open sage slope, some sites are in among the aspens along a small stream (the South Fork of Bishop Creek); bordered by hills and mountains dotted with sage and small pines; lofty peaks rise from behind the local hills; elevation 8100´.

Season, Fees & Phone: May to October; $9.00; 14 day limit; White Mountain Ranger District, Bishop, ☎(619) 873-4207 or Bishop Creek Entrance Station (619) 873-6829 (summer only).

Trip Log: Shortly after you leave town, the highway crosses an enormous sage flat. The east slopes of the Sierra rise dramatically from the far end of the flat. Fabulous panoramas from along this drive. If you're lucky enough to nail down a creekside site among the aspens at Four Jeffrey, you'll have a fairly large and private site to spend your weekend, week, or whatever.

♠ California 150

SABRINA
Bishop Creek/Inyo National Forest

Location: Eastern California southwest of Bishop.

Access: From the junction of U.S. Highway 395 & California State Highway 168 in midtown Bishop, cruise west and southwest on Highway 168 for 10 miles to the Bishop Creek Canyon Entrance Station; obtain a camping permit, then travel another 8 miles (past the hamlet of Aspendell) to milepost 0.0; turn northwest (right) into the campground; or continue on the main road for another mile to the Lake Sabrina day use area. (Note: the last couple of miles are quite steep; at 9000´, it might be a bit of a job for a heavily laden vehicle.)

Day Use Facilities: Small picnic area, drinking water, vaults, small parking area at Lake Sabrina.

Camping Facilities: 20 campsites; sites are small to small+, slightly off-level, with minimal to fairly good separation; parking pads are sandy gravel, short to short+ straight-ins or pull-offs; medium to large tent areas on a surface of course, packed sand; fire rings; b-y-o firewood; water at central faucets; vault facilities; paved driveway; camper supplies in Aspendell, a mile north.

(On the way up to Sabrina you'll pass two small camps: 20-site Bishop Park and 12-site Intake 2; Bishop Park's sites are mostly streamside park n' walk tent sites; both camps have drinking water and vaults.)

Activities & Attractions: Fishing for regularly stocked trout on Bishop Creek and on Lake Sabrina.

Natural Features: Located on a flat along the bank of Bishop Creek, a mile downstream of Lake Sabrina, in a crag-rimmed canyon on the east slope of the Sierra Nevada; majority of sites are in a long, narrow clearing bordered by aspens and some pines; most campsites receive some shelter from wind, but not much midday shade; elevation 9000´.

Season, Fees & Phone: Mid-May to September; $9.00; 7 day limit; White Mountain Ranger District, Bishop, ☎(619) 873-4207 or Bishop Creek Entrance Station(619) 873-6829 (summer only).

Trip Log: The scenery gets better and better as you travel southwest along the one-way-in/one-way-out highway. There's a good chance that *your* tripmates will also exclaim "Wow!" more than once on this trip.

⚑ California 151

WHITNEY PORTAL
Inyo National Forest

Location: Eastern California south of Bishop.

Access: From U.S. Highway 395 in midtown Lone Pine (59 miles south of Bishop, 69 miles north of Inyokern), turn west onto Whitney Portal Road (paved) and proceed 12.5 miles to the recreation area; (the last 5 miles are curvey and somewhat steep.)

Day Use Facilities: Small picnic area; drinking water; vault facilities; parking area.

Camping Facilities: 44 standard campsites, plus 10 trailhead walk-in sites; (a group camp is also available); sites are small to medium-sized, with minimal to fair separation; parking pads are hard surfaced, mostly short to medium-length straight-ins; small to medium-sized tent areas; fireplaces or fire rings; some firewood may be available for gathering, b-y-o is recommended; water at several faucets; vault facilities; paved driveways; adequate supplies and services are available in Lone Pine.

Activities & Attractions: Trailheads for wilderness trips, including popular day-hike trails up to Lone Pine Lake and other alpine lakes; fishing for small trout; day use areas.

Natural Features: Located along Lone Pine Creek in a canyon on the east slope of the Sierra Nevada at the eastern boundary of the John Muir Wilderness; sites are lightly sheltered by conifers; closely bordered by very high mountains; elevation 8000´.

Season, Fees & Phone: Mid-May to mid-October; $11.00 for a standard site, $6.00 for a trailhead site; 7 day limit for standard sites, 1 day limit for trailhead sites; Mount Whitney Ranger District, Lone Pine, ☎(619) 876-6200.

Trip Log: Whitney Portal is literally in the shadow of 14,496´ Mount Whitney, the loftiest peak in the Sierra Nevada. (The mountain was named for a California state geologist.) But don't positively count on getting a site in this very popular place. Whitney Portal usually is filled by backpackers who are either on their way into, out of, or passing through this superscenic region.

🏠 *California* ⚑
Death Valley National Monument

"Death Valley". Just whispering the foreboding name evokes mental sketches of stark landscapes, lifelessness, and hardships, (especially in imaginative youngsters). Death Valley's "season" is the reverse of most other recreation areas in the West. Roughly Thanksgiving to Easter is the time the vast majority of visitors come to enjoy, and marvel at, the Valley's awesome reality.

⚑ California 152 ♿

SCOTTYS CASTLE
Death Valley National Monument

Location: Southeast California north of Barstow.

Access: From the main north-south park road at a point 31 miles southeast of the road's junction with U.S. Highway 95 in Nevada, and 58 miles northwest of Furnace Creek, turn northerly into the parking lot.

Day Use Facilities: Small picnic area; drinking water; restrooms; large parking lot.

Camping Facilities: Nearest park campground is Mesquite Spring, 3.5 miles south.

Activities & Attractions: Park Service tours of the interior and grounds of Scotty's Castle; tours of the interior during the winter months may require a substantial wait.

Natural Features: Located in a small side valley in the Grapevine Mountains at the north tip of Death Valley; the mansion's grounds are landscaped with a broad assortment of desert plants, bushes, and trees; elevation 2500´.

Season, Fees & Phone: Open all year; tours $8.00; park headquarters, Furnace Creek, ☎(619) 786-2331.

Trip Log: Scotty's Castle is an early twentieth Century mansion built by "Death Valley Scotty", who struck it rich here in the Valley. Taking one of the Park Service guided tours may indeed be the best way to see the Castle. But just stopping by for a while to admire the tastefully designed structures (and maybe peek through a window or two), and to walk the meticulously landscaped grounds is well worth the time and effort.

♠ California 153 ♿

MESQUITE SPRING
Death Valley National Monument

Location: Southeast California north of Barstow.

Access: From the main north-south park road at a point 3.5 miles southwest of Scotty's Castle and 54 miles northwest of Furnace Creek, turn south-west onto a paved access road and proceed 1.8 miles to the campground.

Day Use Facilities: Facilities are shared with campers.

Camping Facilities: 53 campsites; (a group camping area is also available); sites are generally small, with no separation; parking pads are paved or gravel, mostly medium-length straight-ins; adequate space for a large tent in most sites on a gravel/rock surface; fireplaces and barbecue grills; b-y-o firewood (gathering in the park is prohibited); water at central faucets; restrooms; disposal station; paved driveways; camper supplies at Stovepipe Wells, 43 miles south; limited to adequate supplies are available in Beatty, Nevada, 60 miles east.

Activities & Attractions: Scotty's Castle, 3.5 miles northeast; Ubehebe Crater, 6 miles northwest.

Natural Features: Located on a gently sloping flat at the upper end of Death Valley; vegetation consists of a grove of large mesquite trees that form a canopy at the entrance, plus small desert bushes and a lot of rock in the rest of the campground; the Cottonwood Mountains stand to the west, and the Grapevine Mountains are to the east; elevation 1800´.

Season, Fees & Phone: Open all year; $8.00; 30 day limit; park headquarters, Furnace Creek, ☎(619) 786-2331.

Trip Log: One of the mesquite trees here is believed to be over a thousand years old. Primarily because of a two thousand feet difference in elevation, it is typically 11°F cooler here than in the camps farther south. This is one of only three campgrounds in the national monument that are open all year.

♠ California 154 ♿

STOVEPIPE WELLS
Death Valley National Monument

Location: Southeast California north of Barstow.

Access: From California State Highway 190 at milepost 85 +.6 (7 miles southwest of the junction of Highway 190 & the main north-south park road, 75 miles northeast of Olancha), turn north into the camping area.

Day Use Facilities: Drinking water, restrooms, small parking area at the ranger station.

Camping Facilities: Approximately 200 campsites in a parking lot arrangement; sites are small-, nearly level, with zero separation; parking surfaces are gravel, short to long straight-ins or pull-throughs; ample space for free-standing tents in designated sites; a few sites have fireplaces; (would it be superfluous to mention b-y-o firewood?); water at central faucets; central restrooms; ranger station; paved driveways; camper supplies and showers are available nearby.

Activities & Attractions: Unique landscape.

Natural Features: Located on a desolate plain on the floor of Death Valley; a few small desert bushes are around the perimeter of the camp lot; sizable sand dunes are in the vicinity; the valley is flanked by the barren Panamint Range a few miles to the west and the Amargosa Range to the east; sea level.

Season, Fees & Phone: October to April; $8.00; 30 day limit; park headquarters, Furnace Creek, ☎(619) 786-2331

Trip Log: Two other campgrounds in this section of the park are certainly worth a look. Emigrant Campground is 8 miles southwest of Stovepipe Wells at Emigrant Junction, on the north side of California 190. Emigrant has 10 campsites, drinking water and restrooms nearby; Wildrose Campground, at an exhilarating elevation of 4000´ above sea level, is 21 miles south of Emigrant Junction via Wildrose Road (paved). Wildrose has 36 sites, vaults, no water. Wildrose is the highest campground in the park.

♠ California 155 ♿

FURNACE CREEK
Death Valley National Monument

Location: Southeast California north of Barstow.

Access: From California State Highway 190 at milepost 110 +.1 (0.2 mile north of the Furnace Creek Visitor Center, 2 miles north of the junction of State Highways 190 & 178, 25 miles southeast of Stovepipe Wells), turn west into the park visitor center parking lot; or a few yards north of the visitor center, turn west and go 0.15 mile to the campground.

Day Use Facilities: Small picnic area; drinking water; restrooms; large parking area.

Camping Facilities: 105 campsites, plus overflow areas; sites are generally small and level, with nominal to minimal separation; parking pads are sandy gravel, medium-length straight-ins or pull-throughs; good-sized tent areas with a sandy surface; fireplaces; b-y-o firewood (gathering in the park is prohibited); water at central faucets; restrooms; holding tank disposal station; paved driveway; ranger station nearby; gas and camper supplies are available at a nearby store.

Activities & Attractions: Visitor center, with exhibits and audio-visual programs; museum; interpretive trails.

Natural Features: Located on a flat in the center of Death Valley; vegetation consists primarily of rows of large, full trees which provide shade for some campsites; barren hills surround the area in the immediate vicinity; most sites also have quite striking views of the classic desert mountains for which the region is famous; elevation 196´ *below* sea level.

Season, Fees & Phone: Open all year; $8.00; 30 day limit; park headquarters, Furnace Creek, ☎(619) 786-2331.

Trip Log: Furnace Creek is the park's nerve center. The visitor center features some really excellent displays and a-v programs. However, unless you enjoy a festival atmosphere, you might consider coming to the park at a time other than the second weekend of November. That's when the Death Valley 49ers hold their annual rendezvous, and the park swells to capacity (and beyond). Most winter holidays and three-day weekends are also congested. Even in midsummer (midsimmer?), a surprising number of people visit the valley, but few camp.

♠ California 156 &

TEXAS SPRING
Death Valley National Monument

Location: Southeast California north of Barstow.

Access: From California State Highway 190 at milepost 111 (0.6 mile south of the Furnace Creek Visitor Center, 1 mile north of the junction of State Highways 190 & 178, and many miles north of nowhere else in particular),

turn northeast onto a paved access road and proceed 1 mile to the campground.

Day Use Facilities: At the Furnace Creek visitor center.

Camping Facilities: Approximately 80 campsites; (a group camp area is also available); sites vary in size, with minimal separation; parking surfaces are sandy gravel, short to medium-length straight-ins or pull-offs; adequate space for medium to large tents in most sites; fireplaces; b-y-o firewood; water at central faucets; restrooms; gravel driveway; gas and camper supplies in Furnace Creek.

Activities & Attractions: Desert panoramas; shade.

Natural Features: Located in a grove of trees on a gentle slope above the floor of Death Valley; sites are minimally to lightly shaded; sea level.

Season, Fees & Phone: October to May; $8.00; 30 day limit; park headquarters, Furnace Creek, ☎(619) 786-2331.

Trip Log: Texas Spring is one of three campgrounds in the Furnace Creek vicinity. Seasoned Death Valley campers prefer Texas Spring's environment and layout to Furnace Creek Campground's slightly more deluxe accommodations. The third camp area, Sunset, offers parking lot stopovers for upwards of a thousand campers during the winter months. Sunset has drinking water and restrooms on a huge, gravelly, unsheltered, gently sloping flat just across the highway from the visitor center.

🏠 *California* ⅄
Joshua Tree National Monument

Joshua Tree is primarily a huge desert wilderness park on the edge of a rapidly advancing civilization. Described below are the only developed recreation areas in the national monument. The monument's main visitor center is located on Park Boulevard (the park's main north-south road), less than a mile south of its junction with California State Highway 62 on the east side of Twentynine Palms.

♠ California 157 &

BLACK ROCK CANYON
Joshua Tree National Monument

Location: South-central California east of San Bernardino.

Access: From the junction of California State Highways 62 & 247 in the city of Yucca Valley, (21 miles north of Interstate 10, 54 miles, as the crow flies, due east of San Bernardino), turn south onto Joshua Lane; proceed south, then east, for 4.5 miles to a 'T' intersection at San Marino Drive; turn right (south again) and go a final 0.35 mile (following a short jog in the road) to the recreation area.

Day Use Facilities: Small picnic area; drinking water; restrooms; small parking area.

Camping Facilities: 100 campsites in a complex of loops; sites are small to medium-sized, with fair to good separation; parking pads are gravel, short to medium-length straight-ins, pads are level to slightly sloped; adequate space for a large tent in most sites; fire rings; b-y-o firewood; water at several faucets; restrooms; holding tank disposal station; paved/gravel driveways; ranger station; complete supplies and services are available in Yucca Valley.

Activities & Attractions: Trails to Black Rock Spring (1.5 miles), Eureka Peak (5 miles), and other, more distant, points in the park; equestrian facilities.

Natural Features: Located on a gentle slope at the mouth of Black Rock Canyon near the northwest end of the Little San Bernardino Mountains; the area is situated within a veritable forest of Joshua trees, junipers, cholla cactus, and desert bushes; elevation 4000´.

Season, Fees & Phone: November to April; $8.00; 14 day limit; park headquarters, Twentynine Palms, ☎(619) 367-7511.

Trip Log: Joshua trees are fascinating in that each has its own individual shape or character. Look around, and you'll rarely, if ever, find two adult trees that are alike. Black Rock Canyon contains a classic assortment of high desert plant life. It almost certainly ranks near the top of the tally of desert camps.

⁂ California 158

INDIAN COVE
Joshua Tree National Monument

Location: South-central California east of San Bernardino.

Access: From California State Highway 62 at milepost 27 +.4 (6 miles west of Twentynine Palms, 15 miles east of the junction of State Highways 62 & 247 at Yucca Valley), turn south onto Indian Cove Road (paved), and

proceed 3.2 miles (continuing past the ranger station) to the campground.

Day Use Facilities: None.

Camping Facilities: 110 campsites in 2 loops; (a reservable) group camp is also available); sites vary in size, but many are large and well separated; parking pads are sandy, short to medium-length straight-ins and pull-offs; some pads will require additional leveling; tent areas are medium to large, and many are acceptably level; fire rings; b-y-o firewood; water is available at the ranger station, 1.8 miles north; vault facilities; paved driveways; adequate supplies and services are available in Twentynine Palms.

Activities & Attractions: Unique setting; campfire circle; foot trail; park visitor center in Twentynine Palms.

Natural Features: Located among a large cluster of interestingly eroded rock formations at the base of the hills along the northern edge of Joshua Tree National Monument; many sites are situated in their own little rock alcoves; campground vegetation consists of a sparse population of Joshua trees and small desert plants; elevation 3200´.

Season, Fees & Phone: Open all year; $8.00; 14 day limit in winter, 30 day limit in summer; park headquarters, Twentynine Palms, ☎(619) 367-7511.

Trip Log: In addition to being in a really distinctive setting, the campground offers some really terrific vistas out across a wide valley to the north. Indian Cove is on the north edge of the national monument's Wonderland of Rocks. Summer temps throughout the monument can be expected to be well into the 100's by day and may cool into the low 70's at night.

⁂ California 159

JUMBO ROCKS
Joshua Tree National Monument

Location: South-central California between Riverside and Blythe

Access: From the park's main north-south highway (called Pinto Basin Road by some sources) at a major junction 8.5 miles south of the park's visitor center near Twentynine Palms and 32 miles north of the Mecca/Twentynine Palms Exit on Interstate 10, turn west onto a paved park road (listed as Quail Springs Road on some maps); proceed 3.8 miles, then turn south (left) for 0.2 mile to the campground.

Alternate Access: From California State Highway 62 in the town of Joshua Tree (near the west edge of Twentynine Palms), head south/southeast on Park Boulevard (which soon becomes Quail Springs Road) for 22 miles (passing Hidden Valley, Ryan and Sheep Pass Campgrounds along the way) to the Jumbo Rocks Campground turnoff; turn south and continue as above.

Day Use Facilities: Several small picnic areas and pullouts are located along the park road.

Camping Facilities: 128 campsites; sites are small and closely spaced; parking surfaces are sandy, short straight-ins or pull-offs; small to medium-sized areas for tents; fire rings; b-y-o firewood; no drinking water; vault facilities; sandy driveways; adequate supplies and services are available in Twentynine Palms.

Activities & Attractions: Scenic drives; rock climbing; hiking.

Natural Features: Located amongst a massive rock formation on the high desert east of the Little San Bernardino Mountains; vegetation consists of Joshua trees and small desert plants; elevation 4400´.

Season, Fees & Phone: Open all year; $8.00; 14 day limit in winter, 30 day limit in summer; park headquarters, Twentynine Palms, ☎(619) 367-7511.

Trip Log: The campground is named for the humongous heap of stones among which the campsites are sequestered. Jumbo Rocks is the largest of a cluster of a half dozen camps in the central park area. The others: Belle, Hidden Valley, Ryan, Sheep Pass, and White Tank, are within 7 miles east or west of Jumbo Rocks and offer a total of some 130 sites. All have similar facilities in essentially comparable surroundings. (According to reliable local reports, several of these campgrounds are solidly in the Land of the Site Savers. Rock climbers, hikers and others eager to help their fellow recreationers often manage to pass good campsites along to an unbroken succession of friends and acquaintances over an extended period.)

⚲ California 160

COTTONWOOD
Joshua Tree National Monument

Location: South-central California between Riverside and Blythe.

Access: From the park's main north-south highway (called Cottonwood Springs Road in this section), at a point 7 miles north of the Mecca/Twentynine Palms Exit on Interstate 10 and 39 miles south of Twentynine Palms, turn east into the Cottonwood Visitor Center parking lot; or a few yards south of the visitor center, turn east onto a paved road and go 0.7 mile to the campground

Day Use Facilities: Small picnic area; drinking water; restrooms; medium-sized parking area.

Camping Facilities: 62 campsites in 2 loops; (a reservable group camp is also available); sites are small, with minimal to nominal separation; parking pads are paved, short to medium-length straight-ins, or narrow, medium-length pull-offs; tent areas are medium to large, level, with a sandy base; fireplaces; b-y-o firewood; water at central faucets; restrooms; holding tank disposal station; paved driveways; ranger station; gas and minimal supplies at Chiriaco Summit, 7 miles south, then 4 miles east on I-10; adequate supplies and services are available in Indio, 25 miles west.

Activities & Attractions: Interpretive center; hiking trails; 4wd trail to Pinkham Canyon; amphitheater.

Natural Features: Located on a high desert plain, with dry, high mountains to the east and to the distant west, and low hills directly south of the campground; a profusion of low-level, brushy plants, (but no Joshua trees) occupy the campground area; elevation 3000´.

Season, Fees & Phone: Open all year; $8.00; 14 day limit in winter, 30 day limit in summer; park headquarters, Twentynine Palms, ☎(619) 367-7511.

Trip Log: Oddly enough, the Joshua tree is botanically classified as a distant relative of the lily and not as a tree at all. It is actually a large yucca, and it does bloom in spring. The armed plant supposedly was named by the early Mormons to whom its outstretched extremities fancifully resembled the biblical character Joshua pointing toward the Promised Land. Cottonwood Campground looks like an excellent place for tent camping. This region seems to be a favorite of European visitors (German, Dutch, Scandinavian), even in summer. The 'word' here is that arrival on or before Thursday is practically mandatory on winter weekends.

California ⚊

Mojave Desert

⚊ California 161 ⚊

PARK MOABI

San Bernardino County Regional Park

Location: Southeast California along the California-Arizona border east of Needles.

Access: From Interstate 40 at milepost 153 +.3 (1.3 miles west of the Arizona-California border, 11 miles east of Needles), take the Park Moabi Exit (the easternmost exit in California); turn north onto Park Moabi Road, and proceed 0.6 mile; turn left into the park.

Day Use Facilities: Large picnic area; drinking water; restrooms; large parking lot.

Camping Facilities: 664 campsites, including 31 sites with partial or complete hookups; sites are all fairly level, and vary considerably in size and separation: from small to very large, from close to quite private; hookup sites are parking-lot style, on a gravel surface; tent spots are generally large and level; tenting not permitted on the grass on weekdays (because of automatic sprinkling); some sites may lack tables and/or fire facilities; barbecue grills in most sites; b-y-o firewood; water at several faucets; restrooms, some with showers; holding tank disposal station; gravel driveways; adequate supplies and services are available in Needles.

Activities & Attractions: Boating; large boat launch area; marina nearby; fishing; small playground.

Natural Features: Located along the west bank of the Colorado River; campground vegetation consists of some watered grass and short-to-medium height, bushy trees; sandy beach; surrounded by desert mountains; elevation 600´.

Season, Fees & Phone: Open all year; $12.00 to $17.00; 14 day limit; park office ☎(619) 326-3831.

Trip Log: Although it often gets pretty busy at this park, they've reportedly never had to turn anyone away. The average camper here travels 250-300 miles for a weekend stay. Park Moabi's campground may prove to be very handy for I-40 travelers. For all practical purposes, the next-nearest public camps along the Interstate are more than a hundred miles from here in either direction.

⚊ California 162 ⚊

MOJAVE NARROWS

San Bernardino County Regional Park

Location: Southern California north of San Bernardino.

Access: From Interstate 15 at the Lucerne Valley/Bear Valley Road Exit at milepost 37 +.6 in Victorville (32 miles north of San Bernardino, 36 miles southwest of Barstow), turn east onto Bear Valley Road (called Bear Valley Cutoff farther east); proceed 3.9 miles to Ridge Crest Drive; turn north (left) onto Ridge Crest Drive and continue for 2.6 miles, then turn left, and go 0.1 mile to the park.

Day Use Facilities: Large picnic area; shelters; group picnic area; drinking water; restrooms; large parking lot.

Camping Facilities: 87 campsites in 2 sections; some sites are in a string along a lake shore; other sites are in a parking lot arrangement; sites are small to average in size, level, with minimal separation; parking pads are paved, and vary from short straight-ins to longer pull-offs and pull-throughs; plenty of excellent tent-pitching possibilities on a grass or sandy base; fire rings and/or barbecue grills; b-y-o firewood; water at central faucets; restrooms with showers; holding tank disposal station; complete supplies and services are available on Bear Valley Road.

Activities & Attractions: Fishing (extra fee); paved, self-guided nature trail; trout derbies in winter; Roy Rogers & Dale Evans Museum in Victorville.

Natural Features: Located on the shore of Horseshoe Lake in a large valley ringed by high and dry mountains, at the southern edge of the Mojave Desert; large hardwoods provide shade/shelter in some sites; most sites are in the open; typically breezy; elevation 2700´.

Season, Fees & Phone: Open all year; $12.00; long term rates are available; park office ☎(619) 245-2226.

Trip Log: You might not think that a park on the "edge of the Mojave Desert" holds much attraction, but this is actually a nice place, even in the warmer months. Reportedly, there's usually room for drop-in campers, even in winter when the park hosts many 'snowbirds'.

⚶ California 163 ⛬

AQUA CALIENTE SPRINGS
San Diego County Park

Location: Southwest corner of California northeast of San Diego.

Access: From San Diego County Highway S2 at milepost 38 +.3 (26 miles north of Ocotillo, 21 miles south of the junction of Highway S2 & California State Highway 78 west of Julian), turn south onto Aqua Caliente Hot Springs Road (paved), and proceed 0.4 mile to the park.

Day Use Facilities: Small picnic area; shelter; drinking water; restrooms/bathouse; medium-sized parking area.

Camping Facilities: 126 campsites, including many with partial or full hookups, in 2 sections; (group camping is also available); sites are medium-sized, with nominal to fair visual separation; parking pads are sandy gravel, fairly level, medium-length straight-ins; adequate space for tents in most sites; fire rings, plus a barbecue grills; b-y-o firewood; water at faucets throughout; central restrooms; paved driveways; gas and camper supplies at a nearby store; gas and groceries in Julian; limited supplies and services are available in Ocotillo.

(Vallecito Park, a smaller county park 4 miles north of here, has 44 spacious, fairly well shaded campsites, water and restrooms in an attractive desert setting.)

Activities & Attractions: Very popular hot springs and mineral pools; recreation building; numerous trails and scenic views within surrounding Anza-Borrego Desert State Park.

Natural Features: Located at the foot of the Tierra Blanca Mountains in the Anza-Borrego desert area; some sites are on open hilltop, others are on a sloping flat among small to medium-height bushes and trees which provide some shelter/shade; Aqua Caliente Hot Springs are a few yards from the camping area; elevation 800.

Season, Fees & Phone: October to May; $9.00 for a standard site, $12.00 for a partial-hookup site, $13.00 for a full-hookup site; 14 day limit; reservations recommended for holiday weekends, contact San Diego County Parks Department, San Diego, ☎(619) 565-3600; for general information(619) 565-5928.

Trip Log: Four natural springs—one cool and fresh, the others warm and sulphurous—are the center of attention here. People from all over come to soak up some warmth and minerals in the reportedly therapeutic hot springs.

⚶ California 164 ⛬

BORREGO PALM CANYON
Anza-Borrego Desert State Park

Location: Southwest California northeast of San Diego.

Access: From San Diego County Highway S22 at milepost 17 +.5, at the intersection of Palm Canyon Drive and Montezuma Valley Road, (1.4 miles west of the town circle—called "Christmas Circle"—in the city of Borrego Springs) proceed 0.2 mile west on the park access road; turn north onto the campground access road and continue for 1 mile to the campground entrance station; or continue west past the turnoff onto the campground access road for another 0.2 mile to the visitor center.

Day Use Facilities: Medium-sized picnic area near the west end of the campground, with ramadas (sun shelters) for all sites; drinking water; restrooms; parking at each site; good-sized parking lot at the visitor center.

Camping Facilities: 117 campsites, including 52 with full hookups, in 3 sections; (an equestrian camp and a number of group camps are also available, by reservation); sites are generally medium-sized, with fair to fairly good separation; hookup sites tend to be larger; parking pads are paved, level, long pull-throughs in the hookup section; parking pads in the tent section are gravel/earth and tend to be slightly sloped; adequate space for large tents; ramadas (sun shelters) in many of the tent sites; fire rings; b-y-o firewood; water in the hookup units and at central faucets; restrooms with showers; paved driveways; limited+ to adequate supplies and services are available in Borrego Springs.

Activities & Attractions: Visitor center with a large botanical garden and interpretive exhibits and slide programs about desert vegetation, wildlife and geology; Borrego Palm Canyon Nature Trail (an excellent guide pamphlet is available); hiking trails; campfire center.

Natural Features: Located at the east edge of the San Ysidro Mountains overlooking the vast Borrego Valley to the east; visitor center area has an extensive and varied collection of desert trees and plants; picnic/campground vegetation includes large, desert bushes and a few palms; the park is highly regarded for its spectacular early spring wildflower bloom; elevation within the park varies from 15´ to 6200´; elevation at Borrego Palm Canyon is about 1200´.

Season, Fees & Phone: Open all year; please see Appendix for reservation information, day use and campground fees; ☎(619) 767-4684 or ☎(619) 767-5311.

Trip Log: Try to plan your itinerary so the visitor center is one of your first stops when you come to Anza-Borrego. Detailed information and maps covering the park's 600,000 square miles of wilderness and near-wilderness can be readily obtained at the visitor center. The center is an underground operation. (Well it really *is*— the earth berming helps to keep the place cool.) The excellent exhibits and information inside, and the botanical displays outside, will strengthen your appreciation of the park's unique environment. Borrego Palm Canyon is the largest and most highly developed area in the park. There are some tremendous daytime and nighttime vistas of the valley from here. Some of the palms look like characters from Sesame Street.

♣ California 165

TAMARISK GROVE
Anza-Borrego Desert State Park

Location: Southwest California northeast of San Diego.

Access: From San Diego County Highway S3 at a point 0.3 mile northeast of the junction of Highway S3 with California State Highway 78, 18 miles northeast of Julian and 12 miles south of Borrego Springs, turn south into the picnic area and campground.

Day Use Facilities: Small picnic area; drinking water; restrooms nearby; small parking area.

Camping Facilities: 27 campsites; (small, primitive camp areas are available nearby at Yaqui Well, 0.3 mile southwest, and just north of the summit of Yaqui Pass, 2 miles northeast) sites are level, about average in size, with fair to fairly good separation; parking pads are paved, short, but extra wide; adequate space for a medium to large tent in most sites; all sites have ramadas (sun shelters); fire rings; b-y-o firewood; water at central faucets; restrooms with showers; paved driveway; limited + to adequate supplies and services are available in Borrego Springs.

Activities & Attractions: Cactus Loop Trail; campfire center; interpretive garden; small visitor center/ranger station.

Natural Features: Located in a desert canyon flanked by Pinyon Ridge to the west and Yaqui Ridge to the east; most picnic and camp sites are fairly well shaded/sheltered by huge Tamarisk trees; other local vegetation consists of a good cross-section of typical desert plants; Yaqui Pass, 2 miles northeast; elevation 1400´.

Season Fees & Phone: Open all year; reservations available October to May, and advised for holidays and weekend; ☎(619) 767-4684 or ☎(619) 767-5311.

Trip Log: Anza-Borrego's 600,000 acres make it the largest state park in the contiguous United States. Weekend traffic during 'perfect' weather in spring and fall can make it seem a little smaller than that, but it's pretty quiet on weekdays during most of the year. Although a lot of people don't think so, it can even be thoroughly enjoyed in summer, provided you bring your sense of adventure (and, of course, your standard complement of hot-weather supplies as well). While summer picnicking and camping in the desert isn't for everyone, you might consider doing it at least once. (There won't be any crowds.)

Special Note:

For information about the best spring wildflower viewing periods in Anza-Borrego Desert: Sometime during the winter enclose a self-addressed, stamped post card in an envelope, and mail the envelope to:

Wildflowers,
Anza-Borrego Desert State Park
P.O. Box 299
Borrego Springs, CA 92004.

The card will be returned to you about 2 weeks before the expected peak bloom.)

🏠 Appendix ⛺

🏠 *West Coast Standard State Park Fees*

State park systems in most Western states have standardized fee schedules set or authorized by their respective state legislatures, so we have encapsulated them in this section for easy reference.

🏔 *Washington*

Primitive campsite	
w/motorized vehicle	$7.00
w/non-motorizid vehicle	$5.00
Standard/developed campsite	$10.00
Hookup campsite	$15.00
"Popular Destination Park Surcharge"	$1.00

(April 1 to September 30, most state park campgrounds)

🏔 *Oregon*

Primitive campsite (i.e., no showers)	$10.00-$14.00
Standard/developed campsite	$13.00-$17.00
Partial hookup campsite	$13-$20.00
Full hookup campsite	$17.00-$20.00
Designated hike/bike campsite	$5.00
Daily park entry fee for certain parks	$3.00

🏔 *California*

Daily park entry fee (per vehicle)	$5.00-$7.00
Primitive/semi-developed campsite	$9.00
Standard/developed/enroute campsite	$15.00-$18.00
Hookup campsite	$18.00-$22.00
Additional for "premium" & south coast camps	$2.00-$13.00
Additional for an extra vehicle in campsite	$5.00-$6.00
Additional for a power boat or sailboat over 8´	$5.00
Backcountry campsite (per person)	$3.00
Group campsite	$36.00-$187.50
Walk-in fee (per person)	$1.00-$2.00

📄 *West Coast Recreation Reservations*

🌲 *National Forest Reservations*

The USDA Forest Service has established a reservation system which affects hundreds of national forest campgrounds nationwide. Continuous changes can be expected in such a large system as campgrounds with reservable sites are added or removed from the list. For additional information about campgrounds with reservable sites, and to make reservations, you may call (toll-free) the independent agent handling the reservation system.

☎ **800-280-CAMP** **(800-280-2267)**

Reservations can be made from 10 days to 120 days in advance. It is suggested that you take advantage of the full 120-day period for any forest camp associated with a lake or sizable stream, or near a national park, if you want to be assured of a campsite there on a summer holiday weekend.

⋏⋏ *National Park Reservations*

For information about campsite availability and reservations at certain campgrounds in *Joshua Tree National Monument*, *Sequoia National Park*, and *Whiskeytown National Recreation Area* call:

☎ (800) 365-CAMP   (800-365-2267)

For reservations in *Yosemite National Park*, you may call:

☎ (800) 436-PARK   (800-436-7275)

Reservations for national park area campgrounds are available from 10 to 56 days in advance. (Campsites in some national park campgrounds, particularly in *Yosemite NP*, are available *only* by reservation 'year round.) To be reasonably assured of securing a site, it is suggested that you take advantage of the full 56-day advance period.

As of this edition, reservations are not available for national park campgrounds in Washington and Oregon, as they are in some other Western regions. You may want to periodically check with MisTix to determine if national park reservations are being taken for Northwest parks.

For national forest and most national park reservations, a fee of $6.00-$7.50 is charged for a campsite reservation. In addition to the reservation charge, the standard campground user fees for all nights which are reserved also need to be paid at the time the reservation is made. (Reservations for consecutive nights at the same campground are covered under the same fee.) If you cancel, you lose the reservation fee, plus you're charged a cancellation fee. Any remainder is refunded. They'll take checks, money orders, VISA or MasterCard, (VISA/MC for telephone reservations).

Reservable campsites in national forest and national park campgrounds are assigned, but you can request an rv or a tent site; rv sites are generally a little larger and most will accommodate tents. When making a reservation, be prepared to tell the reservation agent about the major camping equipment you plan to use, (size and number of tents, type and length of rv, additional vehicles, boat trailers, etc.). Be generous in your estimate. In most cases, a national forest campground's *best sites* are also those which are *reservable*. Most of the national forest campgrounds which have reservable sites still can accommodate a limited number of drop-ins on a first-come, first-served basis.

🏕 *State Park Reservations*

Reservations may be made for individual and group campsites at certain *Washington* and *Oregon* state parks. Reservations should be initiated *at least* several weeks in advance of your arrival date.

Reservations for sites in Washington and Oregon state parks may be obtained 3 days to 11 months in advance by calling the independent agent handling the reservations system, Reservations Northwest:

☎ 800-452-5687

Reservations for individual and group campsites in most *California state parks* may be obtained 10 to 56 days in advance by calling:

☎ (800) 444-PARK   (800-444-7275) or ☎ TDD (800)-274-7275

A reservation fee of $6.00 is charged. A VISA or MasterCard is required for a reservation confirmed on the phone. Campers without credit cards must prepay by check, so three weeks extra processing time is required. Cancellation fees are charged if you bow out.

Reservations for other camp and day use areas in the states covered in this volume *may* be obtainable directly from the public agency responsible for the recreation area, as indicated in the text.

For additional information about reservations, availability, current conditions, or regulations about the use of recreation areas, we suggest that you directly contact the park or forest office in charge of your selected area, using the *Phone* ☎ information in the text.

Please remember that all reservation and fee information is subject to change without notice.

Washington

N

Blue Mtns

61 Sullivan Lake
62 Noisy Creek
50 Evans
51 Marcus Island
Newport
Colville
Kettle River Range
Spokane
Clarkston
67 Chief Timothy
395
90
12

53 Gifford
54 Hunters
55 Fort Spokane
56 Spring Canyon
57 Steamboat Rock
Kettle Falls
52 Kettle Falls
Republic
Ritzville
Walla Walla
64 Charbonneau
65 Fishhook
66 Fort Walla Walla
2
395

59 Osoyoos Lake
60 Bonaparte Lake
58 Sun Lakes
Coulee City
Grand Coulee
Moses Lake
Pasco
Richland
Kennewick
63 Plymouth
20

Oroville
Okanogan
39 Colonial Creek
44 Loup Loup
43 Pearrygin Lake
42 Early Winters
41 Klipchuck
40 Lone Fir
46 Wenatchee River
47 Lincoln Rock
45 Lake Wenatchee
Winthrop
Wenatchee
Vantage
82
97
36 Maryhill
The Dalles, OR
97

38 Newhalem Creek
37 Goodell Creek
Newhalem
Cascade Range
Leavenworth
48 Denny Creek
49 Wish-Poosh
Cle Elum
Ellensburg
Yakima
31 White River
34 Pleasant Valley
30 Ohanapecosh
32 La Wis Wis
35 Indian Creek
33 Iron Creek
27 Sunshine Point
Naches
12

Rockport
Mount Vernon
15 Deception Pass
23 Camano Island
Everett
16 Fort Casey
North Bend
90
Seattle
2
Cascade Range
Enumclaw
28 Cougar Rock
29 Paradise
Mt Rainier
Longmire
Tacoma
22 Kopachuck
21 Penrose Point
13 Millersylvania
Chehalis
Kelso
14 Battle Ground Lake
Cascade Range

Bellingham
24 Birch Bay
25 Larrabee
26 Moran
18 Fort Flagler
17 Fort Worden
Port Angeles
9 Sequim Bay
10 Seal Rock
19 Scenic Beach
20 Belfair
Olympia
12
5

4 Fairholm
6 Altaire
2 Hoh
5 Elwha
7 Hurricane Ridge
Olympic Mtns
8 Staircase
Fairholm
Forks
3 Mora
Queets
1 Kalaloch
11 Ocean City
Aberdeen
Westport
12 Fort Canby
Illwaco
Vancouver
5

Oregon

N

Snake River

Columbia River

Blue Mtns

Jordan Valley
95

52 Wallowa Lake

Baker
84

Huntington
53 Farewell Bend

Ontario

Vale

La Grande

20

Unity

John Day

Blue Mtns

Burns

395

Pendleton

Ukiah
395

Mt. Vernon

Riley

395

Lakeview
54 Goose Lake

Arlington
84

Fossil
38 Lepage

26

Prineville

20

47 Cinder Hill
46 East Lake
45 Little Crater
44 Paulina Lake

The Dalles
40 Hoodview
97

Hood River
39 Trillium Lake

36 Eagle Creek
37 Wyeth

35 Rooster Rock
34 Bridal Veil Falls
33 Crown Point

Madras
41 Cove Palisades
48 Crane Prairie

Bend
43 Blue Bay & South Shore

La Pine
49 Shadow Bay
50 Trapper Creek
51 Diamond Lake

Sisters
42 Big Lake

Estacada

Cascade Range
25 House Rock

Portland
22 Tryon Creek
23 Champoeg

24 Silver Falls

Salem
20

Astoria

Nehalem

Tillamook

Lincoln City

Newport

8 Yaquina Bay

Coast Range

Albany

Springfield
26 Elijah Bristow

Sweet Home

Eugene

Cottage Grove

Oakridge

Cascade Range
28 Joseph Stewart

Roseburg

5

30 Crater Lake
29 Union Creek

97

Chiloquin
31 Doe Point
32 Aspen Point

Klamath Falls

Grants Pass

27 Valley of the Rogue

Medford

Ashland

Coast Range

North Bend

Coos Bay

Bandon

Port Orford

Gold Beach

Brookings

1 Fort Stevens
2 Ecola
3 Nehalem Bay
4 Cape Mearas
5 Cape Lookout
6 Sand Beach
7 Devil's Lake
9 Tillicum Beach
10 Cape Perpetua
11 Jessie M. Honeyman
12 Tahkenitch
13 Umpqua Lighthouse
14 William M. Tugman
16 Shore Acres
15 Bastendorff Beach
17 Sunset Bay
18 Bullards Beach
19 Cape Blanco
20 Samuel H. Boardman
21 Harris Beach

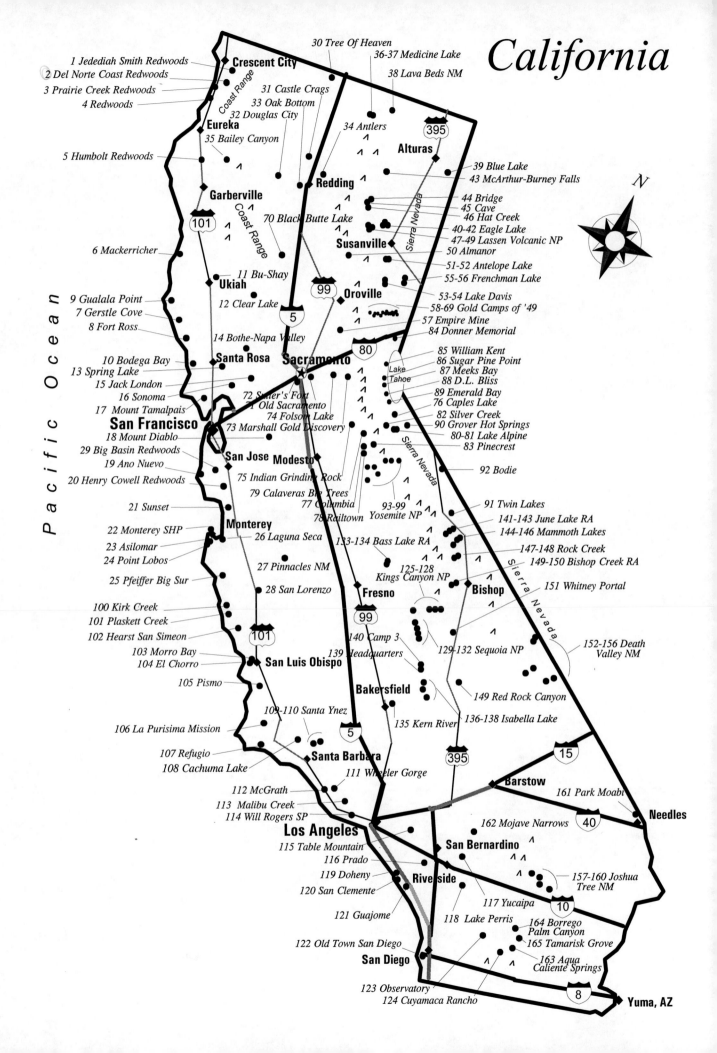

California

1 Jedediah Smith Redwoods
2 Del Norte Coast Redwoods
3 Prairie Creek Redwoods
4 Redwoods

5 Humbolt Redwoods

6 Mackerricher

9 Gualala Point
7 Gerstle Cove
8 Fort Ross

10 Bodega Bay
13 Spring Lake
15 Jack London
16 Sonoma
17 Mount Tamalpais

18 Mount Diablo
29 Big Basin Redwoods
19 Ano Nuevo
20 Henry Cowell Redwoods

21 Sunset

22 Monterey SHP
23 Asilomar
24 Point Lobos

25 Pfeiffer Big Sur

100 Kirk Creek
101 Plaskett Creek
102 Hearst San Simeon
103 Morro Bay
104 El Chorro

105 Pismo

106 La Purisima Mission

107 Refugio
108 Cachuma Lake

112 McGrath
113 Malibu Creek
114 Will Rogers SP

115 Table Mountain
116 Prado
119 Doheny
120 San Clemente
121 Guajome

122 Old Town San Diego

30 Tree Of Heaven
36-37 Medicine Lake
38 Lava Beds NM

31 Castle Crags
33 Oak Bottom
32 Douglas City

34 Antlers

35 Bailey Canyon

70 Black Butte Lake

72 Sutter's Fort
71 Old Sacramento
74 Folsom Lake
73 Marshall Gold Discovery

75 Indian Grinding Rock
79 Calaveras Big Trees
77 Columbia
78 Railtown

11 Bu-Shay

12 Clear Lake

14 Bothe-Napa Valley

26 Laguna Seca

27 Pinnacles NM

28 San Lorenzo

133-134 Bass Lake RA

125-128
Kings Canyon NP

140 Camp 3
139 Headquarters

109-110 Santa Ynez

111 Wheeler Gorge

135 Kern River

39 Blue Lake
43 McArthur-Burney Falls
44 Bridge
45 Cave
46 Hat Creek
40-42 Eagle Lake
47-49 Lassen Volcanic NP
50 Almanor
51-52 Antelope Lake
55-56 Frenchman Lake
53-54 Lake Davis
58-69 Gold Camps of '49
57 Empire Mine
84 Donner Memorial

85 William Kent
86 Sugar Pine Point
87 Meeks Bay
88 D.L. Bliss
89 Emerald Bay
76 Caples Lake
82 Silver Creek
90 Grover Hot Springs
80-81 Lake Alpine
83 Pinecrest

92 Bodie

91 Twin Lakes
141-143 June Lake RA
144-146 Mammoth Lakes
147-148 Rock Creek
149-150 Bishop Creek RA
151 Whitney Portal

152-156 Death
Valley NM

93-99
Yosemite NP

129-132 Sequoia NP

149 Red Rock Canyon

136-138 Isabella Lake

161 Park Moabi

162 Mojave Narrows

157-160 Joshua
Tree NM

117 Yucaipa
118 Lake Perris

164 Borrego
Palm Canyon
165 Tamarisk Grove

163 Aqua
Caliente Springs

Pacific Ocean

Coast Range

Sierra Nevada

Lake Tahoe

Crescent City

Eureka

Garberville

Ukiah

Santa Rosa

Sacramento

San Francisco

San Jose   Modesto

Monterey

San Luis Obispo

Santa Barbara

Los Angeles

San Bernardino

Riverside

San Diego

Redding

Alturas

Susanville

Oroville

Fresno

Bishop

Bakersfield

Barstow

Needles

Yuma, AZ

N

101

395

99

5

80

99

5

395

15

40

10

8

123 Observatory
124 Cuyamaca Rancho

Notes & Sketches

INDEX

Important Note:

* A thumbnail description of a recreation area marked with an asterisk is found in the *Trip Log* section of the principal numbered recreation area.

Washington

Oregon

California

The Double Eagle Guide to
1,000 GREAT!
▲ WESTERN RECREATION DESTINATIONS ⛺

__Volume 1 **West Coast**   ISBN 0-929760-58-1
         Washington∗Oregon∗California   Hardcover $19.95^

__Volume 2 **Intermountain West**   ISBN 0-929760-18-2
         Idaho∗Nevada∗Utah∗Arizona   Hardcover $19.95^

__Volume 3 **Rocky Mountains**   ISBN 0-929760-60-3
         Montana∗Wyoming∗Colorado∗New Mexico   Hardcover $19.95^

__Volume 4 **Great Plains**   ISBN 0-929760-20-4
         The Dakotas∗Nebraska∗Kansas∗Oklahoma∗Texas Hardcover $19.95^

__

^ **Save $3.00** Softcover, spiral-bound editions are also available. Recommended for light-duty, personal use only. Subtract $3.00 from standard hardcover price and ✓ here: ❏

Available from: *Double Eagle*™ guides are regularly updated.

Discovery Publishing
P.O. Box 50545   Billings, MT 59105   Phone 1-406-245-8292

Please add $3.50 for shipping the first volume, and $1.50 for each additional volume.

Please include your check/money order, or complete the VISA/MasterCard information in the indicated space below.

Name_____

Address_____

City_____ State_____ Zip_____

For credit card orders:

VISA/MC #_____ Expiration.Date_____

Thank You Very Much For Your Order!

Prices, shipping charges, and specifications are subject to change.

(A photocopy or other reproduction may be substituted for this original form.)